MEDIA PERFORMANCE

MEDIA PERFORMANCE

MASS COMMUNICATION AND THE PUBLIC INTEREST

DENIS McQUAIL

SAGE Publications

London · Newbury Park · New Delhi

© Denis McQuail 1992

First published 1992   Reprinted 1993

SAGE Publications Ltd
6 Bonhill Street
London EC2A 4PU

SAGE Publications Inc
2455 Teller Road
Newbury Park, California 91320

SAGE Publications India Pvt Ltd
32, M-Block Market
Greater Kailash – I
New Delhi 110 048

British Library Cataloguing in Publication data

McQuail, Denis
  Media Performance: Mass Communication and
  the Public Interest
  I. Title
  302.23

  ISBN 0–8039–8294–1
  ISBN 0–8039–8295–X pbk

Library of Congress catalog card number 92–50228

Typeset by Photoprint, Torquay, Devon
Printed in Great Britain by The Cromwell Press Ltd,
Broughton Gifford, Melksham, Wiltshire

CONTENTS

Part II MEDIA PERFORMANCE NORMS

Contents

Part VI   **OBJECTIVITY**

14   CONCEPTS OF OBJECTIVITY   183

15   A FRAMEWORK FOR OBJECTIVITY RESEARCH   196

Contents

Part VII MASS MEDIA, ORDER AND SOCIAL CONTROL

Part IX IN CONCLUSION

23 CHANGING MEDIA, CHANGING MORES: IMPLICATIONS FOR ASSESSMENT   301

PREFACE

The principal origins of this book date back to the mid-1970s, when, on secondment from the University of Southampton, I directed research into the content of British newspapers on behalf of the 1974–77 Royal Commission on the Press, which included in its terms of reference the task of inquiring into the 'editorial standards of newspapers and periodicals'. This was the first time that I had tried to grapple systematically with the concept of media performance in the sense of expectations concerning the broader public role of mass media. I discovered that there was rather little relevant social or media theory suitable for the task and few coherent attempts had been made to connect social theory with the sort of empirical enquiry called for by the terms of reference cited. Nevertheless, I enjoyed the challenge and the present book is, in some respects, a belated contribution to making good some of the deficiencies of the work done at that time. The many changes that have since taken place in mass media, especially as a result of new communications technology, have stimulated much wider debates about 'public interest' in the media and the topic has taken on a renewed significance.

Immediate plans to follow up the interest engendered by the press research were postponed when I moved to the University of Amsterdam to take the Chair of Mass Communication. Despite changed circumstances, I found myself drawn back to similar questions in a new context in the early 1980s. This context was influenced by debates over the future of the Dutch broadcasting system, then subject to intensive review. I was fortunate to find as a research colleague Jan van Cuilenburg, who had similar experience of evaluative research into the social and political role of newspapers and with whom I was able to collaborate on research into the diversity of mass media in The Netherlands. His own research and ideas have made an invaluable contribution to my thinking. In general, The Netherlands has provided a stimulating and congenial environment for considering questions of media performance, especially because of the high value placed on diversity in media policy and law and because of the lively atmosphere of public debate which surrounds all the media. My renewed concern with questions of media assessment was reinforced by what has proved a long-term engagement with questions of media policy in a comparative European setting, along with fellow members of the Euromedia Research Group. A seminar offered at the University of Amsterdam on 'Media Evaluation' helped to take my thinking some steps further and to broaden its scope.

The present book constitutes a link between several long-standing interests of my own: theory about communication and society; empirical research into media content and media audiences; development of media policy; everyday reading of newspapers, watching television and listening to the radio. A central aim of the book is to address the problem of the gap between normative social theory of the media and applied research. The book began with rather limited intentions and ended with the unrealizable ambition of dealing with very different mass media and being relevant to many times and places. However, it will now have to speak for itself and readers will have to make of it what they can. I hope that it will at least provide a useful source and starting point for others in this field.

I am very grateful to the Gannett Center for Media Studies at Columbia University, New York, for practical help and stimulation in realizing the plan to write this book. During a semester as Senior Fellow in early 1989 I was able to make a substantial start on what has proved a much longer and more demanding task than I had anticipated. Aside from time and space to work, I found in New York the library resources I needed and congenial, like-minded company. I am especially appreciative of the support of Everette Dennis and Jane Goodman. Amongst others who helped in different ways, I would like to mention my assistant, Vera Azar. Since then, the Department of Communication at the University of Amsterdam, all the while in a state of vigorous growth and change, has continued to provide favourable conditions for completing the project. I was permitted a last opportunity to reflect on the manuscript in a more detached spirit during a stay at Seijo University, Tokyo, in the spring of 1991, under the auspices of the Japan Society for the Promotion of Science and as a guest of Professor Seigo Yamanaka. A first version of the final chapter was presented at a seminar in the Department of Journalism and Communication Studies at the University of Tokyo.

Too many have helped me in one way or another for me to name them all individually, but I remain grateful to the Secretary and the Chairman of the Royal Commission on the Press, respectively Mr P.C. McQuail and Lord McGregor, for their part in setting me out on this particular intellectual journey. I also want to thank especially those who were kind enough to provide detailed comments on a late draft of the manuscript: Jay Blumler, Ev Dennis, Marjorie Ferguson, Karl Erik Rosengren and David Weaver. In different ways they each helped me to see errors and omissions and to take more account of the needs of the reader. More importantly, all five have made their own independent and long-standing contribution to the broad enterprise of exploring the public interest in mass communication and I have learnt from them as well as from many others who are cited as references. I have dedicated the book to Joseph Trenaman, whose own research was guided by the conviction that mass media have a positive and practical role to play in the slow journey towards a more just and decent society. Thirty years on, this remains a worthwhile lesson for anyone setting out to study mass communication. This book would not have been completed without the continuing confidence and practical support of the publishers, Sage. Sara McCune, David Hill, Stephen Barr and Nicola Harris have each, at different stages, played a vital role. As always, my family, especially Rosemary, has made a personal, though no less important, contribution.

Denis McQuail
Amsterdam, March 1992

In piam memoriam

J.S.M. Trenaman, 1910–1961

Friend and first mentor in communication research

PART I
MASS COMMUNICATION AND SOCIETY

1
PUBLIC COMMUNICATION AND PUBLIC INTEREST: CONTESTED TERRITORY

Mass communication in the information society

Significant changes in the 'traditional' mass media of press and broadcasting are currently being signalled. These changes are due most directly to technological advances in the means of electronic distribution and handling of information, but they also reflect more fundamental and longer-term social and economic changes. The term most often used to describe the emerging social order of the more economically developed states is that of an 'information society'. Most briefly put, this refers to a form of society in which there is a high and increasing dependence of individuals and institutions on information and communication in order to be able to function effectively in almost every sphere of activity.

It is a basic premise of this book, in line with this definition, that there will be an increasing rather than a decreasing 'public interest' in communication and information, although the nature of this public interest requires redefinition, both as to objectives and the means for securing them. One purpose of what follows is to help in this process of redefinition by examining past and present ideas of what counts as being in the public interest, as far as mass media are concerned.

The main source material for this examination is a particular tradition of communication theory and research which has grown up around the public interest task or responsibility of communications media, from newspapers to electronic data services. The research tradition (identified as 'media performance assessment') is a broad and loosely constructed one. The precise content and meaning given to the idea of a public interest within it is very variable from place to place and time to time and also variable in respect of the means proposed for attaining it. The ground covered is also contested and controversial, for reasons which can readily be appreciated.

Most fundamentally, perhaps, it is because communication has a very ambiguous character in respect of the claims of 'society', or those made on behalf of the 'public interest'.

Communication has several relevant dimensions: the same act of communication can have a private and personal character as well as a public significance; it can have a social-political as well as an economic value; it may be regarded as either a matter of necessity – a fundamental right – or as an optional private indulgence – a matter of wants rather than needs. On most matters, there is no objective way of determining the 'correct' identification and it is impossible, in general, to say when and where the activities of mass media belong to the public or to the private sphere, and thus whether or not they are proper matters of public concern. This allocation can only be made in specific cases according to subjectively chosen criteria. Such sources of confusion aside, there are often strongly opposed economic or ideological interests at stake which influence the definition of situations and of problems, the choice of criteria and the interpretation of any evidence.

Ideas of the 'public' and of public communication

The concepts needed in order to organize further discussion are familiar enough. They include the terms: (communicating) *public*; *public communication* as such; and *public space*. As an adjective, the word 'public' indicates what is open rather than closed, what is freely available rather than private in terms of access and ownership, what is collective and held in common rather than what is individual and personal. As a noun, the word refers (according to social and political theory) to an informal, voluntary, autonomous and interacting set of citizens who share and pursue objectives and interests, especially in respect of forming opinion and advocating policy (Blumer, 1939). A necessary condition for the existence and activity of a public is the availability of adequate means of communication.

For the most part, 'public communication' refers to the intricate web of informational, expressive and solidaristic transactions which take place in the 'public sphere' or public space of any society, as described above. In its expanded modern meaning, this space refers mainly to the channels and networks of mass communication and to the time and space reserved in the media for attention to matters of general public concern. It also involves a reference to a *domain* of subject matter of general interest, about which it is relevant and legitimate to communicate openly and freely. When topics are said to belong to this 'public domain', there is a legitimate claim to a right to receive information and also to publish.

A definition of the term 'public communication', in the sense of what the media do in their public capacity, has been suggested by Ferguson (1990: ix) as 'those processes of information and cultural exchange between media institutions, products and publics which are socially shared, widely available and communal in character'. This definition covers not only the 'traditional' mass media, but also many of the new publicly available data and communication services, based on telecommunications. It also covers much of the activity of public libraries, exhibitions and of the advertising and marketing industry. In other words, it is a very broad concept which is continually widening in its reference.

We may also, provisionally, use the term 'public interest' to refer to the complex of supposed informational, cultural and social benefits to the wider society which go beyond the immediate, particular and individual interests of those who participate in public communication, whether as senders or receivers. Even so, these two key expressions are both vague and contentious and will need further attention.

Mass media and the public interest

While we are assuming that there *is* a fundamental public interest in communications media, however difficult this is to specify, it is also the case that the notion of 'public interest' is sometimes used or seen as an ideological device designed to cloak unjustified regulatory ambitions on the part of governments or even as a weapon in the assault on more fundamental liberties of expression and of business enterprise. For those holding this view, the 'true' public interest will be best achieved by giving more freedom to media market forces, which are supposed to maximize benefits to suppliers, consumers and to the community as a whole (Fowler, 1982; Veljanovski, 1989).

The idea of public interest sometimes connotes one particular form or media arrangement, that of 'public service broadcasting', and is invoked in defence of that system. There is indeed some overlap between the idea of the public interest in communication and public service broadcasting, since the latter is often defined in terms of benefits which it is supposed to deliver to society: universal provision and wide-ranging appeal; services to regions and minorities; attention to national interest, identity and culture; the provision of informational and educational services beyond what the market would require, etc. (cf. Peacock, 1986; Blumler, 1992). But this identification of public interest with one form of arrangement is too limiting and neglects the fact that private communication media are also expected to deliver similar benefits for society on 'public interest' grounds.

While the underlying assumption of this book places it nearer to the supporters than to the opponents of media regulation in 'the public interest', this also happens to be the position adopted by many of the researchers and social theorists who have constructed the tradition of enquiry under review. Without the assumption of a potential service to the public good there would have been no research tradition. No polemical intention is intended and no side is taken in respect of the current debate about media deregulation, or about the need for more, or less, control of the media. It is, nevertheless, impossible to deal with the question of the *standards* which might be appropriate for assessing the performance of the media, in their self-chosen public role, without becoming involved, in some degree, in current conflicts of belief and policy. The larger question of the future of mass media and their public communicative role, under changing circumstances, is addressed separately in the final chapter.

The general idea that some aspects of public communication are of wide concern to the society and may have to be looked after by government or by other public agencies, especially where the needs of the democratic political system are concerned (Lichtenberg, 1990), is neither very new, nor, as such, controversial. According to Johnson (1987), all forms and kinds of human communication tend to be regulated by convention, rule or agreement in order to assure proper functioning and to prevent abuse. For instance, in respect of broadcasting in the United States, Johnson writes: 'reference to the "public interest" at least *contemplates* a public purpose, public "ownership", public impact of consequence, and a declaration of public policy that, whatever else it may be, broadcasting is not just "any other business" ' (Johnson, 1987: 31, italic added).

Much the same could be said about broadcasting in most European countries. For instance, the report of the British Peacock Committee (1986), even though working to a liberalizing brief, endorsed the importance of public service purposes, especially in respect of providing universal service of the kind noted above. The history of debate and policy concerning the newspaper press also suggests that there is a good deal of agreement both on the *need* for extensive and good public information services and also on what counts as 'good' press performance for society. What has usually been missing is any consensus on the *means* for achieving this by way of any public policy (Hutchins, 1947; Picard, 1985b).

Melody's (1990) account of the public interest in the emerging 'information society' refers to the historical notion of certain industries being recognized in law and custom as 'businesses affected with a public interest'. These were often connected with transport and other public utilities, in which monopoly conditions were likely to arise and where needs for service were likely to be pressing. In these circumstances, public regulation was often applied in order to ensure *equity* and *efficiency* – fair, as well as adequate, provision to all at reasonable prices. Regulation was often part of the price paid by service providers in return for advantageous monopoly terms. It is quite easy to place essential public information and communication services within this framework (see Chapter 3), although the special character of information and communication raises some issues which do not apply to normal industries.

The existence of *some* kind and degree of public interest in the operation of mass media has clearly been widely accepted, and it has much to do with the rise of democracy and of a 'public sphere', in which opinions are formed and expressed by citizens on the basis of common knowledge and of widely held values. There are still problems in moving from these ideas to the identification of criteria which are relevant to communicative 'performance' by mass media in their public role. The main difficulties are, first, that of specifying the intended collective beneficiary and, secondly, to specify the rules for determining the balance of benefit or harm. Not surprisingly, there is little consensus on what counts as being 'in the public good', when it comes to the *content* and uses of public means of communication.

The rise of a public sphere: from communication 'warfare' to 'welfare'

Unitary beginnings

In medieval times, the metaphorical 'space' for unrestrained communication in public was very limited, hemmed in and overlooked by the power of church, state, ruling class and local community. Restraints were placed on communication in the name of some good greater than that of the individual – that of true religion, sovereignty of the prince, privilege of the nobility, order in the community. The virtues of *public* communication, other than the largely one-way communication from church and state and the public celebrations of power and ritual, were little regarded. The history of communication is also, in part, the story of the steady enlargement of this public space. At the same time, it is one of continual conflict between established authority and those individuals and collective interests (especially the town and merchant classes) seeking freedom of expression and action.

The 'original', ideal-typical, solidaristic form of society has been depicted (by Emile Durkheim (1947) in *The Division of Labour in Society*) as one in which distinctions cannot be made between public and private spheres. Society is an organic whole in which individuals have few rights or needs distinguishable from the good of the whole. Late medieval European society was already far removed from this theoretical condition. Nevertheless, when printing was invented in the mid-fifteenth century, much of this kind of social theory survived in the attitudes of state and church authorities to the public uses of the new technology. All forms of public expression and publication were, in principle and practice, answerable to authorities which were backed by physical or spiritual violence.

Growth of public communication

The first age of printing The period from the invention of printing until the mid-seventeenth century saw an extensive challenge to, and the fragmentation of, this first 'communication order'. The religious disputes of the Reformation turned initially on the claims of individual conscience against the monolithic authority of the Roman church, but became inextricably involved in the dynastic and inter-state feuding of the period. Aside from the warfare and violence against persons, the Reformation was characterized by propaganda, counter-propaganda and intense dispute over texts and acts of public communication.

During the sixteenth century, printing also became a minor industry and its products a significant item of commerce (Febvre and Martin, 1984). These activities generated a set of much-contested (thus internally inconsistent) principles and practices concerning communication, especially: individual rights to publish; the rights of self-governing communities of like-minded believers to control the communications of their own membership; tolerance for differences of belief; the licensing of printers and their accountability for the views and opinions which they published; the commercial tradeability of cultural or scientific works; the issue of censorship or other forms of control.

Debates on these issues led both to non-conformity and to the reassertion by church and state of their right to control public utterances. The whole period of 'communication warfare' also stimulated much intolerance on the part of adherents of one or other set of religious and political beliefs. As a result, the time cannot simply be characterized as one of steadily increasing tolerance or 'liberalization', even though the foundations were laid for a libertarian philosophy of communication (Siebert et al., 1956).

The early industrial age   The second main period in the development of public communication, lasting until the mid-nineteenth century, saw the emergence, in political thought, of the concepts of a 'public communication' and of the 'public sphere', more or less as we now understand the terms (Gouldner, 1976; Garnham, 1986; Curran, 1991). The political theorist Jürgen Habermas (1989) has done most to conceptualize the nature of the 'public sphere', viewing it largely as an achievement of the new bourgeois, or capitalist, class in Europe, and an outcome of its successful struggle against feudalism. The term refers to the metaphorical space available to all, legally protected from state or church oppression, for the free expression of views and interest claims, for rational debate and public decision-making on political and judicial matters. Intimately connected with the emergence of this space is the large and unrestricted circulation of books, pamphlets, news sheets, etc.

Characteristic of this whole period was an increased recognition of the shared interest, between individual citizens and authorities, in having some channels and forums for the public expression and exchange of information and opinion. By the mid-nineteenth century, the open expression of opinion had been established as a legitimate and normal feature of political life and even as a right, especially after the wave of revolution in Europe in 1848. The spirit of the Enlightenment strongly supported the need for an educated populace, for rational public discussion, as well as for the speedy advance of science and knowledge. Holmes (1990) cites arguments from Kant, Hume and Locke for the benefits of open public debate. According to Locke, for instance, deputies are elected in order to 'freely act and advise, as the necessity of the Commonwealth, and the Publick Good should, upon examination and mature debate be judged to require. This, those who give their votes before they hear the debate, and have weighed the reasons on all sides, are not capable of doing' (Locke, 1681/1965: 441–442).

The emergence of this more benign climate for public communication found many expressions in public and private acts, including: the encouragement of education, the founding of libraries and other cultural provisions for the benefit of a wider public; the rise of popular political parties, with their networks of clubs and organizations and their proliferating publications, meetings and demonstrations; great improvements in postal communications.

This 'intermediate' period in the emergence of the modern public communication sphere is also marked by clearer statements of expectation about rights to communicate. These are early versions of what came to constitute the foundation of the 'public interest' in mass communication. They often have a dual character, on the one hand recognizing essential rights to freedom of expression and political association, while on the other hand setting limits to publication in the interests of state security, law and order or good morals. Classic statements of press freedom can be found in the Declaration of the Rights of Man, the (1791) First Amendment to the US constitution, as well as in many European constitutional documents after 1848.

The age of mass media   The third period of development of the public sphere of communication, taking us to the present day, has been the age of *mass* communication proper, during which many new claims and expectations, and some new reservations, have been voiced. The early part of this long century and a half was dominated by the print media, the latter period by broadcasting, and television in particular. The early period was also marked by intense political communication activity (the 'age of ideology') as well as by enormous popular demand for the novel products of the new media industries – story books, magazines and newspapers. Consumer advertising played a key part in expanding and also shaping the new public communication institutions. The indispensability of the part played by the press in a modern society was increasingly accepted (Hardt, 1979).

Until the First World War, there seemed little that could hold back the advance of the new 'information' and 'culture' industries. The break in this 'progressive' sequence had several causes, aside from war itself. Much of Europe came to experience new forms of autocratic rule, a reminder that mass communication, while historically associated with freedom, also lends itself very well to control. Critics of the new (capitalist) newspaper monopolies drew much the same conclusion. At the very least, events of the early twentieth century, as well as the 'sensationalist' direction often chosen by the mass popular newspaper press, led very widely to a loss of (informed public) confidence in the media as the only or best representative and defender of the public interest in communication.

Ideas about public communication were also influenced by developments within communication itself, especially by the rise of film and broadcasting and the earlier electric technologies of telegraph, telephone and wireless. Each of these media was found to need legal definition and some kind of regulation, of a kind which the newspaper press had managed to avoid or shake off (Pool, 1984). The immediate needs of the customers of new communication services and of the state (since the communications were seen as an essential military, strategic and commercial infrastructure) played a key part in the regulatory process. The cinema everywhere attracted some form of control over content and over rights to exhibit, especially because of possible influences on the behaviour, ideas and morals on the young. Radio broadcasting, very soon after its introduction, also came to be regarded as an invention of immense potential significance for society and its adoption was everywhere accompanied by public control and legal definitions of its aims and scope of operation.

Conflicts over 'communication welfare'

By the mid-twentieth century, the uncomplicated liberal or 'progressive' view of the virtue of unfettered expansion of the means of communication had been replaced by more complex and more ambivalent attitudes. Commercial exploitation, on the one hand, and political or state manipulation, on the other, offered cautionary lessons. There developed around press and broadcasting a complex web of assessments and expectations, which were expressed at one time or another in the name of 'the good of society' or of the 'public interest'. These expectations were often mutually inconsistent (e.g. freedom versus constraint; collective versus individualist values; secular versus moralist claims). They were also applied inconsistently to different media. The situation was further complicated by the growing strength of media industry and media professional interests, able to speak out for themselves and seeking autonomy for their own activities according to their self-chosen aims, whether professional or commercial. As a result, there has been a state of considerable confusion and conflict over the norms which should apply to communication arrangements and to performance, from the point of view of 'society'.

The most fundamental conflict has remained that between the outlook of established authorities (responsible for maintaining the current order) and media demands for unrestricted freedom of expression. Secondly, a new set of disputes has arisen over cultural and public education issues between upholders of 'elite' conceptions of what is 'good' in culture, who are usually also proponents of an educational role for the media, and those who see the media primarily in terms of entertainment and show business (or business of any kind). Both kinds of dispute intersect with an argument over arrangements and structure: essentially between a public utility model and a free enterprise model of media systems. Most generally, there has been continual warfare between the controllers of communication 'gates' in society (especially proprietors, editors, journalists) and all those voices which want control over, or access to, the media channels for their own purposes.

Shifting frontier between freedom and control

In the basic matter of conflict between authority and freedom, the historical progression might be summarized in terms of a move from *suppression* (in the name of state and religion), to *prohibition* (selectively applied), to *permission* (of a limited kind, in the name of liberty and of business), to *prescription* (encouraging educational and cultural goals); to *libertarianism* (a market-based claim to unhindered freedom of operation). Inevitably, the present state of media institutions offers a mixture of all these elements, even if suppression is no longer a legitimate or viable modern option. In addition, the media institution is having to adapt to great changes in communication technology and to changes in the global political economy.

2
MEDIA PERFORMANCE: TRADITIONS OF ENQUIRY

Looking for quality criteria

The contestation and confusion which have arisen over the public task of the media, have not prevented critics and commentators from applying their own self-chosen criteria of quality to what the media do, nor has it held back the growth of ubiquitous and complex systems of regulation of the mass media, on grounds of a supposed 'public interest'. Research into what is here called 'media performance' (defined below), according to diverse criteria, seems to proliferate rather than diminish, for reasons which go beyond the fact of growth in the media sector itself and in the size of the research community. The reason may well be the increased dependence of citizens on public communication for their everyday needs. However, more directly influential is the dependence of political and economic institutions on the media both for instrumental communication purposes (advertising, information dissemination, etc.) and for purposes of securing status, influence, positive 'image', visibility (or invisibility) in public life.

This mixture of motives and interests still further clouds the issue of what the public interest really is, and the very trends towards privatization and commercialization, which reduce public control over mass media, have placed the question of responsibility of the media to the society even more insistently on the agenda of public debate. The shift of balance from public control and regulation (especially of broadcast and telecommunications media) to private ownership and management has typically led to more, rather than less, explicit specification of standards and expectations.

The issue of the 'quality' of what the media do, which was once supposedly guaranteed by public control or 'trusteeship', but now feared to be under threat from 'commercialism', has been widely addressed by policy-makers, regulators and researchers, wherever the old system undergoes major change. An example is a research project of the Japanese public broadcasting corporation (NHK), designed to monitor the effects of change on broadcasting quality (Ishikawa and Muramatsu, 1991). The framework for assessment which they have developed distinguishes three levels at which assessment of quality can be applied and four 'social levels', or perspectives, from which performance may be viewed. The three levels are those of the whole media *system*, of the *channel* and of the *programme* (which identifies the content or service to be examined).

The four 'social levels' are those of state; society; audience; and professionals (the communicators). Each of these may be considered either as potential beneficiaries of the media, or as potential adjudicators of quality (or both). In terms of this four-fold division, the idea of 'media performance in the public interest', as it is used in this book, calls for the deployment of criteria which represent the values and needs of 'society' (rather than of the state, audiences or communicators). However, each of the other three may have to be looked at as a source for defining criteria of public benefit (especially the state, in official, legal and regulatory documents) or as providing some relevant evidence about performance quality (especially audiences and professionals).

This explanation yet again exposes the uncertainty and ambiguity of the enterprise of performance assessment, especially since 'society', in whose interest assessment is conducted, is least likely to speak directly for itself with a single identifiable voice. Its 'point of view' has always to be inferred and is bound to be multiple and divided. No a priori assumption has been made at the outset of this enquiry about what specifically might count as 'in the public interest', or about how the interest of society should be recognized or realized (see Chapter 3). For the most part, it has to be determined by reference to conventions, laws and evaluative claims which surface in public debate according to local circumstances (Chapters 4 and 5). Alternatively, the criteria adopted will be those which researchers have chosen to apply, for differing reasons. There are simply no universal evaluative criteria to hand and many of those chosen often owe their relevance to chance and passing circumstances of time or place.

Other approaches to evaluating the media

The main purpose of this book is to set out and examine the record of a particular, though very broad, tradition of enquiry into the working of the mass media in their potential 'public interest' capacity. At the core of this tradition is the view that public communication, as carried out mainly by way of the mass media, has a significant contribution to make to the general welfare of society and carries a corresponding 'social responsibility', which is recognized, pursued (sometimes enforced) and attained in varying forms and degrees and by many different means. The focus, however, is less on the social responsibility of the *media* than on criteria of their performance in the public life of societies and on how we may assess this. Research can make a contribution by helping to monitor the detail of media performance according to any of the claims, preferences and values that might arise. It has also helped by clarifying the criteria applied and the nature of expectations from society.

The research under review is marked, not only by having itself a certain 'public interest' purpose of its own, but also by its independence from the immediate aims and self-interest of the media. It has to adhere to the canons of social scientific enquiry, especially consistency, objectivity and reliability.

This commitment to objectivity has to be maintained, despite the fact that most of the standards of performance which are applied to the mass media in policy debates, within the framework sketched, are normative, prescriptive and, in the end, subjective – a matter of preference, perspective and value judgement.

The expression 'performance assessment', in discussions of mass media has a wide currency, but no single or precise meaning. It can refer to any of the following: the self-assessment by the media industry in achieving its economic, product or audience goals; evaluation of the working of public policies for mass media (for example, in respect of monopoly or cultural standards); critical evaluation of many possible aspects or cases of the work of media; evaluation of the success of campaigns to inform, persuade, mobilize, sell, etc.

The field of research identified here has a hybrid, even mongrel, character. There are different ways of approaching the problems tackled and whichever approach is chosen is unlikely to suit all purposes or preferences. The diversity of values, claims and criteria generated by the normative framework adopted (see Chapter 6), as well as the differences of *level* at which research can be directed, calls for a multiplicity of methods and can also lead to inconsistency. For the would-be researcher, the task is further complicated by the need to deliver systematic and *objective* evidence on matters which will have many subjective components. A review of the major approaches and traditions of media evaluation helps to explain the main elements of the chosen option.

Organizational efficiency

One possible research model could be to follow the example of a media organization which examines its own performance in terms of efficiency, profitability or level of consumer or client satisfaction. This model is of limited value for the present purpose for two main reasons. First, the standards of performance of an organization are set *internally*, rather than externally, according to organizational self-interest; secondly, in such cases, there are *objective* standards which can usually be applied, partly because management can decide unilaterally on aims and priorities. From a public interest perspective, it is rare to find objectively fixed standards for assessing performance (the requirement for impartiality in public broadcasting is one exception). Even so, research is often carried out by media organizations for their own purposes, or with a view to their public responsibilities. The results can also contribute to independent evaluation.

Media effect model

A second model, originating within communication research itself, is offered by the tradition of enquiry into the possible connection between mass media and crime, disorder, violence, immorality and anti-social or deviant behaviour generally. In this model, performance is equated with the *effects of the media.* While questions of effect do obviously fall within the range of 'public interest' concerns, this particular kind of research usually focuses on the *unintended* and also *negative* consequences of media work. By contrast, we are more likely to be concerned here with the *intentional* aspect of what media do and with positive goals (informing, entertaining, educating, etc.). The idea of a *public good* refers, first of all, to *benefits* for the wider society and only secondarily to avoiding harm to society.

Marxist–critical approach

A third possible model is offered by research which has followed a Marxist-critical line of thought, according to which, *inter alia*, capitalistic or state-bureaucratic media systems are deemed intrinsically incapable of genuinely serving the public welfare, because of their class character. While the focus is on quite different kinds of effect, this approach is also mainly concerned with the *negative* effects of structure on performance (e.g. class-biased content) and, by implication, with further negative consequences for the audience (as citizens). Despite these disqualifying limitations, the research approach has made an important contribution to the overall 'public interest' research enterprise, mainly by supplying ideas and giving a critical edge to media analysis (Rosengren, 1983).

Media cultural studies approach

The approach represented broadly by the 'culturalist' school or tradition of enquiry has its roots in literary criticism, film theory and social critical theory generally (Carey, 1989; Real, 1989). It has an uncertain and uneasy boundary with sociology and psychology, on the one hand, and with the traditional humanities, on the other, but it has undoubtedly acquired a secure and challenging place in the 'communication sciences' (Dervin et al., 1989). While the tradition has several schools, and no 'dominant paradigm' of its own, it has been characterized, in varying degrees, by four main features: an engagement with social issues, usually involving an oppositional, critical, sometimes populist stance (Fiske, 1987); an emphasis on 'ritual', expressive or consummatory versions of communication, as against instrumental or utilitarian views (Carey, 1989); a central concern with the 'text' – the particular content as it is experienced, and thus with methods appropriate to textual 'decoding' in the line of structuralism and semiology (Hall, 1980); finally, an interest in the relation between the reception of texts and the sociocultural context, leading to a preference for ethnographic method (Ang, 1990).

This extensive and internally diverse tradition is certainly concerned with 'performance', but it differs from the variant proposed in several respects. One difference is the rejection of the basic rules of objective, 'scientific', procedures in matters of culture and meaning. This is very roughly, if inadequately, captured by saying that the approach is qualitative and interpretative rather than quantitative. Even more important is the rejection, in this tradition, of the notion of media content as a finished 'product'. Media content only takes on meaning when received and interpreted. There is more interest in *audience* performance than in *producer* performance.

The differences over method and evidence are also important, especially since the methods characteristic of cultural media studies are not yet easy to deploy in public policy debates about the media. Findings are hard to communicate directly outside the community of media scholars, not very usable in political (policy) arguments because of the high subjective component and, often, the complexity of argument involved. It is also relevant that the main *purpose* and driving forces of cultural media studies are not very directly concerned with the politics of the public interest. They lie in trying to explain and understand human communication experience.

Social cost–benefit analysis

At first sight the mode of research practised under the label 'evaluation research' seems also to offer a relevant option. This is generally concerned with assessing the achievement of goals in broad public policy fields such as health, education, welfare, prisons, etc. and it might appear applicable to communication policy. However, communication differs from other public policy fields and the policy evaluation approach is consequently not suitable, mainly because there are rarely any agreed, enforceable or even specific policy goals for the media in their general public role. Thus there are no *optimal* outcomes against which to judge the goals pursued or the expenditure of resources. At root, as has been emphasized, there is *no single* public interest and the media pursue many divergent and even inconsistent aims, which are likely to be valued differently by different 'agents of preference', especially at the audience 'end' of the process.

Even though media may broadly be expected to serve the long-term public good, they are not working *for* society to achieve goals set *by* society. An essential characteristic which has been attributed to mass communication is *purposelessness* (Westley and MacLean, 1957). They *facilitate* and mediate communication by others, provide services to audiences and clients, but much of the rest is chance or the outcome of their own creativity. It is simply not appropriate to investigate the media within a framework of cost–benefit analysis, when the means are so diverse and the goals open-ended and variable.

Media ethics approach

Finally, a relevant alternative to mainstream research approaches is also offered by way of the study of media *ethics* (Rubin, 1978; Thayer et al., 1979; Christians and Rotzell, 1983; Goodwin, 1983; Meyer, 1983, 1987; Mills, 1983; Elliott, 1986; Lambeth, 1986). Many media-ethical issues clearly impinge on the public interest (for instance, matters of privacy, taste and decency, methods of acquiring information, dealings with criminals, etc.). Codes of ethics of journalism can be drawn upon as one source of current ideas of standards for media performance (see Chapter 4). It is clear that 'society' takes an active interest in ethical standards of the media. It is also clear that normal social scientific research methods can be usefully applied to investigate the state of thinking about journalistic ethics and to evaluating actual performance (Weaver and McCombs, 1980; Weaver and Wilhoit, 1986; Meyer, 1987).

Even so, certain features of the 'media ethical' tradition do limit its wider applicability for present purposes. First, it also adopts a predominantly *internal* perspective and is concerned with *self-regulation*, even if according to wider criteria and with a view to broad social responsibility for the consequences of the media (Thurston, 1981). Secondly, many of the ethical matters which are debated are more to do with standards of personal or professional conduct than with public concerns. Thirdly, the typical problem definitions, methods and types of evidence called for are closer to legal than to social scientific research, often involving case histories and depending more on argument than on evidence.

A distinctive approach to media assessment

Origins

None of these variants captures what is central to the research tradition which this book draws on, although each does imply a systematic evaluation of what the media are doing according to some independent criteria of achievement. The type of media performance assessment discussed here belongs to a long tradition of applied media research concerning the working of the mass media in modern democracies, a tradition which has significant origins in the American Commission on Freedom of the Press (Hutchins, 1947). This sought to evaluate the American press of the time and to establish a framework of standards of quality of performance appropriate to 'socially responsible' press media. Although the Commission itself engaged in very little empirical research, the idea of social responsibility and the principles it enunciated have guided much subsequent work.

There have been commissions of inquiry into the functioning of the mass media in several other countries which have combined a similar task of public assessment with programmes of empirical research, for instance in Britain (Royal Commissions on the Press Reports, 1949 and 1977), Sweden (Gustafsson and Hadenius, 1976), Canada (Davey, 1970; Kent, 1981), The Netherlands (McQuail and van Cuilenburg, 1983). The character and scope of research can also be understood by reference to Lemert (1989), who suggests that we can distinguish four main schools of media criticism: marxist; cultural/critical studies; social responsibility; empiricist. His own chosen purpose is to show 'how social science techniques can be used to evaluate and criticize the performance of present and future news media' (Lemert, 1989: 11).

This is one aim of the current work and 'media performance assessment' might be described as a hybrid of the social responsibility and the empiricist schools of criticism. Curiously, media performance assessment, as identified here, compounds two elements which were opposed to each other in a classic statement by Lazarsfeld (1941), namely the 'administrative' (by which he meant media organizational) and the 'critical'. The term 'administrative critical research' might well be a description of one strand of the tradition of assessing media 'in the public interest', certainly the strand practised by press commissions and the like.

This study tries to forge such a 'union' by linking a set of normative principles with a set of research procedures, with the intention of illuminating both. Performance research 'in the public interest' has acquired several distinctive 'biases' of its own in respect of problem definitions and choice of research methods. In particular, there have been biases towards the *cognitive* (news and information) and the *political*, although in relation to television, questions of cultural quality and morality have been just as prominent. The potential relevance of research to public policy-making (regulation of, or intervention in, media systems) has put a premium on evidence which seems 'hard' enough to stand up in political or legal debate and which is also 'communicable' to a lay audience: members of the public, politicians, media practitioners.

Defining characteristics

The particular version of a research model chosen for the task of assessing performance is not an exclusive *alternative* to all other approaches, but it is a distinctive, hybrid, variant which borrows features from some of those described variants. Its main features are as follows:

- A motivated choice from the relevant performance criteria (see Chapter 6 below), in keeping with a clearly defined version of positive social purpose.
- The adoption of a standpoint and a problem definition external to, and independent from, the self-chosen goals and interests of the media, although taking account of their aims and necessary conditions of operation.
- The deployment of strategies and methods of research characteristic of 'mainstream' social science, especially: a neutral attitude and clear statement of values; a search for general and typical, rather than unique or idiosyncratic, features of performance; application of systematic, generally quantitative, methods to data collection and analysis.
- A primary focus on performance in terms of the *content* or product offered by the media, or to overall quality of *service* provided, rather than on media structure or effects.
- Taking some account of alternative perspectives on performance, especially those of sources, producers, clients, audiences.

Media performance analysis according to these specifications can then be defined as

> The independent assessment of mass media provision according to alternative 'public interest' criteria, by way of objective and systematic methods of research, taking account of other relevant evidence and the normal operating conditions and requirements of the media concerned.

The research model which would implement this definition is, in particular, designed to meet the typical requirements of public policy debate, formulation and evaluation. It should have the best chance of communicating relevant and dependable evidence to the main parties to such debates – usually legislators, politicians, governments, 'opinion-makers', the media themselves and the general public – and thus the best chance of influencing public policy or the self-chosen aims and conduct of the media themselves.

Aims and plans of the book

The chosen definition has influenced the overall strategy of this book and especially the selection of performance criteria and indicators, the methods and the research examples which are discussed. The first aim is to develop as comprehensive a framework of normative principle as possible, consistent both with the historical record of social concern with public communication and with the requirements of coherence and economy of presentation. It is not the intention to advance any *new* social or normative theory of media or to make a plea for any one particular version of what the public interest in the working of the mass media might be. The days of unitary, normative theories are (or should be) over (as will be argued). Different, sometimes opposed, claims have to be examined and described in order to propose and apply appropriate measures of performance.

It is an ancillary purpose to help clarify *thinking* about the public interest in communication and about the varied aims and values which are advanced by advocates and critics of what the media do. The need to specify some observable outward sign of supposed merit or public benefit from communication is a powerful incentive to clearer thinking. Research in this tradition has encountered three main kinds of difficulty: one is the diversity of perspectives and values which has to be encompassed; a second is that of establishing the precise criteria which might express any given 'public interest' perspective; a third is to find operational indicators of the criteria which are likely to yield systematic, dependable and communicable evidence for deployment in public debate or policy formulation. The search for solutions to these three problems has helped to expose the meanings attached to the idea of 'public interest' on communication matters.

The book as a whole can also be seen as seeking to bridge the gap between normative (and thus subjective) standards and objective research.

This can only be done by setting limits to its scope: in practice, by attending only to the media systems of a relatively few Western societies during the recent past, which share somewhat similar traditions of liberal democracy. It is for the reader to judge how far what is offered is relevant to the many cases and places which are not discussed and also how far the past of media theory and performance research has a continued relevance for the emerging future of communication in society (see Chapter 23).

The aims which have been described will mainly be accomplished by dealing in turn with the major themes of public interest which relate to the media, especially matters which have to do with their *independence, diversity, objectivity* and also their contribution to the *social and cultural order*. For each of these broad themes, the intention is first to specify relevant concepts and criteria of performance and, secondly, to see, by way of examples drawn from research, how assessment might be carried out and what general conclusions have been drawn in the past. Before proceeding, some basic questions need to be tackled in more detail.

The main problem faced at the start of this study has been the inadequacy of existing social theory of media performance. There is no firm or agreed basis for carrying out a study of this kind, even if it is quite easy to name the broad themes of enquiry. In part, this deficiency stems from relative neglect in the past or from the very spasmodic, local and narrowly defined focus of most research. In part it also stems from the diversity of social contexts and of media institutions. Perhaps, most of all, it is due to the basic conflicts of interest and outlook referred to above.

The difficulties mentioned cannot all be surmounted, but an attempt will be made to lay some more secure foundations. In the chapter which follows, the 'public interest' concept is tackled directly and a working definition established for present purposes. In Chapters 4 and 5, a pragmatic solution is found to the problem of choosing and defining criteria of performance by reviewing the record of public regulation of mass media in a number of societies. The assumption made is that expectations on the part of 'society' are most likely to be expressed by the institutionalized 'voice' of the society, when it prescribes and proscribes for the media in their public role. After this review, Chapter 6 offers a more formal and general statement of the outcome in terms of basic values applicable to the media and of the concepts and sub-concepts which can be derived from them. This is described as a 'framework of principle' for the assessment task.

Before dealing with the substantive issues, Chapter 7 fills in another basic element for the apparatus of enquiry by proposing a general model of media organization and a review of assessment research options and strategies. The point of the media organizational model is to be able to locate the specific problem of performance in terms of its *level* in the system and also to help identify the empirical reality of media work to which the principles of performance can be applied. The chapters which follow proceed as described, issue by issue, and conclude with a view of media changes currently under way. At issue is the continuing relevance of the various principles of performance outlined, under changing environmental and operating conditions of the mass media in general. As media performance inevitably changes, we can expect a corresponding adaptation of public expectations, as definitions of the public interest in communication continue to evolve.

3
THE 'PUBLIC INTEREST' IN COMMUNICATION

Conceptual clarification

According to some political philosophers (e.g. Barry, 1965), the expression 'public interest' has been so long and so loosely used and misused, that it would be better to abandon it altogether. The relevant entry in the *International Encyclopedia of the Social Sciences* (Sills, 1968) says that the notion is 'elastic and relative . . . [and] . . . has no apriori content waiting to be revealed . . . [It] serves to remind parties immediately concerned that there are considerations extending beyond their goals . . .'. Further, 'it assumes the existence of a common interest, although specific manifestations cannot be agreed upon.' Despite its problematic status, Held (1970) has argued that even if we were to abandon the concept, we would not evade the complexities and problems which are associated with the idea of a public interest. These arise in almost any political or legal debate on issues of wide or deep public significance.

One of the most problematic features of the concept is that conflicting proposals can be advocated according to *someone*'s version of what is in the general good. According to Smith, with reference to telecommunications:

> at one level, all policies, plans and purposes on the part of government . . . are manifestations of the public interest . . . Public interest is a field in which parties struggle to establish policy. Public interest implies the invocation of social purpose in all matters in which there remains a territory of discussable collective policy within a society. (Smith, 1989: 23)

In practice, there is no a priori way of distinguishing a valid from an invalid claim. 'Everyone', writes Downs (1962: 3), 'talks about the public interest . . . but few agree fully about the particular policies it comprises.' Downs points out that the concept has three specific functions in a democratic society (the primary reference here is to government actions): it 'serves as a device by which individual citizens can judge government actions and communicate their judgements to one another'; secondly, 'Since the concept implies that there is one common good for all . . . appeals to the public interest can be used to justify what may be against some immediate individual interest'; thirdly, 'the concept serves as a guide to and check on' actions.

The main reason for re-opening this unresolved issue is to help in identifying specific manifestations of public benefit from communication which go beyond the immediate purposes of the media themselves, of their clients or of their audiences. In turn, this helps to set research priorities and to choose relevant criteria of performance.

Lessons of economic regulation

The origin of the public interest concept lies in economic regulation, where it is still widely applied. Mitnick (1980) traced the term to medieval social theory, which gave normative support to ideas of economic justice (e.g. a 'just' or 'fair' price), sufficient to support collective controls, over and against the free play of market forces. Moreover, these controls often stated obligations to the community, which were required in return for certain rights or privileges. Typically, the obligations concerned such matters as: providing service to all equally; the adequacy of goods and services offered; levying reasonable prices. In return, business could expect protection of property, liberty to trade and, in some cases, limited forms of monopoly.

Medieval law also recognized certain occupations as 'common callings', which were subject to particular rights and duties. These occupations included such trades as those of surgeon, carrier, innkeeper, baker, etc. The idea of a 'common calling' implied some essential service to the wider community, thus a general interest, sufficient to override some of the normal rules of the market place. Some things were considered too important to be left to the vagaries of the market and, significantly, several of the 'callings' were related to communication (in the form of physical transportation).

There are numerous modern examples of public utilities which are similarly regulated for the common good, including basic telecommunication services. Melody (1990) reminds us that these belong to a wider class of businesses which in law or convention are regarded as 'businesses affected with a public interest', because of the essential nature of the service provided, their tendency to (natural) monopoly and the requirements of universal service on an equitable basis. The difficulties now encountered in applying such ideas to the media stem mainly from disagreements about what features of mass communication are essential (many are clearly not) and about whether special arrangements, interfering in the free market, are needed at all to secure a fair and efficient provision of those services which are agreed to be essential. In addition, the mass media have special claims to freedom which regulation may deny.

The simple faith in regulation and the granting of monopolistic privilege as a means of securing 'the public good' has long expired. However, as Mitnick also points out, the *laissez-faire* doctrines of the classical economists did not contest the belief, as such, that there *is* some 'general welfare' beyond that of individuals. Adam Smith and other founders of the new political economy supposed, two centuries ago, that the market would provide for this, by way of the 'invisible hand' which would see to the greatest good of the greatest number. The failure of this hidden hand to provide adequately led to a reassertion of regulation of many economic activities in the nineteenth century.

Mitnick, citing Bonbright (1961), mentions two main reasons for conferral of 'public utility' status, both of them relating to the protection of the public. Conditions for receipt of economic privilege are: (a) where the privileges are viewed as necessary to ensuring adequacy of service; and (b) where there are technical characteristics leading to *natural monopoly*. Most modern societies do in fact require support from extensive communication infrastructures (post, telecommunications, mass transit). These, in turn, do frequently have certain natural monopoly characteristics, namely: their unit costs would be higher for the same quality of provision under conditions of competition.

The main conditions for allocating 'public utility' status to basic public communication arrangements do often seem to be present. Regulation can also protect the public from exploitation stemming from monopoly, while promoting the efficient working of the services in question. A common requirement of communication services (both physical and informational) is that they should be available to all on fair terms. 'The criteria of universality and equity supplement those of efficiency and fair price. However, this line of thinking becomes problematic when extended beyond the question of structural (or infrastructural) arrangements.

Typologies of the public interest idea

Several typologies of the public interest concept have been suggested as ways of ordering the main alternative meanings of the concept. Downs (1962) describes three main schools of thought about how the public interest can be identified. One derives from 'the will of the people': the public interest is what the people (the majority of citizens) want. A second version holds that the public interest is decided according to some absolute standard of value regardless of what citizens want. A third, 'realist', school finds the public interest in the 'results of certain *methods* of decision-making' – a 'pragmatic outcome, involving no ethical implications'. In Downs' view, each version has some validity. For our purpose we can follow a similar classification scheme suggested by Held (1970), who also identified three main variants of public interest theory: 'preponderance' theories; 'common interest' theories; and 'unitary' conceptions.

Preponderance theory The expression refers to cases where the *sum of individual interests* is held to be paramount. Public interest is defined in a *majoritarian* way, in line with what Downs refers to as 'the will of the people'. The public interest will be held to lie with the majority choice, or with what is believed to maximize the number of individual preferences. This can be known in different ways: through the working of the market; by voting; by expert calculation of aggregate costs and benefits; by the weight of 'public opinion'; by the assertion of some dominant power to determine a result. Whatever happens, the public interest cannot, according to this definition, be on the 'losing side' in the sense of being demonstrably contrary to the interest of a majority. One of the weaknesses of this class of theory, according to Held, is the potential conflict between a particular *means* of identifying the public interest (for example, a majority vote or mass consumer demand) and the broader notion that public interest means something more than the sum of individual preferences.

Common interest theory 'Common interest' theories refer to cases where the interests in question are ones which *all* members are *presumed* to have in common, with little scope for dispute over preferences. Typical examples are: basic services of transport, power, water; and things held to be necessary for ordered society, such as a system of government, defence, law and justice, policing, monetary systems, etc. The general idea of a 'public space', as discussed above, would also qualify, according to most informed thinking, as a necessity in a democratic political system and thus in every citizen's interest. Rousseau's notion of the general will can provide a philosophical basis for assumptions about what is in the common interest, but problems arise when significant numbers of supposed beneficiaries do not welcome what is claimed, or done, on their behalf.

While majoritarian theory is strong on means (e.g. following the evidence of a popular vote or market choice) and weak on substance (it does not discriminate between alternatives in a logical or rational way), the reverse is true for common interest theory. It opens the way to a persuasive claim for certain objectives (for example, adequate means of public communication) but does not *demonstrate* the necessity (or the demand) for meeting any particular claim. There is some correspondence with Downs' 'pragmatic' class of theory (according to which public interest is what political institutions arrive at by their decision-making), although Held's version puts the attribute of believed general welfare above the institutionalized means for identifying and reaching it.

Unitary theory The third of Held's categories is, in effect, the assertion of some absolute normative principle, usually deriving from some larger social theory or ideology. It is much the same as the 'absolute standard of value' theories referred to by Downs. The public interest is seen as what is most in accordance with a single ordered and consistent scheme of values under which what is valid for one is valid for all. Held cites Plato, Aristotle, Aquinas, Hegel and Marx as having led in this direction, all sharing some notion of an ultimate good, towards which all should aspire in their own ultimate best interest.

The special case of mass communication

It is far from obvious which class of theory is most appropriate for handling public communication issues. We can think of examples which place one or other communication issue in any of the three categories. In the category of 'preponderance' or 'majoritarian' thinking, ideas of 'giving the public what it wants' can be placed, as well as support for free market media provision (thus 'populist', consumerist, media policies in general). This would be in line with the proposal of the libertarian one-time Chairman of the Federal Communication Commission (FCC) to replace the concept of 'public interest' with that of 'the public's interest' – the wishes of different groups of media consumers (Fowler, 1982; Fowler and Brenner, 1983).

Preponderance theory would also support the wide use of public opinion poll findings as a guide to various policy interventions in the media, which might include: censorship (or not) of media representations of sex and violence; protection of an existing public broadcasting service for which a large majority are willing to pay for by licence fees (e.g. Tracey, 1986); the introduction, or the exclusion, of advertising. The examples illustrate the difficulty of using the *means* of determining the public good as a guide to evaluating the possible aims or the content of public communication arrangements. Long-term and fundamental matters would have to be settled on the basis of very time- and place-bound evidence. In general, this line of thinking would lead to a preference for audience and opinion research (which are notoriously manipulable and hard to interpret) as tools for the assessment of performance and putting all proposals to the test of the popular vote or the free market. There would be little chance to take adequate account of deeply held views or of very salient interests of small minorities.

Examples pertaining to the 'common interest' type of theory (the 'middle way', as it were, between 'majoritarian' or 'unitary' concepts) are easiest to find in relation to issues on which public opinion is not well developed or where it is little invoked. Basic features of national media structures and the services they provide (for example, technical standards, press subsidies, frequency allocations, access to political parties, rules for advertising) are often justified on grounds of a wider 'common good', transcending individual choices and preferences, with more reference to experts or to tradition than to the balance of popular opinion. The principle of freedom of speech and publication may itself have to be supported on grounds of long-term benefits to society which are not immediately apparent or clear to many individuals.

The 'common interest' category of theory does not only favour collective interests of society. It may also cover proposals designed to protect or advance consumer interests. For instance, Cass (1981: 61) cites a liberal economic definition as follows: 'Ideally, then, what would be in the public interest is the presentation of all the programs that could command payments in excess of their costs of production and distribution, regardless of the similarity or dissimilarity of the programs and the size or composition of their audiences.' This view contrasts sharply with more frequently heard claims which propose intervention to secure the distribution of programmes which would be unlikely to receive payments in excess of their costs of production, but which satisfy some ideal or value.

There are even more divergent claims for public benefits which can be identified by reference to one or other kind of 'unitary' theory, as described by Downs and Held. For example, theoretical support can be found both for total public and for total private ownership of media. The most vocal unitary theory at the present time may well be a plea for maximum market freedom for all media, in line with constitutional guarantees to the printed press (Fowler, 1982; Fowler and Brenner, 1983; Pool, 1984; Peacock, 1986; Veljanovski, 1989). The claim for media freedom is a good example of the invocation of unitary theory in relation to communication, but there are many other claims which invoke normative support for control of the media. These relate to matters such as: education, protection of the young, national language and culture (Blumler, 1992). In each case, a well-established and fundamental value principle is at stake.

A compromise proposal

Two of the three approaches to defining a public interest in public communication which have been discussed can be ruled out: those which depend heavily on the voice of the people expressed in opinion polls or market research and those which rely equally heavily on some absolute value commitment. The first type is generally insensitive, or just irrelevant, to some key issues, especially matters of a longer term, minority or technical character. It is very doubtful if one can ever rely on majority votes to settle complex issues, when public communication has to serve so many and such divergent purposes. The second type may have a reverse weakness of insensitivity to popular wants, but even more problematic is their frequently authoritarian, paternalistic or ideologically contestable character.

There is no longer (in most countries) a unitary value system to which we can appeal in order to settle broad issues. These two versions of public interest theory will have to be abandoned, by default, although they will not entirely go away and will play a part in the argument on particular issues. Instead we should concentrate on those versions of theory which belong either to Downs' 'pragmatic' ('realistic') category or Held's 'common interest' variant, where specific objectives and mechanisms of achievement can be named and deployed in argument.

It is easy to appreciate how elastic the notion of public interest is and will remain, whatever choice of concept one makes. Held (1970: 163) even suggests that we avoid using the term altogether, wherever a precise alternative is available. If we do mean 'majority preference' or our own chosen value position, it is better to say so. Unfortunately for common sense, it can often (as Downs reminds us) be advantageous in argument to introduce a claim of wider public benefit on behalf of almost any partial interest. An obvious example is the frequent appeal to 'public interest' both in support of, and in opposition to, sensationalist or intrusive reporting.

Held has other suggestions, aside from the avoidance of the term 'public interest'. Most centrally, she proposes that we think in term of competing *claims*: 'public interest' claims are normative assertions that something (e.g. an action or a goal) is *justifiable* on grounds of wider benefits, within the terms of a given political system and framework of norms. The main elements in such a claim are, thus: a set of principles and norms (on which there does not have to be unanimity); a proposal or claim (made with reference to these norms) for something (x) as having wider merit than satisfying individual wants (singly or in aggregate); and a machinery for testing the claim and putting it into effect, if so decided.

She writes:

> To assert that a claim is justifiable is not, however, to make a normative judgement in a final sense that it is *justified*. It is rather to put forward something close to an initial claim, or prima facie finding, or statement of what might be said to be justified prima facie . . . The justification appealed to may simply be that within a political system individuals are normally entitled to favor those actions and policies they think will satisfy their wants'. (Held, 1970: 164)

She adds, 'This interpretation of "interest" is proposed independently of any particular ethical theory about how moral judgements ought to be arrived at . . .' An important aspect of this proposal is the reference to a political and legal system which can act as a 'validating system'. Held stresses that 'meaningful use of the term public interest presupposes the existence of a political system, however primitive or complex'.

By adopting these suggestions, we might agree to treat various statements of public interest concerning communication as a set of competing claims or proposals with a normative component. It will be for the political or legal system to adjudicate between conflicting claims, although decisions may be delegated to authorities, such as the FCC, or a national postal or broadcast regulatory body (such as the British Independent Television Commission (ITC), the French Conseil Supérieur de l'Audiovisuel (CSA), or the Dutch Media Council) to make professional determinations of what will best serve the public as a whole, in accordance with political and legal decisions. Most questions of structure tend to be settled politically, while details of content provision are usually left to specialized agencies of media institutions. Most of the issues of media performance dealt with in this study do in fact belong to the latter territory: they lie within the competence of media organizations themselves (as matters of editorial policy or practice) as well as being at issue in the public domain.

A framework for identifying public interest claims

Mitnick (1980) chooses a more neutral and more concrete term than that of 'interest' to handle the details of claims which might be made concerning public communication. He refers to a 'preference' and to a 'preference schedule':

central to the concept of 'interest' is the notion of 'preferences' . . . there may be a reduction in ambiguity by focussing on one aspect of 'interest', the more neutral concept of 'preference'. A set of preferences or preference schedules are terms taken to mean, in effect, a set of instructions specifying what would constitute successful pursuit of the desired goal or objective. (Mitnick, 1980: 265)

Mitnick also distinguishes between the details of a particular claim or objective and the fundamental value which might justify a proposed act. Some definitions of public interest veer towards broad value judgements (and could thus lead to multiple sets of preferences) while others are very specific about preferences and vague about the fundamental values on which they are based. This new element is consistent with the borrowings from Held and helps in the empirical task of drawing up an inventory of relevant assessment criteria. The general conceptual scheme which can be constructed on the basis of the previous discussion of public interest theory can now be presented, starting from the assumption that claims about the public interest have first to be made by identifiable *claimants* ('agents of preference'), whether in an individual or a collective capacity. First, a verbal summary of the central ideas derived from the theory discussed here can be given, as follows.

Various actors or 'agents of preference' make claims within a political system on behalf of goals (favoured end-states) which are said, in the light of certain fundamental, or commonly held, values to be of general benefit to the whole society, community or public, over and above individual wants, satisfactions or utilities. These claims are specified in terms of preferences about a communication system or its performances which correspond to the advocated end-state. The specifications offered should indicate evaluative criteria for recognizing whether or not preferred conditions are present or goals reached.

The various elements are represented schematically in Figure 3.1. This scheme should be interpreted generally as inter-relating all the main elements named above, which can be further explained, as follows.

- The *polity* refers to the particular political forum or locus of decision-making in which a claim has to be made or settled. It may often be a national parliament or legal system, especially when questions of media structure are at issue. Otherwise, claims may be made in other kinds of public forum, or in the context of professional and voluntary self-regulation (for instance, press or advertising councils, with reference to codes of conduct). The nature of the forum will determine which 'rules of the game' apply concerning the type of claim which can be adjudicated and type of decision which can be made.
- *Fundamental communication values* can refer to any widely held general principle about individual or general good to be sought, or expected, from communication. Most societies recognize a wide range of communication 'goods', especially those which have to do with freedom and diversity of expression, education, information, the arts and

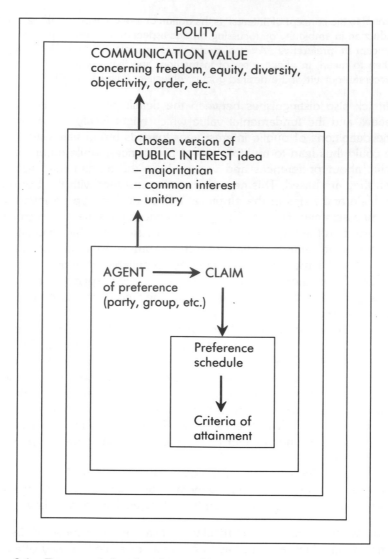

Figure 3.1 *Framework for identifying public interest claims in media assessment*

entertainment, social participation and cohesion, cultural identity, services to democracy, rights to communicate, etc. In general, such values are not themselves in dispute, but there can be conflict about their relative precedence and their applicability to particular circumstances.
- *Public interest concept*: according to Banfield (1955), something 'is said to be in the public interest if it serves the ends of the whole public rather than those of some sector of the public'. As we have seen, there are alternative versions of what would constitute, demonstrate or support a particular claim, especially: majority demand; a fundamental value or a

social theory; common interests as pragmatically determined. An appeal to the public interest settles nothing as such, but its invocation helps to distinguish matters of potential relevance to media performance research from purely sectional, individual or idiosyncratic points of view.

- *Agents of preference*: the potential claimants, those who actually propose objectives or standards for media and argue for them on public interest grounds, are numerous, diverse and often competing with each other. They often include: the state or other public authority; major social institutions with a communication interest of their own, such as political parties, business or trade union bodies; vulnerable social institutions and organized minorities; critics and various kinds of 'media watcher', including reviewers, academic researchers, professional commentators; the media themselves, whether as owners, managers or professional communicators; the audience of the media, speaking in various ways. These 'agents' are all quite likely to have a *self-interest* of their own in media performance, but can also all claim some legitimate right to speak for a wider constituency – thus to make an appeal on behalf of the public interest.

- *Claims:* these are the central elements in the scheme, referring 'back' to basic values and to ideas on the public interest and 'forward' to detailed expectations of preference (preference schedules). Claims at this level are usually expressed in terms of goals or broad purposes which are said both to fulfil some communication values *and* also to merit support on one or other ground of the wider and greater long-term benefit to community or society. Such claims are, inevitably, often divergent or contradictory.

- *Preference schedule*: the expression, borrowed from Mitnick (see above), refers to the set of 'instructions' which specifies the requirements for achieving the objectives of a public interest claim. A preference schedule would normally name certain preferred kinds of information or cultural provision, or condition of access or free operation, etc. It might also specify restrictions (e.g. on advertising, pornography, etc.).

- *Criteria of success in attaining goals:* the final element, necessary to assessment research (although less necessary for political argument) is the translation of the main terms of a preference schedule into even more specific indicators of performance. The criteria should be detailed enough to enable relevant objective observation, an accounting and evaluation of actual performance. They should, thus, allow conclusions to be drawn about progress, or lack of it, in achieving objectives. Aside from this, detailed specification of this kind can help to clarify the meaning of claims and their relation to basic communication values.

A feature of this general scheme is the implication that the number of alternatives and also of conflicts tends to increase as we move from the boundary to the centre of the frames in Figure 3.1. There are relatively few forums where claims can be pursued (although more if we include those of professional judgement alongside more political forums), several possible fundamental communication values and versions of the public interest. Beyond that, we can expect rather more claimants, a large number of specific claims, a proliferation of detailed preferences and even more potential criteria and indicators of performance.

Media policy debates: past and present

This formal presentation of the components of any discussion of mass media and the public interest is meant to help in locating research within a wider framework of 'media politics', the concrete terms of which will be discussed in the next two chapters. While the mass media have long been viewed as playing a vital part in the public life of most societies, they have also been viewed ambivalently, because of potential harmful as well as beneficial influences. In the media politics of Western societies during the recent past, debate about the 'public interest' in mass media has turned, consequently, on the central issue of whether they are either too important or not trustworthy enough to be left to the working of the free market.

There are other questions built into this formulation, especially about the precise benefits or harm that may be expected and about the goals of any intervention which might be contemplated. Between them, these constitute the 'preferences' about media performance referred to above. There are also questions about the *means* which can legitimately be used to advance public interest objectives and values. These means may consist either of 'positive' acts – subsidies, monopoly or other privileges, concessions, etc. – or of negative sanctions, especially rules and regulations designed to oblige media (whether in private or in public hands) to service public ends.

Within the limits of a national political system (for the most part), the advocates and opponents of regulation and deregulation, control or libertarianism, including those with vested economic interests in the outcome, have argued about the failings and successes of private and public media, often with appeals to certain fundamental values. There have often been high political or economic stakes, which have served to cloud issues and subordinate reasoned argument. The overall framework also represents the arena in which media performance-related research has been con-ducted, with evidence deployed to support or resist diverse claims. Not surprisingly, it is not an arena in which sweet reason and the calm weighing of evidence have been much in evidence.

Media policy as a source of norms for performance

According to the framework of principle for identifying public interest claims sketched in Figure 3.1, we have several choices of starting point and perspective. We can define and apply some set of fundamental communication values or we can proceed more pragmatically by following the view of particular 'agents of preference', examining particular claims and applying selected criteria of performance. As the field of performance research has developed in a rather arbitrary and fragmentary way, fuelled by local and particular motives, it is difficult to find a more systematic and coherent approach, except one driven by a 'unitary' value or by an exclusive ideology (whether libertarian or socialistic).

In so far as research has been theoretically grounded, it has usually been guided by reference to 'middle range' principles such as 'social responsibility', 'objectivity' or, less often, 'diversity' and 'cultural quality'. The nearest to a comprehensive framework of norms and values is probably that offered by one or other of the 'four theories of the press' of Siebert et al. (1956) and those who have followed in their footsteps (Merrill, 1974; Hachten, 1981; Altschull, 1984). For reasons which are discussed in Chapter 6, these normative press theories do not seem to provide an adequate foundation for performance research.

The practical utility of the four theories for guiding policy or research has always been extremely doubtful and is even more so at a time when media technologies and distribution systems are multiplying and when there is less consensus about basic values than in the past. Of course, the verbal constructions which the theories comprised were largely confined to the pages of academic writings and had no status in law, regulation, self-regulation or policy. In contrast, for decades, specific normative issues concerning the media have been fought out in the political and judicial arenas of most national societies. As a result, a wide-ranging body of principle concerning what media ought, or ought not, to do in their public capacity has emerged.

This is to be found in laws, regulations, court decisions, reports of commissions in so far as it concerns what society expects of the media. The extensive regulation of broadcasting (and even its deregulation) had produced a very large body of proscription and prescription which was largely ignored in the earlier tradition of theorizing referred to above. The media themselves have produced yet more numerous codes of journalistic practice (e.g. Nordenstreng and Topuz, 1989) and there has also been a gradual extension of regulation and of the normative discourse to the international level (globally and regionally).

In short, this body of material does provide an empirical basis for a normative enquiry into the media, however diverse in form, ramifying and uncodified it may be. We may expect to find the clearest expressions of the 'public interest' and also the clearest statements of fundamental values about communication from the point of view of 'society' in such material. The main purpose of the next two chapters is to sketch the main universe of meanings which ideas of a public interest in communication have been given in a number of different countries. The intention is to describe the most common principles of media performance which have been deployed in public policy discourse, in relation, first, to the newspaper and, secondly, to broadcasting.

In general, media policy has been directed at forms of publication which are closest to the concerns and interests of established power and authority (thus relating to matters of politics and religion more than to fiction and entertainment, and to public or national affairs rather than personal or business uses of communication). For this reason, it remains difficult to find normative theory relevant to the newer forms of the 'consciousness industry'. Vestiges of early policy also often survive beyond the circumstances which may once have justified them, for instance concerns about threats to national or state security, which reduce the relevance of some components of this body of 'media doctrine'.

Despite the extension of free market principles, the media remain very 'politicized' in the broad sense of the term. This is due to a continuing belief in the 'potency' of the media, however difficult to pin down, the seeming impossibility of *not* regulating the medium of television, for a variety of reasons, the growing industrial and economic significance of communication and information and the expanding set of international obligations (relating to 'software' as well as 'hardware' issues) which cannot be met without extensive domestic regulation.

A summary of mid-twentieth century policy issues

The foundations for a developing body of public communication policy and the accompanying normative discourse were already laid by the middle of the twentieth century and can be summarized in terms of several broad themes, which are recognizable in similar form in most post-war liberal democracies, albeit with varying priorities and specific expressions. The oldest issue was that of *national security and the maintenance of public order*, expressed in reserved government powers to supply or withhold information or even to censor, under conditions of emergency and 'in the national interest'.

The theme of *press freedom* was animated both by fear of state control and by the perceived dangers of large commercial monopolies. Radio regulation led to a particular emphasis on *univeralism* and *equity* of service, especially in matters of political conflict, but also in response to claims for *diversity* of provision on grounds of locality, taste and social needs. The potential *moral and cultural* impact of print, radio, music and film media, especially on the young or otherwise vulnerable, was another large subject of normative debate and a basis for regulation and self-regulation.

The standards of commercial print media in respect of their *information quality* or lack of it (e.g. alleged 'sensationalism') were also much discussed, though with little regulatory consequence. Finally, the *international tasks and obligations* of national media were beginning to be recognized, especially after the unhappy early history of propagandist use of the media in global, imperialist, rivalries.

Varieties of national expression of media norms

In order to appreciate the range of expression of communication values and principles of policy we need to look at how these issues have been handled in particular countries. The core principles relating to media performance have often found clearest expression at crisis or turning points in national or media history; for instance, when media were re-established in many European countries after enemy occupation during the Second World War; when the new and powerful medium of television was being introduced; when monopoly tendencies in the press appeared to be getting out of hand; at the time of upheavals in American society in the 1960s; or, more recently, when the established European broadcasting order is being challenged by the appearance of new distribution technologies. Such occasions have given rise to much contemporary evidence about normative expectations from the media.

Considered statements of principle concerning the public interest and the expectations of 'society' from the media are rarely found in systematic form. The nearest equivalents are encountered in the reports compiled by various national commissions and committees charged with the task of assessing media performance according to the issues named above, or of charting paths for change in media systems as a result of new technology. Other sources are codes of media practice originating within the media themselves, statements of public policy, or the actual requirements of performance entered in laws, regulations or similar instruments of public policy.

The status and availability of sources varies from one national situation to another and the discussion which follows in Chapters 4 and 5 draws on a variety of such sources from a limited number of countries, chosen mainly on the basis of the availability of relevant material and of a generally shared concern with the issues named above. There is a clear 'Anglo-Saxon' bias, partly the result of being accessible to the author, and partly stemming from historical circumstances of media development, including two world wars, which gave 'Anglo-Saxon' media theory a certain primacy over continental European variants in the past half-century (Homet, 1979). It is impossible to explain the full context of each reference or to deal with more than fragments of the policy 'discourse' which is uncovered. But enough can be done to assemble the main component items in a broad universe of principle relating to the social responsibilities and rights of the media in the time and place under review.

PART II
MEDIA PERFORMANCE NORMS

4
PERFORMANCE NORMS IN MEDIA POLICY DISCOURSE: THE NEWSPAPER PRESS

Policies for freedom and democracy

In modern times there has been virtual unanimity that the press should enjoy full freedom of publication, within the limits set by the individual rights of citizens and, ultimately, the need to safeguard the integrity and security of the state which guarantees freedom in the first place (Emerson, 1970; Lichtenberg, 1990). There is less consensus on how to provide in law for this freedom, since the forms range from an absence of specific law (as in the UK), through a prohibition of any law which would limit freedom of publication (as in the USA), to specific constitutional guarantees of freedom (as in Germany, France and many other countries). Quite widely, the most essential aspect of freedom, however secured, is thought to be the absence of any form of pre-publication censorship or any requirement for a licence, or permission, to publish.

If this were the only issue with respect to the public interest, there would be a limited and repetitive policy discourse, little policy and no particular reason to include the topic in a discussion of media performance. However, there are also disputed issues, most of which ultimately relate to the great power which has been attributed to the newspaper press and also the importance of the press to the health and routine conduct of modern democracies. These circumstances have generated a set of concerns about the responsibility for exercising press power, expectations about its positive use, questions of equity and ownership in respect of access to the benefits of power.

Nearly everywhere, the economic freedom of the press is viewed as essential, but the potential effects of market freedom are also viewed with concern (Keane, 1991). The market liberates, but its 'laws' also lead to concentration of ownership, reductions in diversity and commercial failure, leading to closure. In so far as the newspaper press is not just 'any other business', these normal contingencies of free market life may not be acceptable, even when the benefits of competition are valued. Much of what passes for press policy, when not designed to guarantee freedom, has been activated by the wish to protect the newspaper press from the full rigour of market forces.

The contours of debate are well indicated by a much-quoted phrase from a judgement of Judge Frankfurter in the case of *Associated Press* v. *US* (1, 28, 1943): 'In addition to being a commercial enterprise, it [the press] has a relationship to the public interest unlike that of any other enterprise for profit . . . The Business of the Press . . . is the promotion of truth regarding public matters by furnishing the basis for an understanding of them.' This view is echoed in documents and pronouncements around the world, perhaps even more forcefully in countries with less firm commitments than has the USA to the primacy of the market.

The USA: basic principles of policy

The First Amendment to the Constitution of the United States (1791) states that 'Congress shall make no law . . . abridging freedom of speech, or press . . .' This has usually been interpreted as outlawing censorship, although taken at face value it would seem to make all laws concerning the press unconstitutional and to rule out policy for the media altogether. This interpretation has certainly had an inhibiting effect, but it has not closed off all possibilities for government to play a role, in response to what are seen as imperatives of the wider public interest (Ernst, 1946; Lieberman, 1953; Bollinger, 1976; Brenner and Rivers, 1982; Hess, 1984; Glasser, 1986; Holmes, 1986; Dennis, 1989; Bennett, 1990; Lichtenberg, 1990).

Two other features are characteristic of media policy debates in general in the United States: the strongly economic flavour of regulation, stemming from the overwhelmingly commercial character of communications media; and the importance of the courts and of legal decisions in establishing and applying normative principles. The United States is, in addition, both more decentralized and more self-sufficient than are most other nations and it has never experienced any sharp discontinuity of the kind caused by military defeat, occupation or revolutionary change.

According to Pool (1984), in line with Kalven (1967), the country has known three different types of media regulatory regimes, in succession, but now overlapping each other: (a) the press freedom model applied to print media, which constitutionally forbids regulatory intervention; (b) the 'common carrier' model for telecommunications, which calls for regulation of infrastructure, but not of content; and (c) the broadcasting model, which involves extensive regulation, to the extent of influencing content and restraining some kinds of freedom of expression.

The newspaper press in the United States

Largely because of constitutional protection from any governmental interference, there have been no official inquiries into, or recommendations about, the standards appropriate to newspaper performance. Nevertheless, there has been no shortage of criticism, assessment and suggestions for codes of practice. The only example of a general inquiry (albeit a private venture) into the state of the American press is provided by the Commission on Freedom of the Press (Chafee, 1947; Hocking, 1947; Hutchins, 1947). Although its report was heavily criticized at the time by the press itself (Knutson, 1948), it had an enduring influence by way of its closely argued claim that the press owes something to its society (thus a 'social responsibility') and by its statement of the standards of performance which would be appropriate for responsible news media.

According to Blanchard (1977), the appointment of a Commission, convened and paid for by publisher Henry Luce, was initially welcomed by the press because it came at a time of increasing friction between the press and government and of increasing demands for limitations on the freedom of the press, despite First Amendment immunity (Seldes, 1938; Ickes, 1939). The stated aim of the Commission was to 'examine areas and circumstances under which the press of the United States is succeeding or failing; to discover where free expression is or is not limited, whether by government censorship, pressure from readers or advertisers or the unwisdom of its proprietors or the timidity of its management'.

When the report was published in 1947, it came out strongly for continued freedom from government, but contained unwelcome messages, concluding that the failings of a free press could lead to government-imposed control. The report was very critical of press 'sensationalism', the heavy concentration of ownership, and a failure to provide citizens with information they might need in a democracy (Desmond, 1947). The Commission concluded that the time had 'come for the press to assume a new public responsibility'. Specific recommendations were made for standards of performance which would be called for in order to fulfil the proposed new norm of 'social responsibility' (Hess, 1966; Anderson, 1977; Dennis, 1986; Hodges, 1986).

The press, it was argued, should first of all provide 'a truthful, comprehensive, and intelligent account of the day's events in a context which gives them meaning'. In doing so, newspapers should separate fact from comment and present both sides of disputed issues. Secondly, the press should 'provide a forum for the exchange of comment and criticism'; newspapers should be 'common carriers of the public expression'. Thirdly, the press should project a 'representative picture of constituent groups in society', avoiding stereotypes and explaining group values. Fourthly, the press should present and clarify 'the goals and values of society'.

The report contained a good deal of criticism of the sensationalism of the press and of its subordination to commercial criteria of performance and to vested interests of proprietors. It spoke in favour of more diversity of press outlets and more 'vigorous mutual criticism' of the press by itself, as a means of discouraging the slanting of news to fit editorial policies. Despite the negative reception of the report in many press quarters, including the influential American Society of Newspaper Editors (ASNE), Blanchard (1977) concluded that it had a longer term influence in providing, by way of the 'responsibility' thesis, the goals for future aspirations (especially by means of professional education) and in making 'press criticism socially acceptable'. The Commission also helped to provide a foundation for much future research on the press, even if it carried out little research itself and was not strongly based on empirical data.

One of the neglected but most interesting aspects of the work of the Commission on Freedom of the Press was its early attempt to address the question of international obligations and standards in the reporting of foreign news. A separate report of the Commission entitled *Peoples Speaking to Peoples* (White and Leigh, 1946) made a plea for higher standards of reporting than market forces alone might justify, in order to represent the United States in the world and also to report back adequately from the outside world to the United States, in the interests of establishing 'a stable, peaceful world society'.

Specifically, the report asked for in-depth, contextualized, balanced, truthful reporting of events and the avoidance of reporting which would promote hatred, suspicion and hostility between nations, allowing for the need to report conflict and evil in the world. To these ends, the report asked for improved physical conditions for reporting, reduction of political barriers to the flow of news and 'improvement of the accuracy, representative character and quality of the words and images transmitted in international communication'. These recommendations were, according to Blanchard (1986), turned into a crusade to export American conceptions of press freedom worldwide.

The idea of self-regulation of performance by the press was not a complete novelty in 1947. The ASNE had adopted its first code of standards (Canons of Journalism) in 1923, and it has continued to be an active promoter and monitor of press performance (De Mott, 1980; Meyer, 1987). Its 1975 revision of the Canons of Journalism provides a good indication of what is currently regarded as good practice. The main items, in brief, are as follows:

1 Responsibility: the aim of serving the 'general welfare' by informing people and enabling them to make judgements about issues of the time.
2 Freedom of the press.
3 Independence from vested interest.
4 Truth and accuracy.
5 Impartiality, in particular a clear distinction between news reports and opinion.
6 Fair play, meaning respect for the rights of people involved in the news,

observing standards of decency, giving opportunities for reply, respecting confidentiality.

In keeping with the 'non-policy' tradition of press freedom, there are few other substantial or authoritative sources of normative statements concerning press responsibility, apart from a few significant court decisions (for example, the 1969 Red Lion decision, which upheld the constitutionality of various forms of broadcast regulation; and the *Miami Herald* v. *Tornillo* case of 1974, which upheld a newspaper's right to deny access; see Holmes, 1990). There is, nevertheless, an enormous and continuing volume of critical attention to the press, owing its main impulse to the active, voluntary self-regulatory tradition and the professionalization of journalism, including the rise of journalism education and research (Dennis, 1989).

Despite the sparsity of legislation or court judgments impinging on the press in their public capacity, there are some policy instruments relating to the operation of press industries which imply certain expectations. The instruments include tax and postal concessions (see Picard, 1985a), anti-cartel legislation and the 1973 Preservation of Newspapers Act, which sought to exempt economically weak newspapers from some provisions of anti-cartel legislation by allowing joint operating agreements (Barvis, 1980; Patkus, 1984; Busterna, 1987; Picard, 1987). In general these measures were designed to give some economic protection to the press, and therefore some privilege which was justified according to 'public interest' principles concerning the quality, independence, diversity and volume of information available in society. Policy has shown much ambivalence and inconsistency in recognizing the threats to freedom of expression arising from monopoly tendencies in the press (Holmes, 1990).

Canada: press policy for democracy and cultural identity

The Canadian experience has resulted in a somewhat different perspective on what counts as being 'in the public interest', despite its sharing a similar tradition of press freedom with the United States. The main differences stem from facts of geography and history. Canada is a more recent and more vulnerable nation state; it is more evidently divided culturally and linguistically than is the United States. It is more extensive and thinly populated and a large majority of its citizens live within easy and effective reach of an attractive foreign media system. There is a high degree of concentration of the press industry, partly as a consequence of economies of scale in a relatively small total national market; there has also been the influence of European thinking about press accountability, as a result of British and French connections; and policy traditions which have a more 'social' or collectivist character.

From these features, we can readily understand why issues of media structure and performance in Canada have been dominated by three or four main themes, within the framework of issues named in Chapter 3. One of these is the problem of national integrity and identity; a second is that of media concentration and its consequences; a third is the matter of securing adequate provision for a dispersed population; a fourth is the question of maintaining the balance and integration between the two language communities and the health of the more threatened French language minority media sector. This concern has subsequently extended to other language and ethnic communities and led to a policy of 'multiculturalism'.

We can also appreciate why there has been much public scrutiny of press structure and performance, including several major inquiries at national and provincial level as well as extensive programmes of empirical research designed to evaluate the condition of press (and broadcasting) in their public service roles. Only the key points resulting from this vast public scrutinizing activity can be picked out, with a view to *enlarging* the range of normative principles for media performance that have been identified (thus additional to those shared with the USA and which have already been mentioned).

The clearest impression of concerns about the Canadian newspaper press can be gained from the report of the Royal Commission on Newspapers (known, after its chairman, as the Kent Commission), set up in 1980 and reporting in 1981. The Commission was primarily established to consider the degree and consequences of the increase in chain ownership of newspapers, and thus the decline in independent editorial control. Its terms of reference required it to assess the degree to which economic trends (concentration and loss of individual newspapers) were affecting the newspaper industry's 'responsibilities to the public'. There is a reference to the possible consequences of current trends in the industry for 'the political, economic, social and intellectual vitality and cohesion of the nation as a whole' (Kent, 1981: 259).

The performance criteria applied by the inquiry in taking evidence and conducting research are not especially original or unique to Canada. Most relevant to the present purpose are the following factors: the need to contribute to the democratic process; the danger of 'editorial concentration' and loss of independence in media chains; the need for a wide international perspective; the need for diversity and a broad spectrum of representation; the threat to adequate news coverage as a result of 'sensationalism'. Although the report asks for accountability to the public, it also warns of what it calls 'market-survey' journalism, in which papers seek to follow rather than lead public opinion. Although the standards of performance in news which were advanced by the Commission are already familiar, they received a very clear definition in several of the research studies which were carried out to assess the effects of press concentration (Fletcher, 1981; and see below).

The Kent Commission (1981) also cited approvingly the 'Statement of principles' for Canadian daily newspapers (the work of the Canadian Daily Newspapers Publishing Association) which, in some respects, goes further than similar US codes. For instance, in addition to provisions concerning freedom, accuracy, fairness, ethics and privacy, it has detailed entries on 'responsibility', 'independence' and 'access'. On responsibility, the code states that 'The operation of a newspaper is, in effect, a public trust, no less binding because it is not formally conferred, and its overriding responsibility is to the society which protects and provides its freedom.' On access, according to the code, 'The newspaper is a forum for the free interchange of information and opinion. It should provide for the expression in its columns of disparate and conflicting views. It should give expression to the interests of minorities as well as majorities, and of the less powerful elements in the society' (Kent, 1981: Appendix VII).

Press policy in Britain

The press in Britain experienced a rapid commercial growth and a strong trend to monopoly in the early part of the twentieth century, much as occurred in the United States. The response of journalists, intellectual critics and the labour movement caused this to become a political issue, with calls for government intervention in the organization of the press, especially after the Second World War (Smith, 1974b; Seymour-Ure, 1991). The experience of extensive controls on the press during the war (especially on newsprint supply) and the political colour of the post-war administration made intervention a real possibility, despite strong traditions of press freedom and the power of the press itself to influence opinion against such an eventuality. Parliament established a Royal Commission in 1947 to examine the degree of press monopoly which had developed and, especially, 'whether such concentration as exists is on balance disadvantageous to the free expression of opinion, or the accurate presentation of news'.

In its report (Royal Commission on the Press, 1949), the Commission (like Judge Frankfurter quoted above) took the view that the press is more than just a business, and has a public task and a corresponding public responsibility, being 'the chief instrument for instructing the public on the main issues of the day'. It gave a statement of normative principle, as follows:

> The democratic form of society demands of its members an active and intelligent participation in the affairs of their community, whether local or national. It assumes that they are sufficiently well-informed about the issues of the day to be able to form the broad judgements required by an election, and to maintain, between elections, the vigilance necessary in those whose governors are their servants and not their masters ... Democratic society, therefore, needs a clear and truthful account of events, of their background and their causes; a forum for discussion and informed criticism; and a means whereby individuals and groups can express a point of view or advocate a cause. (RCP, 1949: 100–101)

The standards by which the performance of the press should be judged in the light of this public responsibility were made clear by the Commission, although it also acknowledged the requirements of the press to be run as a business and an industry and its need to respond to the wishes of readers. The emphasis was placed on standards which were widely shared within the press itself, especially: full and up-to-date information together with explanation and comment; accuracy; and the clear separation of fact from comment. The Commission also endorsed the view that newspapers should not allow their general policy or particular reporting to be influenced by advertisers, or by government information services.

Particular emphasis was put on three other matters, which are not so consistently represented in the press's own view of the standards of performance: *truthfulness; diversity;* and avoiding *sensationalism.* The first was interpreted essentially as avoiding 'excessive bias'. Bias, in turn, was said to have three aspects: first, the deliberate suppression or omission of relevant facts; secondly, the distortion or mis-stating of facts; thirdly, exaggerated or highly coloured and emotive presentation of facts. According to the Commission, newspapers have a right to hold and express opinions, but should make their opinions known in commentary, not in headlines or news itself. The standard of what counts as 'excessive' bias is set at going beyond that which can be justified by news values alone, taking account of the relative significance of events and the likely political and other interests of the readership.

'Diversity' was defined as a requirement that 'the number and variety of newspapers should be such that the Press as a whole gives an opportunity for all important points of view to be effectively presented in terms of the varying standards of taste, political opinion, and education among the principal groups of the population.' 'Sensationalism' was dealt with as a 'tendency to abandon rational standards of relative importance and to magnify the trivial and the irrelevant', a tendency attributed to undue deference to the immediate interest of the reader.

Three undesirable features are covered by the reference to 'triviality and sensationalism'. One is applying what are called 'peculiar values' in selection (a quaint example given by the Commission is the tendency to give as much space to sport as to 'serious' news). A second feature is giving undue attention to crime, scandal, entertainment and human interest. A third feature relates to the manner of presentation and lay-out. The use of bold headlines, pictures, variations of type and display are mentioned as examples of seeking 'eye-appeal'. The report remarks that 'in times of tension . . . it may dangerously stimulate public excitement.'

The third Royal Commission on the Press (1977) was appointed to 'inquire into the factors affecting the maintenance of the independence, diversity and editorial standards of newspapers and periodicals and the public's freedom of choice of newspapers and periodicals, nationally, regionally and locally'. It applied much the same criteria of performance as had the first Commission, with particular reference to the possible negative effects on standards of press mergers and concentration. It too stressed the degree to which there was a 'public interest', going beyond claims of proprietorial liberty, sufficient, in principle, to justify some forms of regulation of the market, should the need be demonstrated.

There is little in the report in the way of extension of 'normative discourse', but the Commission did initiate a good deal of research – into attitudes of the public and of journalists as well as into press content – as a way of testing standards of performance. It produced a clearer and more concise statement of principles than has been typical of such bodies. It also paid attention to a wider range of matters, including the alternative press, the education of journalists, media cross-ownership, and the quality of local and regional newspapers.

The most recent event in British press policy history has been the report of the Calcutt Committee (1990), appointed to look specifically at standards of press behaviour in matters of sensational reporting and 'invasion of privacy', another case of an economically liberalizing administration being also conservative and restrictive. The main outcome has been the establishment of a new (still voluntary and self-regulatory) Press Complaints Commission to replace the Press Council and a new threat of compulsion if the press does not mend its own ways. Between the setting up of the Committee and its reporting, the press, for the first time in Britain, published its own code of conduct, to which most editors subscribed, dealing in a similar way with the same issues.

The continental European contribution

The factors which influenced media policy in the cases described – especially growing press concentration and the need to regulate broadcasting – were common to many other countries, especially in Europe. Although responses have varied according to local circumstances and traditions, the basic principles and array of normative terms of the Anglo-American model were largely shared and again influential in the restructuring of the media after the Second World War. A fuller understanding of the norms widely invoked on behalf of the 'public interest' in communications can, however, be gained by looking at some principles of performance which have been under-represented in North American and British experience.

Sweden: support for the political role of the press

Swedish press policy has been distinctive for its clear support of a press system fundamentally based on political diversity and for the extent and range of economic support. Sweden may also be distinctive for the key role which communication research has played in guiding and evaluating press policy. Moves towards protection of the press were first stimulated in Sweden, as elsewhere, by the worrying experience of post-war newspaper concentration and loss of titles. The very dominant position of the Social Democratic party in government over many years clearly played a role in shaping the response to economic pressures. The basic aim of this response was to reconcile press freedom (constitutionally guaranteed in 1949) with economic support for newspapers (Andren, 1968; Gustafsson and Hade-nius, 1976; Hollstein, 1978; Gothberg, 1983; Hadenius, 1983; Hulten, 1984; Nieuwenhuis, 1991).

The primary goal was to protect the *political role* of the press (regarded as crucial to democratic liberty). The traditional pattern of the Swedish press was of party alignment and local or regional competition among independ-ent, politically opposing, newspapers. This pattern was threatened by economic forces and two parliamentary commissions (1963–65 and 1967–68) examined ways of giving aid without limiting freedom, especially aid to *second* newspapers in a weak competitive position (low penetration rate) in a given region. A complex set of subsidy provisions (largely based on the example of Norway) was instituted and is still in force. In total there have been six commissions, the most recent in 1985–88, whose main task has been to assess the working and effects of support mechanisms for the press.

It was the third parliamentary commission (1972) which, on the basis of social, as well as economic, research, extended thinking about the role of the press and the need for support. A statement of the proper functions of the press in a democracy was made. These were said to be: providing all-round information; commentary on the events of the day; scrutinizing holders of power; facilitating communication among and within organized groups.

While this is not very different in principle from the view of press functions set out, for instance, by the British 1977 Commission, the emphasis is much more strongly on the (party) political role of the press and its distinctiveness (compared to what broadcasting might have to offer). In particular, the press can offer much *more* information, it can take up partisan positions and comment freely, it has better access to information held by power-holders and it is closely related to the structure of political and other social groups.

Nieuwenhuis interprets the aims of press policy in Sweden as follows: 'The essence of the theory of social responsibility seems in Sweden to come down to a social responsibility *for* the press and not *of* the press. Normative tasks are not laid upon the press, but are attached to functions which the press factually fulfils' (1991: 265). These functions relate to opinion-forming and information and can be determined empirically. This interpretation (which applies more widely in Europe) leaves the press quite free, in principle, but allocates the right, even duty, to a society to secure the conditions necessary for the press to perform its 'natural' tasks.

Other national experience: France, Germany and The Netherlands

Post-war experience of trends towards newspaper concentration in several other European countries was not dissimilar to the cases described, although responses varied. There was, in several countries, an additional factor stemming from the need to re-establish a free press after a period of dictatorship or foreign occupation. In France, for instance, ownership rules were drawn up after the liberation designed to exclude press owners who had collaborated and to dispose of some titles (Albert, 1990). A comparable process took place in The Netherlands (Wieten, 1988), demonstrating a powerful feeling (overriding considerations of economic freedom) that the newspaper press is too important to be in the hands of 'unsuitable' elements, from the point of view of nation and society. The same principle guided the reinstatement of a free press in Germany during the occupation period.

Post-war press policy in France was guided additionally by a wish to exclude foreign influences in newspaper ownership and by a growing concern about concentration and the general weakness of the national (Paris-based) press in particular. A number of measures of economic support, including postal and tax concessions and some direct subsidies to individual titles, were introduced. Since 1970, provision has also been made to limit the degree of concentration and cross-media ownership. Of three official commissions which have inquired into the press since 1970, the Vedel Commission (reporting in 1979) gave the clearest statement of the goals of press policy, under the familiar headings of: Freedom, Independence and Pluralism. In respect of freedom, more emphasis was placed on the right of the public to be informed than on the rights of the publisher. Independence was construed as relating both to relations with government and with hidden financial interests. Pluralism was named as a priority for a modern press support system. However, the Commission resisted the idea that press policy should be based on a concept of 'public service'. Pluralism was essentially equated with what would be delivered by an effective free market (Nieuwenhuis, 1991).

In Germany, debates about press functions and policy were also stimulated when the re-established free press came to experience much the same sort of economic pressure and concentration tendency as elsewhere. However, fears of the revival of press barons came into conflict with stronger fears about government intervention and the result was to inhibit public intervention of the kind described. Within the constitutional framework guaranteeing complete freedom of the press, each *Land* was able to make its own laws for the press, and some of these did give verbal support to the democratic political functions of newspapers. For instance, the Hamburg Press Law has a section on 'social functions of the press', which refers to news collection, opinion expression and formation, criticism and education (Lahav, 1985). Two parliamentary commissions during the 1960s made recommendations for more economic support, but these were not well received, especially because of fears of press dependence on government. In 1976, however, anti-cartel legislation was sharpened up to make it easier to apply to newspapers.

In The Netherlands, a principle valued on a par with freedom of the press has been 'pluriformity' – essentially the diversity of press structure and content, as manifested in alternative opinions and outlooks which reflect the key differences in the national society (McQuail, 1992). The main guarantee for this desirable condition should stem from society itself, but marked concentration trends, reinforced by the fears (as in Germany) of the impact of television advertising (after 1967) led to a range of measures for helping weaker newspapers, paid for by some of the television advertising revenue. The main aim has always been to preserve as many independent titles and as much choice for readers as possible. The measures have been incorporated into the 1988 Media Law. As in other countries, a main point of debate has been how far such measures of support should be general, addressed to the industry as a whole, or targeted at particular newspapers.

Norms for international news

Expectations of the press in regard to its treatment of other countries have provided an additional focus for normative discourse. The 1947 American Commission on Freedom of the Press (see above) gave the issue a place in wider discussions of press responsibility. However, there is no international press *institution* as such, no agreed body of norms, no agency which can exert any effective pressure or restraint on the press, as routinely happens in a national domestic context. Discussions on the issue have been both controversial and unsuccessful in going beyond statements of principle which are in themselves unlikely to be effective in practice.

The case of international news reporting is problematic for many reasons, especially because it is closely tied in with press fears of limits on its freedom, with international enmities and alliances as well as economic competition and relations of dependency. The terrain is very complex and highly politicized.

At the core of the problem of establishing possible performance standards is the fact that the media are *nationally* organized to serve their own publics and national or state interests. The media generally regard themselves as owing no responsibility to 'foreigners' or other states and, in the 'West', do not accept that the state can legitimately interfere in any news reporting concerning non-domestic events, although accountability and even intervention may be accepted on some points of national 'public interest'. In brief, the media generally recognize no other constituency than what is provided by their own public or, at most, their country.

This basic fact has made the media themselves reluctant even to recognize the legitimacy of any normative criteria for their dealings with the rest of the world, and to view even the most toothless move in this direction with great suspicion. This attitude has come increasingly to seem at odds with the 'shrinking' of the world, the acknowledgement of increasing interdependency in economic, and 'security' (war, peace and terrorism) issues, and matters to do with the environment. The typical nationalism of the media has contrasted strongly with the growing internationalism of politics. Nevertheless, Nordenstreng's (1984) account of international legal documents extending over 40 years reveals a surprising level of normative expectation concerning news treatment of international matters (see also Jones, 1980). It also draws attention to the close similarity between what the American Commission on Freedom of the Press opined on this matter in 1947 (White and Leigh, 1946) for home consumption and what UNESCO said in 1978 in its Media Declaration.

Indeed, many of the standards concerning news already mentioned, including those freely adopted by the press itself as general codes of conduct, could lead one to assume that foreign news will be treated with the same care for fullness, truth and accuracy as home news. In the event, it appears from research and experience that media are generally more arbitrary, 'biased' (in every sense) and less 'responsible' in dealing with news from abroad than in dealing with home news, standards varying a good deal according to which medium and which segment of the domestic public is being served (Kivikuru and Varis, 1985).

The main principles outlined in the 1978 UNESCO Media Declaration, albeit rather pious and unrealistic, do express a set of expectations about performance which are not unreasonable, nor out of line with mainstream journalistic norms of 'good performance'. The Declaration indicates prescriptions as well as proscriptions based on widely acknowledged principles of human rights, including a 'right to communicate'. The media are asked *not* to: incite to war, or make propaganda for aggression; seek to subvert other governments by misinformation and subversion; advocate hatred on the basis of nationality, religion or race; provide biased or distorted information about other countries. On the positive side, media are asked to: promote efforts towards peace, disarmament and *détente*; promote free and balanced flow of diverse information; give expression to the claims of oppressed peoples in the world; make their public aware of world problems of hunger, poverty, sickness, underdevelopment; allow access and rights of reply to international voices.

These claims appear to go beyond normal concepts of what a domestic public might expect from international news coverage and imply limits to freedom of opinion and comment on the international scene. Even so, the gap between these norms and what is thought appropriate for equivalent domestic issues is not so great (for instance, not promoting social conflict or inciting hatred and positively working for community and national harmony – all typically regarded by most media as normal in a domestic context). The same (unwritten) norms might be largely agreed in relation to news attention in and between closely allied nations, as in the European Community. The question is one of the relative sense of responsibility of national media for effects which might occur beyond the national frontier or beyond the expected audience.

Changing status of the press

For most of the twentieth century, the newspaper press has been at the centre of attention, from the point of view of public interest concerns, largely because of the key role it played in the historic movements of the Enlightenment, reform and revolution from the eighteenth century to the present. There are clear signs that this situation is changing and the newspaper, in its traditional form, is no longer as important to society as it once was because of the rise of electronic media and the commercialization of the newspaper press itself. We are at an uneasy juncture, when development of normative thinking about the press seems either ritualistic or simply 'stuck' in a groove, while normative thinking about the new, and not so new, media is fragmentary or lacking legitimacy (Lichtenberg, 1990; Keane, 1991).

5
PERFORMANCE NORMS IN MEDIA POLICY DISCOURSE: BROADCASTING

Media on a leash

Broadcast media in most countries have taken a very similar path of development, following the adoption of radio in the early 1920s as a means of communication to the general public. Access to the use of the airwaves and the permitted uses to which radio could be put were governed by law, licence or regulation, even where the free market reigned, as in the United States. The same can be said of television in its post-war rise and, despite deregulation and proliferation, television and most other audiovisual media still do not enjoy the degree of freedom of publication granted to the print media.

The reasons are much the same everywhere: especially the widespread assumption that these media have great power in respect of the morals of the young, public decency and order, and also the views, as the political and social significance of television became appreciated, that access to limited airwaves (as sender or receiver) should be allocated in a equitable manner. Technical reasons and arguments from efficiency and from the need to manage national resources have also played a part. Beyond a consensus approach along these lines, public expectations from the broadcast media have varied a good deal according to national traditions and circumstances.

The USA: regulating the airwaves

The first act of communications policy which consciously involved restrictions on free speech was the Radio Act of 1927, which set up the Federal Radio Commission, the body which was to issue licences and oversee the development of radio after its early unregulated few years (Mander, 1984). This step was undertaken because, without regulation, communication through the airwaves would have been impossible, given the shortage of spectrum and the need to allocate access on some fair principle, as well as to maintain acceptable standards. In the selection of licensees, the Act required the new Commission to pay particular attention to issues of free speech. These were expressed in terms of a bias against monopoly ownership, rules against private censorship (which had become common before the Act, see Simmons, 1978), rules requiring 'equal time' (later known as the Fairness Doctrine). In general, the standards required of licensees were summarized under the expression 'public convenience, interest or necessity', a phrase which still guides the work of the successor to the Radio Commission, the Federal Communications Commission (FCC), and still leads to much dispute as to what it means in practice (see below).

The Federal Communications Act of 1934, which established the FCC, largely confirmed the provisions of the Radio Act and still remains in force, although modified by the deregulation of 1984 and various provisions for cable television made since the early 1970s. The arbitrariness of the broadcasting model, its inconsistency with First Amendment provisions, its lack of economic logic (licences are given, not sold), its ambiguity about the nature of the public trust involved have often been criticized (for example by Owen, 1975, 1982; Cole and Oettinger, 1978; Fowler and Brenner, 1983; Pool, 1984). Even so, the body of law, regulations, decisions and court cases which has grown up embodies a number of principles which have had to be taken seriously by broadcasters and are relevant to research on media performance.

The main principles are fairly clear, even if their application to cases is often uncertain. Firstly, there is no doubt that the legislation, in the name of the 'public interest', and in return for the grant of a licence to operate, was intended to place the broadcaster in a position of public *trustee* (Rutkus, 1982). According to a statement of the FCC in 1960:

> The licensee is, in effect, a 'trustee', in the sense that his license to operate his station imposes upon him a non-delegable duty to serve the public interest in the community he has chosen to represent as a broadcaster . . . The confines of the licensee's duty are set by the general standard of 'the public interest, convenience and necessity' . . . The principal ingredient of such obligation consists of a diligent, positive and continuing effort by the licensee to discover and fulfil the tastes, needs and desires of his service area. If he has accomplished this, he has met his public responsibility . . . (Barrow, 1968: 451)

Krugman and Reid (1980) made their own assessment of the criteria of public interest which were used by the FCC over a period of years in its evaluations of applications for licences or of performance by licensees. Their conclusions were based on interviews as well as on documents (e.g. the FCC 'Blue Book', 1946). The main items were as follows:

- *balance* as between various interest groups in respect of some controversial policy issue;
- *heterogeneity*: a value attached to the attention given to the number of diversified interests;
- *dynamism*: adaptability and evolution;
- *localism*: favouring broadcasting at the local level and local content;
- *diversity*: of programmes and services to the public.

These terms crop up repeatedly as standards of performance and they are supplemented by other specific principles, especially the 'equal opportunities doctrine' and the 'fairness doctrine' (Barrow, 1968; Simmons, 1978; Rowan, 1984; Powe, 1987; Lichtenberg, 1990). The former has its origin in the 1927 and 1934 Acts and relates especially to candidates for political office who should be given equal opportunities to broadcast, involving not only equal time, but comparable conditions of scheduling, facilities, charges, etc. This provision is not only supposed to protect candidates, but also to serve the public need to know their candidates, a duality of purpose which can place broadcasters in difficulty. The 'fairness doctrine' (deriving from the 1934 Communications Act) required licensees to aid dialogue on vital issues by providing reasonable opportunities for the presentation of opposing viewpoints on controversial issues of public importance. Barrow (1968) cites the FCC decision on the Mayflower Broadcasting Corporation (1941) as representing a more or less definitive statement of the doctrine:

> Freedom of speech on the radio must be broad enough to provide full and equal opportunity for the presentation to the public of all sides of public issues. Indeed as one licensed to operate in a public domain, the licensee has assumed the obligation of presenting all sides of important public questions, fairly, objectively and without bias. (Barrow, 1968: 462)

This statement of principle has had several side effects on the general norms governing broadcasting in America. One has been to put a general premium on a reasonable provision of news and of programmes dealing with public issues of interest in the communities served. It has also contributed to the concept of the right of the public to be informed on matters of significance. Barrow quotes another (1949) statement of principle by the FCC which contains the following passage: 'It is the right of the public to be informed, rather than any right on the part of Government, any broadcast licensee or any individual member of the public to broadcast his own particular views on any matter *which is the foundation stone of the American system of broadcasting.*' (Interestingly, this version of fairness seems the one which receives most support from public opinion, to judge from Comstock, 1988.)

When regulations for cable were being drafted in the 1970s, similar kinds of criteria of performance were applied, although particular significance was attached to *localism* and to *access*. The first of these put a premium on local ownership, production and content. Access provisions required a separate channel to be reserved for 'non-commercial public access . . . available on a first come, non-discriminatory basis', together with channels for local educational authorities, local government and for local leased access services. There would be no control over programme content on these channels by the cable television system. Subsequent deregulation has largely abolished all content requirements.

There has long been concern about the possible harmful or disturbing effects of film and television, especially on the child audience (Blumer and Hauser, 1933; Wartella, 1988). This has led to much research, some wide-ranging, high-profile inquiries, as well as to various codes of practice for broadcasting, in the absence of formal machinery for control of content. In a volume of evidence relating to the Report of the National Commission on the Causes and Prevention of Violence (Kerner Commission, 1969), Baker and Ball (1969) evaluated the codes of practice concerning television which were then mainly the responsibility of the National Association of Broadcasters (NAB), to which the main networks and most affiliates belonged. The NAB code was intended to maintain acceptable levels concerning standards of film and television in America on matters to do with morals.

According to Baker and Ball:

> a distinctive characteristic of the (NAB) code is its insistence that television programming have a moral theme. Drug addiction, cruelty, greed, selfishness, criminality, murder, suicide and illicit sex relations are to be portrayed in an unfavorable light. With respect to children's programming, the Code called for avoidance of the 'techniques of crime in such detail as to invite imitation' and recommends against the portrayal of violence and sex unless 'required by plot development or character delineation'. (1969: 600)

A more difficult issue for American television was raised by the widespread outbreaks of civil violence in American cities during the mid-1960s which led to the Kerner Commission inquiry. It was more difficult because it concerned not fictional portrayals of violence, but news reports of actual violence, which some suspected of stimulating or disseminating more actual violence (yet which could claim First Amendment protection). While these charges were not sustained, the Kerner Commission did make some criticism of the performance of news media and some recommendations for improvement.

Two points in particular were singled out. One was the importance of not distorting the truth by a disproportionate emphasis on dramatic and violent aspects of the reported events (the riotous behaviour and response of the police). On this matter, the Commission noted a tension between news values and considerations of social responsibility. A second issue was the relative absence of minority (or 'black' community) points of view in the reporting, which was largely carried out from the perspective of a dominant (and white) majority. These remarks underline the value placed on balanced and objective reporting on the one hand and diversity and access opportunity on the other.

In a supplementary staff report to the Kerner Commission, Baker and Ball (1969) made a number of specific recommendations for action by government and media, which enlarged on the performance criteria mentioned. They asked, *inter alia*, for: less sensationalism (reporting of violence for its own sake); more interpretation of events reported; more continuous coverage of 'minority' news; more attempts to establish contacts with police and potential dissidents; more precision about demonstrations and violence; more coverage by the media of alternative means of expressing grievances.

This account of statements of expectation concerning broadcasting performance can be supplemented by reference to the establishment of a public broadcasting service (PBS) by the Public Broadcasting Act of 1967 (Carnegie Commission, 1978; Comstock, 1989). Public broadcasting had its origin in the educational broadcasting movement and was established to supplement normal commercial programming, rather than compete with it, by offering educational and cultural programmes (including provision for minorities) which might not appeal to a mass audience (and should not be intended to make a profit). The values which PBS is designed to uphold (and for which it is publicly subsidized), in addition to those of education and 'culture', are those of *participation, community, localism* and *access*. The form of organization and funding – local and voluntary – is designed to fulfil these ends.

Canadian broadcasting: multiculturalism and autonomy

The Canadian approach to broadcast regulation has been shaped even more by its proximity to the United States than has its press policy. With 70 per cent of its population living within easy reach of television broadcasting from the United States, Canada has had a most difficult task in developing and protecting a broadcast system which can effectively serve national cultural and social needs. French-speaking Canada has a natural defence against the inroads of foreign television, but the linguistic and cultural division of what is a huge territory has also added to the burdens of maintaining an adequate and autonomous broadcasting service.

All these factors have influenced Canadian views about the public interest served by radio and television. They also help to explain why Canada has had such an active and articulate tradition of media policy-making, with much use of research to help monitor performance. Broadcast policy has been high on the political agenda and informed public debate has for long been conducted on questions which have elsewhere been taken for granted (Ferguson, 1991). Because of its situation in relation to the United States, Canada has long experienced conditions of threat to broadcast sovereignty which are only now emerging in Europe (Hoskins and McFadyen, 1989). This has lent particular interest to the way in which Canadians have defined and tackled problems of cultural integrity.

Canadian broadcasting has known a mixed private and public system since 1932, although both sectors have fallen under the same regulatory regime. The Broadcasting Act of 1968 is the main legislative instrument and it is not constrained by constitutional provisions concerning freedom of speech from regulating matters of broadcast content, as in the United States. The Act established a Canadian Radio-Television Commission (CRTC) which supervises public (CBC) as well as private stations, including the more recent cable systems. The main aim of the regulation of broadcasting has been to ensure that programming should be 'varied and comprehensive, of high standard and predominantly Canadian' (Peers, 1975: 78). Peers identified six main aims of regulation: Canadian ownership of stations; setting limits to foreign-originated programming; achieving maximum reach of the national broadcast services; identification of private stations with their community; limiting the concentration of station ownership; ensuring high quality in terms of service to community, variety, integrity of news presentation, fairness in matters of controversy.

Very prominent in the Canadian case is the emphasis placed on the contribution of media to national integration and cultural integrity. The Broadcasting Act provides a specific mandate to promote these goals. The Davey Committee (1970) endorsed the view that 'the Canadian media – especially broadcasting – have an interest and obligation to promote our *apartness* from the American reality'. Since that time, Canadian policy-makers have struggled, without great success, to hold back the tide of American media influence.

There has been a series of major national inquiries into the aims, performance and organization of broadcast media, including two Committees on Broadcasting (1957 and 1965), a Special Senate Committee on Mass Media (1970, known after its Chairman as the Davey Committee) and an influential Review Committee of Federal Cultural Policy (Applebaum and Hébert, 1982). The concerns and normative assumptions of the 1965 Broadcasting Committee, which preceded the 1968 legislation, were summarized in its report in terms of four 'fundamental objectives' which Canada was said to have accepted for its national broadcasting system: 'the public should be offered a wide and varied choice of programmes; all programmes should be of high quality; broadcasters should be responsible for the great influence of their programming on individuals and society; broadcasting has national responsibilities and must awaken Canadians to Canadian realities (Fowler, 1965: 11). This last stipulation includes a reference to what later became a distinctive feature of Canadian broadcasting policy – its 'multiculturalism' – in asking that the two Canadian national cultures should be able to express themselves and that 'every ethnic group and region' should be able to 'recognize itself through the broadcasting system' and 'be known by every other group or region'.

The concerns of the wide-ranging Davey Committee (1970), whose main report was published under the title *The Uncertain Mirror*, can be deduced from the main headings of questioning in the survey research that it commissioned. These dealt with the following: freedom of the press from bias towards government; fairness to politicians; privacy generally; informativeness of news media; the influence of advertisers; the portrayal of violence, sex and crime; foreign ownership of the media; monopoly and chain ownership; the preference for American media. The Cultural Policy Review Committee (Applebaum and Hébert, 1982) specified the kind of television programming which would fulfil the public responsibility of

Canadian broadcasting, including: a truly Canadian alternative to American programming; an end to excessive sports coverage; attention to specialized areas such as business, the arts, international affairs and politics; more cultural programming, including Canadian drama; more regional programming; programmes explaining cultural diversity and shared experience; more exchange between English and French programming; more experimental programming; more classical foreign series.

British broadcasting policy: from public service to consumerism?

The modern era of politics of the media in Britain begins, during the 1920s, with the establishment of a public corporation, the BBC, to run radio broadcasting. Paradoxically, the BBC was based on the 'rejection of politics' (Curran and Seaton, 1988). Certainly, in its early years it was run as if it was above politics – an instrument of public enlightenment, close to the Establishment of government, monarchy, church, but without overt links to any political party. One reason for this notional 'depoliticization', aside from it being the strong personal preference of the BBC's first Director General, John Reith, was that broadcasting began, as in most countries, without any clear sense of social or political purpose.

Social and political significance was gradually discovered through experience of events, such as the crisis around the General Strike of 1926 and the political conflicts of the 1930s. Significance was also discovered by the early, inter-war, Committees (Sykes, Crawford and Ullswater) which confirmed the public constitution and public service role of the BBC. The Sykes report (1923) said that broadcasting was 'of great national importance as a medium for the performance of a valuable public service'. The outcome of experience, public scrutiny and BBC policy all seemed to confirm the wisdom of continuing on the course somewhat fortuitously chosen at the start (Briggs, 1961; Smith, 1974a). The BBC was to be a public monopoly operated in the public (and the national) interest, its goals being to take a leading role in the provision of education, information and entertainment of high quality and good taste and to remain aloof from party politics and matters of controversy.

The standing of the BBC was at its peak in the immediate post-war years after it had been seen to play its part in the national war effort and to have enhanced its own international reputation and that of Britain (Seymour-Ure, 1991). The tasks expected from the BBC were set down very briefly in its Royal Charter and licence (first in 1927 and periodically renewed), documents which are permissive and vague about aims and limitations (see Smith, 1974c). More specific indications of goals are to be found in the BBC's own policies and activities. The most recent version of the BBC Charter and Licence contains a resolution of the Board of Governors recognizing their 'duty to ensure that programmes maintain a high general standard in all respects (and in particular in respect of content and quality), and to provide a properly balanced service which displays a wide range of subject matter'. Obligations to political impartiality and to showing concern for the needs of the young are also recognized.

What the BBC tried to do, it was thought to do well: to provide news and information of high professional quality, fully, without bias and in a range to suit the varying requirements and capacities of its audience; to give time to culture (especially music and drama) and to education, also at different 'levels' of taste and capacity; to offer popular entertainment in the form of comedy and variety. The BBC, which was examined and in the end approved once more by the 1949 Beveridge Committee, was a seemingly unshakeable national institution which, on the whole, managed to satisfy its audience, the national Establishment and the political left.

The first main challenge to the BBC monopoly arrived with the liberalizing policies of the first post-war Conservative administration in 1951 and, despite widespread misgiving and scepticism about success, a commercial television (though not radio) alternative was established by the Television Act of 1954. The tenor of official public expectation from the new commercial television service can be judged from the terms of the 1954 Act, which laid down stringent rules and requirements to be applied by a new and powerful public licensing and regulating body, the Independent Television Authority (ITA). These regulations display a considerable suspicion of the probable cultural and political tendencies of commercial broadcasting, left to itself, and a wish not to depart from the BBC-established norms of quality, taste and political impartiality.

The main content (thus, performance-relevant) provisions of the 1954 Act (largely taken over in subsequent legislation, though with some modifications, most recently in the Broadcasting Act of 1990) were contained in clause 3, requiring:

(a)   that nothing is included in the programmes which offends against good taste or decency or is likely to encourage or incite to crime or to lead to disorder or to be offensive to public feeling or which contains any offensive representation of or reference to a living person;

(b)   that the programmes maintain a proper balance in their subject-matter and a high general standard of quality;

(c)   that any news given in the programme (in whatever form) is presented with due accuracy and impartiality;

(d)   that proper proportions of the recorded and other matter included in the programmes are of British origin and of British performance;

(e)   that the programmes broadcast from any station or stations contain a suitable proportion of matter calculated to appeal specially to the tastes and outlook of persons served by the station or stations;

(f)   that due impartiality is preserved on the part of the persons providing the programmes as respects matters of political or industrial controversy or relating to current public policy; and

(g)   no matter designed to serve the interests of any political party is included in the programmes (aside from special 'party political broadcasts' and other 'properly balanced discussions or debates . . . of a political character').

In many respects, the rules laid down for independent television were simply specifications of norms extrapolated from BBC practice, plus additional rules to deal with advertising and commercial ownership. The main revisions of the legislation of 1974 to allow the addition of commercial radio, in 1981 to authorize an additional commercial television channel (Channel 4) and in 1990 to establish a new channel and a new financial regime, have not taken much away from, or added much to, the spirit or letter of the original 1954 Act, although the actual standards applied (or what counts as permissible in most of the areas legislated – taste, decency, controversy, advertising) have changed a good deal. In some respects, the 1990 Act has sharpened requirements concerning impartiality and 'decency'.

There have, nevertheless, been significant additions to the 'normative discourse' concerning British television as a result of the three committees of inquiry which have reported since 1954 (Pilkington, 1962; Annan, 1977; Peacock, 1986). The Pilkington Committee was strongly critical of the performance of independent television, especially on grounds of the 'trivialization' of content (attributed to the effects of commercialism and described in the report (p. 35) as 'more dangerous to the soul than wickedness'). The concept was hardly new, but it was given great prominence and something close to a definition. According to the report (sections 98–99):

> Triviality is not necessarily related to the subject matter . . . [it] resides in the way the subject matter is approached and the manner in which it is presented. A trivial approach can consist in failure to respect the potentialities of the subject matter . . . or in a too-ready reliance on well-tried themes, or in a habit of conforming to established patterns, or in a reluctance to be imaginatively adventurous . . .

The 1977 Annan Committee had, as its principal outcome, the establishment, in 1982, of Channel 4. This was intended to represent a new concept in British broadcasting, a channel acting as a publisher rather than as producer and relying on the work of independent producers. It also has a specific statutory remit to extend the range of broadcasting, and to embody the new ideas of openness and of social and cultural *diversity* which were espoused by the Annan Commitee. The 1981 Act says that Channel 4 programmes should contain 'a suitable proportion of matter calculated to appeal to tastes and interests not generally catered for by ITV'. It is also required to encourage 'innovation and experiment in the form and content of programmes' and to have a 'suitable proportion of programmes of an educational nature'.

The Peacock Committee was appointed in 1985 primarily to inquire into the desirability and feasibility of alternative forms of financing for the BBC. It decided against immediate change, but strayed into a number of other areas relevant to this discussion. Its main conclusion was that British broadcasting should 'move towards a sophisticated market system based on consumer sovereignty' (in effect, some version of subscription or pay-TV). On the whole, the Committee appeared to be convinced that the immediate effect of enforced commercialism would lead to less rather than more consumer choice. It identified the interests of 'consumer welfare' with some of the things the BBC had long been doing, namely: providing a 'considerable range of broadcast programmes, particularly that which concentrates on matter of serious national concern' (S.570); and 'exposure to programmes which expands their [the consumers'] range of taste and preference'.

The Peacock Committee also looked more closely than had previous committees at what the public interest and 'public service' might actually mean in the context of broadcasting. They cite, at the outset, the view of the Broadcasting Research Unit that the 'public service idea' of broadcasting involves eight principles: of geographic universality; catering for all interests and tastes; catering for minorities; concern for national identity and community; detachment from vested interests and government; direct funding of at least one broadcasting system by the corpus of users; competition in good programming rather than for numbers of viewers; having guidelines which 'liberate rather than restrict' programme-makers. In the end, the Committee appeared not to dissent, in the name of the consumer, from these principles, but it concluded that the principles do not have to be achieved by way of a *public service institution*. A sophisticated market system should do as well.

The policy tendencies in broadcasting in Britain during the 1980s have been generally in the direction of increasing competition by way of commercially funded alternatives (Syvertsen, 1991; Seymour-Ure, 1991). This has added little to the range of performance norms, although it has changed priorities towards the goal of consumer satisfaction as the main measure of success and towards self-regulation as the preferred means of gaining conformity to the expectations of 'society'. In the process, the stigma once attaching to advertising and commercialism has been lifted. However, the editorial freedoms of broadcasting have not benefited from the more liberal commercial climate, rather the reverse.

There has also been some reaffirmation of the claims of conventional morality in respect of sex and violence, partly as a result of fears of the possible consequences of deregulation, partly as a conscious ideological choice. One result has been the institution of a Broadcasting Standards Council (1989) with the task of drawing up a code for the portrayal of violence and sex on television, monitoring content accordingly, considering complaints, undertaking research and making annual reports. This body has, from its inception, been controversial and generally unpopular with existing television authorities and broadcasters. Its establishment and its published programme guidelines, although not very novel in substance nor essentially illiberal, provide a good indication of one significant strand of thinking about performance standards in Britain.

Varied national experience in Europe

The issues which have called for broadcast regulation in most of Western Europe have been similar to those raised in Britain, but the circumstances and the priorities are often different. In fact, accounts of principles and values which have been pursued in different countries show remarkable divergences of emphasis underneath an apparent common concern with maintaining a general service (information, entertainment, culture) of good quality and managing the boundary between public service and commercial interests (see Shaughnessy and Cobo, 1990; Blumler, 1992; Siune and Truetzschler, 1992). What Blumler has referred to as the 'vulnerable values' which broadcast regulation seeks to protect in different national systems are also noticeably varied.

In particular, there has been variation in the relative significance attached to the following: the *independence* of broadcasters; the *diversity of access* of systems; the protection accorded to *national language and culture*; the promotion of *regional, local and community media*. Often it has been the pressure of change, especially as a result of new media and more commercialization, which has led to values and principles being much more explicitly declared and embodied in public documents and guidelines. Only a sample of the evidence can be touched on here, with examples from Germany, Sweden and The Netherlands.

Germany: democracy, regionalism and cultural obligations

The most important principles of German broadcasting, as reconstructed after the Second World War, were, first, to ensure a high degree of decentralization of the system and of autonomy for the eleven *Länder* in matters of broadcasting policy and, secondly, to achieve, by way of public broadcasting structures, a system of representative democratic control of the medium. The introduction of private commercial competition during the 1980s, by way of cable and satellite especially, has threatened both principles and stimulated efforts to ensure, by way of regulation, a continuation of the same principles (Holz-Bacha, 1991). The new regulations are, if anything, more extensive and detailed than before, although enforcement is likely to be another story.

Private commercial television was formally legalized in Germany in 1987 by means of a 'States Treaty' between the governments of the eleven *Länder*, which regulate all broadcasting matters in the Federal Republic. Each *Land* has its own laws and statements of conditions for the operation of a television licence, most of them stating in detail a number of expectations and performance criteria. The results have been reported by Shaughnessy and Cobo (1990) and their summary provides a source for the main separate headings of performance principle, which are listed as follows, in the most commonly used forms of words. Positive value is placed on:

- Diversity of opinion and of culture
- Attention to the culture and politics of region and locality
- Respect for personal dignity
- Respect for opinions of others
- Aiding peace and international understanding
- Contributing to the peaceful reunification of Germany
- Appropriate amount of German cultural production
- Promoting local participation in management
- Promoting free individual and public formation of opinion
- Promoting social justice
- Allocating time to charitable and non-profit organizations
- In-house production
- Employee participation in decisions
- Defence of democratic freedoms
- Avoidance of any dominant influence or opinion
- Contributing to equality between men and women
- Allocating time to non-commercial and esoteric cultural groups
- Allocating time for party broadcasts
- Allocating time to specific religious groups
- Attention to significant political, philosophical and social forces
- Adequate time to controversy on matters of general interest.

Things to be avoided include:

- Racial hatred
- Glorification of war
- Harm to children
- Pornography
- Undue cross-media ownership
- Bias to any one party or vested interest
- Undermining the constitutional order.

While such a list does not indicate the actual or relative importance attached to different principles nor their varying enforceability, it does suggest that the normative framework applied has been influenced by special features of German post-war history as well as by older national traditions. Particular attention seems to be paid to respect for constitutionality and democratic principle, to regional culture and values of localism, political decentralization and the promotion of arts and culture generally. The values of political diversity as well as of individual freedom and social equality are also stressed. The impression created is of an emphasis on positive expectations rather than of negative control, but realization of these ideals in practice is perhaps another matter (Hoffman-Riem, 1992).

Sweden: support for culture and politics

The case of Sweden is instructive because it introduces somewhat differently formulated principles. Broadcasting policy in Sweden has similar overall aims to those of other European countries, but there is rather more emphasis on the role of critic and monitor of government and business than is found, for instance, in Britain, where a more neutral and mediatory role is favoured. The following statement of obligations is found in the Agreement between the State and the Swedish Television Company (Sveriges Radio).

- To convey news and to comment upon, or otherwise illustrate, events and processes, providing the all-round information that the population needs to orient itself, and to form an opinion on social and cultural issues.
- To stimulate debate on important social and cultural issues.
- To scrutinize authorities, organizations and private enterprises which have an influence upon decisions affecting the general public, and to monitor activities within these and other organizations.
- To utilize and develop the specific potentialities of television to offer experiences and stimulate the imagination, thus affording opportunities for empathy, involvement and amusement.
- To promote artistic and cultural involvement, and make creative use of the medium in artistic forms of expression.
- To monitor and scrutinize events and developments in the arts and, in interplay with Sweden's cultural life at large, make known and stimulate various cultural activities.
- To cater to a reasonable extent to a variety of interests in such areas as religion, culture and science.
- To pay special consideration to the linguistic and ethnic minorities.
- To pay special consideration to various groups of handicapped.

Some further clauses call for: close attention to facts and to relevance in news; respect for privacy of individuals; a right of reply; access to be given to government authority for messages of public importance. There is also a prohibition on advertising, although this is now under discussion (Hadenius, 1992).

The Netherlands and elsewhere: support for 'pluriformity'

Press and broadcasting policy in several other countries has also strongly endorsed the principle of *diversity*, although sometimes in different ways. In a linguistically divided country like Belgium, the language communities are more important than the parties, although one criterion cuts across another, leading to considerable multiplicity. In The Netherlands, diversity (or 'pluriformity') has been the vital principle for press and broadcasting policy, but is interpreted as having an unusually wide reference (McQuail, 1992).

The original basis for emphasizing media diversity was the political settlement achieved to resolve the religious-political conflict between Protestant and Catholic communities (Wieten, 1979). The settlement was referred to as a 'pillarization' – a sharing out of institutional power and resources between the main religious communities. The Dutch broadcasting system is, in principle, open to all significant 'voices' in the society. Successive media laws, since the 1920s, have provided for the recognition of claims to air-time by organized social groups which can demonstrate a sufficient degree of popular support. Initially, the main groups which shared radio time were identified as Socialist, Roman Catholic Christian, Protestant Christian or none of these three. More recently, newer groups have been added, though with a strong trend towards a more secular, liberal or hedonistic basis. The result has been to multiply and water down the requirement for what counts as a relevant dimension of social or cultural diversity, but also to reinforce the value attached to the idea of diversity as such.

Other forms of diversity have been given varying degrees of emphasis and policy support elsewhere in Europe. One of these is *regionalism* and *localism,* expressed generally as support for the idea of broadcasting which reflects the life of its locality, serves the interests of local people and helps to increase identity with and attachment to community and to place. What counts as regional or local as a basis for media varies, ranging from the sub-nation (as Catalonia in Spain), or the German *Land,* through historic provinces and counties, to cities and small towns (Kleinsteuber and Sonnenberg, 1990). In Spain, the Radio and Television Statute calls for 'encouragement of the sense of national unity' and also 'recognition, respect and encouragement of understanding between the different geographical and linguistic communities within the national territory' (Shaughnessy and Cobo, 1990: 63).

Additional goals in European media policy: identity and access

Lastly, we can draw attention to two other principles, which are widely expressed in expectations from media. One concerns protection for *national* language and culture, which is prominent in French, German, Swedish and Spanish laws. Countries whose total language community is small and subject to cross-border incursion often make such provisions. But the attitude of some larger countries is not much different. European (Community) rule-making now requires all countries to give some preference in television programming to European language and culture, and not only as matter of economic protectionism.

Another principle, growing in importance, is that of *access* for minorities of all kinds, although a distinction should probably be made between the idea of access for divergent and dissident voices (especially by way of local radio) and access for minority immigrant or ethnic groups within a larger 'host' society. There is more lip service than implementation on both counts, but the principles usually get normative support. Radio legislation in several countries now makes provision for a 'fourth' kind of service (beyond national, regional and local): that of *community radio*. This was, for instance, defined by the Peacock Committee as 'a fourth tier of radio . . . either in the form of a low power transmitter broadcasting to the immediate neighbourhood, with a close involvement of the community, or a station broadcasting across a wider area to a "community of interest" such as an ethnic minority'. Associated characteristics are usually smallness of scale, non-commercialism, voluntarism, high listener participation. Content and control must be local or specific to the purpose (see Kleinsteuber and Sonnenberg, 1990; Siune and Truetzschler, 1992).

New rules for European television

A new feature of media policy discourse in the 1990s stems from the extension of competence over broadcasting from the national to the international level, in the case of Europe. The Council of Europe, which has 26 member states and the European Community, which has 12, have both developed very similar guidelines which should apply to television services intended to cross national frontiers. The main difference between the two is that European Community rules (Television Without Frontiers Directive) are binding (from 1992) rather than voluntary. The rule-making aim has been limited to reaching a consensus on minimum standards, sufficient to ensure that any broadcast service originating in any one of the member states, and which complies with the guidelines, will be guaranteed the right of distribution in any other member state.

The rules relate to three main areas of performance: advertising amount, programming and content; protection of young people, with particular reference to controls on presentation of violence and sex; due proportions of content of 'European origin' and of independent European productions. The rules themselves are not innovative or wide-ranging, nor are they as restrictive as most existing national regulation, since they represent a cross-national political compromise. However, they are interesting for what they suggest about the universalizing trend of normative discourse, as well as having wider practical consequences for performance in some countries.

A wider policy debate

The media policy debates of the post-war decades have led to considerable extension and specification of the content of the six mid-twentieth century policy issues described in Chapter 3. It appears that we should place three largely new issues on that agenda, which can be summarized as:

1 The question of autonomy for national language and culture, as well as rights of cultural expression through the media for sub-cultural or

minority groups. The need to protect regional and local media, which help sustain the viability of local life, can be included under this heading.

2   The control of commercial communication as such (advertising, sponsored content), especially because of the expansion of private broadcasting and the internationalization of media (for instance, in Western Europe) (Keane, 1991).

3   Economic, industrial aspects of mass communication have become much more salient, leading to policy debates and actions concerned with the protection, stimulation and regulation of media industries and many new questions of information property rights (Melody, 1990; Murdock, 1990).

The large changes which have taken place in the content and climate of media policy discourse since the middle of this century can only be very inadequately indicated by naming these additions to the agenda of concerns. The whole media landscape is vastly different, because of the development of entirely new media forms and major adaptations of structure. The media policy debate has become internationalized, along with the gradual internationalization of the media themselves and the diminished power of national frontiers to shape and contain media experience. Regulation and control in relation to the three 'new' issues of public concern increasingly take place according to cross-nationally agreed principles and sometimes by way of supranational bodies. The idea of a public sphere in which principles of media performance are debated has had to be considerably enlarged as a result of these changes.

6
A FRAMEWORK OF PRINCIPLE FOR MEDIA ASSESSMENT

Four (or more) theories of the press

The policy principles and 'communication values' which have been identified are relatively few in number and they recur from one country to another, despite local variations in their form, formulation and relative salience. The aim of this chapter is to construct, from this material, a general framework of expectations about performance which can serve as a guide to a potentially very large field of research. So far, we have kept to the actuality of public debate about the media; an alternative route might have been found by way of various normative theories of the media (e.g. Siebert et al., 1956; Merrill, 1974; Hachten, 1981; McQuail, 1987; Altschull, 1984; Picard, 1985b).

The 'Four Theories of the Press' (proposed by Siebert et al., 1956) have often been invoked as a normative framework in theoretical discussions of the media, sometimes modified by additions or subtractions. This was a by-product of the American Commission on Freedom of the Press (Hutchins, 1947) and was in part advocacy of a liberal model of a reformed free press operating 'responsibly' in a modern democracy. It was first of all a codification of stages of history of the press (from the 'authoritarian' to the 'libertarian') and also a marking of difference between Western freedom models (whether responsible or not) and the Soviet communist model. While a significant advance in its day, it no longer seems adequate.

Two more variants of theory, one labelled 'development', another 'democratic-participant', can be added to take account of other realities and other models (McQuail, 1987). According to Rosengren et al. (1991), the six resulting theories offer norms about, on the one hand, institutional relationships among media, journalists and society and, on the other, media content. In their view, however, the content norms to be found in such theories are too general to be of much use as a guide to research into the 'quality of media performance': 'they [all] ask for morals, taking for granted what kind of morals is meant.'

More recently, Picard (1985b) made a determined effort to distinguish, within the category of Western models, a distinctive 'social democratic' version of press theory, which, in contrast to 'social responsibility' and 'libertarian' (free market) theory, provides legitimation for public intervention, or even for collective ownership so as to ensure true independence from vested interests, access and diversity of opinion. Whatever else, it is clear that there are always likely to be alternative, inconsistent and changing conceptions of the norms appropriate to the relations between media and their own society.

The attempt to formulate consistent 'theories' of the press is almost bound to break down, for reasons other than underlying conflicts of interest and political ideology present in any society. The suggested frameworks have usually derived from a simple and outdated notion of 'the press' – one which provides (mainly political) news and information within the boundaries of the nation state. They are now inadequate for coping with the great internal diversity of mass media types and services and with changing technology and times.

There is, for instance, little of relevance in any of the variants of theory to the cinema, or the music industry, or the video market, or even a good deal of sport, fiction and entertainment on television, thus to much of what the media are doing most of the time. It is hardly plausible any longer that these things should lie entirely outside the scope of social-normative thinking. The theories have other weaknesses. They can often seem ethnocentric, over-idealistic and even arbitrary. They involve an almost inextricable confusion between: the actual working principles of a given media system; the theoretical ideals of the system; and the dominant ideology of the society (capitalist, socialist, revolutionary, developmental, or whatever).

Basic communication values: a proposal

Although this book aims to break some new ground, it is certainly *not* intended to advance any new normative theory or to advocate the special claim of any particular value or set of values. The aim is only to represent fairly the main evaluative ideas which are actually encountered in public debate and in regulations concerning media performance. These ideas comprise, in effect, the terms of a particular policy (and performance) *discourse*, whose meanings are rooted in typical and recurring circumstances of the working of mass media. As with any discourse (here meaning an identifiable and dedicated form of language usage), the terms are interrelated and overlapping and their specific meanings are dependent on their place in a larger frame of reference. This chapter aims, first of all, to specify the component elements of this frame of reference. It also maps the *space* occupied by expressions of public expectation from mass media and by commonly found evaluative orientations towards the media, showing key distinctions and interrelations.

Although the source material (as represented in Chapters 4 and 5) is empirical (existing in documents and recorded discourse), there is no purely empirical way of drawing such a 'map'. What is offered is no more than one argued proposal for arranging the most frequently occurring normative terms and ideas in a single coherent structure of meaning. There is no implication, however, that this constitutes a closed or unified *system* of values. The most difficult task is to find an entry point: to identify the irreducible core, the most economical statement of key principles, from which other sub-principles can be derived or to which they can be related. This is also the point where there is most risk of introducing the personal views and bias of the author of any such proposal. Some such bias is bound to have crept in.

Fortunately for present purposes, the discussion of media performance is not universal and free floating, but rooted in time and place, and it is reasonable to suppose that the main principles at stake largely coincide with the core values of modern Western society, which, in turn, are likely to govern media institutions. While the particular terms are open to alternative interpretations, it is proposed that these values be named as: *freedom; justice/equality; order/solidarity*. These seem to be the basic principles which lie at the heart of most expectations concerning public communication, just as they shape the discussion of most other fundamental public issues.

Freedom as a value in civil society has often been defined in terms of communication rights: of belief, speech, movement, assembly, association, access to information. The most hated denials of freedom have been those which impinge on the identity and integrity of individuals and on their rights to self-expression. The most practical instruments for protecting freedom and combating tyranny have been the means of communication, used to claim rights, criticize power-holders, advance alternatives. A representative modern statement of human rights, the European Convention, states, for instance, that 'Everyone has the right to freedom of expression. This freedom shall include freedom to hold opinions and to receive and impart information and ideas without interference by public authority and regardless of frontiers' (Article 10). Freedom, according to most current conceptions, also entails economic freedom for media to operate in their public role and in their private business capacity, although government intervention in media arrangements need not be inconsistent with freedom of expression (according, for instance, to the same European Convention).

The value of *equality*, although open to more varied interpretations, corresponds closely with the idea of justice (equality of rights and before the law, fairness of social arrangements). It, too, is connected with public communication in less direct, but no less crucial ways. In brief: the expression of grievances and processes of justice require adequate channels of communication and the means of publicity; the potential to communicate and to receive communication is a social good which should be universally and equally available (or at least fairly distributed, according to accepted standards of justice); democratic political processes designed to increase public welfare and equity also require the services of public channels of communication; the full concept of citizenship presupposes an informed and participant body of citizens (Golding, 1990). Most generally, if we suppose there to be a 'right to communicate', then we also suppose an equal claim for all to hear and be heard.

The third basic value, that of *order/solidarity*, is open to more divergent definitions and evaluations than either freedom or equality. It was, nevertheless, coupled with both, under one of its several names, in the slogan of the French Revolution: *liberté; égalité; fraternité*. It was also a key term, in the sense of the solidarity of workers, in the socialist and social reform movements of the last two centuries. Order, in the sense of peace and rule of law has usually been regarded as a pre-condition for a just and civilized society. It can also be regarded as a central communication value according to the definition of communication as increasing commonality and sharing of outlook and experience.

The interdependence and stability of collective life of a society or community derive from, and depend on, communication processes and call for expressions of identity and belonging as well as involving social control through communication. There is a complex relation between order and culture in which communication plays a central part (see below). At the most general level of analysis, a social order (here equivalent to a whole society or social system), whether or not based on freedom and equality, can only be maintained over time through processes of public communication. The term 'order' is, however,˙used in the present discussion in a much more limited sense as referring to cohesion and harmony (see below). Nevertheless, at whatever level deployed, the notion of order is normatively ambiguous because of its potential association with control, with hierarchy and subordination of the weak to the powerful.

Each of these three basic values has, in fact, a dark and light side, a negative as well as a positive pole. Against the positive connotations of freedom are the negative associations of licence and lawlessness. Absolute individual freedom may imply isolation, *anomie*, alienation, a lack of basic social solidarity. In its individualist formulation, freedom clearly strains against collective solidarity. It may also be inconsistent with equality and have to be restrained on grounds of social justice. A social order supposedly based on total equality may lead to a denial of individual freedom and an excessive resort to restraint in order to prevent a re-emergence of material or social inequality.

It is clear that the three basic values do often come into conflict with each other and an appeal to one may be made in order to counter an appeal to another. Such tensions are often reflected in public debates about the structure, regulation and performance of the mass media, reminding us of the lack of any consensus either about the way in which the values should be applied or about their relative order of precedence.

Freedom as a public communication value

Freedom as a communication principle has often been defined (as in the First Amendment to the US Constitution) in terms of an unrestricted right to publish without prior permission or licence and without reprisal, aside from the normal provisions of the law, which apply to all citizens. It is a *condition,* rather than a *criterion,* of performance, since freedom does not predict any specific performance outcome. According to classic libertarian logic, the media are as free to cooperate with their own potential oppressors (as when they support authoritarian governments or favour their own monopolistic proprietors) as they are to oppose them. Similarly, they are as free to disseminate supposed 'error' (which might turn out to be true) as they are to publish truth and light (which might turn out to be error).

While this interpretation applies to any given case of publication, the media in general cannot entirely escape from the pragmatic demands as well as normative expectations of their various external partners, especially sources, clients and would-be communicators (see Chapter 7). Nor can they ignore with impunity the fundamental norms concerning 'good faith' which underpin their credibility and continuing appeal to their own audiences. Historically, the press did not acquire its freedom because of the irresistible appeal of an abstract libertarian or utilitarian principle, nor simply as a right going with ownership. There were a good many practical advantages in freedom, when 'responsibly' exercised, meaning in practice being relevant, reliable and never fundamentally subversive.

Even so, the advantages of freedom have long been acclaimed for their own sake. According to one authority, Emerson (1963: 4), the human right to freedom of expression stemmed firstly from the 'widely accepted premise of western thought that the proper end of man is the realization of his character and potentialities as a human being'. From this are derived rights to form personal beliefs and to express them. Secondly, according to Emerson, the right to freedom of expression derives from 'basic Western notions of the role of the individual in his capacity as a member of society'. From principles concerning the purpose of the state to promote individual welfare and equity, follow several specific communication rights: of access to knowledge; to hold opinions; to express needs, preferences and judgements in public; to participate in formulating the broad aims of society and in choosing means for achieving them. In this view, freedom of expression is, at one and the same time, a crucial individual right and an indispensable social good.

Although press freedom, in this Western value system, may ultimately derive from notions of individual rights, it can be seen, in its main institutional forms, to offer concrete benefits to society and its members. As a condition of media structure, freedom calls not only for the absence of a legally imposed licensing or censorship mechanism, but a degree of independence (which must actually be exercised in order to count) from the main kinds of pressure and constraint encountered in public life (Chapter 7). According to theory concerning media freedom, although independence can never be absolute, the more it is actually used, the more benefits are likely to accrue for the general welfare as well as to the media's own public and clients.

The main connections between freedom, diversity of opinion and democracy (in the American context) are succinctly put as follows:

> Accordingly, freedom of the press is an important constitutional guarantee not because a free press is inherently valuable but because a free press can best meet the public communication needs of a democratic society; First Amendment protection for the print and electronic press is desirable because it fosters a robust and uninhibited press; a robust and uninhibited press is desirable because it is a press able and presumably willing to accommodate divergent points of view; divergent points of view are desirable because they sustain public debate; public debate is desirable because it nurtures an informed citizenry; and an informed citizenry is desirable because it brings about a more perfect polity and, in the end, legitimates the very idea of self-government. (Glasser, 1984: 137)

The benefits are quite direct and concrete. For instance, the *credibility* of any news and information supplied is largely dependent on confidence that it is not unduly or secretly influenced by partisan or vested interests (of government, advertiser, proprietor, source, etc.). Freedom is also thought to require and promote a diversity of channels, thus more choice for the 'consumer' of information and of other media services. Press independence is also a pre-condition of the exercise of the 'watchdog' role: exercising public vigilance in relation to those with most power, especially government and big business.

Other practical benefits include an openness to new ideas and a readiness to make access available to different voices in the society. Free media will be prepared, when necessary, to offend the powerful, express controversial views, deviate from convention and from the commonplace. Freedom of communication has a dual aspect: offering a wide range of voices and responding to a wide-ranging demand. Similar remarks apply to the cultural provision of media, where independence will be associated, other things being equal, with creativity, originality and diversity. These ideas bring us to an interface and overlap with benefits offered under the heading of 'equality'.

This brief discussion has sought to make a connection between the following: structural conditions (legal freedom to publish); operating conditions (real independence from economic and political pressures and relative autonomy for journalists and other 'communicators' within media organizations); opportunities for 'voices' in society to gain access to channels; benefits of quality of provision for 'receivers', according to criteria of relevance, diversity, reliability, interest, originality and personal satisfaction. The main elements discussed can now be expressed as the first set of components in a larger normative framework (Figure 6.1). The implications of each sub-principle will be worked out in more detail later. It has to be emphasized that these are all *theoretical* benefits flowing from freedom, logically interconnected. They may not be realized in practice because of

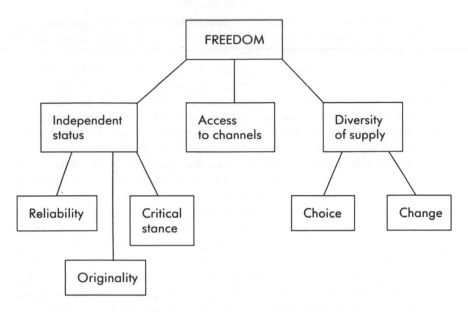

Figure 6.1 *Freedom as a principle of media performance*

contradictory claims and limited opportunities (Schmidt, 1976; Lichtenberg, 1990).

Equality as a public communication value

The value of equality has to be translated into more specific meanings if it is to be applied to the mass media. As a principle, it underlies several of the normative statements, or 'preference claims', which have already been described. In relation to communication and political power, it is equality which requires that no special favour be given to power-holders and that access to media should be given on a fair, if not always an equal, basis to contenders for office and, in general, to oppositional or deviant opinions, perspectives or claims. In relation to business clients of the media, equality requires that all legitimate advertisers be treated on the same basis (the same rates and conditions). Equality also implies, in such matters, that the normal conditions of a free market should apply.

It is equality which supports policies of universal provision in broadcasting and telecommunications and of sharing out of the costs of basic services. Equality will support the expectation of fair access to channels, on equivalent terms, for all alternative voices that meet relevant criteria (the diversity principle again). In short, equality calls for an absence of discrimination or bias in the amount and kind of access available to senders or receivers, as far as is practicable. The real chances of equality are likely to depend on the level of social and economic development of a society and the capacity of its media system. There will have to be *enough* space on different and mutually independent channels which are widely available, for any degree of equality to be realized in practice.

The principle of diversity (also identified as a major benefit of freedom), which can be derived from these meanings of communication equality, is especially important because it underpins the normal processes of progressive change in society (the periodic replacement of ruling elites, the circulation of power and office, the countervailing power of different interests), which pluralistic forms of democracy are supposed to deliver.

In accounting for diversity of *provision*, the extent to which real alternatives are on offer can be registered according to several yardsticks of difference: kinds of media (e.g. press, radio, television, etc.); function or type of content (e.g. entertainment, information); geographical level of operation (national, regional, local, etc.); the audience aimed at and reached (differentiated by income, age, etc.); language, ethnic or cultural identity; politics or ideology. Glasser (1984) cites John Dewey to the effect that 'Only a culturally plural society can embody the spirit of democracy; and only the spirit of democracy can nourish a sense of community and an appreciation of the integrity of diverse values.' In general, a media system is more equal in character the more diverse the provision, according to the criteria mentioned.

Two basic variants of the 'diversity-as-equal-treatment' principle have been identified in research (McQuail and Van Cuilenburg, 1983). According to one version, a literal equality should be on offer – everyone receives the same provision or chances for access as sender to media channels. This equality is realized, for instance, where contending parties receive equal time in an election, or in those countries (such as Canada or Belgium) where separate language groups have their own, parallel, media services. An alternative, more common version of diversity means only a 'fair', or appropriate, allocation of access and treatment. Usually, fairness is assessed according to the principle of representation or reflection. Media provision should proportionately *reflect* the actual distribution of whatever is relevant (topics, social group, political beliefs, etc.), or just reflect the varying distribution of audience demand or interest. The differentiation of media provision (content) should approximately correspond to the differences at source or to those at the receiving end (the audience).

A consideration of equality as an evaluative principle also takes us into the territory of *objectivity*, although this has other meanings and potential sources of support, especially those stemming from the value of *independence* and from media professionalism and autonomy. Most centrally, objectivity is a form of media *practice* and also a particular attitude to the task of information collection, processing and dissemination. It means adopting a position of detachment and neutrality from the object of reporting (thus an absence of subjectivity or personal involvement and also of partisanship). It calls for attachment to accuracy and other truth criteria (e.g. relevance, completeness) as well as lack of ulterior motive or service to a third party.

The process of observing and reporting should, accordingly, not interfere with the reality being reported on. In some respects, objectivity has an affinity, in theory at least, with the ideal of rational, 'undistorted' communication advocated by Habermas (1989).

This version of an ideal standard of reporting practice has much support and has become the dominant model for the role of professional journalist (Weaver and Wilhoit, 1986). Objectivity has links with the principle of *freedom*, since independence is a necessary condition for detachment and truthfulness. Under some conditions (e.g. political repression, crisis, war, martial law), the freedom to report can only be exercised in return for a guarantee of objectivity (especially factualness, neutrality of direction and tone). The link with *equality* is just as strong: objectivity requires a fair and non-discriminatory attitude to sources and to objects of news reporting – all should be treated on equal terms.

In the set of interactions which develop between media and their operating environments, as described in Chapter 7, objectivity may be crucial. Agencies of state and advocates of various interests are able to speak directly to their chosen audiences by way of the media, without undue distortion or intervention by the 'mediators' themselves and without compromising the independence of channels. Because of the established conventions of objectivity, media channels can also distance their editorial content from the advertising matter which they carry and advertisers can do likewise in respect of editorial content. In general, media audiences appear to understand the principle of objective performance well enough and its practice helps to increase their credence and trust in information and opinions which the media offer. The media themselves find that objectivity gives their own news product a higher and wider market value. Finally, because the objectivity standard has such a wide currency, it is often invoked in claims and settlements concerning bias or unequal treatment.

The main sub-principles related to the value of equality can now be entered (Figure 6.2).

Values of order and culture

The ambiguous standing of the order concept in discussions of media and society has already been noted. One of the difficulties in using the concept is that, in its largest sense, 'order', along with 'culture', properly belong to a more general and higher level of analysis than either freedom or equality. The 'social order' is equivalent to the whole society or the social system. It is often characterized in terms of a particular 'culture', in the more anthropological sense of all systematically related ideas, actions and artefacts. A culture, in turn, is usually characterized by having its distinctive symbolic (meaning) system or order. In the present context, the term 'order' is used in a much more limited sense of 'cohesion' or 'harmony', at particular levels of social organization, and also as the processes which

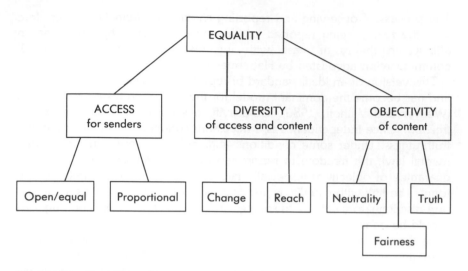

Figure 6.2 *Equality and its main components*

stengthen or weaken this cohesion. Communication is one of these
processes. The degree of harmony or coherence which exists is also
manifested in communication content and patterns of flow.

From the standpoint of established authority, the media are sometimes
viewed as potentially disruptive of the normal 'order' of the society,
although they are also widely regarded as indispensable to the maintenance
of order, in the wider sense of social 'harmony' and the normal running of
things. For individuals and the component sub-groups of society, the media
are also perceived ambivalently. Mass communication helps in forming and
maintaining personal identity and group cohesion, but it can be a source of
disturbance when it intrudes with alien values or when it is used as an
instrument of control. Theory of mass communication has drawn attention to
the dual effect of media in society – both centrifugal and centripetal:
differentiating and individualizing on the one hand; centralizing and unifying
on the other (Carey, 1969, 1989; McQuail, 1987).

Claims pertaining to the value of order are sometimes framed negatively,
in requirements to limit the exposure of children or other vulnerable groups
to possible moral or cultural harm. Positively, the media are expected to
promote education and traditionally valued culture, or to promote cultural
autonomy and authenticity for social groupings based on language, region
or nation.

The concept of order (as a quality of cohesion, integration or harmony)
can apply both to symbolic content and to forms of social organization
(community, society, any established structure of social relations). In the first
of these meanings, the primary reference in the present context is to the
content produced and disseminated by the mass media and to the
'environment' of cultural and social meanings which the media make
available. In the second (social relational) meaning, most relevant is the

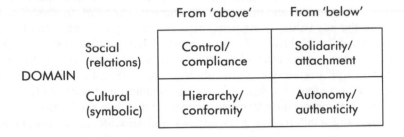

Figure 6.3 *Ideas concerning order*

contribution (or not) of communication to a sense of belonging to a significant social group and to the capacity to deploy and enjoy an authentic and personally valued culture (language, dress, activities, etc.).

This broad dichotomy of meaning (symbolic environment and social relations) may also be cross-cut by a distinction of perspective – from 'above' or from 'below', as it were (see below). This divide is essentially that between established authority on the one hand and ordinary people and minority groups on the other. At issue is the question of *whose* coherence and harmony is promoted by public communication: that of the more or of the less powerful. In turn, the distinction also corresponds approximately to that between order, in the sense of control, and order in the sense of solidarity and cohesion – the one 'imposed', the other voluntary and self-chosen. The complexity of communication values in this territory stems from the underlying conflicts within class-stratified and hierarchical societies which are still with us. These ideas about order (in the sense of social and cultural cohesion) can be arranged as Figure 6.3.

The assessment of media performance in terms of order is more dependent on the choice of perspective than is the case with concepts of freedom and equality. The question '*whose* order?' has first to be settled. In practice, the kind of media assessment most frequently applied has adopted a conventional standard, shaped by the dominant perspective (of established authority). More attention has usually been paid to *disruption* of order (conflict, crime, deviance, etc.) than to the failings of the established order itself as perceived by more marginal social and cultural groups in society.

The scheme proposed in Figure 6.3 makes a distinction between the *social* and the (symbolic) *cultural* domains. Both domains can, in turn, be treated according to a second distinction – between the view from 'above' and that from 'below'. The social 'space' identified by the 'top-down' perspective is characterized by communicative efforts to establish control and compliance. As far as media performance is concerned, this implies either very 'negative' portrayals of conflict, disorder and deviance or in the differential access and support given, symbolically, to values and institutions of the established 'order': the law, church, school, police, military, etc.

When the social domain is located according to a 'bottom-up' ('grass-roots') perspective, we are dealing with concepts (and also qualities) of mutuality, cooperation and voluntary attachment. The term 'solidarity' helps to capture the key value, recognizing also that society is composed of many sub-groups, different bases of identity and of different interests. Standing against a unitary perspective of a consensual 'good order' in a nation state (the view and preference from above) are a number of alternative perspectives on what is a desirable social condition and way of life.

A correlative expectation from mass media is that they ought sympathetic-ally to recognize alternative perspectives and provide some access and support for social groups and situations which are marginal, distant or deviant from the dominant, national, point of view. This implies symbolic support for the aspirations of sub-groups in society, by giving either access or positive forms of representation. The same media tendency should find expression in empathy for 'victims' and for the disadvantaged, the public recognition of shared risks, sorrows and hardships, the linking of private and local experience to wider experience.

The domain of the 'cultural' is clearly not easy to keep separate from these matters. As used here the term refers primarily to any set of symbols organized by way of language or in some other meaningful patterning. We can locate cultures in any of three main ways: as characteristic of a set of people, identifiable by language, gender, class, ethnicity, etc.; as a set of activities (work, home-related; politics; sport, etc.); or as represented in and by symbolic texts and artefacts (books, films, types of performance, genres, etc.). The first of these three is already largely covered by reference to the 'social' domain and we are not directly concerned with activities (behaviour). This leaves the symbolic cultural artefact, especially the mass media 'text' as the main focus of attention.

Media assessment has typically been concerned either with matters of symbolic cultural 'quality' (usually defined according to standards of 'high culture') or with 'authenticity' in terms of society or group (and with cultural identity). The subdivision of the cultural domain is not easy to achieve in a neat way, although the presentation in Figure 6.4 indicates one line of division: between a 'dominant' or established set of cultural values, based on traditional criteria of quality, and a set of 'alternative' values relating to cultural or sub-cultural identity, in which intrinsic (aesthetic or technical) quality plays no significant role. In practice, the former implies a *hierarchical* view of culture, according to which certain cultural values and artefacts have been 'certified' by established cultural institutions and are privileged accordingly.

Typically, such an established culture implies a set of absolute values and quality standards according to current professional or expert criteria. The cultural virtues relevant to identity mainly refer to recognition and boundary markers (our culture versus others) but no necessary aesthetic or moral gradations. There are further possibilities, explored in Chapter 19, of assessing the content of symbolic culture according to 'uncultural' or socially

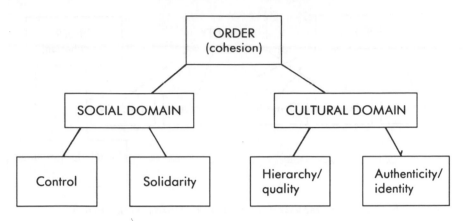

Figure 6.4 *Order and its main component principles*

disapproved features: those considered not only unconventional but also uncivilized.

The component normative principles relating to 'order' can now be summarized in Figure 6.4.

An overall framework of communication norms

The three basic principles of freedom, equality and cohesive order have been worked out separately in terms of their implications for media performance. Nevertheless, they are intimately inter-connected and inevitably overlapping. Thus, the main concepts of access and diversity appear both under the heading of 'freedom' and under that of 'equality'. While the 'order' principle stands somewhat apart, the connection between the 'solidaristic' component of order and the principle of equality is very strong and, in practice, solidaristic communication values can only be realized by access to channels and by some degree of diversity in the media system.

The logic of the composition of the framework involves a progression of increasing specificity from the most abstract and general level (the three basic values), to the implications of these for media system and performance (independence, diversity, etc.), to yet more specific sub-principles or concepts which provide a link to the application of assessment procedures and research. This stage is reserved for later chapters, when each of the main 'second order' principles is discussed in detail. In conclusion, the three main component elements can be brought together to offer a view of the upper levels (really the foundations) of the unified framework of principle promised at the outset of the chapter (Figure 6.5).

The apparent symmetry and coherence of this framework is largely an illusion. The key principles named embody potentially deep internal inconsistencies (e.g. liberty v. licence; absolute equality v. unequal, but 'fair', shares; social control v. solidarity) and they may be mutually contradictory.

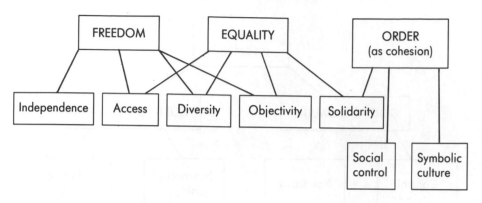

Figure 6.5 *Summary framework of principles of media performance*

Each value is open to self-interested interpretation. For these reasons, there can never be any straightforward 'reading' of the 'public interest' from these values and their sub-concepts. This can only be established, case by case, by argument and evidence, according to the proposal made in Chapter 3. This applies, for instance, to the competing claims of proprietorial or editorial autonomy versus the demands for open access to public channels of communication. It also relates to the gap between benefits of full and objective information and the virtues of group loyalty, solidarity or ideology. In both cases, support can be found for quite different versions of the 'good of society'.

Other perspectives on media performance.

While there may be some consistency in what has been thought to constitute the universe of values relevant to assessing media performance 'in the public interest', we cannot expect much consensus about which values are relevant in any given case, their order of priority or how they should be worked out in precise criteria of performance. The 'public interest' is never a *given*, but always open to debate and counter-claim. The same conclusion follows from the potential incompatibility of several of the values embodied in the normative framework just sketched.

Nevertheless, assessment research practice can only proceed on the basis of clear choices (however debatable) about which norm to apply and how it should be operationally defined for a given purpose. The question of perspective, or standpoint, from which to assess a media situation and define a 'problem' for assessment is crucial at the initial stage when choices are made, when working definitions are arrived at and also when the results of assessment are being interpreted. The framework of performance norms offered can only be 'activated' selectively, on the basis of a partial, or even partisan, point of view.

The most obvious difference of position from which the performance of the media might be viewed is that between a media *insider* and a media *outsider*, given the normal relation of multiple (and mutual) tension between a media organization and its operating environment (see Figure 7.1 below). There are also predictable differences according to ideology, usually separating liberal or left-wing critics and would-be reformers, on the one hand, from conservative defenders (or even critics) of the status quo, on the other.

Despite local divergences, the main alternative positions which are relevant to public interest claims about media performance can be plotted approximately in terms of these two factors. *External* to the media, a typical political/ideological division (and also dimension) is that which separates three common positions: 'progressive' (and interventionist) *reformers* (on the left); *liberals* (in the centre); and *conservatives* or traditionalists (on the right). Typically, reformers make the running in calling for public accountability and for changes in structure of practice 'for the public good'. A 'liberal' concern for freedom and a faith in the market usually makes for resistance to the more interventionist 'reformers'. While 'conservatives' oppose change, they may also see the need for accountability, although typically with a different normative agenda from that of 'reformers'. Their emphasis is likely to be on possible abuses of freedom and on the alleged promotion by the media of 'disorder' or moral decay.

While the media *insider* view is normally opposed to any external monitoring or regulation on principle, there appears to be a similar division of internal views on questions of performance. The nearest to the 'reformist' view is the 'participatory' or 'advocacy' conception of the journalistic role. This perspective expresses a view that journalism ought to 'take sides' and play an active, campaigning, critical role in society. In culture and the arts, there should also be a degree of social engagement for ends beyond those of the media industry. Some sympathy is also likely to be found, amongst those who adopt such a standpoint, for external critical views. There is probably a good deal of inter-cultural difference between national media systems in the strength of such views among media professionals (Fjaestad and Holmlov, 1976; Donsbach, 1981; Kocher, 1986).

An alternative, 'middle', position is represented by what has sometimes been called a 'pragmatic', or a 'professional' outlook, which favours detachment and neutrality, the practice of the craft of journalist (or producer, etc.), emphasizing the goal of providing an adequate service to the main customer: the audience. A preference for the values of diversity and objectivity is likely to be involved, although external assessment is not likely to be favoured. This view is also likely to give support to professional codes of ethics and to self-regulation. Thirdly, there is what might be called the 'proprietorial' view, which emphasizes the commercial aims of the media industry, disclaiming social purpose. It is the ultimate *management* outlook, to which external normative assessment is likely to be irrelevant.

These remarks are not only intended to underline the lack of fixed point of view or agreed criteria for media performance. They also point to the need to pay attention to the circumstances of media organizational work and the process of production. While the differences between the views from inside and outside the media have just been stressed, on many points public expectations about performance are often matched by normative and ethical orientations within the various media. The latter are generated in the daily experience of media work and deserve special attention. The view 'at the coal face' of media work helps the observer to formulate realistic standards of assessment by uncovering the common *obstacles* to 'good performance', as judged against many of the criteria discussed. It is the struggle against such obstacles that has often led media 'insiders' to formulate performance norms for themselves. The media are, for the most part, autonomous industries (as opposed to branches of the public service) which have to respond according to their own logic to diverse demands from society, as well as to their own internal problems.

PART III
RESEARCH MODELS AND METHODS

7
MEDIA ORGANIZATIONAL PERFORMANCE: MODELS AND RESEARCH OPTIONS

Obstacles to performance as viewed from within

There is much evidence that the media operate under conditions of considerable pressure and constraint. Figure 7.1 represents the 'field of social forces' (after McQuail, 1987: 142) in which they typically have to operate. According to this model, the media are often at the receiving end of a number of sources of 'power leverage' (Gerbner, 1969). The same situation may also be represented as a hierarchy of influences, ranging from the very 'distant' and very general (such as requirements of international regulation or the traditions of past performance) to the immediate and particular (such as the pressures of competition from rivals or those from local political and business interests) (Dimmick and Coit, 1982).

A strong awareness of, and sensitivity to, external pressures and demands is reported in many accounts of the media at work (Cantor, 1971; Tunstall, 1971; Elliott, 1972, 1977; Sigal, 1973; Johnstone et al., 1976; Burns, 1977; Engwall, 1978; Schlesinger, 1978; Tuchman, 1978; Gans, 1979; Weaver and Wilhoit, 1986; Carroll, 1987). Such accounts often emphasize the extent to which those who work in organizations develop defences against such pressures in order to protect their autonomy. They also make clear that autonomy is always severely limited and that what the media do (their 'performance') is often shaped by others, especially by powerful institutions and irreplaceable 'sources'.

There is enough evidence, in any case, to enable us to identify the main potential 'agents of influence' in the environment of a *typical* media organization, with whom relations of conflict or cooperation are generated. Against this background, the circumstances in which media operate seem less than ideal for attaining 'idealistic' standards.

Figure 7.1 typifies the situation of a media organization such as a

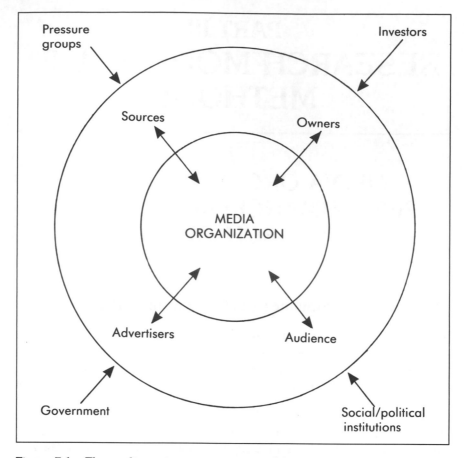

Figure 7.1 *The media environment: sources of demand and constraint*

newspaper or television channel. The key is provided by the ideas of *demand* and *constraint*. An organization tries to meet conflicting demands, or expectations, in the face of obstacles and limitations. According to many accounts, the main goals of a newspaper (or similar news organization) are themselves mixed and even inconsistent (Tunstall, 1971). The main 'partners' in the environment of the media, as showing in Figure 7.1, also vary in the degree of power or influence they can exercise (Gerbner, 1969). For this reason, the agencies with most immediate power or leverage (especially owners, advertisers, sources and audience) are shown as closer to the media 'core' than investors, social institutions, suppliers, governments or pressure groups. A highly regulated industry, such as public broadcasting, may have government much 'closer' and, in general, the disposition of forces displayed will vary according to industry type.

In a situation like this, day-to-day problems can only be handled by, on the one hand, developing work routines which simplify the tasks and decision-taking (Engwall, 1978; Tuchman, 1978) and, on the other, by referring to a set of occupational or operating norms, which often connect with wider norms of conduct for public life. It is these which are of interest here, since there is a good deal of evidence about the principles of conduct which help to map out the normative landscape of media work. It is not only the external relations of the media which give rise to conflicts with normative dimensions. Such conflicts also occur *within* organizations because of mixed, in some cases barely compatible, goals.

The most economical account of internal conflicts about the goals of a media organization is probably to be found in Engwall (1978), who made a three-fold division of work cultures into: management; editorial, creative or writing people; and technical, design and production staff. Each of the three groups is likely to have somewhat different goals, different normative priorities and different kinds of relationship with the various 'agencies' in the media environment. The existence of variations in normative outlook according to task or function has also been widely reported (e.g. Burns, 1977; Weaver and Wilhoit, 1986; Meyer, 1987).

Normative responses to organizational pressures

The normative issues which recur in daily practice can be described according to the main types of relationship, as represented in Figure 7.1; in particular, relations with sources and selection decisions; economic pressures; relations with the wider society; relations with the audience.

Relations with sources and selection decisions

The key problem is how to behave as a 'gatekeeper' (Dimmick, 1974; Hirsch, 1977) under circumstances of varying ease or difficulty of obtaining material from sources. On the one hand, media are pressed to accept a large supply of ready-made content from well-organized and sometimes powerful sources (like government departments, large firms, major social institutions). On the other hand, there are many sources and voices which are poor in resources, but not necessarily less deserving of attention on grounds of relevance or significance. Apart from this power imbalance between those seeking access, the collection of news and the acquisition of material has widely varying costs to the organization. There may be a resulting bias, other things being equal, towards accepting content (thus giving access) where content is both free and well organized to suit press needs (Gans, 1979). Similarly, there may be pressures to avoid possible indirect offence to powerful interests.

The media are thus continually faced with a set of essentially normative dilemmas. In relation to the state and branches of *government*, with whom media are potentially in a state of tension (in their 'watch-dog' role), the situation is especially sensitive. What government does is often significant, relevant and interesting and the media are, consequently, always dependent on government and its agencies for large and convenient supplies of news. However, the government has its own informational purposes which go beyond the objective needs of the media or the audience. The media can be assimilated to these goals or sometimes compromised by a state of dependence and resulting compliance (Gieber and Johnson, 1961; Sigal, 1973, 1986).

For their part, the media usually assert the principle of their own right to determine, in their publication policy, what is in the interests of their audience and, indirectly, of society. In other words, they claim the rights as well as the obligations of citizenship in a free society. Similar problems can arise in relation to the many special interests and pressure groups which seek to acquire (or to evade) publicity on their own terms (Gandy, 1982). Aside from their power, such groups or interests may claim attention on the basis of legitimacy, appeals to altruism or of acknowledged general public esteem.

Although the general question of access covers a very diverse set of situations, a limited set of basic norms has emerged to deal with these matters, as seen from the media perspective. These can be summarized as follows:

- Media should not be influenced in what they do or do not publish primarily by fear of offence to the powerful or because of convenience, or of other rewards of collaboration.
- Competing claims for access should be assessed by the media mainly according to criteria of relevance to the audience or significance for society.
- Media should not unfairly 'penalize' (e.g. by denial of, or by negative, attention) the resource-poor, marginal or deviant groups and causes.

Response to economic pressure and support

The main sources of media finance which can give rise to normative problems are those from third parties: owners (or other paymasters) and would-be advertisers or sponsors. For the most part, income direct from 'consumers' is not regarded as normatively problematic since the audience is presumed to pay for what it gets and to get what it pays for. Proprietorial influence on content, although defensible as a property right, may conflict with media claims to offer fully disinterested truth or independent opinion (Meyer, 1987). There may also be objections on grounds of resulting political bias, especially bias towards business interests and right-wing government. Dependence on advertising revenue places media under a potential obligation to major advertisers (Turow, 1984).

A similar situation arises in relation to direct or indirect sponsorship. As with ownership ties, the central issue is that of the *autonomy* of the media: the independence of decisions about content from the commercial self-interest of the media. Subsidies may sometimes be received from public funds, either in the form of exceptional economic help (tax relief, loans and grants, direct payments, etc.) or (as with many public broadcasting bodies) as general income from taxation or licence fees raised from the public. These sources of income can also raise the issue of reduced independence. The principle that content decisions *ought* not to be directly influenced by this kind of support is usually recognized. Other sources of income, from political parties, churches, etc. are less problematic, as long as the connection between outside interest and the medium is made clear. In such cases, 'sponsors' and media public are assumed to have a shared interest.

A set of somewhat disparate normative propositions serve to represent this complex territory, especially:

- Editorial judgements should not be subordinated to economic pressures, whether from proprietors, advertisers, sponsors, public funds, or other financial sources (e.g. other business interests of a media firm).
- Where there is potential influence from financial source on content this should be controlled and revealed; for example, by a clear separation of advertising from editorial content, by reporting sponsorship, by general openness about vested interests, etc.
- Owners should not use their economic power on a day-to-day basis, or in idiosyncratic and personally motivated ways.

Relations with the wider society: public interest or self-interest?

The many and varied demands of society have generally been matched by an equally diverse set of responses on the part of media organizations themselves, usually informally and as a process of continuous response to the interests of their own audience and to the requirements of clients and sources. Not surprisingly, the only special obligation attributed to the media is to satisfy customers and clients as efficiently as possible, from which wider benefits to society will flow, as guided by the 'hidden hand' of the media market. Nevertheless, amongst newspeople at least, a basis of normative dimension does seem to separate the purely organizational and task-orientated obligations from wider social commitments (e.g. Tunstall, 1971; Janowitz, 1975; Johnstone et al., 1976). There is evidence of a wish to serve the 'public good', because of the semi-public status of the media.

Several different versions of the self-perceived social role of journalism have been indicated in research (see Cohen, 1963; Janowitz, 1975; Kocher, 1986; Weaver and Wilhoit, 1986). The most commonly chosen version is that of neutral observer, transmitter and interpreter of events of significance in society – the role of public *informant*. A second version is that of *participant* or *advocate*, involving the aim of engaging in political and social life and of having a purposeful influence on events. This may include an *altruistic* element (Gans, 1979) – an impulse to speak up for society's victims, minorities and underdogs. A third kind of involvement is as critic, adversary, *watch-dog* of any sphere of public life. Fourthly, there is a widespread view that the media have a task as a platform or *forum* for the diverse voices of society, allowing the expression both of varied opinions and of cultural streams. The media, in this view, are less a channel for separate messages than a public resource to allow society as a whole to speak to itself. Fifthly, there is the role of responsible *guardian* which is sometimes adopted in matters of public order and morals, culture or personal conduct (for example, Burns, 1977, on the BBC). This has been described as a 'sacerdotal' role (Blumler, 1969) which finds its expression in a commitment to public duty and traditional values over commercial success or popularity.

Relations with the audience

Relations between the media and their audiences, under conditions of free choice and diverse supply, are usually thought to be self-adjusting and unproblematic. The audience cannot 'harm' the media, nor need the media harm the audience, where the latter has freedom to choose. Even so, there is evidence that the audience is often viewed ambivalently by professional communicators, who have little time for most audience research and who construct images of the audience, according to their own self-images (Bauer, 1958; Burns, 1977; Gans, 1979). The demands of the audience are supposed, nevertheless, to provide the ultimate performance yardstick.

For communicators, the main problem is the potential threat posed to their own autonomy and, sometimes, to their professional standards. Situations arise where pleasing the audience (for commercial reasons) may seem to be inconsistent with integrity and where professional norms may conflict with organizational policy. Such problems are often taken care of by division of labour within an organization. Communicators can opt to serve a particular audience, or some goal of the organization according to personal preference and sense of professional integrity, rather than to follow commercial goals. Tunstall, for instance, refers to the 'non-revenue' journalistic goal (for instance, covering foreign news or domestic politics), which gives a newspaper status and social influence without gaining either many readers or advertising income.

Autonomy as a recurrent theme

These comments on the operating environment of the media, as it is reported by research into 'insider' experience and outlook, indicate the most sensitive points at the interface between media and society, the points at which norms of performance are likely to have developed internally or been applied externally. Especially notable, perhaps, is the recurrent theme of *independence*: the emphasis on the need to maintain an essential autonomy and freedom of action so that the *credibility* and good faith of the media as well as personal integrity can be sustained. This claim to autonomy provides a counterweight to the emphasis on demands *from society* and on control and external accountability, although its strength varies according to circumstances and from medium to medium. In a free society, it is the media institution itself which has, in the end, to deliver the social goods of public communication and not governmental or citizen committees and commissions. The attainment of media 'quality' is dependent on the quality of the media themselves, and on their creative and professional freedom.

A media organization model

To examine more closely the constraints on media and also to help map out the research terrain, it is useful to deploy a general model of media organizational structure and process. The aim is also to highlight some relevant features of media as business firms (or public corporations). A basic model of any industrial organization can be adapted for this purpose (Figure 7.2) (in this case, from Busterna, 1988b; Scherer, 1980). This model shows three key features: *market structure* – the essential features of finance, control, market dynamics and constraints; *conduct* – the most common types of organizational behaviour; and *performance* – the main factors relevant to assessing the *output* of a firm.

Market structure

The sub-terms need a brief explanation. *Concentration* refers to the degree of monopoly characterizing a given firm or market sector – the extent to

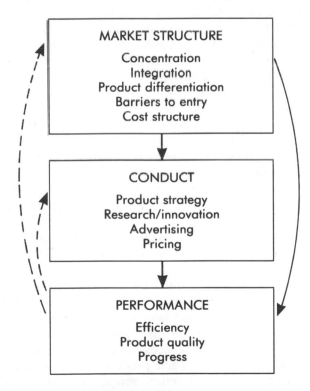

Figure 7.2 *A media organizational model*

which activities belong to the same owner or fall under the same control. *Integration* refers to either vertical or horizontal ownership or control. Vertical integration applies when succeeding stages of the process are in the same hands; for instance, film production and cinema or television distribution, or paper production, advertising agencies and newspaper production. Horizontal integration occurs when competing media or media-related business are jointly owned (the case of multi-media businesses).

Product differentiation refers to the range of products which an industrial concern makes and offers for sale. Typically, the media industry is characterized by a high degree of differentiation of goods and services. Most national media systems are highly interdependent, so that one unit in the system affects another (by competing for a limited audience or supply of advertising). They are also structured according to function (type of product and of target audience) and also geographical and time factors.

The term *barriers to entry* refers to the possibilities for competition from new firms. In some industries, there are almost no barriers beyond some minimum capital requirements. Modern mass media tend, however, to be characterized by high barriers to entry, either because of the need for operating licences, which ration access, or because of public monopolies of broadcasting and electronic media, or from historic and sociocultural features of media, which give advantages to existing media firms (the equivalent to 'good will' and reputation of established firms). Of course, high capital and labour costs of media production are often a very large barrier. Existing mass media, such as major national newspapers or television channels, can in practice only be effectively challenged by new media which have very large initial capital backing.

The last term, *cost structure*, refers to some distinctive and highly variable features of media industries. Typical of many traditional forms of mass media is the high proportion of fixed costs relative to variable costs. The fixed costs for newspaper and television organizations consist mainly of salaried staff (and of contracted 'stars'), physical plant, overheads and readily available supplies of 'software' (films and television programmes). The variable costs are the unit costs per reader or viewer reached (paper and distribution for books and newspapers, discs and tapes for music, performance payments for TV).

While there are variations from case to case, media organizations do tend to share some typical features of structure, on each of these dimensions. They often seek to maximize their share of the chosen audience and advertising markets. They also often pursue both vertical and horizontal integration, stimulated in part by high barriers (natural or artificial) to entry (as with national newspapers and television networks). The typically high product differentiation results in part from providing varied general information and entertainment services to very large audiences (consumer markets) and in part because each product is supposed to be unique (content of news, episodes of series, songs, etc.). This puts additional pressures on media cost structures, which are subject to rigidity (high fixed costs) and vulnerable to fluctuations in consumer demand (for example, audience or circulation loss cannot be compensated for by cutting costs in the short term, and longer-term cost-cutting has a vicious cycle effect on circulation and audience appeal). Without protection through various forms of limited monopoly, the main media would be very high-risk businesses.

Media organizational conduct

Under the heading of 'conduct' in Figure 7.2 are listed the main key features of *product strategy, research/innovation, advertising* and *pricing*. The media are likely to behave somewhat differently from other industries in respect of each of these, partly because of the peculiar method of financing, with a high proportion of income coming not from 'consumers', but from advertisers, to whom the attention of audiences is effectively being sold. The product of the media is also very unusual because it has both to be 'manufactured' in a routine way and yet be endlessly different from day to day. The news product is extremely perishable, not only having to be unique but also having a 'shelf-life' or no more than a few hours. Fiction, drama and entertainment can be 'resold', but only after an interval of time or in a different market.

Product strategies imposed by these conditions lead to a very high degree of *innovation* and also continuous consumer (audience and readership) *research* to provide a basis for product strategies. According to Tunstall (1991: 165), 'media organizations are unusual in being preprogrammed by research findings in so much detail and with such frequent updates.' The need for continuous product innovation and for very flexible marketing takes a lot of management time, especially under highly competitive conditions. There is also a search for products with a high 'utility' value: ones which can be re-used or resold in other markets.

Much *product strategy* is also concerned with manipulating potential audience attention-giving behaviour rather than actually disposing of products, as in other industries. Strategies for maximizing efficiency can often conflict with goals of creativity or information quality.

The *pricing* behaviour of media firms is especially unusual because of the dependence on advertising income, which means that most commercial media offer their product either 'free' (purely commercial television or free sheet newspapers) or at much below production cost price (most newspapers and magazines). Where media are operated as public service monopolies, there is virtually no need to establish a relation between the cost of production and the cost to a consumer (which is paid by way of a fixed licence fee or tax). Mass media in general probably rely neither more nor less than other industries on *advertising* of their products and services, but are unusual in that advertising is one of the media's own main product/ services and because the media often have the means for self-advertising. A good deal of media content is actually devoted to indirect and often unpaid advertising of other media content.

Media organizational performance

The main aspects of performance as they relate to media firms are not very distinctive, except for the consequences which follow from the unusual nature of the media product. Because this product is a public rather than a private good, extremely diverse and exposed to immediate public assessment, response and evaluation, the *quality* of media products is subject to much more scrutiny, according to more diverse criteria than other more typical standardized consumer products. Commercial media have to be as *efficient* in their use of resources and financial returns as other businesses, although the relation between cost of production/distribution and price may be much more complex and variable. Typical of performance indicators for the media are those cited by the Peacock Committee (1986) in relation to British television, especially hours of output per person employed and degree of utilization of crews and equipment. Media firms are also expected to show *progress* in updating and modernizing, perhaps more so because of continuing innovations of technology (computerization, high definition TV (HDTV), cable and satellite distribution, etc.).

Media performance is often assessed by criteria which have nothing to do with normal business criteria, and may even be inconsistent or in conflict (for instance, political criteria), as well as according to the usual *internal* standards of successful operation. This fact lies at the heart of some of the basic conflicts between society and media. The 'public interest' does not necessarily coincide with the organization's own interest as a business firm.

Informational feedback for media and society

An important feature of this model is the essential *interdependency* of the elements (indicated by the arrows of influence in Figure 7.2), especially the connection between the three main features of structure, conduct and performance. Features of structure determine conduct, as when monopoly or horizontal integration allows for broad product strategy and differential pricing. Both structure and conduct will have a direct influence on performance and each may have to adapt in response to 'feedback' at the stage of performance.

Each of the three main levels or 'stages' of the model also corresponds with a distinctive phase or terrain of the 'public interest' discourse and of media assessment. The level of structure corresponds with the discussion and formulation of public policy for the media. Media conduct is often very much a matter for public debate and opinion formation. The sphere of performance is more distinctively associated with *information* provision (rather than argument about principles) – information about market success, audience appeal and product quality. 'Performance assessment', as defined in this study, is essentially an information-gathering activity. Just as business firms in the organizational model described need dependable, thus 'independent', evidence concerning their own economic performance, so public policy should be guided by relevant information, as well as by normative preference (and neither can be a substitute for the other).

Variants of media organizational form

While the media have some features in common with other industrial organizations, they are in many respects quite distinctive. There are also differences of organizational structure and form *among* the main kinds of mass media, which can be relevant to performance assessment. In particular, media organizations vary according to whether their main task is editing, production or distribution, and in the balance between these. An outline of four main variants is offered as a guide to the location of relevant performance problems. The four variants are composed of much the same basic elements, representing different organizational 'actors' or 'tasks', as shown in Figure 7.3.

Of particular relevance for present purposes is the variable degree of *interconnection* between the main actors and tasks. The more these are linked together and 'under one roof', the greater the probability that the organization concerned will have a significant public 'presence', give rise to public interest claims and be an object of performance assessment. The variants are labelled according to four types: newspaper; broadcasting; book; and common carrier (telecommunications). Each model can have a wider application than the labels imply and there are many deviations from the typical forms described. Thus the newspaper model also applies to some magazines and the 'book' model has some relevance for the film, music and video industries. Each 'model' represents a conventional type of organization which developed during the 'industrial age' of mass media. However, these forms are becoming anachronistic, especially under pressure of new technology and forces of internationalization (see Chapter 23).

The newspaper press model

The main defining feature of the traditional form of newspaper organization is that a large number of different functions are gathered together, often literally, 'under one roof': especially management, editorial and production (printing) tasks. This is indicated in Figure 7.3 by the dashed line enclosing core elements. Only the distribution function has usually been (in part) in separate hands. Additionally, the newspaper works to a very short and tight time scale of production, which requires a high degree of coordination of tasks.

The issues of *structure* which are most relevant to newspaper performance concern relations between owners/publishers and editors and links between different titles which may be operated by the same concern (questions of monopoly, diversity and resources). Issues of *conduct* mainly concern relations between management and editorial staff (autonomy) and also relations between the newspaper and its advertisers and sources. Questions

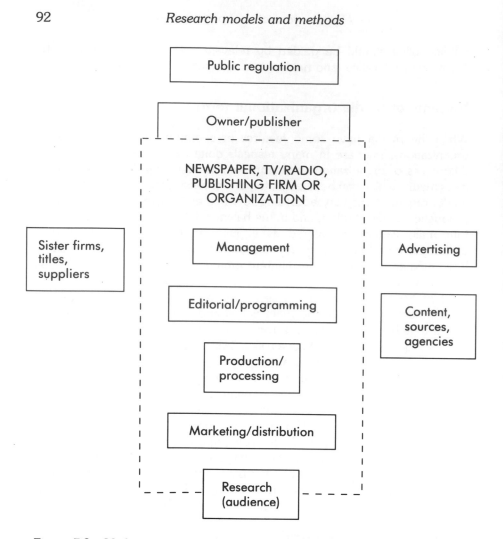

Figure 7.3 *Media organizational components and tasks*

of *performance* apply to the quality of press content. The typical newspaper, according to the traditional model, produces a high proportion of its own editorial content on a daily basis, but this is changing, with increasing concentration, rationalization and buying or sharing of services from outside.

The broadcast model

Broadcasting operates in very different forms, according to variations of national system and of scale and range (national, regional or local). A near universal operating condition, however, is a framework of detailed public regulation and control unknown to the typical newspaper. Broadcasting may or may not have a single organizational home but the trend is away from this. In general, the more commercialization, the more fragmentation and independence of organizational elements. The key media tasks shown in

Figure 7.3 are most likely to be closely linked in the case of the traditional national public broadcasting organization. It is difficult, otherwise, to typify the broadcasting form of media organization, although the following characteristics are often present:

- monopoly or oligopoly conditions of market structure;
- a potential or actual separation of editorial/programming, production and distribution tasks;
- an extreme diversity of product;
- diversity of financial support (advertising, licence fee, sponsoring, subsidy, subscription).

For present purposes, the main issues of *structure* concern the degree of monopoly and the relations between editorial actors and their owners or public regulators (which may extend to the political system). The issues of *conduct* are also similar to those which apply to the newspaper organization (especially relations with advertisers or sources and internal questions of journalistic and artistic autonomy or integrity). The difficulty of establishing a direct financial link with the audience/consumer poses some of these issues in sharper form. In respect of *performance*, the limited number of broadcast channels (in the past, at least, as a result of scarcity or monopoly) has led to relatively more attention being given to questions of diversity of programming and of opportunities of access for 'voices' from outside the organization itself. In addition, the regulation of many aspects of broadcasting conduct and performance 'in the public interest', for whatever reason, has led to many more claims and much more public scrutiny of performance.

The book model

This is the oldest and simplest media organizational form, but it too occurs in many different variants, depending on which medium is involved (it may also apply, for instance, to the cases of music, film and video production). In so far as they are present, the elements shown in Figure 7.3 can come together under one roof or be quite separate organizationally. The earliest form typical of book publishing was for ownership, editorial selection, production (printing and binding) and the initial stage of distribution to be carried out in one workshop (although authorship was always independent).

The separation of the publishing (editorial selection) from the printing and binding task occurred quite early in the history of the industry. Since then there have been further tendencies: towards a large degree of concentration and conglomeration; towards much more division of labour and contracting out of tasks. Publishing firms are essentially editorial and production organizations and are totally dependent on outside sources (authors) for a supply of content. A basic feature of the organizational form is that it produces a large number of unique products which are individually sold to individual consumers, who are the only significant source of income.

The model applies in general terms to the music industry, where song and music writers are the independent sources of content to be produced and disseminated. The main difference lies in the appearance of another element – the performer – and, generally, the greater fragmentation of the whole system. While a few large multinational companies now control the music industry in economic terms, the different elements are still usually organizationally independent. A second difference is that income is derived not only from unit products sold to consumers, but also from performing rights.

The film industry deviates rather too far to be adequately captured by the same organizational model, although it shares some typical features with books and recorded music. It has always been characterized by fragmentation, with production and cinema distribution (originally the only channel of income) always separated. The alternative ways of gaining income (especially broadcasting, cable satellite and video) now make the industry even more organizationally disparate.

In respect of this set of media, the relevant public interest issues have mainly concerned aspects of *structure* (in which varieties of concentration and their consequences have gained most attention). Only limited aspects of *performance* (content), especially where issues of public morals or decency might be involved, have been subject to public scrutiny. The amount and focus of interest in performance has varied a good deal from time to time and country to country, with the printed book largely escaping scrutiny.

The common carrier model

For completeness, a sketch is given of the 'common carrier' model (Pool, 1984), so called because it refers to a public communication distribution facility available to all, especially telegraph, telephone, mail. The main additional organizational features are:

- It is a point-to-point service, not openly disseminated.
- Management of the distribution infrastructure is separate from any control of content carried.
- Most content is private and not controlled at all.
- Conditions of natural monopoly and other 'public interest' factors usually lead to close regulation of the service.

The model is not, in origin, a mass media model at all and is still of only marginal relevance to the present task. However, it does apply to some public communication services, especially videotex and similar consultative services. It is also likely that common carriers will play an increasing role as channels of distribution for signals which are now carried by broadcasting, cable and satellite, aside from any growth in videotex and similar services. In principle, for instance, an electronic newspaper can be delivered by broadband cable. An increasing, if small minority, share of public communication will be provided within this organizational form, which is currently characterized as having a very limited 'editorial/selection' function, little or no production of its own and a high degree of external public regulation.

The basic logic of social research into media performance

The model shown in Figure 7.2 contains several implications for the role of assessment research. It is, fundamentally, a sequential, 'cause-and-effect' model, with structure leading to conduct leading to performance, as indicated. The main terms of the public policy debates about media, described in Chapters 4 and 5, help to add some flesh to the bare bones of this causal sequence. They also remind us of the ways in which social research on media policy is often patterned according to the media organizational sequence. The connections are typically as follows.

Features of *society* (for instance, industrialization, large-scale capitalist organization of industry) powerfully shape the basic nature of media *structure* (e.g. concentration of ownership, degree of public control), which becomes an object of public policy (e.g. limits on monopoly, public regulation, licensing) which then directly affects *conduct* (e.g. the terms of competition and corresponding product strategies), which affects *performance* (especially variations in product quality), which, in turn, affects society and its culture.

Research (even when independently sponsored or conducted) is often an extension or adjunct of public *policy* (though it may be independently sponsored or conducted), which is, in essence, the main expression of 'society's' views and intentions concerning *structure*. From this perspective, 'society' is seen to have an influence on media conduct and performance by way of policy. The main role assigned to research in this highly general model is to collect *evidence about performance* which can inform or guide public policy, typically the only legitimate instrument by which society can directly limit or control the autonomy of media conduct on behalf of the public interest. According to this view, research is mainly a form of diagnostic feedback which may serve to signal problems of performance relevant to 'society', generate particular policy proposals, or evaluate how public policy is working. The model in Figure 7.4 is intended to summarize these main points.

Less self-evident presuppositions built into this model are: that a media 'system' normally reflects and interacts with its social and cultural environment and that society as 'receiver' may respond differently from society as 'source' (put another way, policy may propose, but people will, in the end, dispose).

The implications for assessment research are, first of all, that account has to be taken of the perspectives of audiences (and other interests in society) as well as those of would-be policy-makers (or the media themselves). Secondly, there are various sources of tension in the connections and loops

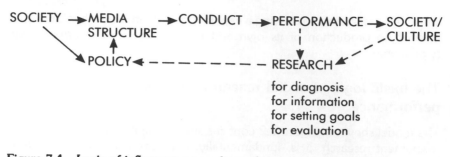

Figure 7.4 *Logic of influences on media performance and the role of social research*

shown in Figure 7.4. It is not a smoothly working, self-adjusting system. Policy is nearly always contested in 'society' and between society and media, nor does it necessarily work on structure, conduct and performance as planned (there can be unwanted side-effects as well as no effects). The criteria by which performance should be assessed are not usually agreed, as among policy-makers, media and the 'general public', who form the body of consumers. Performance assessment may aspire to the role of neutral informant, but it cannot escape from the normative and material conflicts which are endemic in the structure and dynamics of media work.

Strategic research options: choice of level and of explanatory variables

While, by definition, the main focus of performance research has to be at the stage or level of *performance*, some account has to be taken of *structure* and *conduct* in defining problems and designing research. Even where content is the main object of enquiry, a decision about which *level of media structure* to study has to be made. In practice, we are likely to differentiate three main levels:

1 The *macro*-level, referring to an entire (usually national) media system (or simply all relevant media).
2 The *meso*-level, referring to a particular 'sector' of media (for instance, national daily newspapers, or periodicals, or local radio, etc.).
3 The *micro*-level, referring to any one media channel, such as a single newspaper title, a television station, a publishing company, etc.

The first of these would be an unusual choice, given the extent and range of most media systems, but one may wish to consider the condition of an entire media system or to make comparisons between one national media system and another, or to compare the same national system at two points in time. A macro approach may also be appropriate for looking at the full range of media in one region or city area. Some of the normative principles mentioned, especially those of independence and diversity, can be applied to the assessment of complete media *structure* as well as to content performance. A meso-level enquiry, for instance into the national daily newspaper press, might also have to take account of the location of the press in a larger national 'system' of media.

The most frequent location of problems for performance assessment has been at the meso-level – with enquiries into a distinct sector of media provision. This stems mainly from the way in which problems have been posed, since policy concerns tend to relate to only one media sector at a time. It is also methodologically much easier to conduct research confined to one media sector, than to cross sector boundaries (different media require different sampling and different kinds of measure).

Micro-level research is often the option chosen by a media organization itself, in evaluating its own performance, but it can also be a suitable choice for 'public interest' research. Examples of such occasions include the case of a prestige national newspaper, a dominant broadcast channel or a monopoly city newspaper, where the object of research is a uniquely significant component in a media system. Situations where altered circumstances (e.g. disappearance or appearance of a competing title or channel, or takeover by a chain), which may have a significant impact on a particular title or channel, may also call for a micro (single channel) enquiry.

This division according to structural 'level' of a media system does not exhaust the possibilities for defining a particular research terrain or performance problem. Equally relevant are variables of *form of ownership*, where these are posited as affecting conduct or performance, especially various kinds and degrees of concentration. Some other variables of structure have been hypothesized as relevant to performance, for instance the effect of different sources of revenue (dependence on advertising, sponsorship or subscription income).

Variable features of the *conduct* of media organizations have not been much deployed in performance research, although they are often thought to be relevant. Research into media organizations suggests that several matters internal to the working of the organization and not accountable under the heading of *structure* are relevant to performance (e.g. Becker et al., 1978). These include the perceptions and attitudes of media communicators about their own tasks and their social background and identifications. Levels of staffing and resources and the varying 'climate' or 'culture' of the media workplace have also been examined for possible effects on performance. There seems to have been little success in connecting these variables in a systematic way with specific features of performance in terms of content, partly because of the complexity of the research task.

There is therefore a limited number of main options or variants of empirical research strategy. The key building blocks can be reduced to four main items, each indicating a certain kind of evidence and typical method of research, which can be named as relating to structure, conduct, content and audience.

Inter-media comparisons

The option of comparing different *media* (for instance, newspapers, radio and television) in terms of their performance has not often been followed, although for particular purposes inter-media comparisons have been made, usually by reference to audience perceptions. For instance, there is a tradition in political campaign research of asking electors about the differential credibility or information value of newspapers and television (e.g. Carter and Greenberg, 1965; Blumler and McQuail, 1968). There has also been continuing debate about the relative merits of press and electronic media as general sources of information for the public (see Chapter 16) (Robinson, 1972; Clarke and Fredin, 1978; Gaziano, 1983; Robinson and Levy, 1986).

Otherwise, the relative absence of comparisons between the media, according to the normative framework discussed above, stems firstly from the institutional differences between broadcasting and the press, such that broadcasting has less editorial freedom and is usually required to provide certain basic services and to be fair, balanced or neutral. Secondly, it is due to obvious differences of structure function and technology. Compared to the press, television is almost unavoidably less likely to carry deep and diverse information and more likely to be oriented towards sensation (in the widest sense) and to entertainment. In these circumstances, performance comparisons have limited relevance.

Multiple methods needed

It is obvious that performance research has no distinctive method of its own, since it has to deploy evidence of disparate kinds: about public policy, organizational structure, communication content and audiences. The only indispensable data have to do with content, which is at the heart of performance. For this reason, methods of content and text analysis have dominated the field, and the challenge of performance research has often led to significant advances of method. However, for many of the questions which have been posed about performance, content analysis is not enough. This points to another characteristic feature of the research tradition: a high level of creativity in designing indicators of performance and combining different methods. The problems of evaluation are also often so specific to time and place that they require continuous invention of instruments and strategies. Many of the problems posed (especially those to do with media) call for qualitative research methods and multiple approaches to the same problem.

PART IV
MEDIA FREEDOM

8
CONCEPTS AND MODELS OF MEDIA FREEDOM

Degrees of freedom

Because freedom of the media is first of all a structural condition, it has to be approached somewhat differently from other evaluative principles, with relatively more attention to the *conditions* of independence at the levels of *structure* and of *conduct* (as shown in Figure 7.2) and rather less to performance in terms of output. While some measures applied to media content can help to indicate independence of performance, no single 'utterance' in the media can be said to be intrinsically more or less 'free' than any other, in the way that some media messages might be said to be more, or less, truthful, accurate or balanced, etc. In any case, the principle of freedom of expression protects error as well as truth, even if not all content has an equal claim to protection (see below). Nevertheless, there are expectations and claims about freedom inscribed in media institutional arrangements (although variably and with large margins of uncertainty).

All established media are locked into systems of considerable constraint which offer little chance of exercising the kind of freedom available to individuals or even to alternative, grass-roots media whose main *raison d'être* is to resist established power (see Downing, 1984). There are also differences between the main models of media organization (outlined above), according to the kind of constraint experienced and the kind of opportunities available for editorial freedom. In general, the book model offers most freedom and broadcasting least. The newspaper model recognizes no limit on freedom but, in practice, there are severe social and economic limitations on action. Any view on what is *reasonable* to expect from media in the way of use of freedom has to take account of these differences, of the subject matter involved and of circumstances of time and place.

Questions of structure

At the level of structure, the freedom of operation of the media is often guaranteed (or limited) by provisions of society, in the form of constitutional clauses or media laws. The boundary markers of the 'free space' granted to the media can, up to a point, be seen in the formal, written, arrangements. This is one obvious source of 'reasonable expectations' about ultimate performance. However, most constitutional guarantees of freedom specific-ally refrain from stating any conditions concerning the positive expectations of performance (Lahav, 1985).

Press laws usually just offer a legal framework, within which freedom can be enjoyed. They are likely only to state certain exceptions to complete freedom, by reference to other laws or to national security and order. From considerations of structure, we can also derive other, more concrete, expectations and criteria concerning media freedom. Thus, in general, the more varied types of media there are, the more separate channels, the more diversity of owners and forms of control, the more real availability of media to the public – then the more freedom is likely to exist. These aspects of media systems can usually be investigated in objective, quantitative, ways.

Questions of organizational conduct

At the level of *conduct*, the central issue is the degree of independence which is available to different kinds of potential 'communicator' – especially to editorial decision-makers, the staff inside the media, whether as reporters, writers, performers or presenters and those outside the media seeking access to channels, whether as artists, advertisers or 'advocates'. In general, editorial decision-makers are most directly constrained by the structure and, in turn, they may have power over the freedom of (external) 'access-seekers' and of (internal) media staff. The degree of autonomy of each group is, however, shaped by additional factors.

The freedom of media personnel is, inevitably, very variable from one organization and one work task to another, although two general factors operate. Most obviously, seniority and status within the organization and (audience) market value will play a large part in the matter. Secondly, the available 'free space' can be enlarged by the development and recognition of professional ethics and sometimes by local agreements about autonomy for communicators (as in so-called 'editorial statutes' which in some countries define editorial goals and ideals, offering some protection for editors and journalists).

In some circumstances high journalistic autonomy, based on strong professionalization or unionization, has been regarded as a threat to the freedom of expression of editors and proprietors, especially where it is associated with an alleged liberal or left-wing bias on the part of journalists (e.g. Lichter and Rothman, 1986). There is scattered evidence from some countries (e.g. the USA, Sweden, Germany, Britain) that journalists as a professional group have somewhat more liberal sympathies than the general public. This may well influence the selection and treatment of some controversial issues, although it is not obviously illegitimate. Editorial freedom of expression is inevitably limited by social norms and conventions and there is little agreement about where the balance of any resulting news consensus actually lies (see Chapter 19).

Not all external or hierarchical lines of influence are only *constraining*. Sometimes, editorial discretion in giving access, or freedom to staff, can even be *facilitated* by political, proprietorial or market forces. There may, for instance, be political pressure to observe diversity. Economic success can allow for more freedom of opportunity, just as economic failure is usually restrictive. The power of private ownership need not only limit freedom but can extend possibilities for the media, if the choice is made for this, even against market disciplines or political obstacles.

The chances of access (and thus of effective freedom to communicate) for those outside the media depend on several different factors. Some can buy access or be better organized to supply what the media want in a usable form. High social status or legitimate claims to speak to society (e.g. governmental or political) can secure attention. In general, the more the goal of the access-seeker coincides with the audience goals of the organization, the better the chances of access for self-chosen purposes, on self-determined terms. It is deficiencies on all these factors which typically characterize 'low resource' groups (minority, poor, marginal, unorganized), whose effective communication freedom is correspondingly low.

Components of the press freedom idea

The Western press tradition does not offer any uniquely coherent or fully agreed version of the various elements which make up 'freedom of the press'. One, rather arbitrarily chosen, version of what this concept means can be derived from the replies to a question about the meaning of press freedom which was submitted by the first British Royal Commission on the Press (1949) to over a hundred editors and publishers. From many replies, a limited number of separate items can be distilled, referring to *rights*, *duties* or *conditions* of freedom, as follows.

Rights
- for corporations and individuals to publish news and views and offer them for sale;
- to start a newspaper;
- to refuse to publish material;
- to attend and report on public meetings;
- to gather information;
- of the public to hear alternative views;
- of the public to receive fair, full and objective information.

Conditions
- absence of licensing, censorship or discriminatory taxation;
- absence of interference by proprietors, advertisers, editors, printers, etc.

Table 8.1 *Press freedom*

	Whose freedom?	From what?	To do what?
Level of structure	Proprietor	Censorship; unfair taxes;	Publish/sell news and views; not to publish; start a new publication
Level of conduct	Editor	State; proprietorial and outside interference (advertisers, sponsors, etc.)	Print news and views; gather information; not to print; advocate views; criticize
Level of performance	Public	Lack of choice; bias in news and views	Hear news and views; express own views

Duties
- to give chances to the public to express their views;
- to serve the public good;
- to present alternative points of view, including unpopular or disagreeable matter;
- to act as a trustee on behalf of the public.

This covers the universe of components mentioned without representing any agreed overall consensus. Bearing in mind the time when these points were formulated and the bias towards the perspective of publisher and editor, this is not a bad guide to key elements of what is still widely understood under the heading of 'right to communicate'. It also helps to locate the main objectives of press freedom and the main potential barriers to its attainment. These matters can be presented summarily in Table 8.1.

The sources of potential inconsistency and conflict in this universe of ideas about press freedom can be deduced from this summary. An initial and basic question concerns the *location* of the freedom right. Does it lie with owners of the media (as an economic right), or with editors, journalists and artists, or with the public, as audience or body of citizens in whose interest the media are thought to operate? Embedded in these questions is an ambiguity about whether freedom can be claimed by an *organization* (e.g. the media firm) or only by individuals. The wide differences of view amongst the original respondents to the 1947 questionnaire are concealed by summarizing the outcome in this way, but it is clear that even in one time and place, with a fairly homogeneous set of informed participants, no single or simple model of press freedom was shared by all publishers and editors.

Four editorial models of media freedom

Quite different media systems can and do make a supportable claim to advance freedom, without necessarily meaning the same thing by it (see

Altschull, 1984). Often the difference turns on the question of *whose* freedom is advanced or protected. According to the distinctions just noted, the essence of freedom means something different to different potential beneficiaries. For owners, it means property rights in the means of communication production; for editors and staff, it means professional autonomy and freedom to select, write and produce; for voices in society, it means the possibilities of access or adequate representation to the wider society; for audiences, freedom stands for wide choice of all kinds.

Following the distinctions of type of organization model described in Chapter 7, four *editorial models* are discussed below, representing the main variants of core structural conditions in which media freedom is exercised. The term 'editorial' is used because it refers to the publication (content) decisions, which make up the key editorial task. Most performance is, from this point of view, the direct result of editorial activity, in the broadest sense. Assessment of performance has to take account of the conditions which apply to different media.

The press market model of editorial freedom

This has also been described as a 'libertarian', or simply 'free press', model. Its essence is support for the maximum freedom for any person to express and disseminate information and opinion. There should, in particular, be no 'prior restraint', in the form of advance censorship, screening or licensing, nor any retribution for what is published, aside from what any citizen might have to answer for before the law. The freedom offered is essentially an individual right to free speech which has been translated into an economic right to run a publishing business with as much freedom as any other business, and often with certain special privileges added (Ernst, 1946; Lieberman, 1953; Brenner and Rivers, 1982; Chamberlin and Brown, 1982; Lahav, 1985). The notion of a 'free market place of ideas' has sometimes been invoked in order to establish the connection between the two, although there is rarely any true economic market in ideas (in the public sphere, at least). The phrase is more a metaphor and also a rhetorical device to legitimate private ownership of media (Keane, 1991).

The case for equating press freedom with property rights is far from conclusive, especially since property rights are generally conditional and are often subject to intervention on grounds of 'public interest' (see Lichtenberg, 1990). Other arguments for press freedom, in the Western value system, are actually much stronger. Even so, it may well be true that property rights are a necessary, though not a sufficient, condition for media freedom. According to Kelley and Donway (1990: 79), 'Any action whatever involves the use of physical resources ... The exercise of any right, therefore involves an exercise of property rights, and some system of property is required in order to define any category of rights, including those of speech.'

More pragmatically, the unhindered working of the market of supply and demand for communication can be thought to best serve the public interest in, and need for, a free flow of information and ideas (the 'free market place of ideas' again). The market form also *appears* to resolve potential conflicts of interest between the rights of communicators and the rights of receivers. Thus the communication market, left to itself, should ensure that the communication needs of receivers as well as of senders are fulfilled as far as is practicable (unmet needs will generate alternative supply). This also appears to take account of the view that press freedom is a right of the public to have its information needs met. According to the press market model, intervention (by government or law-making), even if ostensibly on behalf of consumers or of the 'public interest', in undesirable, either in principle or because it distorts the relationship between supply and demand.

Authoritative accounts of the theory of the American First Amendment do not always support the equation of economic freedom with press freedom nor the argument for private ownership as a necessary condition. According to Emerson (1970: 115), for instance, 'the essence of a system of freedom of expression lies in the distinction between expression and action.' On this interpretation, the operation of media businesses belongs to the sphere of 'action', and can properly be regulated, in societies which, otherwise, do seek to protect individual freedom. One simple and far-reaching consequence of exercising property rights has been increased concentration of media ownership (Lichtenberg, 1990). Particularly relevant is the fact that the exercise of property rights inevitably limits the freedom of others, while legitimate expression of views can take place without impinging on other people's freedom. It is also obvious that modern mass media are not equally available to all as a means of publishing ideas, nor can they even be equally received by all. Schmidt (1976) has provided an extended account of conflict between advocates of pure First Amendment freedom and advocates of rights of public access to the media.

The broadcasting editorial model

The second main variant of an editorial model (see Figure 7.4) has been slow to receive recognition as a distinctive form of media structure, although Pool (1984) treats it as having a status equivalent, in regulatory practice, to free press arrangements. Pool views the broadcast model as a deviant and undesirable result of temporary technological bottlenecks. Even so, it is now a pervasive form of organizational arrangement worldwide and shows few signs of withering away. It is certainly an *editorial* model, because it presumes a process of selection, production and dissemination, often centralized within the same organization.

In general, it departs from the press market model, mainly in being posited on a presumed scarcity of channels which have a high social and economic value. In turn, this entails the need for rules for access and some regulation of content. Scarcity of channels and 'natural monopoly' conditions (where free competition is inefficient and inconvenient for the consumer) would make it impossible (so runs the theory) for the market mechanism to deliver, via broadcasting, the benefits claimed for the press market model (Rundell and Heuterman, 1978; Powell and Gair, 1988).

In organizational terms, the broadcasting model has already been described as monopolistic and subject to strong public regulation of operation and content. In general, it is characterized by editorial policies which are designed to ensure that communication needs, over and above those which an unregulated monopoly would provide, are adequately met. In addition, we usually find some mechanism of accountability to society as well as some provision for securing editorial autonomy in the face of regulation.

The difficulty of reconciling accountability with autonomy is very obvious. Even so, the record of regulated public broadcasting is not necessarily discreditable when viewed against expectations that media should play a critical, watch-dog or investigative role. Public broadcasting often uses its autonomy to provide access to views which governments may find very uncomfortable. Curran (1991), for example, concludes that in Britain, during the 1980s, both the BBC and ITV, without overstepping their legal limits, performed the expected critical role at times of crisis and on sensitive issues at least as well as the newspaper press.

The broadcasting model can take either a public service or a regulated commercial form. In the public service variant, the *raison d'être* is to deliver communication benefits which are thought to be 'in the public interest', usually including an adequate and diverse supply of information, access for minorities and the resource poor and provision of various cultural services. Such goals are clearly stated in founding documents. In the commercial case, there may be editorial obligations to society as conditions of operation, but they are likely to have a much weaker, or even nominal, force and to depend on self-regulation. The broadcasting model gives relatively more priority to the rights of the receiver than to those of the communicator and also establishes rights of access for would-be 'external' communicators.

This bias has been supported by US courts, the Red Lion judgment stating, for example, that 'It is the right of the viewers and listeners, not the right of broadcasters, which is paramount', including rights to 'receive suitable access to social, political, aesthetic, moral and other ideas and experiences' (Bazelon, 1982). Thus, several features of the model entail material restrictions on the freedom of those who operate broadcasting services, often expressed as specific obligations, with a view to enlarging the freedom of receivers, especially those in a weak market position.

The book market model

This form of publication usually enjoys the same (or even greater) rights to freedom as the newspaper press, based on the right of free expression. It is, however, much more unambiguously, a right of *communicators* (authors and publishers) and not a public 'right to receive'. In some respects, it is less clearly an *editorial* model than the two described, more a particular industrial and marketing form for individual authors. While in some respects organizationally similar, video, film and music media are less likely, in practice, to have the same freedom as the book because of their dependence on complex technology and distribution arrangements.

Common carriage

The common carrier model (see Kalven, 1967; Pool, 1984) applies to channels which, in principle, offer a universal communication facility. In its main historic forms, it is not an *editorial* model at all, nor one that applies much to mass media. However, it is becoming adapted to new media and new types of information traffic, especially consultative and interactive communication. Because of this, editorial decisions are increasingly being taken about what content services to offer and questions both of freedom and of performance will also come to apply.

The classic media examples representing the model are telephone, mail service, telegraph, all point-to-point services, in which access is open to all and there is little or no control of the communication content carried. It now applies to some 'telematic' services (e.g. videotex) and it *can* be the future model for many cable television or sound radio services (where sender access is simply leased, without editorial rules). Its inclusion in this set of models is a reminder that concepts of editorial freedom have continually to be rethought and are not rooted for all time in the newspaper model.

Varying conditions of constraint: finance and freedom

The one variable in each model which is always relevant to independent performance is that of source of *finance* (see Altschull's, 1984, 'second law of journalism', which states that 'The content of mass media always reflects the interests of those who finance the press'). The main sources of media finance which are usually thought to impinge on editorial freedom are: *public subsidy* (including receiver licence fee), which gives some power to the state, but also to the public via the political system; commercial (as opposed to personal) *advertising*, which gives some power to economic third parties; *senders*, who may provide, subsidize or sponsor content (including governments, political parties, private individuals, pressure groups and public relations (PR) agencies); *consumers* who pay directly for the costs of content and/or distribution.

The degree of leverage accompanying each source of finance will vary according to editorial model and from case to case. In practice, media often rely on several different sources of income at the same time – a condition which conventional wisdom holds to be better for freedom. Another commonly held view is that freedom (independence) is more secure where consumers pay all the costs (approximated in the case of the printed book medium, if not always the book market model as a whole).

In the case of the newspaper, the more that finance is derived from a third party (e.g. government, advertisers or sponsor), the less plausible is the claim to full independence. The extreme case is probably that of the commercial free newspaper (or its PR magazine equivalent), which rarely even claims 'real' newspaper status). Even so, newspapers in the United States, which are often 80 per cent financed from advertising yield little or nothing of their claim to be independent.

It can be argued that the more a newspaper is dependent on reader income, the more it will be constrained to please these readers and the less inclined to offer them unpopular or disagreeable news and views, whatever professional integrity or the need to report 'reality' might call for. However, there are different kinds of reader-dependency. A party political (or similar) newspaper, for instance, which aims to propagate particular views usually reflects and responds to the opinions and tastes of its self-selected readers. But this is a consequence of pursuing self-chosen editorial goals and need not entail conflict with, or limitations on, editorial freedom (though there can be problems for individual journalists who are more interested in objective reporting than in the political purpose of the undertaking as a whole).

On the other hand, a commercial mass popular newspaper, which aims to please and flatter its readers/consumers, usually does so as a means to more audience revenue and thus profit. In this case, the commercial objective of increasing reader income comes first and is more likely to conflict with editorial or media-professional goals. It may then represent a restriction on the freedom of journalists. It is quite possible for the two types to merge in a publication which is both propagandist *and* 'commercial'. The examples illustrate the virtual impossibility of drawing firm conclusions about the condition of independence solely on the basis of data about media structure and sources of revenue.

Broadcasting is everywhere more restricted than print media, for reasons already given. Historically, the most common editorial limitation applied to broadcasting franchises and licences is that broadcasters should be even-handed or neutral and avoid serving any single dominant interest. This restriction stems mainly from conditions of channel scarcity and natural monopoly, but also from lingering beliefs about the irresistible power of broadcasting over its audiences. The main principle of regulation in the United States, for instance, where government interference is anathema, has been that broadcasters should act as 'trustees of the public interest' by providing for a wide variety of views, a measure of access and 'balanced' coverage of controversy (Bazelon, 1982).

The exercise of broadcasting autonomy does differ according to the main sources of finance, especially as between licence/subsidy support and advertising income. Autonomy in the former (public service) type of system depends more heavily on their being scope for professional judgement in carrying out the trustee role in matters of selection and quality. Commercial forms are more likely to follow the logic of the market, especially audience demand, with freedom being associated with more choice for the audience and thus with supposed 'consumer sovereignty'. Professional autonomy (of editorial decision-makers) in public service systems usually entails resistance to political and financial pressure as well as to some of the demands of the audience market, if 'public interest' requirements of independent and fair news are to be met. Commercial broadcasters have mainly to contend with economic pressures (freedom is limited by owners, advertisers, profit motives). They are more free to yield to audience market demand, or to use this as a yardstick for meeting public regulatory requirements.

The position of other media is less clear cut and shows more variation between cases, over time and across societies. The cinema/film carries no clear social definition, or public expectation, concerning freedom, either for the maker/exhibitor, or for the film-viewer. It is essentially a case of 'caveat spectator'. Exhibition of film is widely subject to some form of censorship (especially by way of content and age-related classification schemes) and films themselves are often openly or covertly propagandistic in tendency or intention, penetrated by the interests of authorities and special interests (for instance, facilities may be given by the military or big business, props and settings can advertise commercial goods and services, tourist attractions, etc.).

In the end, even so, it is the film-viewer who provides the overwhelming source of finance and of profit and the freedom of the commercial film-maker depends on assessments of likely consumer demand. Whether this has a liberating or a constraining effect depends on the market circumstances which apply. The enormous cost of professional film production and the nature of the mass market for films suitable for public showing or for television and video release almost certainly limits chances of exhibition for many kinds of independent-minded films. But alternative film circuits also offer opportunities for free expression.

The situation is not so different from that which applies to book publishing (aside from different cost structures), which is completely free in principle, but where chances of publication are assessed according to numerous potential sub-markets. Similar remarks apply to recorded music and video in respect of their freedom claims. It is easy to appreciate that the principle of 'free publication' as such is not much related to the real chances for an individual to get something both published and widely distributed.

Variable claims to freedom: information versus art; fiction versus reality

Claims and expectations of independence also vary according to media types and form of content. Some kinds of content do not raise issues of independent performance, or do so only to a minor degree. They make no strong 'freedom claim', for one reason or another and are, consequently, less privileged within the media institution or society. Custom and convention usually indicate where claims to independence are strong or weak and whether or not they matter. The variation is not, however, arbitrary, but derives from the link between form and content, on the one hand and the protection of some relevant values on the other.

In the US press institution, according to Emerson (1970), the key values supporting the claim to freedom, aside from that of attaining truth, are individual self-fulfilment and the participation of citizens in social and political decision-making. Where these values are not at issue, there is less force behind any claim to free expression in media, especially if a claim to restriction can be lodged on the ground of some alternative values (e.g. morals, protection of minors or public order). Typically, only weak freedom claims can be made for explicitly 'commercial' *content* (such as advertising) or for a large territory of popular fiction, amusement and entertainment, even if the right to publish all of this is, in general, acknowledged.

There are two main classes of content which *do* give rise to especially strong claims to protection of their independence. One comprises any information or opinion (news and views) which clearly belongs in the 'public sphere'. The other covers artistic and aesthetic content, which is protected according to a different, but not weaker, tradition of respect for creative integrity. The individual right to free expression is reinforced, in the case of news and public opinion, by considerations of public interest (especially the need for informed citizen participation in democratic politics), in the second case by notions of the integrity of 'works of art'. On the whole, however, the *mass* media are not regarded as channels of creative artistic expression (the main exception is book publication), principles of artistic freedom are less respected, and censorship is often tolerated.

For more practical purposes of assessing media performance, according to public interest concerns, we are dealing with content of current social reality, whether portrayed in factual or fictional forms. The implications of this distinction between fiction and reality are complex. For instance, Elliott (1972) explored the relative degree of autonomy available to (British) broadcasters, who typically act as mediators or editorial decision-makers, rather than original communicators. According to his analysis, they have least autonomy where channels are simply put at the disposal of outside 'voices', according to externally established rules or conventions (e.g. to advertisers or political parties). Most autonomy exists when they offer original television drama where conventions of artistic/authorial freedom are held to apply (in Britain, at least, in the 1960s). The claim to artistic freedom can be an additional defence against attempts at control of fiction. In any case, fiction more easily evades control, because its meaning is more ambiguous and its relation to reality more uncertain.

In between 'direct access' and 'art', as indicated by Elliott, are the two categories of most likely relevance to performance assessment: first, *news*, where a medium offers its selection of information (filtered access for society), according to its own criteria of relevance, but generally purporting to portray things 'as they really are'; secondly, *documentary*, in its various forms, which generally claims to portray reality, but usually 'remade' according to the partial viewpoint of the reporter or documentary maker. The growing category of 'docudrama' – fictionalized portrayals of real events – raises problems for any attempts to impose standards of impartiality

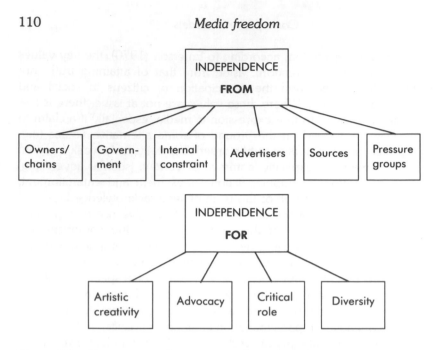

Figure 8.1 *Component indicators of media independence*

in broadcasting, or for the assessment of the information quality of content using such formats.

Extending the normative framework

We can now show how the norm of independence can be further specified in ways which lend themselves to empirical research and the choice of appropriate indicators of performance (Figure 8.1).

There is no simple way of 'reading off' the (absolute or relative) degree of independence of media systems or sectors from even the most detailed information about their structural arrangements. There are too many variable features for this to be possible. Differences of tradition and convention often defy outside interpretation. Different expectations concerning freedom often attach to different kinds of publication and types of content. The sources and kinds of pressure are too variable to be captured by standardized indicators.

The task of establishing reasonable expectations about independent performance is very complex, involving a good deal of subjective judgement. This does not mean that the relation between structure and freedom cannot be sensibly examined, but it does imply that, beyond the simplest facts of constitutional and legal arrangements, only very detailed case studies, supported by evaluation and argument can support any conclusion about the scope and active exercise of freedom by the media. There will be no 'quick fix' from research.

However, a more interesting conclusion can be drawn – which is that there is a fair degree of independence, or 'play', between structure and performance. Formally free media can submit to constraint and fail to use their freedom. Structurally more controlled media (whether public or commercial) may actively use and extend whatever scope the structure permits (sometimes by devious means). Media freedom cannot be established by constitutional or legal decree, but has to be constantly developed and re-affirmed in daily practice.

This means that there is every reason for applying tests of performance to media of all kinds. In the two following chapters, evidence about performance is assembled which bears on the two most central questions at issue: whether constraints of ownership (especially conditions of concentration and monopoly) can be shown to limit freedom and whether the more routine, but even less avoidable, restrictions in the organizational environment of media organizations lead to effects of a similar kind.

9
MEDIA FREEDOM: FROM STRUCTURE TO PERFORMANCE

Conditions of freedom of structure

Much research on media freedom has been motivated by fears about the effect of concentration and monopoly, especially in relation to the newspaper press. In the immediate post-war period, American research was also influenced by ideological motives since press freedom was held out as one of the great benefits of liberal society and there was cause for concern at the growth of newspaper monopoly within the United States. International comparative research into press freedom was one response, with typical conditions of the Western free press model taken as the norm or standard for judging the degree of freedom elsewhere (Horton, 1978; McCoy, 1979). Generally, this has meant taking the absence of government control as the main condition of freedom. Several studies (e.g. Nixon, 1960; Farace and Donohew, 1965; Weaver et al., 1985) have examined correlations between social system variables and a 'dependent variable' of degree of press freedom, the latter typically measured on the basis of 'expert' judgement and documentary evidence.

Alternative approaches to assessing the relative degree of structural freedom are to be found. One is by case study (e.g. Jansen et al., 1982), which allows a diversity of criteria to be applied and a sensitivity to many forms of interference in freedom, but does not lend itself easily to generalization or quantification. Another approach is to look at the range and incidence of government interventions in the press, often those intended to increase press freedom (e.g. Smith, 1977; Picard, 1985a). Tabulation and systematic comparison of these measures have helped both to widen the notion of freedom to include 'positive' interventions designed to widen publication diversity, as well as to differentiate between systems which are otherwise registered simply as 'free' in crude nominal scales.

The international comparative approaches mentioned have rarely been applied to broadcasting (although see Katz and Wedell, 1977; Browne, 1989; Blumler and Nossiter, 1991). The reason lies in the universality of some form of regulation of broadcasting and the lack of any commonly agreed standard of freedom beyond, perhaps, the relative scope offered for private enterprise, the degree of monopoly and the extent of the system (the more different 'channels', the more potential for freedom).

By contrast, there has been a good deal of research into independence, measured in terms of economic ownership and control of particular sectors of national media systems. Pioneering work was carried out in the United States in the wake of a rapid post-war decline in the number of independent newspapers (e.g. Nixon, 1945, 1966; Baer et al., 1974) and the rise in the number of 'one-paper cities' in the USA (Rosse and Dertouzos, 1979). Nixon and Hahn (1971) extended the scope of such research by comparing trends in 32 countries. In several European countries, a wave of concentration also took place, especially during the 1950s and 1960s, followed by research into press structures (especially in Germany, Sweden and The Netherlands). Research into press concentration has involved attention to the number of independent titles, the growth of large groups and chains, especially where this leads to local monopoly ownership (absence of competition from another independent paper) in a single circulation area or to cross-media ownership (e.g. newspaper and radio). There is a large literature on these matters of press structure, well surveyed in Picard et al. (1988) and with important contributions from Bagdikian (1988), Compaine et al. (1982) and various national press inquiries referred to elsewhere (e.g. Royal Commission on the Press, 1977; Kent, 1981).

The main issue in respect of press freedom has been the extent to which a given geographical public (or media market) is served by a range of media which are independent of each other (in terms of ownership and editorial policy). General trends in several countries towards greater economic concentration have been established beyond much doubt. For instance, the Canadian Royal Commission on Newspapers, aside from documenting a marked increase in the degree of chain ownership of newspapers in Canada, cited a Council of Europe report which reported that between 1955 and 1973 the number of 'independent editorial units' in the member countries had declined by 35 per cent, while the circulation had increased by 95 per cent over the same period (Kent, 1981: 14).

The task of estimating the real degree of editorial independence has been complicated by changes in press organization, sharing of editorial services, etc. There can be varying degrees of editorial independence within the same group ownership and there is no fixed standard for adjudicating the degree of editorial autonomy. New forms of structural (economic) concentration are also appearing by way of ownership of new media and by vertical integration, which may or may not have any direct implication for editorial functions. It is the latter which usually lie at the heart of concerns in this area. Since the degree of concentration or monopoly is the main causal variable in studying effects of media structure on independent performance, more precise measurement of the conditions of freedom in groups and in editorial units is urgently needed.

Seeking signs of independent performance

It is exceptionally difficult to deliver systematic evidence about the degree of freedom of mass media (in structure or performance), except by way of

detailed description, case study and argued evaluation. Although the scope
for applying communication science research is limited, this brief discussion
of structural conditions of freedom and the models sketched in Chapter 7 do
indicate a number of ways forward. In general, the bridge from structural
analysis to performance research has to be constructed by reference to the
consequences for content, which are, implicitly or explicitly, supposed to
follow. We have to ask, in particular, what will be the 'outward signs' of free
media.

Most attention has been paid to the supposed *negative* effects of media
monopoly. According to Entman (1985), research, as well as belief,
concerning competition and monopoly conditions:

> suggests that competition a) enhances the *quality* of newspaper, meaning . . .
> more cosmopolitan, in-depth news and editorials, b) provides more *diversity* of
> views on public issues, c) encourages more *fairness* or balance in presentation of
> political controversies, with less one-sided, propagandistic or biased news and d)
> stimulates greater *responsiveness* to the interests of citizens – providing stories and
> editorial that help encourage enlightened and rationally participant citizens.

Fletcher (1981), on behalf of the Canadian Royal Commission on
Newspapers, provides a similar statement of expectations from a free press.
After references to accuracy and diversity of outlook, he writes:

> A third criterion for assessing the press relates to the role of the newspapers as the
> 'Fourth Branch of Government' in D. Cater's (1964) phrase . . . For him the
> newspaper's role in public affairs is that of critic and investigator. Newspapers
> much maintain some distance from institutions on which they report and must
> serve to stimulate public debate and to organize public conflict in respect of the
> major issues of the day. (Fletcher, 1981: 7; see also Hachten, 1963; Rivers and
> Nyham, 1973)

It seems that the *effects* of independence are to be looked for in a wide
range of qualities and not simply in the fact of being free from obvious
constraint. Even the limited degree of independence which is enjoyed by
broadcasting is expected (by its audience at least) to lead to fairness, diversity
and resistance to pressures from government, advertisers, sponsors and
outside advocacy groups. Publicly regulated broadcasting, in free societies,
is still expected to give proper attention to conflict and controversy in society
even though it is supposed to avoid taking sides. Emerson (1963) notes that
'a system of free expression is designed to encourage a necessary degree of
conflict within society.'

The discussion suggests several lines of enquiry which can be turned into a
series of questions about influences from owners and controllers on editorial
decisions and content (whether factual or fictional). There is a second set of
questions about influences which derive from pressures in the operating
environment of media, especially from advertisers, news sources and
organized pressure groups or public relations. These matters are taken up in
Chapter 10.

In addition, we can ask how far the media actually deal with controversial matters, engage in criticism and risk antagonizing either powerful interests or their own audience. As an extension of this, we may ask how far the media play an active, participant, campaigning or investigative role in their society or community. In the end, it is only answers to such questions which can really tell us about the degree to which the freedoms granted to media are actually exercised.

Does monopoly affect content?

Questions of freedom *from* pressures and constraints, on the one hand, and the positive use of freedom (freedom *for* some chosen goal), on the other, have both attracted attention. Rather more attention has been paid to the first than the second question, partly because it is easier to investigate the implied process of cause and effect, where the main variables can be identified in a fairly precise way. There has also been more demand for knowledge which might help to safeguard the exercise of media freedom than for information about how this freedom might actually be used.

There are several variants of research design for comparing the performance outcome of media situations according to the degree of competition or monopoly. One is to compare the same paper before and after the loss of a local competitor (e.g. Bigman, 1955; Willoughby, 1955; McCombs, 1987a, b); another is to compare papers before and after they were acquired by chains (Grotta, 1971; Thrift, 1977; Romanow and Soderlund, 1979; Trim et al., 1983; Browning et al., 1984; Demers and Wackman, 1988; Hale, 1988); another is to compare chain and independent papers on one or more performance indicator (e.g. Hicks and Featherston, 1978; Dizier, 1986; Litman and Bridges, 1986); a fourth is to compare the content of papers under a local monopoly and those which have competition (Borstel, 1956; Nixon and Jones, 1956; Rarick and Hartman, 1966; Baldridge, 1967; Stempel, 1973; Baer et al., 1974; Schweitzer and Goldman, 1975; Weaver and Mullins, 1975; Donohue et al., 1985; Lacy, 1987).

Most research examples relate to the newspaper press under naturally occurring situations of increased monopoly ownership or control. The main aims have been to measure the consequences for performance of increased concentration, according to the following main hypotheses:

1   Acquisition of a newspaper by a national chain or group diminishes its service of *locally* relevant news and opinion.
2   Loss of a competing newspaper reduces the *diversity* of information and opinion available to readers in the area concerned.
3   Transfer from independent to group status (or a move to monopoly status) diminishes the independence and *editorial vigour* of a newspaper.

The first hypothesis is relevant to the question of independence because of the implication that content is dictated by remote, group policy rather than what is judged relevant by the local editor. It is possible to interpret the degree of diversity shown in content (second hypothesis) both as an outcome of independent editorializing and as an indicator of freedom, especially if the diversity in question is found amongst the titles/channels owned by the same chain or group. Its opposite – homogeneity – can be equated with conformity (Bigman, 1948), whether or not caused by monopoly or chain ownership. The third hypothesis directly equates 'vigour' and activity with the exercise of editorial freedom.

Of more concern here than the results of specific investigations are the indicators which have been deployed for assessing the effect of monopoly, especially those which relate to independence, as a quality of performance. The main indicators are the provision of: more local news; firm and even partisan opinions on issues of local relevance; more 'hard' news, especially dealing with local public affairs; more editorial 'vigour', argumentation and conflict; more international news; greater diversity of type of content and of opinion expressed. In addition, positive signs are taken to include having a high ratio of editorial/news content to advertising (equals proportional 'news-hole'), having multiple news agency subscriptions and showing a degree of financial commitment to editorial quality (Litman and Bridges, 1986).

Despite the amount and ingenuity of research, it is hard to avoid the conclusion that it has failed to establish clear general effects from monopoly conditions on the balance of costs and benefits, in performance terms. Where there *is* evidence, the effects seem to be quite small. Litman and Bridges (1986), for example, examined 100 newspapers in varying kinds of ownership to test the relative merits or demerits of monopoly in terms of performance variables, but especially, the size of news-hole and the number of news agency subscriptions. They found little conclusive evidence of effect from ownership condition, whether positive or negative. According to Picard (1989), this probably reflects a reality in which general industrial conditions on the one hand and a shared journalistic professionalism, on the other, largely conceal or suppress potential effects from ownership conditions.

Some positive effects of chain ownership or increased monopoly on the quality of performance are also possible. Improved economic position going with monopoly *can* lead to better staffing levels and widen the scope for good reporting (Busterna, 1988a). It can also strengthen the position of an editor *vis-à-vis* local economic or political pressures. Similarly, the resources of many kinds available in a large chain can improve the quality of support services. The more such benefits accrue, the more they can compensate for negative effects and the fewer differences will show up when the indicators mentioned above are deployed.

There has been relatively little attention up till now to the effects of monopoly or competition in broadcast media, even in the United States (but see Gormley, 1977, 1980; Prisuta, 1977). The conditions for this kind of research are emerging in Europe, as a result of the multiplication of channels and the entry of commercial firms into television provision. There are strong indications that competition is leading to less rather than more content diversity, as both public and private channels compete for the same peak-time audiences (see De Bens et al., 1992). In more monopolistic days, a degree of inter-channel diversity was enforced for reasons of public policy, if need be in defiance of audience market tendencies.

Proprietorial versus editorial freedom

At the heart of the matter for a newspaper press which operates on free market principles is the question of the degree to which private *commercial* ownership uses the power which goes with ownership to direct or influence editorial decisions. The question does not arise in the same way in the case of political party ownership (where influence is expected) or where government has legitimate control over media (as in most European broadcasting systems) and sets legal limits to freedom. While freedom of expression is not generally a zero sum good, in certain kinds of publication decision, where there can only be one outcome (i.e omission or inclusion, positive or negative opinion), one person's freedom is another's constraint. If the owner/publisher uses his/her ultimate power to choose a certain line of opinion or content policy, then editors are also denied some of their scope for taking decisions.

Despite the widespread (press institutional) norm that proprietors ought to refrain from using their power to interfere with editorial decisions (ultimately this would destroy credibility and, some would argue, business effectiveness), most theorists, especially those critical of monopoly media, hold that proprietorial influence is ever-present, even inevitable (Altschull, 1984; Shoemaker and Mayfield, 1987) as a latent force. Most close observers of the media can also cite and document instances of this power being used from time to time on particular matters (Hetherington, 1985; Curran and Seaton, 1988). In the lore and history of journalism, for instance, there are stories of newspapers keeping 'blacklists' of persons who are *non grata* in the eyes of proprietors and not to be mentioned.

There are many obstacles in the way of empirically testing expectations about the influence of ownership on what media actually *do*, however well founded in everyday experience they happen to be. In part this stems from the multiplicity and varying time-scales of (interacting) influences on content decisions and the difficulty of isolating any one influence (Shoemaker and Mayfield, 1987). The relevant theory also tells us that the exercise of corporate power does not have to translate itself directly into newsroom decisions for it to have an overall effect on the character of the newspaper owned (Dreier, 1982). At the newsroom level, investigation is hampered by the specificity and multiplicity of immediate influences (Hetherington, 1985), by the difficulties of gaining access and by the limits to what can be inferred from content analysis, especially where many effects may involve omission rather than inclusion.

Evidence from editors

The situation is also clouded by the fact that editors often willingly follow the lines preferred by their proprietors and that such intervention, while generally frowned on, is not entirely illegitimate, nor always covert. In a famous instance, Lord Beaverbrook told the 1947 Royal Commission on the Press that he ran newspapers in order to 'make propaganda' (RCP, 1949). This has often been assumed of many other proprietors who have been less open in admitting it. The direct approach to investigation, by asking editors about their experience, does not take us very far, although it does confirm the existence of a strong *norm* opposing direct proprietorial intervention. Bowers (1967), for instance, investigated this issue by surveying 600 managing editors of US dailies. These reported fairly modest degrees of publisher direction of content, with more direction likely in small papers and in relation to local content or content touching revenue or the personal affairs of proprietors.

Evidence from a survey by Meyer (1987) also shows editors to claim a fair degree of actual autonomy *vis-à-vis* publishers. Thus, 61 per cent of editors recorded that publishers 'never' order editors to undertake a major investigation on a specific subject. More indirect publisher influence was, however, acknowledged by way of a different question concerning the frequency with which a publisher 'demonstrated by selective use of praise and criticism what he wanted the editor to do'. Of editors, only 22 per cent replied 'never' on this point and the modal occurrence of this kind of influence seems to be a few times a year. In Britain, the replies of editors to a questionnaire of the Royal Commission on the Press firmly rejected the idea that owners interfered (RCP, 1977).

The case of electoral politics

Evidence about the degree of systematic and covert proprietorial influence on newsroom decisions has always been elusive, but there are some issues and cases which have yielded to investigation. The requirements for research usually comprise: a high-profile and high-volume news event or issue on which the preferences and interests of a proprietor are known and where there are opportunities for making relevant cross-media comparisons. These requirements are not often met, although the case of political endorsements, especially in two-party systems, does seem to qualify. In the United States, where large media groups own numerous different titles and where ownership generally goes with Republican leanings, group-wide endorsement practices have been investigated.

Wackman et al. (1975), for example, looked at American presidential endorsements by most American newspapers for the presidential elections of 1960, 1964, 1968 and 1972, comparing chain with non-chain papers. They showed that 'the vast majority of chains exhibited homogeneous endorsement patterns in the four elections years studied'. In 1972, chain homogeneity of endorsement stood at 91 per cent, significantly higher than for non-chain papers. In three of the four election years, the chains preferred Republicans, the exception being 1964, when Johnson opposed the somewhat maverick Goldwater. They concluded that chain papers do generally favour the preferred candidate of the publishers and that 'chain ownership of newspapers discourages editorial independence in endorsing presidential candidates'. Gaziano (1989) followed up this study for the 1971–88 period and found a continued, although diminished, tendency towards homogeneity on the part of chain newspapers in their presidential endorsements (see also McCombs, 1967; Robinson 1974; Pilegge, 1981, for evidence of systematic candidate and party endorsement).

The situation in other countries is less clear cut, partly because the phenomenon of chain ownership of significant newspaper titles and of one-newspaper cities is less pronounced, partly because different traditions of press–party alignment have legitimized certain patterns of political endorsement. In Canada, where conditions and expectations about political independence are much the same as in the USA, a small-scale study of one seven-paper chain and one election found no consistency in election coverage or endorsement among papers owned by the same chain (Wagenberg and Soderlund, 1975). Fletcher's enquiries for the Canadian Royal Commission found apparent variation among chains in their tendency to endorse but, crucially, there was also 'a lack of uniformity in any of the major chains' (Fletcher, 1981: 85).

There are few other countries where chain ownership of the press has developed on such a scale (although it is not uncommon to find large publishing groups dominating national newspaper circulation in several European countries (Murdock, 1990). In Britain, where concentration of ownership has been high for a long time (Northcliffe had a higher share of national daily circulation than the 35 per cent enjoyed by Murdoch in 1990), the politics of the owner often do determine the political line of national and regional newspapers (though it is less likely at city and local level) (Seymour-Ure, 1991). The case of Beaverbrook has been noted above. The mantle has, more recently, fallen on Rupert Murdoch, whose News International owned three (out of eleven) national daily and two (out of eight) Sunday newspapers in 1990, controlling over a third of national daily circulation. The Murdoch papers consistently supported the Conservative party and government through three elections and eleven years, although editorial freedom is still proclaimed (and the claim is difficult to counter).

Other evidence of owner influence

Beyond the case of party politics and elections, systematic research evidence is more scarce. It is not difficult to find isolated examples where there is prima facie evidence of undue proprietorial influence. One relates to the competitive launch, by Murdoch's News International, in 1989 of a new direct broadcasting television service (Sky Television), directed at the British market. This received extensive publicity before and after the launch in all

British media. However, the Murdoch-owned press gave differentially more and more positive attention to the Sky TV venture. Certainly, most other newspapers thought so, as did Sky's main prospective competitor (BSB) and a prominent editorial resignation at *The Times* seemed to confirm the story (Seymour-Ure, 1991). The existence of undue proprietorial pressure was contested by News International itself, which claimed that editorial policy was shaped only by considerations of their readers' interests. They also pointed out that they were not doing anything covertly. Curran (1991) documents the case of pressure on *The Observer* newspaper by its owners, Lonhro, to avoid reporting which might damage some of their interests in Africa.

Another example is provided by the coverage in the US press of the UNESCO proposals for a New World Information Order, universally hated by press proprietors. Giffard's (1989) study of US press content showed not only consistently negative treatment, but also presumptive evidence in patterns of content of systematic proprietorial influence on what was published (see below). From time to time it is possible to investigate the hand (or voice) of the media proprietor in some particular tendency of content, but there is rarely a criterion for distinguishing the policy of editors from that of owners, except perhaps where a business interest of an owner is very apparent.

The typical inconclusiveness of the evidence concerning the effects of concentration is not just the result of a balancing of positive and negative effects from concentration or of the commitment of media conglomerates to the values of editorial freedom. Absence of competition in a given newspaper market exerts a pressure on newspapers to respond to the varied needs of local business, politics and readers without undue interference from 'head office'. Editorial autonomy is also a matter of managerial autonomy allocated to those who know their 'markets', and the various benefits of autonomy (especially credibility and diversity of appeal) are often also marketable commodities. In addition, the quality of performance is likely to be more directly influenced by the practices, traditions and organizational requirements of journalism than by ownership structure. The indicators of performance noted above are often less likely to register group 'policy' than to reflect the normal routines of the profession and requirements of the industry (McCombs, 1988; Picard, 1989).

The media as watch-dog and critic of government

Possibly the most important requirement of performance in respect of freedom is that media should deliver on the promise to stand up for the interests of citizens, in the face of the inevitable pressures, especially those which come from government (Martin, 1981) or from big business. The view of mass media as a watch-dog against the abuse of power and against corruption in a public life has long been a staple ingredient of journalistic self-image, press mythology and of Western democratic political theory.

Criticism of office-holders has indeed always been a major topic of newspapers in both commercial and party-political press systems. Views of press functions from the point of view of society, or of journalists, or the general public, have consistently given a prominent place to this task (e.g Cohen, 1963; Hachten, 1963; Fjaestad and Holmlov, 1976; Curran, 1991). It has often been described as an 'adversarial' role (Cater, 1964; Rivers and Nyhan, 1973) or as an 'antithetical' role, especially in respect of government, big business or other authority. If we are to assess the independence of the media, we should look for evidence that this role is being carried out.

Applied research into the critical role of the media

There are scattered examples in the research literature of how assessment on this matter might be conducted. The type of reporting involved has been variously labelled as 'advocacy', 'participative', 'active', 'investigative' and 'critical'. All these imply that the news media should go further than just observe and report (although these too imply the exercise of freedom) (Culbertson, 1979, 1983). Even the FCC Broadcast Fairness doctrine includes 'controversiality' as being in the public interest. It is worth noting, at least, that the attachment to controversiality is not universal. Edelstein and Larsen (1960) found in their local media research that the general public (as opposed to a vocal elite) have a preference for consensus in their community media.

The main evidence in content (performance) of these inter-related concepts has been sought in one or other of the following:

- clear expression of editorial opinions on 'difficult' issues, especially where the opinions offered are unpopular or deviate from the consensus;
- paying attention to subjects of a conflictual, 'negative' and uncomfortable kind, which are not likely to be immediately rewarding in audience terms;
- adoption of a challenging and enquiring stance against claims made by business, government or other power-holders;
- carrying out investigative campaigns on difficult issues;
- conducting advocacy campaigns on behalf of some cause or group;
- being active, enquiring and enterprising in the approach to news;
- reporting news which records strong disagreement between the protagonists;
- reporting of criticism, praise, evaluation of policies or persons, rather than simply giving the 'facts'.

There is an implied continuum of critical activity, ranging from partisan advocacy on difficult issues to a more routine option of alert and inquisitive reporting. Beyond that, of course, the continuum might be extended to reach the completely supine or the active collaboration in the propaganda goals of the powerful. Since the extreme positions of radical opposition and sycophantic assimilation are usually self-proclaimed or self-evident, it is the middle ground of normal reporting and comment which needs most attention from research. It is, for example, the terrain likely to be most relevant in evaluating the performance of public service broadcasting, which is generally denied a partisan or advocacy role but which does have a limited watchdog role carried out under close scrutiny (possibly threatening to journalistic freedom, see above). The main challenge to research is to be able to discriminate, within the normal 'objective' mode of reporting, between the more and the less active uses of whatever editorial freedom is available.

It may be that only the most detailed, well-documented, historical case studies of situations of conflict can be adequate to the task (e.g Curtis, 1984, on the British media and Northern Ireland), but some more routine, objective approaches can also be helpful, at least for purposes of *comparative* assessment over time or across media.

The active editorial role

Fletcher (1981), drawing on Bogart's (1979) survey of 'editorial ideals', defined a quality of editorial 'vitality' in terms of five main content variables: a high ratio of staff-originated to wire copy; a large news-hole; a high ratio of news interpretation and background to spot news; an adequate number of letters to the editor; diversity of political columnists. A similar concept of editorial 'vigour' employed by Thrift (1977), in investigating the effect of chain ownership, included four main variables of the content of selected newspapers. These were: localness of topic; argumentativeness of form of news report; controversiality of topic of news; the extent to which editorials provided 'mobilizing information'.

This last measure was originally developed and applied by Lemert (Lemert et al., 1977; Lemert and Cook, 1982; Lemert and Ashman, 1983; Lemert, 1989) and it proved both reliable and discriminating. Lemert has defined mobilizing information as 'any information which allows people to act on the attitudes they already have'. In effect, this refers to giving practical information about names, times, dates and places which enable them to do something about an issue. It is distinct from advice or opinion intended to shape attitudes.

Clarke and Evans (1980) used their interview and observation study of political reporting to develop another index of 'journalistic activity'. This differentiated between reporters and styles of reporting, rather than content, and was derived from measures of:

-   frequency of interviewing candidates;
-   talking with campaign managers;
-   contacting supporters' groups;
-   using libraries and other sources.

Other researchers have commented on the extraordinary degree to which political reporting uses none of these, relying only on routine sources or other media.

Research into the amount and kind of media editorializing (in the sense of opinion-giving) presents relatively few methodological problems, since the 'editorial comment' format and its conventions are well understood and the intended direction of comment can be measured (see Chapter 17). Logically, an active press editorial performance is most likely to show itself in clear endorsements, adoption of positions or expression of opinion on current issues. Entman (1989), investigating news quality, introduced a measure of 'responsiveness' in editorials. This referred to 'liberal' stand-points (e.g. support for the 'have-nots') and any praise or criticism levelled at politicians. However, this is only a necessary, not a sufficient, condition for active, participant journalism. Active editorializing, on its own, might as easily consist of propaganda for outside vested interests as fearless advocacy of controversial causes. It is hard to say what more would be required to identify forms of advocacy which tell of a fearless, independent, press. However, additional 'outward signs of inward grace' can be sought in editorial willingness to deal with divisive issues and readiness to take unpopular stands.

Conflict reporting as an indicator of freedom

There are several possible indicators of *degree of conflict* (as a measure of independent reporting) to be found in the research literature (Cony, 1953). Donohue et al. (1985) looked at *local conflict* reporting as a key variable of a press active in opinion-forming and defined it as 'space devoted to reporting about manifestly different positions or statements about a public issue from at least two persons or interest groups in the community'. In practice, this is less a measure of controvery of subject matter than of a *form* of treatment which might provoke debate. The wider context of their research did allow them to assess the issues in question according to their degree of implied conflict or consensus. Entman (1989: 158) defined conflict in terms of 'the presence of disagreement among the actors quoted in a story'. The more clashes the stories reported, the higher the score.

Research into the treatment of deviant or outsider minorities in society has also helped to identify reporting or comment which adopts an independent line towards unpopular groups in society. In general, independence is though to be demonstrated where there is positive or sympathetic attention to such groups (e.g. Fedler, 1973; Golding and Middleton, 1982; Shoemaker, 1984). In doing this, the media are considered to be rejecting (however temporarily) the social control task which is so often allotted to them (Ericson et al., 1987). It is possible, of course, that such content is no more than conformity to a liberal orthodoxy. Extra-media data may be needed to contextualize the evidence of content.

Investigative reporting

The cases of *investigative reporting* and advocative campaigning (which has attracted little research attention) help to illustrate this point. Both activities sound as if they should count towards 'high' performance scores in respect of active use of freedom. Journalistic exposés, according to Chibnall, 'give reporters the sense that they are autonomous actors in touch with the finest traditions of their craft – crusaders in the cause of truth, protectors of the peoples' freedom' (1977: 61). Ericson and co-workers' (1987) account of Canadian news media shows that little reporting really qualifies as 'investigative', partly for lack of resources, partly for lack of access to other organizations, and partly through self-imposed limitations relating to objectivity.

Paletz and Entman (1981) point out that journalistic investigation usually helps to support, rather than challenge, the status quo, largely neglecting the whole area of private business as a terrain for investigation, for conventional as well as practical reasons, but with little justification in public interest terms. For these reasons, the surface appearance of investigative reporting activity cannot be taken at face value. Glasser and Ettema (1991) are more inclined to recognize the dual tendency of investigative reporting – both towards conservation and change of the moral order. The actual 'quality' of performance depends largely on the *target* of the investigation or of the critical campaign and perhaps also on the instigation behind it. Investigations can often pursue 'soft' targets, which are already unpopular and of dubious relevance to serious issues. They can also serve some outside vested interests. Investigation can also be sensationalism (see Chapter 17) in another guise.

Similarly, campaigning may be no different from conformism when it promotes some entirely consensual goals (e.g. child welfare) or from social control when it opposes some widely agreed evil (e.g. drug-taking or drunk-driving). Genuine, active, independent, advocacy journalism would need to involve pursuit of powerful, or even just popular, figures, or support for the powerless and the unpopular. Investigative reporting will normally call for the pursuit of reluctant sources and concealed information. As well as being difficult, it may be expensive and thankless (see above and Chapters 10 and 14). A sign of genuine and successful investigative effort may well be an angry response from the parties investigated. It would be possible, although not easy, to develop research tools for identifying relevant targets and causes, taking account of these variables, although not without a good deal of local and contextual knowledge (see, e.g., Murphy, 1976).

Structure and performance only weakly linked

It is fairly clear from this account of attempts to pin down the effects of media concentration in performance that it is very difficult to demonstrate any conclusive link between the two, beyond what is apparent from the facts of a given case. In part this is due to the very different kinds of evidence involved, often at different levels of analysis. In part it is because the process which links structure to performance is complex and influenced by more variables than can be taken adequately into account.

10
MEDIA FREEDOM: THE ORGANIZATIONAL ENVIRONMENT

Conduct and performance: perceptions of autonomy

This chapter is concerned with potential limits to freedom which derive from the normal working environment of the media (matters of 'conduct') rather than from conditions of ownership and structure, although the two sources of pressure and constraint are not easy to keep apart. It is also difficult to separate out the 'internal' from the 'external' pressures, as these are experienced on a day-to-day basis. Most of the indicators of independent performance discussed so far have referred to the extent to which editorial decision-makers are able to exercise their own choice and judgement. The degree of autonomy obviously varies from case to case and it is largely closed to outside observation as well as difficult to quantify. However, there are numerous case studies, reports of participant observation and some survey evidence from the 'communicators' themselves. There is enough evidence at least to support McCombs' (1988) conclusion, that variable conditions of any given organizational structure are less important than more universal tendencies which apply to a branch or sector of media activity.

One comprehensive survey of theory and evidence concerning influences on news content leans heavily to the view that economic and political pressures leave little scope for individual freedom of action within the 'system' of news production (Johnstone, 1976; Shoemaker and Mayfield, 1987). The less numerous studies of entertainment media tend to a similar conclusion about limitations on autonomy which are imposed by commercial and audience-seeking pressures (e.g. Westen, 1978), although Ettema and Whitney (1982) found some real scope for creativity under conditions of competition and constraint. According to their account, a common response to economic and audience market constraints is creative problem-solving and product innovation. Elliott (1977a), while generally pessimistic about the internal autonomy of mass communicators, also identified several, limited, sources of creative 'space'.

Journalists were asked (by Weaver and Wilhoit, 1986) about the degree of freedom that they enjoyed on two main matters: the selection of news stories on which to work; and decisions about which aspects of the stories to emphasize. They also asked about the extent of editing which their copy received. The results showed a rather high degree of perceived autonomy on story choice and emphasis (60 per cent or more, on average, feeling 'free'), very close to levels observed ten years previously, the results varying somewhat from medium to medium. These outcomes can partly be explained in terms of self-recruitment to chosen media (Sigelman, 1973) or by in-house socialization (Breed, 1955). Whatever the explanation, the matter does at least seem open to investigation by methods which discriminate between type of journalist and type of medium (for instance, news agency journalists were reported by Weaver and Wilhoit to have much lower expectations about freedom).

In a survey dealing with press ethics, Meyer (1987) compared the responses of publishers, editors and staff members to a series of questions concerning editorial autonomy, offering hypothetical situations for comment. In general, staff consistently chose the most 'independent' line of behaviour offered on any given option, possibly more indicative of the prevailing norm than of actual behaviour. However, staff also believed that publishers actually exert more influence on choice and treatment of stories than do either newspaper editors or readers. For instance, in reply to the question 'How often does the publisher of your paper ask for special handling of an article about a company or organization which has some economic clout over your newspaper?', 58 per cent of publishers, 54 per cent of editors and only 32 per cent of staff replied 'never' (Meyer, 1987: 219). Participant observation research by Gans (1979) reached similar conclusions. His journalist respondents perceived themselves as having a reasonable degree of autonomy, but at each level they were conscious of pressure from within the organizational hierarchy.

US data concerning perceived autonomy cannot be assumed to apply elsewhere, although there is some similar evidence from other places. For instance, the British 1977 Royal Commission on the Press inquired into the attitudes of editors and senior journalists on some of these matters. When asked what they liked or disliked about working in journalism, the two most frequently mentioned matters were 'variety and interest' (by 46 per cent of journalists) and 'creativity and scope for initiative' (39 per cent). Only 8 per cent mentioned 'distortion of stories' as a disliked feature. When asked about undesirable pressures on their work, none out of 103 editors of national or provincial papers mentioned 'proprietors and owners' and none mentioned advertisers. In Britain at least, actual experience seemed then (1975) to match the theory of press freedom, although circumstances may have changed since and there have been several documented instances of proprietorial autocracy (e.g. Evans, 1983; Curran and Seaton, 1988; Seymour-Ure, 1991).

Relations with routine news sources

Over-reliance on limited news sources has often been cited as a potential cause of constraint on the independence of journalism. Non-news media may also be dependent on other kinds of source: for example, on organizers of major sports events, suppliers of feature films for television showing, diverse holders of performance rights, etc. Obviously, some degree of such 'dependence' is a natural and inescapable feature of organizations which mainly *mediate* (rather than originate) a supply from source (often other media, including news agencies) to eventual receiver.

Even so, the special role of the media as channels of public information presupposes a need for independence in the relations between journalists and sources. Reliance on a restricted range of sources can itself result in bias (Shoemaker, 1983). Early research into the relations between reporters and their frequent, routine sources (e.g. politics, law enforcement agencies) suggested that collaborative links tended to develop, with sources more or less coming to 'assimilate' reporters (Gieber and Johnson, 1961). Elsewhere, the source–media relation has been referred to as 'symbiotic' (Sigal, 1973; Miller, 1978). Essentially, what was thought to occur was an undue degree of cooperation, with sources being allowed to place their version of events in (often tacit) return for the ready supply of useful news copy (Tunstall, 1970; Chibnall, 1977; Ericson et al., 1987).

Participant observation studies (e.g. Miller, 1977; Gans, 1979; Ericson et al., 1987) have indicated that gaining access to media channels is related to the source's own efficiency in organizing the supply of suitable material, as well as to the power and status of the source (the greater the power, the better chance of access on own terms). Weaver and Wilhoit's (1980) long-term study of the content of reporting of US senators suggested, for instance, that effective staff work and offering what the media wanted were more likely to achieve access than actual political power. Clarke and Evans (1980) pursued a similar line of enquiry. Ericson et al. (1987: 364), in their study of Canadian news media, stressed the extent to which powerful sources can 'mobilize strategically to variously avoid and make news . . . a limited range of sources can pry it [the news media institution] open and sometimes harness its power to advantage . . .'. The question of relations with powerful sources in society is taken up below.

Public relations as source

The public relations industry would agree that news media are open to penetration and manipulation by efficient sources (see Paletz and Entman, 1981: 134–146) and would find some support from research which has systematically sought to trace the success of press releases or PR handouts in influencing content as published. Several American studies (Chittick, 1970; Hale, 1978; Martin and Singletary, 1981; Lacy and Matusik, 1984; Turk, 1986a, b) and a German enquiry (Baerns, 1987) all reported a rather high degree of use of material derived from (in these cases, public institutional) handouts to the press (see also Sigal, 1973; Grunig, 1976; Sachsman, 1976; Atwater and Fico, 1986). Baerns' research model was based on earlier gatekeeping and diffusion research, in which a body of content is traced through successive stages of selection and reduction or where the results of 'success', in gaining access, at successive stages of selection, are compared (e.g. Cutlip, 1954; Robinson and Sheehan, 1986; Shoemaker, 1991).

Baerns focused on the coverage, by several media, of political affairs of one German *Land*, thus a topic area open to direct reporting as well as served by official handouts, press releases, etc. For each medium, the research assessed the origin of each relevant news item published, according to whether the source was a press release or news conference (both PR sources) or 'journalistic' in origin (e.g. reporting public or closed events, investigative activity). Approximately two out of three items were found to be from the PR sources, with little variation between the media of press, TV or radio. The main explanation offered was in terms of the superior efficiency of the PR (saving media costs) as well as the funnelling of information through news agencies. The situation investigated is probably fairly typical and must often arise. However, research of this kind is very laborious and can only give an occasional indication of a process at work.

While there is no objective way of deciding on the level at which PR usage becomes inconsistent with the norm of independence, these findings raise doubts about what independent performance really means to journalists. The latter, who generally perceive themselves to have reasonable freedom to select and treat stories may be thinking more of their personal autonomy (e.g. freedom to cover a story as they like) rather than their real independence from power-holders in the society.

Media self-origination of content

Statements of quality criteria for news performance (e.g. Ghiglione, 1973; Becker et al., 1978; Fletcher, 1981; Meyer, 1987) often place much weight on the degree to which a news medium produces its *own content with its own resources* and this has been used as an approximate indicator of performance of news channels, following the same logic as the German research just described. The approach has the advantage of simplicity, although it is not always possible to allocate content to source by inspection alone. Even items attributed to an 'own correspondent' may be heavily dependent on agencies and sources. There are also significantly different types of external source used or quoted, for instance between 'routine' sources and those which require more activity on the part of the journalist (Clarke and Evans, 1980; Berkowitz, 1987). In his study of relations between reporters and government officials, Sigal (1973) distinguished between 'routine' and 'enterprise' channels for finding material, the former proving to outnumber the latter by more than two to one (which seems to be a recurring ratio in these matters).

'Routine' sources mainly refer to press release and conference material, 'enterprise' ones to interviews and investigative content. Material from 'enterprise' sources is likely to be different, if not unique, increasing the diversity on offer to audiences as well as demonstrating independence. A similar distinction has been used as a criterion in several other studies, namely that between news agency and non-agency material. In general, the second is more expensive as well as having the potential of adding diversity to the total news offer. However, such content is not necessarily 'better' information than agency material, by the standards named above or by the criteria of 'information quality' discussed in Chapter 16.

A related form of content analysis has been used to assess the degree of *independence* of papers owned by the same chain or group. The more *overlap* in the actual content used by different titles under common ownership, the less editorially independent they really are (Donohue and Glasser, 1978). Comparisons can also be made, along similar lines, between different papers covering the same events on the same day to produce a measure of diversity, which is also an indirect measure of independence (Glasgow Media Group, 1976; McQuail, 1977). The more a channel offers its own distinctive version of events, the more likely that it is pursuing some independent line of reporting, and vice versa. Again, this says nothing in itself about whether it is, in any sense, a *better* version of events.

The criterion of 'self-origination' as a measure of quality has been widely used in respect of content other than news (see Chapter 21), and some television regulations require a certain proportion of output to be self-produced. Aside from the merits of independence which are thought to go with self-production, such content is often more expensive to produce and its presence signals a financial commitment to quality goals.

Powerful sources

An important aspect of independence concerns the relationship between media and powerful outside interests. While it is relevant for media to report news about and from the powerful, a heavy or undue reliance on powerful sources, or just excessive attention to them, can entail a reduction of freedom. Normal reporting procedures place a great emphasis on certification of 'facts' by authorities and involve a 'bias' to institutional power (Tuchman, 1978; Fishman, 1980). Innumerable studies of content which involve classification of sources, attributions, etc., have reached the conclusion that news is very much a 'top-down' flow in society, with media telling the general public largely what 'responsible' officials or spokespersons, or leaders in institutions decide to say.

A fairly typical example is offered by Brown and co-workers' (1987) study of the sources behind 846 stories in six newspapers (cf. Sigal, 1973; Culbertson, 1983). Despite the apparently large number of sources, 55 per cent derived from national or foreign governments and a further 24 per cent from 'affiliated' citizens, in effect, pressure groups or public relations sources. It appeared to the researchers that newspapers, through their subordination to elite (and male) sources, were failing to live up to the 'expectations of the media in a pluralistic democracy'. Similar conclusions emerged from a study by Whitney et al. (1989) of US network news content during the 1980s. Of 5483 sources for 5190 news stories, 72 per cent were of an official character and 86 per cent were male.

The assessment of independence in relation to sources can be further refined by including the variables of *conflict* and *criticism*, or that of evaluative tendency of content (see Chapter 17). The situations which present themselves for analysis are complex and require careful 'unpacking'. Powerful sources are often self-interested parties in matters of dispute (Donohue et al., 1985). However, material *derived* from them *can* be used in a critical as well as a supportive way. We are reminded of the difficulty of 'reading off' answers about the independence of media from such research, without reference to other contextual data concerning media structure and the actual circumstances of news events. As Sigal (1986) reminds us, access gained by virtue of authority is no guarantee of a 'good press', from the source point of view. It is also true that content which the media produce themselves can be sycophantic to power-holders as well as critical of them.

There are possibilities of making comparisons in respect of reliance on powerful sources between media channels, types of subject matter, across time and between countries. Variations in performance can be indexed according to the relative share of content which draws on non-elite, powerless, grass-roots or deviant sources and content. Self-origination of content (as noted above) can also provide an indicator of performance. Research into international news coverage has often found a high degree of reliance by national media on their own governments as sources (e.g. Batscha, 1975; McQuail, 1977; Adams, 1982; Larson, 1984). Often it seems that mass media are effectively assimilated into the goals of national foreign policy (e.g. Becker, 1977; Morris, 1980; Paletz and Entman, 1981; Vilanilam, 1989). Herman and Chomsky (1988) explain this in terms of a 'propaganda model' of media–state relations. An alternative view is that such limitations on editorial independence stem from ethnocentricity or just response to public opinion.

War and patriotism

Limitations from powerful source control combine with pressures from public opinion in cases of (limited) war to set powerful constraints on media freedom and to apply the 'test of reality' to the media claim to autonomy. International conflicts in an age of increasingly copious international television news coverage have focused attention on this issue, most recently in the case of the Gulf War, following the Iraqi annexation of Kuwait. Somewhat similar cases have been provided by the Falklands War in 1982 and the US invasion of Panama in 1984.

In the case of the Gulf War in 1991, the relevant conditions for assessing the independence of the media, particularly in the main combatant countries of Britain and the USA, were: a *de facto* Anglo-American dominance of international television news reporting resources; a near-monopoly control of the supply of news of the war by US military and government sources, involving strict censorship; and a high degree of popular support for the war by publics at home. The media had very little opportunity to collect or report news freely and were serving domestic audiences which might not be very receptive to critical or 'unpatriotic' reporting. In such circumstances, even objectivity is hard to maintain.

While the evidence is still very incomplete, early assessments seem to agree that the US and British media reported the war in a highly supportive and 'patriotic' way, largely as the authorities would have wanted it and that control of information was almost total. In practice, this meant that there was little hard news of any significance and little diversity on essentials of information or of opinion, especially after the armed conflict began in January 1991. Thoughtful commentary has widely cited the expression 'the first casualty of war is truth' and the media have not emerged, in the eyes of many journalists and commentators, from the episode with much glory (Dennis et al., 1991). Most of the American and British media (with 'allied' media following in varying degrees) seem to have collaborated enthusiastically in the war propaganda effort, with little attempt to offer detached or alternative versions of facts or evaluations of what was going on.

If this is the outcome of a 'test of reality' of media independence, it suggests rather mixed conclusions about performance. First, it has to be recalled that there was an unusual degree of unanimity (in Western eyes) about the justice of the cause and legitimacy of war aims. Military action seemed even to be a rather popular option. Secondly, the event demonstrates the power and efficiency of military and government when they choose to control information. Thirdly, this seems to be a clear case where the media *freely* chose to collaborate with their controllers. Much the same conditions applied in Britain at the time of the Falklands War, although public service television, in particular, helped then to maintain a degree of detachment (Morrison and Tumber, 1988) and was positively rated by its audience for its performance (Harris, 1983).

All this is a salutary reminder of the degree to which established mass media are incorporated into their nation states and likely to be carried along uncritically in popular international enterprises, where national 'honour' and 'interest' is thought to be involved. The critical, watch-dog role is easily subordinated to other interests and aims. The reasons are not so hard to find. One telling fact to emerge from survey evidence in the United States is that most Americans knew and approved of military censorship of news (Dennis et al., 1991). The statement that 'the military should be given more control over how news was reported' was endorsed by 57 per cent of the public. There was also overwhelming approval of the way the press covered the war. In the absence of strong voices from their own societies urging caution, national media seem to have voluntarily followed the line of least resistance and possible profit.

Other options for assessment

There are few routes to systematic assessment of source dependence other than those mentioned, leaving aside the rare possibility of detailed ethnographic study of the kind conducted by Gans (1979) or Ericson et al. (1987). While this kind of participant research helps in understanding how the system of source–reporter interdependence works, it is not easy to carry out on a broad front over a period of time. Survey research amongst journalists can probably do little more than demonstrate the general distribution of the *norms* of independence from sources (Meyer, 1987).

It is almost impossible for the media audience to have any clear perception of the degree of independence from sources. Schlesinger (1990) recommends the adoption of a 'source perspective' if we are to understand source dependence. He emphasizes that typical situations of source competition for access involve the deployment of *different* resources, especially institutional power, money and legitimacy (cultural capital). He also warns against drawing conclusions about the degree of media dependence solely on the basis of what eventually appears in the media. In the end, all the same, that is what matters.

Advertiser pressure

Much dispute surrounds the potential influence on media content of the commercial advertiser or sponsor (Jamieson and Campbell, 1983). Shoemaker and Mayfield (1987), for instance, underline the view that sources of finance (including, of course, advertisers) are generally strongly influential on all aspects of news production and that a funder's ideology is likely to have an ultimate effect on editorial decisions relevant to this ideology. The *potential* of a threat to independence is well supported by the literature. There is also plenty of evidence of a powerful norm within the media condemning such interference.

For instance, Meyer's (1987) survey evidence showed that newspaper people reported that 'pressure from advertisers' was quite frequently discussed as an ethical issue (only 21 per cent said it was never discussed and 46 per cent it was discussed several times a year or more often). The extensive regulation of advertising in European broadcasting is based in part on a widely held conviction that advertising *does* tend to have an affect on other programming and that this effect should be controlled. Several national as well as EC sets of rules forbid sponsoring, oblige clear identification of advertising and limit its chances of being associated with particular programme content.

Effects of advertising on structure and content

It is not really in doubt that advertising has a *general* influence on media content, especially by shaping the structure of markets, the relations between media and their audiences and the balance of types of content offered (e.g. Curran, 1978; Hirsch and Gordon, 1975). Tunstall (1991) argues that economic dependence varies according to the degree of competition for a dominant revenue source. He cites, as an example, US network TV, which 'engages in imitative competition because of its dependence on fierce competition for mass market national consumer advertising'. Although he also warns against extrapolating this particular pattern and effect to other national systems, he states as a general hypothesis: 'competition for a single source of revenue drives programmes towards imitative conformity.'

The logic of commercial media (that is, media operated for profit under free market conditions) works towards maximizing revenue by way of various 'marketing' strategies. One of these will involve the shaping of content and service provided in order to contribute to this goal. Where advertising revenue is being sought, the strategy may be to offer content which is 'friendly' (or even just relevant) to the goods and services likely to be advertised. Where subscriber revenue is sought, the strategy may be to orient content to the largest consumer taste, or towards a selected consumer market (in socioeconomic or demographic terms).

However, there are many different kinds of market situations and a product (content)-related marketing strategy may not always be appropriate. In some cases, the situation may even call for experiment, orginality and independence of publication policy, in order to open up a new market opportunity. Media also vary a good deal, by their own choice, in the degree to which they operate according to a commercial logic. At the heart of this variation is the degree to which an autonomous communication objective is sought. Despite the growth of monopoly capital power over media, many mass-media activities still claim to follow a 'communication logic' first of all, or seek an acceptable and viable balance between this and commercial viability. Under certain conditions, advertising revenue *can* also (as noted above) create opportunities for media to be more independent. These conditions are those where advertisers *follow* the success of media and content, rather than drive it. The balance between limitation and facilitation is extremely hard to strike or to assess from outside.

It is easier to suggest plausible negative (or positive) effects from advertising dependence than to investigate them empirically (especially any direct effects on ideology) or to draw reliable conclusions about the degree of freedom of the media in respect of advertising. The more important variable conditions relating advertising finance, on the one hand, and media freedom, on the other, seems to be as follows. Advertising tends to *limit* freedom:

- the more there is strong competition among the media for a limited pool of advertising revenue;
- the more uniform the main sources of advertising revenue are in a given market (especially where a single source of advertising dominates);

- the closer the correspondence between specific advertising content and the specific media content;
- the more dominant the share of advertising in the revenue of a single medium.

Advertising pressure and editorial autonomy

The problem remains of empirically establishing the degree to which service to commercial clients involves a surrender of independence. Gans (1979) studied elite media in the United States, which, however broadly structured to serve advertising in general (which is not really in doubt), were powerful enough to resist pressure on specific issues. His participant observation evidence suggested that potential offence to important advertisers could be an editorial consideration on certain product-sensitive issues. News outlets in general are constrained not to offend the hand that feeds them – especially large private corporations. It should be recalled as well that governments are often the single biggest source of advertising.

There is no shortage of reports of specific cases where media have experienced or given way to pressures from advertisers in respect of certain content. These range from those of very doubtful legitimacy (e.g. deference to local industrial interest, Hirsch, 1976) to those which belong to the normal working of the self-adjusting commercial system, in which media avoid unnecessary offence to potential advertisers and the latter put their commercial interests first (e.g. the case in Britain during the 1980s of supermarket chains reportedly withdrawing advertising from newspapers considered to have editorially sexist policies which offended the customers the advertisers most wanted to reach, Seymour-Ure, 1991). There is compelling evidence (e.g. Montgomery, 1989) to show that US network entertainment programming is finely adjusted to the needs of advertisers.

There is a large grey area where media define their own editorial goals with a view to generating advertising revenue at the same time as satisfying special audience needs (including the need for information from advertising, as with travel, leisure, motoring or book supplements). The greyness stems mainly from the inevitably thin line between relevant independent comment in the media and promotional advertising copy supplied by business. The case of commercial sponsorship of radio and television programmes, where responsibility for content often rests with an interested (commercial) third party, is usually regarded as involving a surrender of independence, although there are also gradations from total subordination to mutual 'status-conferral'.

The scope for external and independent assessment research on such matters is limited, aside from recording the incidence of overt forms of commercial penetration in the form of sponsoring, merchandising, advertising supplements, etc., and seeking to assess the degree to which editorial and advertising matter are really kept separate. Even where there is scope for research, surprisingly little has been done. This scarcity is, admittedly, due to the low yield which can be expected from studies of content on their own and to the difficulty of getting access to decision-making. If advertising has a limiting effect on freedom, it is likely to take the form of (often routine and unconscious) media self-censorship, the omission of content which might offend advertisers or, indeed, anyone. What is not there to see is not easy to measure and there are often legitimate reasons, other than the wish to please advertisers, for omitting content which will cause offence to advertisers or the audience. Effects from advertising on performance are thus very hard to establish.

It is sometimes feasible to compare content of publications with the expected interests of important advertisers. Tankard and Peirce (1982), for example, showed a relationship between the amount of magazine advertising for alcohol and the favourability towards drinking shown by editorial content. However, the 'system' itself legitimates connections of this kind and the hard part is to show editorial content *reluctantly*, or covertly, *giving way* to the dictates of advertisers. As with news and sources, there is an element of symbiosis which may be accounted as a general restriction on independence, although it is often within the limits of what is acceptable within normal commercial media practice.

Journalists and the audience as sources of evidence

Surveys of journalists have confirmed the occurrence of 'unethical' influence from advertisers. Data reported by Meyer (1987) showed that at least 39 per cent of newspaper staff agreed that on their paper there are sometimes cases where editorial matter is published on behalf of advertisers, at the behest of the business office. Meyer also (p. 39) reports a *Wall Street Journal* survey of business and financial editors in which 23 per cent said they routinely had to 'puff up or alter and downgrade business stories at the request of advertisers'. There is British survey evidence showing that daily newspaper editors were unconcerned about advertiser pressure, although senior journalists were less sanguine (RCP, 1977). Survey research also shows quite widespread suspicion on the part of the general public of advertiser influence on the media (see below). The Time/Mirror survey (Gallup Organization, 1986) reported that 65 per cent of the public thought that advertisers 'often' influence the media in the way they report the news.

Pressures from advocates and special interest groups

Mass media are subject to pressure of all kinds from groups in society seeking to influence media content, especially where it concerns their own media representation. It also seems that these lobbying efforts can be successful in their aim. Content of television fiction is often adjusted to avoid offence to any significant social group or minority, especially in commercial media systems, where negative publicity is feared for its chilling effects on potential advertisers. Montgomery (1989) describes several successful campaigns by advocacy groups, but she also says that 'the most effective groups were those whose goals were compatible with the network TV system' (1989: 217). Success also depended on external conditions of degree of public support or interest.

The restrictions and changes applied to media content, where they occur, are usually imposed at higher management levels in large media organizations and almost certainly constitute a limitation on the creative freedom of writers and programme makers. The *general* effect is likely to show itself in the form of blandness and conformity, a blurring of controversy and ambiguity about meaning. These qualities have often been imputed, but not often systematically measured (but see Gerbner et al., 1982). In any case they can also have quite other causes than advocacy pressure. Often the main result is the absence of controversy and the predominance of positive messages and happy endings, but these are often what audiences want anyway.

The general situation of mass market television still seems similar to that signalled by Breed (1958) when he carried out a 'reverse content analysis' of American local newspapers, demonstrating their avoidance of content which might offend the dominant values and interests of the local community (see Chapter 22). As with potential advertiser pressure, it is usually impossible to distinguish unacceptable interference with creative editorial decisions from the general, and presumably legitimate, wishes of the media to please their audiences and advertisers and to avoid hurt to minorities or vulnerable groups.

Accounts of news-making have also pointed to the understandable motivation on the part of media to avoid exposing themselves to legal reprisal (Tuchman, 1978). The strategies employed to this end are partly procedural (e.g. seeking quotations from authoritative sources and keeping to the 'facts'), but are also likely to involve some degree of avoidance behaviour in sensitive matters. The general result of such tendencies is, inevitably, a *differentially* positive treatment for the better *organized*, as well as the more established, special interest groups (Shoemaker, 1984).

Of 'manipulators outside the government', Paletz and Entman (1981: 124) write: 'The effectiveness of their attempts to shape media messages depends on their capacity to exploit the media's interests and practices.' They identified marginal groups, with little positive access to, or control over, media coverage as 'unofficial strikers, urban rioters, welfare mothers, student militants, radical and impoverished reactionaries'. As a contrary case, they looked at the *New York Times*'s coverage of a well-endowed and high-status 'citizen's lobby' called 'Common Cause', active in the 1970s, which received much attention in the paper, most of it virtually a conduit or channel for the movement's own ideas and information, with almost no criticism or even attempt at evaluation. This seems to be an instance which well illustrates Schlesinger's (1990) argument about some sources having high 'cultural capital' as their main resource.

The audience view of media freedom

The research approaches for assessing media independence which have been described mainly involve participant observation, interviewing or content analysis. The scope for any revealing audience/reader research on the question of media freedom is limited, but evidence from this source can have a part to play. For instance, degree of local audience satisfaction with their media has been applied as a performance criterion of media under different conditions of ownership (Stempel, 1973). Some extensive enquiries have also asked audiences more or less directly for their views about the independence of their own media or the media in general (see Fielder and Weaver, 1982; Immerwahr and Doble, 1982). Hulteng (1969) showed that the public does believe newspapers to be open to influence by outside interests, especially political and business leaders. The public also believed some outside power sources (governor, mayor, etc.) are able to prevent publication of an editorial on a controversial issue. Einsiedel and Winter (1983) showed there to be definite opinions in the public they surveyed about the negative aspects of media monopoly.

There is evidence of suspicion about the lack of independence of the established media, even if it may only reflect a general cynicism. For example, the findings of a major survey of the public conducted by Time/Mirror (Gallup Organization, 1986) revealed widespread doubts about the independence of American media. On this matter, 37 per cent replied that news organizations are 'pretty independent', while 53 per cent thought they were 'often influenced by powerful people'. The main powerful outside influences, each mentioned by over 60 per cent of the sample, were the federal government, business corporations, advertisers and labour unions. Further questioning showed the public attributing poor news media performance to commercial pressures, special interests, government news management and advertiser pressure, in that order.

The British Royal Commission on the Press survey found that around 15 per cent of readers of national newspapers thought that the papers were 'afraid of offending advertisers' and, on average, less than 50 per cent endorsed as 'very true' the statement that 'it [a given newspaper] is prepared to criticise anyone if they deserve it.' The Canadian Royal Commission on Newspapers came to somewhat similar conclusions. Too much should not be read into such general findings, but they do at least suggest that a potentially considerable gap exists between the ideal and the perceived reality of media independence.

We should also bear in mind that the general public, even in the home of press liberty, does not seem to understand it or rate it very highly. Emerson (1963) expressed alarm at the readiness of the American public to approve limits on freedom of speech and publication. Comstock (1988) cites extensive survey evidence to show that the public has little idea of what the First Amendment requires, in general believing there to be extensive rights of access, which do not exist, and assigning more responsibilities than rights to the mass media. A large majority would favour a law requiring both newspapers and television to allow equal coverage to contending political candidates. Large minorities think that Nazis and communists have very limited rights to publish their views. Immerwahr and Doble (1982) found public support for interpreting media freedom in terms of fairness and diversity and also a fair degree of tolerance of deviant views on mass media.

Modest achievements, limited knowledge

The empirical investigation of performance of media in respect of their use of freedom has been carried out in very fragmentary, often oblique, ways in a small number of places and according to a restricted and often unexplicated definition of what freedom for media actually is or ought to be. Most research attention has been directed at the newspaper press and most is North American (for circumstantial reasons: the early growth of communication research and the link between research schools and journalistic education). The concentration on the newspaper is partly due to its special status in liberal democracies as the main instrument of open and competitive politics, especially by way of its informative and opinion-giving task.

While there has often been conflict between democratic governments and news media, usually over matters of state security, or the 'national interest' (and cases of press resistance), most research has dealt with the degree to which the press has shown itself independent in the face of economic or organizational pressures or of the many demands made by other powerful social institutions. The potential for a fearless and adversarial press emerges as held back less by any fearful adversary or Leviathan state than by endemic media organizational self-interest, the appeal of easy (and cheap) routine and sycophancy towards populism and power.

Surveys of journalists and participant observation research repeatedly confirm that outside pressures are constantly experienced which work to modify the condition of pure 'freedom granted by society and to blunt the aspirations of crusading journalism. The work of the media does not seem, much of the time, to call for great enterprise or risk-taking, being often a matter of relaying public knowledge in a way which serves customers and matches standards of efficiency and competence.

Most research appears to tell us that the media do not grossly betray the promise of a free press in an open society, but that they are, to quite a degree, incorporated into the routines of economic and political processes. The media are thus neither independent of, nor fully under the control of, any single power source, *as long as there is some diversity of channels and of forms of ownership*.

It is broadcast media, which are formally less free (and which, for that reason, have rarely been assessed in terms of their freedom) which have often helped maintain the balance and diversity which prevents active suppression of truth. Despite the limited yield of research (for instance, the lack of clear results in charting the impact of monopoly conditions), a range of useful concepts and indicators has been developed which could be adapted to different media types and formats and to other problem situations. There is a potential for comparative research over time and across countries which as yet has hardly been tapped.

PART V
DIVERSITY

11
VARIETIES AND PROCESSES OF DIVERSITY

The diversity principle

The origins of the value of diversity are deeply rooted in the Western version of what counts as a modern society: one in which a premium is placed on individualism, change, freedom of thought and of movement. Societies are typically more diversified and segmented than in the past, whether for good or ill, and the value attached to diversity can, in part, be understood as a response to these changes. It reflects an attempt to make a virtue out of a necessity brought on by modernity, but it also signals resistance to some of the new unifying (and fragmenting) forces of economic power, technology and bureaucracy. Diversity is certainly much more than just a doctrine of economic liberalism or of political pluralism. Nevertheless, it is the latter which frequently underlies the vesting of a 'public interest' in media diversity.

Pluralism has significant philosophical roots in the eighteenth century and it gradually became an important political concept, fuelled by an admiration for American federalism. In general, it stood as a positive reference to any political forms opposed to statism or absolutism of the kind typified by imperial Germany. Breitling (1980) quotes Laski as saying that 'pluralism was born of a reaction from the moloch-like demands of the state in war time', and that it was a protection against excessive state power. In its later history, pluralism came to be identified more simply with central tenets of liberal democracy, in which many different interest groups are thought to compete for power and for access to resources (Dahl, 1967; Tumin and Plotch, 1977).

Although pluralistic political arrangements were held to provide checks and balances and to prevent undue concentrations of power, later critiques of capitalist society from the left tended to treat pluralism as a discredited ideology, because of the relative failure of pluralistic politics either to restrain the rise of capitalist class dominance or to advance working class aims. Nevertheless, pluralism has retained a claim to provide a basis for a tolerable and tolerant form of society, a claim reinforced by the collapse of communist hegemony in Eastern Europe.

The appeal of pluralism in modern social thought also derives from theories of mass society, which also developed as a critical response to totalitarianism (Kornhauser, 1960), to the rise of bureaucracy and of the corporate capitalist state in the twentieth century (Mills, 1956). In highly organized modern societies, old forms of constraint and social ties were replaced with new, more remote, but equally powerful, means of control – among them the mass media. The freedom of depersonalized individuals in mass society was held to leave them vulnerable to manipulation, rather than genuinely at liberty. Pluralistic arrangements for mass media can be seen as essential weapons in resisting trends to centralized control and uniformity.

Alternative interpretations of media diversity and its benefits

Aside from justifications in political theory, diversity has come to acquire the status of an end in itself for mass media – a broad principle to which appeal can be made on behalf both of neglected minorities and of consumer choice, or against monopoly and other restrictions. Media policy (as we have seen) has often sought to promote diversity, especially of expression, opinion and culture, whether by maximizing opportunities for media freedom or by way of intervention in the market place. However, the terms 'diversity' and 'pluralism' as applied to mass media conceal differences of emphasis and of application from one media system to another.

In the United States, for instance, FCC policy sought to promote diversity under two headings: one of maximizing consumer choice; the other of serving the 'public interest' by ensuring an appropriate range of service from broadcasting and 'fairness' in giving access and attention to opposed political groups and views (Brennan, 1989). The Supreme Court, in 1969, supported the view that receivers of broadcasting had rights to 'receive suitable access to social, political, aesthetic, moral and other ideas and experiences' – effectively the core claim on behalf of diversity.

According to Hoffmann-Riem (1987), the diversity principle lies at the heart of broadcasting arrangements in Europe: 'The public service philosophy of broadcasting . . . is oriented towards the accessibility of pluralistic information for citizens and society rather than the freedom of communicators. Diversity of program content, accessible to all segments of the audience must be established and safeguarded.' The pluralistic ideal is interpreted and implemented differently in different countries, according to the kind of priorities discussed in Chapters 4 and 5. For instance, in Britain, media policy has sought to promote diversity on a broad front: not only in terms of political balance and regional representation but also by providing for different cultural tastes, minority access and even by encouraging alternative forms of financing and of control.

In Canada, the main policy aim has been for media which will serve a multicultural society. In The Netherlands, diversity provides for the cultural needs of the traditional component 'pillars' (religious, political, social-cultural) of the national society and also for regular access for many minority voices (Wieten, 1979; McQuail, 1992). The key clause in successive Dutch broadcasting laws states the requirement that any group claiming access as a broadcaster has to show that it represents some distinct and significant political, religious or philosophical stream which is current in the society. There are several examples in European media law of new provision for small-scale, local access forms of local radio, protected in some degree from commercial and political pressures (Siune and Truetzschler, 1992).

In most European countries there have been moves to extend the notion of diversity from its primary reference to political and social-cultural differences, so as to embrace the market-place concept of diversity of products and services available to consumers at different prices (Peacock, 1986; Veljanovski, 1989). This has mainly been caused by the shift from extremely limited channel capacity to relative abundance. A more general 'liberalizing' and deregulation political-economic trend in Europe has also played a part (McQuail, 1990).

Diversity can be considered, not only as an end in itself, but also as a *means* to securing other benefits. There is a two-way link to *freedom*, little argument being needed to support the proposition that public freedom of expression for individuals and self-determination for groups is likely to require (and lead to) a substantial degree of media pluralism. It also seems that freedom and diversity are strongly connected in public opinion to judge from a survey of the American public (Gallup Organization, 1986). When asked what freedom of the press meant to respondents personally, the option overwhelmingly chosen (61 per cent) was that it means 'the public has a right to hear all points of view.' Comstock (1988) found that a decided majority of Americans would favour a law 'requiring both television and newspapers to give equal coverage to the two major party candidates and to opponents and advocates of a controversial policy'.

Progressive social change is linked in several ways to diversity. Innovation, creativity and originality in all fields of social and cultural life are unlikely to exist without diversity within a society and also over time. *Equality* also presupposes diversity (and vice versa), since diversity is a relativizing concept, opposing any claim to dominance or to cultural superiority. In a pluralistic society, all groups should have equal rights, if not equal status. There are many legitimate forms of conflict which can contribute to change and to progress and which may depend on a considerable tolerance for diversity of expression if they are not to lead to instability. For this reason, presumably, the FCC 'fairness doctrine' specifically held the public airing of 'controversial' matters and of opposing viewpoints to be in the public interest. In any case, there can hardly be diversity of opinion on matters of substance without some conflict. Paradoxically, diversity can also help in resolving social conflict and promoting social peace. Without the possibility of *pluralistic* solutions, many conflicts could not be resolved. In general, media diversity contributes to social *order* by promoting free expressions of discontent or disagreement and by offering pathways to compromise.

Media diversity: three standards of performance

Hoffmann-Riem (1987) has identified four main 'dimensions of diversity':

- of *formats and issues*: essentially referring to differences of media function, such as entertainment, information, education, etc.;
- of *contents*: in relation to opinion and topics of information and news;
- of *persons and groups*: essentially access, but also representation;
- of *geographical* coverage and relevance.

There is also wide agreement that pluralistic mass media can contribute to diversity in three main ways: by *reflecting* differences in society; by giving *access* to different points of view and by offering a wide range of *choice*. Each implies a somewhat different version of what diversity means (or standard by which it should be assessed), although they are not mutually exclusive.

Diversity as reflection

Pluralistic mass media are expected to represent or reflect the prevailing differences of culture, opinion and social conditions of the population as a whole. The widely shared culture which is characteristic of most modern societies is likely to be internally varied in ways which find their expression in media structure and content. This principle of reflection largely coincides with what Jacklin (1978) has termed 'representative diversity': 'there is representative diversity when the "structure" of diversity in communications corresponds to the structure of diversity in society.' He puts the emphasis on diversity of social reality in media content, although the structure of the media system can also be considered in terms of its reflection of differences in social structure.

Diversity as access

The media 'make available' channels through which the separate 'voices', groups and interests which make up the society can speak to the wider society, express and keep alive their own cultural identity, where that is relevant. It is often by way of this kind of access that critical, oppositional and deviant voices, which are essential to change and to choice, can be heard (Barron, 1972; Goldenberg, 1976; Bantz et al., 1981; Downing, 1984; Haiman, 1987). Media access can also help people to communicate among themselves, especially where sub-group members are widely scattered. This promotes cohesion and identity, even though mass media provision cannot be a substitute for autonomous and informal networks of internal communication. The most essential conditions for effective access are: freedom to speak out; effective opportunity to speak (there being a sufficient number of independent and different channels); autonomy, or adequate self-control over media access opportunities.

Diversity as more channels and choice for the audience

Choice increases the quality of communication services, viewed as a consumption good. For consumers, it represents greater freedom – a variety or range of products or services available to them – essentially the diversity of formats and contents mentioned by Hoffmann-Reim (1987). Choice for receivers can also be seen as making other opinions, information, cultural forms and ways of living more available, contributing to social change, enjoyment and to the interest of social and cultural life.

Conceptual overlaps

These three principles are obviously inter-related, but they can also be independent of each other. Media can 'reflect' society in their contents without there being much diversity of access. There can be opportunities for access, by some definitions, without the outcome in content terms representing the full range of differences in society as a whole. Consumer choice can easily exist without there being wide access to channels, or even much accurate reflection of a diverse social reality. Media can satisfy modal cultural tastes of consumers without offering a wide range of catering for small minorities.

Sub-concepts of media diversity

In order to guide assessment of diversity we need to make some other conceptual distinctions beyond the trio of reflection, access and choice. Account has also to be taken of the *level* at which these concepts apply, according to the distinction between structure (and organizational conduct) on the one hand and performance on the other (see Chapter 7). Although performance (content and delivery to audiences) is most central in this enquiry, some questions of diversity relate more to structure than to content.

External versus internal diversity

External diversity The 'external' principle of structure (strongly linked to the idea of access) refers to a condition where the full range of relevant differences (political, social-cultural, etc.) in a society is matched by an equivalent range of *separate and autonomous* media channels, each catering exclusively for its own group or interest. It presupposes a high degree of homogeneity or consistency of content *within* each channel, a corresponding degree of audience homogeneity and a high degree of differentiation between one channel and another. In theory, each 'voice' in a differentiated society will have its own channel and speak to its own 'followers'.

While complete media systems of this kind no longer exist (if they ever did), the principle can be seen at work in culturally and linguistically divided societies and those where there has been a strong partisan press system, in which each party has its own organ of opinion which serves and mobilizes a loyal following. In the latter case, we expect sharp political differences of content and a high correspondence between content and the political allegiance of readers. Broadcasting in The Netherlands was, for instance, organized along such lines from its beginning and significant elements of 'external diversity' still remain in place. Television and radio time is shared out between a number of associations, each organized to provide its own distinctive content, primarily for its own membership (Wieten, 1979; Browne, 1989; McQuail, 1992). The newspaper press in Sweden has also been traditionally structured along lines of external diversity, with each region having competing right- or left-inclined titles (Hadenius, 1983; Hulten, 1984).

Externally diverse media systems of this kind have usually been associated with conditions of social conflict or diversion but they are unlikely to disappear completely (they may even be on the rise in Eastern Europe). As the number of television channels increases (because of cable and satellite and new electronic forms of publishing), there is even a potential for a shift towards more 'external' electronic media diversity, especially in the form of 'narrowcasting' – offering specialist content channels to minority interest audiences (LeDuc, 1982). However, there is little prospect of the growth of an externally diverse TV system in political terms, in the absence of necessary social and political conditions. Commercially motivated expansion is not likely to produce this kind of diversity, however technically feasible.

While external *political* diversity of the press has declined, some media sectors do show an increase in external diversity according to dimensions other than politics. The magazine press, for instance, has developed along specialized lines – increasingly seeking to match the content and image of a given publication to a distinctive taste or consumer readership group. The principle of geographical differentiation also offers a version of external diversity which may be resistant to social homogenization. Different media often try to cater for audience (and advertiser) needs related to variations in geographical and social space: the neighbourhood, city, region or nation. By definition, true external diversity is a condition of a media *system* or *sector* and not of an individual 'channel'.

Internal diversity This refers to the condition (of system, sector or single channel) where a wide range of types of content or points of view is offered by the same channel(s), usually with a view to reaching a large and heterogeneous audience. This is close to the principle of *reflection*, as discussed above, although not identical with it. Such arrangements are characteristic of pluralistic societies, where a small number of large circulation newspapers or of television channels compete for much the same large, national audience. The condition is also likely to be found (as in the United States) where city regions are served by only one or two newspapers or a few broadcasting stations.

Conditions of internal media diversity are usually associated with balanced and objective news styles, in line with professional journalistic tendencies. Conditions of concentration and monopoly, whether public or private, tend to encourage internal diversity as does dependence on advertising, rather than consumer, revenue. There is no *necessary* connection between these features and internal diversity, although there is a connecting logic: media which seek to maximize their audiences and their own attraction for advertisers, or which have a degree of monopoly, also seek to avoid exclusivity, to appeal to as many different interests and information needs as possible and to avoid offence to any significant minority (or to powerful government or business interests).

Regulated broadcasting systems often provide a special case of internal diversity, by design of public policy. Because there are limited channels, diversity and balance are usually required as conditions for the granting of operating licences, as a matter of equity in allocating a scarce public resource. They are also a direct outcome of the politics which have given rise to media policy in the first place.

Equal versus proportional reflection and access

This discussion has implied a definition of diversity along the following lines: 'The variability of mass media (sources, channels, messages and audiences) in terms of relevant differences in society (political, geographical, social-cultural, etc.).' It also appears that diversity (the variability referred to) can be promoted by different kinds of media structure – the 'external' variety promoting *access* and the 'internal' sort offering more chance of *reflection*. 'Variability' both of media structure (the channels) and of content (the outcome of performance) can be assessed according to two additional standards – one which values *equality* of access and representation for all significant differences, another according to a principle of *proportionality*.

Equality of access According to the equality principle, the ideal form of diversity is one in which *all* relevant candidate groups or interests have an equal share of access to media channels or receive equal attention in the media. The principle of absolute equality of time or space allocated is an extreme one, literally impossible to realize, but having some applicability wherever a limited number of 'candidate voices' are recognized as having a legitimate claim to media access and attention. Thus, the principle *is* literally applied and realized (in media structure) in countries such as Belgium or Canada, where two language communities have their own parallel broadcasting and press systems. Political and market forces combine to produce this result.

The equality principle is sometimes applied, for reasons of public policy, in allocating access for electoral purposes, where all parties contesting an election may be given exactly the same amount of television time (as in The Netherlands). It is a standard sometimes invoked in claims for access for women in the media. It is also the ideal of equality which supports the view that all citizens should have the same chances of *reception* of the media, and thus be offered the same range of choice of channels and of content. The principle of *universality* of service deployed in telecommunications policy is also derived from the idea of equality (Melody, 1990).

The equality claim may sometimes coincide with that of proportionality (for instance as with gender). More often, it is only invoked to *modify* the working of proportionality, without having to be met in full. In some circumstances, strict numerical proportionality would not even provide small minorities with enough access or visibility to be of any real use to them. More often than not, an appeal to equality does no more than support a move in the direction of proportional reflection, on some motivated ground (e.g. where a particular communication need is strong, or where it gives a basic minimum access to a legitimate voice).

Departures from proportionality and towards equality of access may also result from the free working of the market which, paradoxically, has an 'equalizing' effect by differentially increasing the chances of small, wealthy or powerful minorities. It is the economically privileged minority which, in practice, benefits most from the 'equal access' promise of market-based systems. The working of the market can also have an 'equalizing' (or 'democratizing') effect on the diversity of reflection in society: stimulating a supply of popular content for tastes and interests which an elitist media system would not cater for.

The equality principle of diversity has more potential to promote change and innovation, while reflection tends towards reinforcement of the status quo (or balance of social power). For this reason, we often find claims for more equal access and attention being made by minority or oppositional groups which go beyond their 'fair share'. The beneficial effects of more equal media access for a minority political party in election situations have more than once been demonstrated (e.g Blumler and McQuail, 1968).

Proportionality While proportionality appears to need no arbitrary decision about eligibility (unlike claims for equal access), the standard invoked being simply that the 'media distribution' (e.g. of content voice and image) should match the 'social reality' distribution, there are some concealed problems. One of these has already been mentioned: an achieved proportionality may simply be inadequate to serve any useful communication purpose, where channel capacity is limited and there are no objective standards for judging what would be minimally adequate. Secondly, plausible claims can always be made for giving disproportionately more (or less) access and attention to some topics, groups, actions and institutions, on grounds of relevance and significance.

Moreover, there are numerous overlapping minorities (we all belong to many differently defined categories) and not all can be accommodated in media content all the time. What is uncovered here is the weakness of the *numerical* notion of proportionality as a guide to policy or assessment. The numerical calculation involved in comparing two distributions is simple and objective, but the choice of what to compare is not. It requires account to be taken of relative significance of social or cultural identities and thus involves value judgements. Claims made on proportional grounds alone can be as mindless as claims on grounds of literal equality (see below).

Quantitative versus qualitative diversity of treatment

The distinction just noted – between *amount* and *kind* of treatment – applies with the same force to both equality and proportionality. These are two separate matters: one of access/attention in terms of media space and time; the other of quality of treatment. The second refers to the balance, impartiality, fairness of any direct or indirect valuation in the *manner* and *form* of representation. Even if numerically equal or proportional access and attention is achieved, the implicit balance of evaluation in content may be one-sided.

While the amount of media access and representation may sometimes be hard to distinguish from its quality (for instance, in cases where political parties get both their fair share of access/attention and also receive even-handed treatment in broadcast news), the distinction is usually both clear and important. There is, however, no consistent relation between amount and direction of coverage. Some minorities get a lot of attention, but are also portrayed in a very unfavourable light (Hartman and Husband, 1974; Shoemaker, 1984; van Dijk, 1991). The reverse can sometimes happen to high-status minorities or individuals (royalty, celebrities, the very rich, etc.). Some political parties or social groups get a fair share of attention, but not on favourable terms. Peaks of attention to certain countries in international news coverage can as often be associated with negative as with positive images.

Diversity as consumer choice: the horizontal/vertical distinction

The standard most often applied in assessing diversity of media content from the point of view of consumer choice has been that of quantity and range – the more options and the more different they are, the more diversity for the consumer. However, a distinction has sometimes been made, especially with reference to radio and television choice, between 'horizontal' and 'vertical' diversity (Litman, 1979). Horizontal diversity refers to the number of different programmes or programme types available to the viewer/listener at any given time. Vertical diversity measures number of different programmes (or types) offered by a channel (or set of channels) over the entire schedule (an evening, week, month, etc.). For obvious reasons, the (consumer) diversity of a single channel can only be assessed 'vertically' (over time), although both standards can be applied to sets of media channels. There are some problems in applying these concepts to other media and also in determining what counts as 'different' (for research examples see Chapter 13).

The inter-relation of concepts

Most of the conceptual distinctions just described can be summarized by inclusion in the following description of diversity research procedures. Media diversity in the sense of reflection, access or choice can be assessed:

- according to a chosen dimension of differentiation (e.g. politics, geography, social-cultural);
- at the level of *structure*, according to criteria of 'external' and 'internal' diversity, or range of channel choice;
- and at the level of *performance* (content and audience), according to criteria of *equality* or *proportionality*;
- applied to the *amount* and the *kind* of representation and access;
- taking account of the *horizontal* or *vertical* dimension of time.

Alternative dimensions of media diversity

While every country has its own unique set of diversity priorities and problems, there are some recurring sources of social-cultural differentiation and, correspondingly, some typical features of media systems, which can be accounted as responses to these differences. In practice, much of the policy debate and research on diversity has been concerned with difference of *politics*, *geography* or of some *social-cultural* attribute which contributes to social division.

The political dimension

The value attached to political diversity in media performance needs little explanation. Politics is rooted in differing and conflicting interests which seek public expression. Democratic politics is normally organized around public competition for popular support, in which the mass media now play a crucial role. Electors are supposed to make rational choice among candidates, policies and parties on the basis of information available in the public sphere. Contending parties and politicians use mass media to recruit and keep voter support by presenting themselves and their policies in a favourable light, through information, argument and image-presentation.

Although openly 'politicized' media systems (the party press model) have generally been in decline, it is hard to imagine diverse media which are not also differentiated ('internally' at least) according to political direction in opinions expressed or reported and in the selection of news and informational content. Expectations will vary a good deal from one context to another. A strong (external) version of political diversity is one in which each significant party has its own set of media serving its own loyal followers. In a weak (internal diversity) version, the main mass media, often apolitical themselves, can offer a full range of politically relevant content in an even-handed way (the objective press and broadcasting models). Political diversity often extends to cover other controversial matters in society, including labour and economic conflict, moral and legal issues, women's rights, the environmental debate, etc.

The geographical dimension

Geographical differentiation has always been a key principle of media structure, as it is of social structure. The boundaries of audiences and of media markets are often identified geographically. Differences of geography may also coincide with ethnic, religious or language differences within the national society. Neighbourhood, community, town or region usually call for their own communication channels in order to serve local needs, as well as to help integration into the wider society.

Media serving geographical area are commonly expected to meet certain criteria of structure, provision and performance. They should be locally owned and controlled, provide news and comment about local events and there should be independent competing channels. They should service local institutions (politics, education, etc.) and provide channels for the expression of local culture. Regional and local media have an economic function as channels for advertising and information and by representing the area positively to the outside world. A common expectation of local media is that they will help to form and maintain local community consensus (Janowltz, 1952; Edelstein and Larsen, 1960). Finally, within the area served, local media should also provide alternative access opportunities as well as variety of content for audiences. Where there is real geographical diversity, media serving different areas should also be noticeably different in content (Donohue and Glasser, 1978). In addition, media at national level (thus purporting to reflect and serve a national society) should give adequate attention to all regions (Cranford, 1960; Dominick, 1977; Whitney et al., 1989).

Concerns about geographical diversity are thus of four main kinds, the first two being matters of structure, the second two of performance:

- whether or not localities and regions are in fact served by their own media;
- whether the local media system offers a real choice among channels;
- whether there is, within channels, diversity of information, opinion and 'culture' adequate to local conditions especially in terms of the criteria of access and reflection mentioned above;
- whether regional and local media offer a service (alternative channels

and content) sufficient to form an adequate substitute for national media (especially where these are not readily available);
– whether or not national media give due attention to different regions.

An ideal blueprint for the structure of regional/local media diversity would thus seem to call for other *kinds* of media (press, radio and television) as well as choice and competition among channels.

The social/cultural dimension of diversity

Diversity requirements are not exhausted by reference to politics or geography, especially where societies are open and changing. There are also numerous possible identifications, of varying kinds and salience, beyond the more obvious ones of religion, ethnicity, language and social class. A larger view of social and cultural pluralism has to recognize the potential significance of sub-cultural differences based on gender, generation and many kinds of special interest, which may be important to people themselves. While structural provision is often made for media diversity, either by policy (e.g. legislation for regional broadcasting or the needs of linguistic minorities (or by way of linguistic minorities) or by way of the market (where minorities are sufficiently strong to organize their own media or large enough to attract a 'natural' market provision), quite a few social/ cultural groups are likely to remain unprovided for.

Many countries are now host to numerous and sizeable minority groups of economic, or political, migrants who are ethnically and culturally distinct and who often lack the degree of appropriate media provision which would satisfy the home population. The strength and legitimacy of claims to separate provision for social-cultural minorities, or the chances of them being satisfied by way of market forces, varies enormously. These remarks can also apply to group identities based on class and status. Aside from older class/status differences, which may be diminishing, poor social-economic conditions often produce a marginalized identity (sometimes referred to as an 'underclass'). While the media market may provide adequately for the normal range of social class differences, the least socially integrated and the poorest sectors of society are likely to be excluded from the main range of diversity provision, for economic reasons.

Delivering media diversity: two basic models

Diversity of media structure and performance has been secured in varying degrees and by various means. Most media systems are very complex sets of haphazard arrangements, often accumulated over time and having no single logic. Any given system is as much the outcome of chance as of design and there are always gaps and inconsistencies. Even so, there are two main sources of diversity, one stemming from the demands of the public or audience (the receivers) and the other deriving more from the needs of the 'senders' and the media. The two do not always coincide or reinforce each other. In addition, there are other kinds of structure or model which can embody or promote the diversity principle, one based on market forces, the other on non-market intervention or political policy.

The market model

In several ways, the media market works towards meeting many of the claims outlined. In theory, the free operation of supply and demand should provide for access for all 'voices' which can pay for it and for a supply of content relevant to all consumers. Market mechanisms also lead to a continuous process of trial and error, of innovation, product improvement and of flexible response to potential communication needs. A market system should stimulate the growth of new channels and new audience markets. The outcome can be increased numerical diversity (more channels and more choice for consumers). By the same token, many of the requirements for adequate 'reflection' should also be met by an appropriate supply of content in a market system, under conditions of freedom. The media system should reflect the demands of would-be receivers, whether these are expressed directly in the audience (subscription) market or indirectly through the advertising market. According to market logic, advertisers will have a strong motive to encourage a media provision which corresponds to the diversity of society.

From this account, it seems that a well-functioning market will maximize the benefits of would-be senders and receivers. In practice, the interests of audience and advertisers do not always coincide, nor do the dynamics of advertiser and audience (subscriber) financing work in the same direction or achieve the same kind of diversity. The direct media consumer 'market' (which relies on sales or subscription for income and profit) is likely to produce a much more fragmented (but also differentiated) pattern, which caters best (in volume and choice) for higher income groups. It can be profitable to cater for very many small but wealthy groups of consumers. However, less commercial media, with 'idealistic' communication goals and no profit motive, can also survive on the basis of a small, but committed support from their audiences.

The advertising-based variant of the market model operates best in the interests of one category of sender and contributes most to diversity where the make-up of media content matches the composition of the consumer market for other goods and services. Under market conditions, media provision is shaped by the same factors as consumption generally. Media distribution and content patterns are especially inclined to follow lines of income and of locality. Advertisers can choose vehicles for their messages in order to reach diversified target groups in a way which suits their own needs and which also contributes to 'representative' diversity. Since socio-economic variation also often correlates with mainstream political differentiation, the advertising market variant has some potential for meeting the main requirements of political diversity noted above. Audience demand will stimulate media to give access to, and to represent, the main political perspectives in the community or society.

Because the retail trade is organized on a local basis, reliance on advertising should, in general, also work in favour of local and regional diversity. Social-cultural variation in terms of life-style, fashion, music and similar consumption-based identifications is also likely to be well served on the basis of the media market, because of advertising and marketing 'tie-ins'. Advertising markets are not only organized to service the retail trade and to follow the stratification of purchasing power.

The market model has several drawbacks aside from its 'bias' to the interests of (commercial) senders who finance the system. It often leads to high basic costs of access to the mass media (favouring the rich and leading to concentration of ownership). It is inclined to neglect poor or marginal groups of media consumers, who are not very interesting economically. It encourages the growth of mass or very homogeneous audiences. According to Hoffmann-Riem (1987), for instance, because of its orientation to 'mass appeal', commercial broadcasting is 'likely to reduce the chances for certain kinds of provision, especially content: of a specific local and regional kind, e.g. in a minority language; dealing with minority problems; serving less wealthy target groups, including children, old and poor'. LeDuc (1982), reflecting on the new abundance of channels and the process of media deregulation in the United States, is very sceptical about the market having delivered any significant increase in alternative programming options for the audience.

The non-market (public policy) model

Mainly, though not only, because of the limitations described, public policy has often aspired to equalize chances of media access, to encourage fairer representation and to limit, or redress, some the imperfections, or 'biases', of the market place. Sometimes intervention is openly applied on behalf of groups which are simply unable, for economic reasons, to gain adequate access to the media system. The aims are divergent: either to ensure a varied and representative media supply; or to help 'senders' to overcome the effects of fundamental inequalities in society. Often communication policy for diversity is an adjunct of wider social and cultural policy, aiming to secure not only better access conditions for 'senders', but also a more universal and diverse supply for audiences, than the market, left to itself, would be likely to deliver.

The forms taken by public policy interventions on behalf of diversity vary according to local priorities and political cultures. In general, the broadcasting model (already described, Chapter 7), especially in its 'public service' variant, was developed in order to promote diversity under conditions of limited channel capacity. Press systems are less open to direct intervention, but measures to encourage press diversity are not uncommon, usually by way of general economic support and by setting limits to private monopoly (see Picard, 1985a).

The intended beneficiaries of public intervention are usually political and social groups with less power in the market place. The 'public policy' model is usually thought to be superior to the free market for achieving wider diversity of *access*. It is often equal to the market in achieving *reflection*, although the results are likely to be different. However, it is the market which tends to score higher when performance is measured according to increased *audience/consumer choice*. Drawbacks of the public policy model include an inevitable limitation on choice for some consumers. Interventions in press or broadcasting structure have also been criticized for increasing rigidity – establishing rights to support (or access) which become vested interests and are difficult to change when social needs and other conditions change.

The diversity of media systems may be increased by forms of financing other than that from consumers, advertisers or public subsidies to the media. Organizations, such as political parties, churches, educational institutions and many interest associations also subsidize media channels or content in pursuit of their own aims as senders or on behalf of special minorities. Sponsored corporate, institutional or government advertising, informational or public relations communication activities, which seek to reach very special target audiences, are often 'friendly' towards media diversity. Classified (e.g. occupational or personal) advertising, which is typically aimed at many, varied, but very specific target audiences, also encourages channel and content diversity, without distorting effects or manipulative intention.

Options in diversity research

Few of the many potential questions for diversity research, which are raised by the performance claims and the various concepts of diversity described, have been systematically investigated. Often, findings about diversity have been a by-product of other enquiries. We can, nevertheless suggest a framework for investigation based on the sequential model of the process of communication in society given in Figure 11.1.

Questions about diversity can and have been asked about each of these stages and research designs are based on combinations of these elements.

Source diversity

Three basic meanings can be distinguished. The first ('society as source') is the broadest meaning of the term, referring to society as a whole – its

Society as   Society as
sender   receiver

SOURCES → CHANNELS → CONTENT → CONTENT → AUDIENCE
                          as sent   as received

Figure 11.1 *The mass communication sequence*

general structure and composition as well as the circumstances, events and locations of social life which provide the essential background and subject matter of most media content, whether as fiction, fact or commentary. A second meaning ('advocates') refers to the 'original communicators', the diverse 'voices' of society who are active in social communication as 'advocates' of ideas and interests, or as artists, writers, educators who seek to use the channels of mass communication in order to reach audiences with a message. They can include the media themselves when they choose to act as communicators rather than just mediators, as in editorial opinion columns. Thirdly, there is the more technical meaning ('news source') where the reference is to the contacts of journalists, official spokespersons and other sources of information, news agencies, etc.

Diversity questions have been asked about each of these kinds of source. In respect of 'society as source', at issue is the variety of the picture of social reality portrayed in fiction, advertising or entertainment, as well as the range of locations, events, groups and persons which make up the substance of news and information content. In relation to 'advocates', the same logic applies but attention focuses on the range and representatives of the 'primary communicators' who receive direct or indirect access to channels. Often what matters is the range and degree of access and/or exclusion experienced by alternative voices in society. The question of *whose* definition of reality or whose agenda is disseminated also arises. In the case of 'news source', diversity analysis usually aims to assess the number and range of sources actually cited in news texts, noting patterns of omission, imbalance and over-dependence on certain limited news sources, including news agencies (see below for research examples).

Channel diversity

The term 'channel' refers to any independent mass media distribution agency (newspaper, radio station, cable network, etc.). Investigation of channel diversity is essentially a structural matter, which will depend on the system level at issue and on the relevant standard (access, reflection or choice). At the macro (whole system) or meso (media sector) level what counts is the number of channels and the degree to which they are different from each other: the more channels and the more differentiated they are, the more diversity. The main criteria of differentiation are likely to be: type of ownership and control (e.g. public versus private; chain versus independent); periodicity (e.g. morning versus evening); type of medium (print, audio, audiovisual, etc.); functional or content type definition: news, entertainment, general, specialist, etc.; format and genre of content type; cultural 'quality', however assessed; type of audience demographics sought or obtained; and main financial basis (see above). The diversity of a single channel (micro level) is also open to investigation as an internal matter. In essence, the diversity of a single channel is the same as its *content diversity*, which can be investigated 'horizontally' (at one point in time, e.g. the morning's news in one newspaper edition) as well as 'vertically' (over a period of time) in the case of press media but only vertically in the case of broadcasting.

Diversity of content 'as sent'

'Content as sent' (what is usually measured by content analysis) can provide a basic answer to questions about diversity, following conventional lines of categorization. The universe of content offered by a set of channels, or a single channel (over time), can be assessed according to the number of different types of content (e.g. news, films, advertisements, etc.) and the distribution of time/space between these types. In general, the more different content types and the more even the distribution across them, the higher the level of diversity. Each 'content type' may be further differentiated according to format and variety of genre. Here, 'content diversity' may be much the same as 'channel diversity'. The variables of 'horizontal' and 'vertical' diversity, mentioned above, can also come into play.

The diversity of content can also be measured according to 'extra-media' data, where the intention is to assess diversity according to differences in society, rather than just by internal, organizational criteria (Rosengren, 1977). Thus, diversity of content can be accounted in terms of social groups given access, 'pictures of the world', representations of any aspect of social reality. The question of degree of relevance to social differences is also likely to arise. For instance, we may ask (as did Gans, 1979) whether national news reflects regional and social differences (Morgan, 1986).

Diversity of content 'as received'

'Content as received' refers here to 'content as sent', weighted according to the size of audience reached (it does not refer to differences of perception, attributed meaning, or effect, although this is the next stage in the process). This variable identifies a different universe of content than that sent – what the audience actually selects, although it can be analysed by the same methods. While the result may tell us more about the audience than about media performance, audience selections are, to some extent, an outcome of editorial decision-making about relative prominence, placement, scheduling, publicity, etc. and can indicate the success or not of such decisions.

The systematic difference between the two measures (content sent versus content received) also provides an indicator of any trend towards increasing or diminishing diversity, which may occur during the sequence depicted in Figure 11.1. Typically, content as received will show a narrower range (thus less diversity) than content as sent, as a result of audience selections in favour of more popular types, formats and items. There is plenty of evidence that certain kinds of content are systematically over- and under-represented in audience choices (as they are in the funnelling and filtering which always takes place before content is offered to the audience).

On its own, diversity of supply cannot secure diversity of *reception*, but it is a necessary condition for this. There has been little research attention to diversity of content 'as received', as defined here, although routine audience and reader statistics make it possible to compute the relationship between range of offer and range of audience choice for many basic types of content.

Receiver/audience diversity

The audience can be defined in different ways, but here it is taken to mean the set of regular readers, viewers, etc. of a given media channel, or the set reached by a given media sector (e.g. 'the cinema audience' = regular cinema-goers), as recorded at a given point in time. The assessment of diversity of an audience so defined depends on which version of the concept is chosen and which standard is applied. It also depends on choosing a relevant dimension of audience composition (e.g. age, gender, politics, place of residence, educational background, tastes and preferences, etc.). The diversity of an audience can be assessed either by reference to an 'extra-media' standard (e.g. the representation of the population as a whole in terms of age, education, income) or in terms of its content preferences. In the latter case, the main question is usually whether what is offered by the media matches what the audience prefers. The match, or lack of it, between variables of content as sent and of audience as composed may have practical consequences, when would-be 'communicators' are faced with the problem of targeting a particular set of 'receivers', in a political, advertising or information campaign.

I
Structural diversity of media system
How much external diversity (separate access)?
How much internal diversity (reflection of differences)?
How much choice (number and range of channels)?

II **Channel-audience diversity**	III **Channel-content diversity**
How far a separate channel? How far a separate audience? How far a general channel? How heterogeneous the audience?	Does output reflect social life? Does output give equal access? Does output offer choice (horizontally or vertically)?
IV **Audience diversity**	V **Content as received**
Is composition homogeneous or heterogeneous, according to a chosen dimension?	What is the relation between degree of diversity of content received and as sent, according to the chosen dimension?

Figure 11.2 *Main questions for diversity research according to a chosen dimension of differentiation (political, geographical, socio-cultural)*

The main questions for diversity assessment research

The main kinds of research task identified by this discussion are summarized in Figure 11.2, which shows the connections between them. A necessary condition for setting out on any of the tasks is a choice of relevant *dimension* of differentiation. This provides the point of reference and standard for judging the kind and degree of diversity offered by the media and for reaching conclusions about performance. Almost any principle of variability can be applied, although (as noted) the most commonly encountered have to do with politics, geography or social-cultural difference.

12
TAKING THE MEASURE OF DIVERSITY: MEDIA REFLECTION

Reflective diversity and media structure

The central issue is the degree to which a set of media channels (or the media system as a whole) corresponds to relevant variations in the society. Here, 'society' refers to the 'source' in the first and broadest sense mentioned in Chapter 11 ('society as source'), meaning the composition of society in terms of social groups, major institutions, varying conditions and everyday experience. According to the reflective principle, the more differentiated the media system and the closer the correspondence between variation in media and in society, the more an appropriate form of diversity is thought to obtain. Much assessment relating to diversity happens to have been a by-product of research into political communication, media 'bias' or into the reflection (or not) of 'social reality'. As a result, the issues most frequently raised have concerned politics, place or social class.

Political reflection in media structure

The political balance of any media system – the extent to which it corresponds to the main political divisions in the society – has attracted much attention. These divisions can usually be expressed in terms of the distribution of votes for the main political parties, which are often ranged along a spectrum from left to right or from liberal to conservative. The political differentiation of newspapers in equivalent terms can be measured in any of three main ways: according to the editorial endorsements of political parties or candidates at election times; or the direction of political leaning in content as a whole; or the voting preferences of readers.

The political diversity of the Dutch newspaper press (McQuail and van Cuilenburg, 1983) was, for example, assessed by ranking ten national daily newspapers on a conservative–progressive dimension according to a score of political direction in editorial commentaries. The results showed a mild skew of the national press towards the progressive (leftward) end of the spectrum, compared to the political division of the population: the press as a whole was accounted 76 per cent progressive or moderately so, against 64 per cent for the population, according to its party preferences.

In Britain the political diversity (or lack of it) of the national press has usually been measured according to the editorial endorsements of the main parties at elections, taking account of the average share of circulation which different newspapers control. By this measure, in 1987, Conservative papers accounted for 74 per cent of national daily circulation and Labour papers for 26 per cent (Seymour-Ure, 1991), while the parties' respective share of votes in the General Election of that year was 42 and 31 per cent. This would have to be accounted as a low or inadequate degree of diversity in the sense under discussion. The British national press has for long been skewed in a Conservative direction. In these kinds of calculation, not only the *spread* along a continuum is taken into account, but also the comparison with the 'extra-media' reality. In the examples cited, the Dutch case showed a reverse pattern to that of Britain, but one where the press more closely reflected the political divisions of society.

Local and regional media diversity

The adequacy of media structure in terms of geographical diversity can generally be assessed directly according to the number of national and regional or local media channels which are available. A high degree of press diversity will be present where, in addition to a varied national press, each region or major city has several of its own independent press or other media channels, or has a good locally relevant service from nearby media. The opposite obtains where national or metropolitan newspapers dominate circulation everywhere and perhaps also where the national level is itself missing. An *appearance* of geographical diversity of media structure may obscure the fact that locally available channels can belong to national chains and offer much the same content in different localities (Donohue and Glasser, 1978).

Variations in local media system diversity have multiple causes. Apart from physical extent (as in the USA), historical fragmentation (as in several European countries) has played a part in shaping the geography of the media. The most general explanatory factor is economic. Regions or cities which have the largest, most concentrated and most prosperous populations are likely to be better served by alternative and competing media channels. The older bases of regional differentiation, especially in respect of politics and culture, are declining in Europe, although localized markets for certain kinds of information and advertising services can still provide a support for media diversity of a kind. In general, European regional and local print media have tended to fare better economically than national newspapers, partly because they have less advertising competition from electronic media.

According to such simple accounting methods, trends in diversity can quite easily be monitored, although problems arise as to what constitutes genuine differences between the newspapers or channels which appear to serve different regions (Donohue and Glasser, 1978; Kariel and Rosenvall, 1983). The more that editorial services or contents are shared between regional or local newspapers or television and radio channels, the less real diversity. The networking of local radio content, for instance, greatly reduces the seeming diversity of local radio. The burst of privatization in local radio in Europe in the 1980s was often followed by consolidation and concentration.

Media structure and class structure

Similar principles of reckoning diversity can be applied to social class differences, since variations of media structure still reflect the class division of societies. The printed press began mainly as a provision for the middle classes. Working class papers followed, either as political vehicles for a radical or socialist opposition or as channels for advertising directed at the growing mass consumer market. The rise of advertising as the main source of press income has helped to cement the 'social class' differentiation of newspapers, in so far as class is equated with consumer spending patterns (Hirsch and Gordon, 1975; Seymour-Ure, 1991). Advertising has had much less effect on radio and television structure and provision.

In Europe, the composition of readership of national newspapers is still often clearly differentiated according to socioeconomic status, which provides one guide to the overall diversity of media provision. Where there is little variation between papers in the social class composition of their readership, a situation of 'internal diversity' usually holds, with all papers catering for the same wide range of social class interests. Where papers are strongly differentiated in terms of reader composition, we are likely to find 'external diversity' in respect of social class, with each social stratum catered for by different titles. Which condition is preferable is a matter of value judgement, but the empirical measurement of such matters is straightforward enough.

The effect of market forces is much the same everywhere; the more prosperous social strata are likely to have more choice of media channels directed to their probable tastes and interests, thus to enjoy a more diverse provision, by comparison with the less well-off social groups. For instance, in Britain there are approximately nine national daily or Sunday titles (out of 19) which are mainly directed to middle class readers, compared to about the same number mainly directed to a numerically much larger non-middle class readership. The middle classes have, effectively, more choice. Similar principles of measurement can be applied to media diversity in terms of age groups, gender differences and some categories of leisure time interests.

Reflective diversity and media content

The degree of correspondence between the diversity of the society and the diversity of media content is the key to assessing performance. The criterion of an adequate degree of reflective diversity will be the closeness of this relationship. The history of communication research is full of examples of questions posed in this way, not usually intended to measure diversity as such but to assess whether or not the media give a biased or a true reflection of society and if not why not.

Reflecting political divisions

In political communication research, this particular issue is usually tackled by comparing the balance of media attention to different parties and political figures, especially during election campaigns, with the political balance in the society (e.g. Hofstetter, 1976; Patterson and McClure, 1976; Blumler, 1983). A new issue for assessment has been introduced as a result of the televising of proceedings in parliament, as in Britain (see Blumler et al., 1990). There can be bias of camera attention, not only along political party lines, but also along lines of regional representation and, possibly, unjustifiable attention to prominent national figures. Each of these could offend against the diversity principle.

In order to assess the relative *amount* of attention to different politicians or political positions, samples (sometimes all) of politically relevant media content (generally news, comment, background and political access material, including advertising and parliamentary reporting) are analysed according to amount of space or time which either *originates* from, or simply *pays attention to*, a party or candidate, and the distribution of the 'population' of political actors, as this appears in media content. The results of such measures can be compared numerically with a chosen standard of representation (e.g. equal or proportional reflection).

A second type of question concerns the balance of attention to the *substance* of politics, rather than to the range of political actors. Political content can be more or less diverse in its range of factual coverage or reference to reality. Most evidence on this point comes from so-called 'agenda-setting' research, which seeks to determine the issue priorities in politically relevant media content and to compare the result with either the issue 'agenda' of politicians or that of public opinion (McCombs and Shaw, 1972; Funkhouser, 1973; Chaffee and Wilson, 1977; Becker, 1982; Iyengar and Kinder, 1987; Rogers and Dearing, 1987; Reese, 1991).

The more the media agenda corresponds with that of politicians or the public, the more we suppose (reflective) diversity to be realized. The alternative would be a concentration by the media on a small number, or a narrow range, of subjects, unrepresentative of debate in society. In that case, one supposes that the interests of some politicians and some sectors of the public are being neglected. The methods for investigated these matters are straightforward enough (see e.g. Graber, 1976a; Weaver et al., 1981) and comparisons can readily be made between the content of different channels and the balance of emphasis in public opinion or in statements or speeches made by politicians, as long as one accepts the validity of comparing statistical distributions derived from quite different original material.

Chaffee (1981) has suggested an interesting possibility for measuring the diversity of opinion, which can equally be applied to opinion expressed in media content, following the agenda-setting approach. In brief, he suggests using Shannon's measure of 'entropy' (Schramm, 1955). This measure is based on a computation of two parameters of a set of categories: the total number of categories and the degree of evenness of spread of distribution between categories. These mathematical properties might satisfy an assessment of opinion diversity: greater diversity arises when the range of opinions is wide (more categories); less diversity is apparent when one or a few viewpoints dominate the scene (inequality of categories). The same reasoning may apply to media content (of many different kinds).

Gerbner et al. (1982), following the tradition of measuring 'cultural indicators', tested the proposition that the medium of television (in the USA) exerts a powerful pressure towards homogenization and 'mainstreaming' in social and political attitudes and thus contributes to a reduction of political diversity in society. According to this view, the diversity of television content is noticeably less than that of American society. The economics of television, in particular, and the search for maximum audiences, lead to the avoidance of fundamental controversy and to attempts to balance discordant views. Gerbner et al. write 'these institutional pressures suggest the cultivation of relatively moderate or "middle of the road" presentations and orientations.' The evidence confirmed that those most exposed to television did in fact opt for political outlooks of this kind. Even so, it may simply be that mainstream television simply tries to reflect the consensual views of mainstream 'heavy television viewers'.

The main thrust of theory and evidence tends to support the view that political diversity of daily news media will be limited by the 'environmental' pressures described in Chapter 7, but especially by reliance on the same sources and shared journalistic routines and news values. Journalistic cooperation and imitation ('pack journalism', Paletz and Entman, 1981) and competition for the same audience have a similar effect. News media are not necessarily expected to reflect the 'real world' as it is, but to apply selection criteria of significance and of relevance to the current concerns of their audience. This often results in a similarity in the balance of attention given to events between different media serving the same national audience. It does not necessarily lead to a closer correspondence between media content and that 'reality'. We are reminded, in addition, that 'media pluralism' (many channels) is not the same as 'message pluralism' in the sense of internal diversity of content (Gormley, 1980). A dominant political institution often exerts a strong 'agenda-setting' pressure towards a uniform version of 'reality', despite inter-party rivalry.

Social life reflected in media content

There is much evidence which bears indirectly on the reflection of social diversity in media content. A good example of the general type of enquiry is Martell and McCall's (1964) study of the 'story ethnography' of American mass periodical fiction, as it developed between 1890 and 1955. Their principal method was to characterize the fictional 'population' of a sample of stories, in terms of social-demographic characteristics and to compare this distribution both with the equivalent distribution of the magazine readers and also with that of the American population, each at different points of historical time. Their main conclusion relevant to diversity was that the distribution of fictional population characteristics was *not very* close to the American population reality (thus it scores low on reflective diversity). On the other hand, it was much closer to the distribution of characteristics of the *readers* of fiction. For instance, the fictional population was, like the body of readers, differentially well educated, young to middle-aged, in good employment and ethnically white.

Following similar lines, attention has been paid to other aspects of social experience, with special reference to: race; work; gender; crime; and the portrayal of foreign countries. Content measures of a given universe of media content (whether in fiction or fact) are compared with 'real-world' indicators derived from official statistics of the society (Blackman and Hornstein, 1977; Luttberg, 1983). In one of the most sophisticated versions of this approach, Gerbner and Gross (1976) and Gerbner et al. (1978) have compared a set of 'TV answers' to questions about social reality with 'real-world' answers. For instance, the 'TV answer' (what content analysis indicates) to questions concerning the chances of being involved in some kind of violence is 10 per cent, while the 'real world' chance of this happening is only about 1 per cent. On such a basis, an impression of a very skewed TV picture of the world is arrived at. Some of the issues raised in the following pages are also dealt with in Chapter 20.

Race and ethnicity reflected in media content

So-called 'bad news' is often thought more newsworthy than 'good news' and ethnic minority members are differentially more likely to be identified in negative contexts, even if cast as victims (Hartman and Husband, 1974; van Dijk, 1991). Processes of stereotyping in the mass production of fiction also lead to patterns of this kind (Berelson and Salter, 1946). In general, expectations of large discrepancies between fictional (or news) worlds and statistical real worlds have been confirmed, indicating a general failure of media, by such criteria, to reflect the diversity of the world at all faithfully.

Berelson and Salter's (1946) research design is paradigmatic: norms for the representation of minorities in magazine stories were derived from population statistics and applied to the fictional content, which was treated as if it too had a 'population', made up of the individual story characters (as with Martell and McCall, 1964). For instance, the American black population was then around 10 per cent and only 70 per cent of Americans were accountable as white, native Americans. Findings showed blacks to have 2 per cent of roles in magazine content, while 90 per cent went to Americans. There was a secondary pattern of negative association for black and hispanic minorities in particular. They were differentially in lower status occupations or criminal roles.

Research in many countries since then has told a very similar story of less than proportional reflection and less than equal (or unbiased) treatment (e.g.

Hartman and Husband, 1974; Sentman, 1983; van Dijk, 1991). Symbolic neglect or disparagement are very common, although with some evidence of improvement over time and of variation between media (Poindexter and Stroman, 1981). Such findings do not necessarily indicate a failure of reflective diversity on the part of the media or a performance which could easily be improved. Some minorities are actually too small for a proportional reflection to help very much in gaining visibility or chances for access. Other minorities are actually differentially poor, marginalized, more likely to be criminalized and often the victim of real-life discrimination, even more than they are in media representation. An unflattering picture may thus reflect a current reality without necessarily indicating lack of sympathetic treatment or adverse performance in terms of diversity.

Women in the media

Similar research has reported comparisons of the representation and portrayal (images) of women in different kinds of media content (fiction, advertisement, news) with the reality of experience of women in society (examples can be found in Franzwa, 1974; Busby, 1975; Tuchman et al., 1978; Williamson, 1978; Greenberg and Atkin, 1980; Seggar and Hafen, 1981; G.J. Robinson, 1983; Durkin, 1985; Signorelli, 1985; Vestergaard and Schrøder, 1985; Gunter, 1986; Leiss et al., 1986). Research often calls for detailed specification of complex role situations (e.g. single, young, working) or of role types to which characters can be assigned.

The results have usually shown a pattern of representation which often underestimates the economic role of women, assigns them to lower status or subordinate positions in relation to men or accentuates some statistically uncommon roles (e.g. of mistress or prostitute) while neglecting other roles which are no less common in real life (Miller, 1975; Lemon, 1977; Blackwood and Smith, 1983). The relative invisibility of women in news and their tendency to appear in a limited set of contexts (sport, entertainment, welfare, family, etc.) may also be due to relative exclusion from power roles in society.

The representation of work and social status

Research into the occupational distribution of fictional characters (and persons in the news) compared with that of the actual labour force (e.g. Amheim, 1944; Head, 1954; DeFleur, 1964; Cantor, 1980; Butsch and Glennon, 1983; Cassata and Skill, 1983; Douglas et al., 1985) has also consistently reported a distorted media representation of the statistical reality. Media portrayals accentuate higher skilled, better paid and higher status occupations, both in terms of frequency and often in direction of valuation. Routine or normal working class jobs are rarely seen, except for service roles. An aspect of the distortion is a considerable reduction in the *range* of occupations represented in mass fiction.

The general explanations are not very different from those noted already in relation to gender. Neither elite nor mass culture has even been much inclined to portray the world as it really is – the former often ignoring the lower class, the latter assuming that a vicarious experience of high-status life offers 'escape' or other pleasures to the working class. Most commercial media systems make little separate media provision for working class audiences and inadequate reflective diversity matches and reinforces inadequate media structural provision.

A distorted reflection of the world?

These examples can be matched by similar enquiries, with similar results, into the pattern of crime reporting (Davis, 1952; Graber, 1980b; Sheley and Ashkins, 1980; Fedler and Jordan, 1982; O'Keefe and Reid-Nash, 1987); reporting of industrial relations (Glasgow Media Group, 1976; Kellner, 1990) and the geographical reality of the world and as reflected in the media (Galtung and Ruge, 1965; Gerbner and Marvanyi, 1977; Rosengren, 1980; Womack, 1981; Adams, 1982; Hopple, 1982; Whitney et al., 1989). In respect of crime, for example, the media consistently underplay petty, non-violent and white-collar offences and emphasize interpersonal, violent, high-status and sexual crime. In industrial relations, attention is highly skewed to a few high-profile fields of employment and avoids many labour issues. The media world map places the rich, industrialized nations disproportionately at the centre of attention and bears little relation to relative population size or land area. However, it does matter a good deal whether one takes population, or area, or some other variable (for instance, trade relations) as the criterion for assessing relative attention (Rosengren, 1980).

Most explanations of distortion in crime news reporting (especially the bias towards interpersonal crime) refer to the demands of audiences (for what is interesting, some might call 'sensational') or the requirements of objectivity (see below) which call for attention to what is more significant (therefore to more serious crime or to the kinds of crime which people fear most). It is also clear that the processes by which crime events come to the attention of the media (from the police or justice system mainly) militate against reflection of statistical 'reality' (Chibnall, 1977; Fishman, 1980). The explanations for other distortions of reality are not very different. Coverage is determined by audience interests, widely shared 'news values', technology and organization of news gathering, the differential power of certain news sources. In international news, it is geographical and cultural distance and the reigning pattern of international relations and balance of power which does much to shape news flow.

Reflective diversity and the media audience

In contrast to the wide interest shown in matters of diversity of structure and content, only peripheral attention has been paid to media audiences, despite the wealth of data available as a by-product of routine audience and reader research, should answers be sought. The two most salient questions arising from diversity theory concern the general matter of heterogeneity or homo-geneity of audiences for media channels or types of content; and the relation-ship between audience composition and message content. For instance, in relation to politics, a given audience can share much the same views or be quite diverse in political attachment. An audience can also vary in the extent to which it is in tune with the political direction of a channel or its content. Essentially, both are matters of audience 'selective exposure', which is readily open to investigation, although interpretation of the results may call for detailed knowledge of the context of 'exposure' (Donsbach, 1991).

In general, a situation of high 'internal' audience diversity will be one where a representative range of views reaches an audience which is a cross-section of the public as a whole and where there is little selectivity. By contrast, the more that each political 'voice' reaches its own chosen followers, the more we can speak of 'external' diversity. The first condition did hold, for example, during the British General Election of 1959 in respect of television party broadcasts. According to Trenaman and McQuail (1961: 88), Conservative viewers saw only marginally more Conservative than Labour programmes and vice versa. For instance, the average Labour broadcast drew about 53 per cent of its audience from its political opponents. This was largely the result of an artificial situation in which all party broadcasts were transmitted on two national channels simultaneously at peak viewing times.

An alternative situation (of audience selectivity and external diversity) was demonstrated by research on the Dutch newspaper public in the 1970s, showing most newspapers to have regular readerships disproportionately skewed in political loyalty to their chosen party. At the extreme, for instance, the leading Christian Democrat paper (*Trouw*) drew 82 per cent of its readers from Christian Democrat voters (only 32 per cent of the electorate), while a Labour-leaning paper (*Volkskrant*) had an 85 per cent Labour Party readership (only 38 per cent of the electorate).

In political communication, it can make a difference whether a channel reaches a politically diverse or a homogeneous target – an audience of potential converts or an audience of the converted (Blumler and McQuail, 1968). As far as media performance criteria are concerned, it is a matter for value judgement whether there is greater virtue in heterogeneity or in homogeneity. If external diversity is valued in politics (the tradition of an active, partisan press and a highly contested political arena) then the first is preferable – with each political voice speaking to its own followers. There is a trend both towards more consensual politics and towards general media which are not sharply differentiated by political allegiance, but more according to various principles of media market segmentation.

If the chosen ideal for a society is multiculturalism (as in Canada), there can be virtue in either pattern. A clearly differentiated media audience composition in terms of class, gender, religion, language or ethnic group may be considered as supportive of separate identity for the groups concerned. The alternative pattern of largely undifferentiated audiences, may, however, contribute better to dialogue and mutual understanding between the different groups and cultures. Methods for comparing the content of media with the social characteristics of audiences have already been referred to (e.g. Martell and McCall, 1964) and are not especially demanding. Where the results of routine media research are available, it is usually feasible to assess the degree of audience diversity (in terms of homogeneity or heterogeneity) on matters other than politics.

Reflections on reflection

Most of the research cited has been guided by an expectation of finding much 'distortion' and only limited diversity of structure, content or audience. Both expectations have generally been met. Nearly every group or area of human activity can be shown to be either incorrectly represented statistically or misrepresented, according to some objective indicator. Few researchers have tried to qualify this blanket conclusion or to defend the performance of the media, even though, on some topics, it is likely that the media perform quite well in faithfully reflecting what is going on in the world; for instance, in relation to national politics, sport, big business, popular entertainment, theatre and established arts and in respect of many leisure interests.

Any evaluative conclusion about diversity which can be drawn from the evidence depends on several considerations. The principle of reflective diversity does indeed call for literally *proportional representation*, but it would be unreasonable to expect this on all matters in all media. The media, with limited space and time, are obliged to select on grounds of relevance and significance for the intended audience and this is bound to reduce proportionality. The social world (real or self-perceived) of the intended audience might well provide a more relevant standard of comparison than the statistical average of the whole society.

Schulz (1988) has criticized the view that media fail to reflect the 'statistical' reality of the world. He argues that this is based on an antiquated, 'mechanistic' view of the relationship between media and society, akin to the discredited 'hypodermic needle' model of media effects. It fails to recognize that media actively participate in society and have to construct their own 'media reality', for their own purposes and those of their clients and their audiences. It would be unrealistic and unreasonable to expect a faithful reproduction of some 'pure reality'. He argues for a concept of objectivity which recognizes the autonomy of media accounts and the validity of alternative definitions of reality. The same remarks apply to the question of diversity.

The design typical of research into the reflection of reality has several problematic features. Aside from a need to choose an appropriate universe of content for analysis, account has often to be taken of the various unwritten 'rules' and conventions of different formats. The same approach to measurement is unlikely to be valid across genre boundaries, or even within the same genre. A consideration in choosing content for study will also be that of *time*. A cross-section at a moment of time (for instance, the news of a day or a week) will yield a different result from a sample of the same size taken over a year, and will need to be judged by different standards. Some attention may also have to be given to *cumulative* diversity. Thus, over time, the *range* of attention is likely to widen (more and different events in the news, for instance). This distinction is similar to that between 'horizontal' and 'vertical' measures of diversity described above.

The more that fiction approaches art and the more that art departs from the model of statistical reality, in seeking to express truth about human experience, the more inadequate are statistical measures as an index of adequate representation. Different media genres and formats have their own codes and conventions, according to which they can be interpreted by their audiences. Folk tales and science fiction can tell truth just as well as naturalistic soap operas. Structural and discourse analysis offer alternatives to content analysis in uncovering hidden layers of meaning, although there is little reason to suppose that methods of this kind will make much difference to the general conclusions noted about 'failures' of reflection. They might add an extra dimension to the analysis and help to avoid some of the pitfalls of mechanistic and context-free interpretation.

On not being too literal

Statistics are virtually meaningless to most people – thus to most of the audience, on whose behalf the critique of non-diversity is ostensibly launched. In practice, a statistically correct picture in no more likely to be recognized or accepted as true by its audience than is a highly skewed version. Content as sent is never the same as content received. Meanings will be added and changed, gaps and contexts filled in. There is evidence that audiences do not accept what they see as a single literal truth nor do different audience members experience the same 'reality' as it is represented in the media (Liebes and Katz, 1986; Dahlgren, 1988; Jensen, 1991). Between the 'picture of reality' offered and the 'actual reality', there is usually a third variable of 'perceived reality' which has some independence from the other two because it is self-constructed. This could also be a third dimension for diversity analysis.

13
MEDIA ACCESS AND AUDIENCE CHOICE

Diversity as access: questions of structure

The central performance question can be summarized as 'Who receives access to which channels, in what degree and on what terms?' The *who* referred to is the *source*, in the sense of specific actors, institutions, interests or groups (thus 'advocates' as defined in Chapter 11, p.156). The answer depends, first of all, on the number of independent media channels of different kinds which are available in relation to the population in a media system. In general, the more such channels, the more access opportunities for more and more different sources. Account can be taken, nationally, regionally and locally, of the number of television and radio channels, the hours of broadcasting, the number of newspaper titles, the number of periodicals, the number of books published annually, etc.

Such figures need to be backed up, where possible, by more detailed enquiry into the *quality* of access offered. For instance, the more that different channels are under the same ownership or editorial control (thus less independent), the lower the access potential. We can also suppose there to be less access opportunity in broadcast channels which are largely taken up by repeats, networked overlaps or foreign imports, or in newspapers where there is much syndication or much advertising. More access, on the other hand, is provided in channels which innovate or which offer specific 'access' slots in the form of space for letters or 'forum' pages and for outside contributors generally. It seems, from limited evidence, that 'letters to the editor' can serve quite varied purposes for media and for the audience and that access/selection policies vary from one medium to another (Tunstall, 1977b; Renfro, 1979).

Much depends on the *terms* under which access is given and on the degree of autonomy allotted to system 'outsiders'. A relevant aspect of media structure is the degree to which there exists an 'underground' or 'alternative' press of one kind or another (Downing, 1984). In the case of media under public control (broadcasting in Europe), access is often guaranteed to some groups for their own purposes and different interests are represented in boards of management or advisory councils. In some countries (e.g. France, Italy, Belgium, Germany), broadcasting has, at times, been more or less openly politicized so as to allocate posts proportionately to different political parties, leading to the political colouring of different television channels. In countries where there has been a tradition of a party press (as in Sweden, Denmark, Holland), access opportunities may be built into the structure of the media. The degree of (external) political diversity of a press system, in such cases, is open to observation.

Diversity of access in media content

Political access and inter-channel difference

In order to go further with the assessment of access, attention has to be given to organization *conduct* and to media content, if we are to have a fuller answer to the question posed above. In respect of politics, content analysis can help to establish the sources and the political direction of mass media, especially in the case of news. The more general question of the real *degree of political difference* between media channels can also be approached, using some of the methods and content indicators already discussed in relation to media freedom and diversity (see Chapters 9 and 11). In the United States, where there is often little real inter-newspaper competition on grounds of politics (according to Entman, 1985, there is no 'opposition' press in the USA), the matter has mainly been investigated, either by studying patterns of press editorial endorsements of candidates (e.g. McCombs, 1967; Robinson, 1974; Fedler et al., 1982), or by making comparisons between the three main network television news systems (e.g. Efron, 1971; Hofstetter, 1976; Patterson and McClure, 1976; Graber, 1980a).

Much evidence about the duplication (and thus the lack of diversity) of US network news has accumulated. The CBS network, for instance, was long suspected of being consistently more 'liberal' than other channels (Efron, 1971; Lefever, 1976), although the evidence was always thin (Stevenson and Shaw, 1973). Access for administration or opposition views in the United States was investigated by Foote (1989), who recorded the number of times the opposition response to presidential speeches and addresses was reported on the three networks. Over a 20-year period, opposition replies to all 15 presidential State of the Union messages were covered by all three TV networks, but the rate of coverage for opposition replies to other forms of presidential access was much lower. The findings showed no consistent inter-network difference, but a strong general difference between the amount of opposition access under Carter (less) and under Reagan (more).

In US presidential election campaigns, successive enquiries have reported a high, almost uncanny, similarity in the share of time, of attention and of types of news given to the contenders by the three main networks (Fowler and Showalte, 1974; Foote and Steele, 1986). Even the distribution of story *types* varied *little* (Hofstetter, 1976: 37). Much the same applies to the coverage of party political topics by the British national broadcast news services and for much the same reasons. Both national broadcasting systems are subject to very close scrutiny by politicians and neither has had much freedom to editorialize. Even in the USA, the 'balance' expectation from television news has been enforceable through the courts, although direct political pressures probably have more effect. Often the result of external pressure is to confine the range of political diversity to the main established parties. For instance, Whitney et al. (1989) found, from a study of TV news, that only *two* out of 4886 party political sources were other than Democrat or Republican.

Politically relevant news, outside of election contexts, seems to have followed a similar pattern of inter-channel homogeneity, lending support to the view that multiplication of channels does not do a great deal for the multiplication of access opportunities (or for extending the range of access). For instance, Pride and Richards (1974) examined the 'student movement' on US television news between September 1968 and April 1970 and found no differences between networks in treatment of 'symbols relating to authority'. A study by Pride and Wamsley (1972) found only minor inter-network differences in coverage of the Laos incursion, when a detailed examination was made of cut-to-cut segments of news coverage. Every comparison between the three US networks finds evidence of *some* differences (Frank, 1973; Pride and Clarke, 1973), but there is little to show that the networks have ever offered significantly different versions of the political scene. Comstock and Cobbey (1976) as well as Dye and Ziegler (1982) and Altheide (1982) provide support for this conclusion. Nimmo and Combs (1985) find that such differences as are to be found between networks are matters of *style* rather than of substance.

Duplication of news content

Comparisons between the main US network news services show much actual duplication of items and, inevitably, of sources. For instance, Lemert (1974) found there to be an average *duplication rate* of news stories, between the three networks, of 70 per cent. Where this occurs, there is also a high degree of duplication of sources from one channel to another. Newspapers are more likely to offer more alternative versions of events and to employ more sources, partly because of political choice and other bases of differentiation (e.g. region, social class, etc.), partly because they simply have more space in which to be different.

Evidence concerning British television news, under conditions of competing services, has come to similar conclusions (Glasgow Media Group, 1976; Morrison and Tumber, 1988). While the press should offer more scope for diversity in selection, McQuail (1977) also showed a high degree of duplication of stories and of component items of stories in a sample of national newspapers. The same rather narrow range of actors and spokespersons appeared in competing newspapers. Duplication was highest (and thus diversity lowest) on major political and economic news stories, thus where more significance for the society might be presumed to exist. Most studies of source access in news (see also Chapter 17) report a 'bias' to higher ranks in organizations, to official rather than unofficial sources, to men rather than women and to managers rather than workers (Sigal, 1973).

In interpreting such results, account should be taken of contextual factors. For instance, the more the channels concerned are competing for the same 'market' of people or region at the same time, the more we should expect duplication of content and sources. Competitive imitation will play some part in this (and what Paletz and Entman (1981) have called 'pack journalism'), as well as considerations of relevance to the target audience (Hetherington, 1985). Even so, one might reasonably expect to find differences in sources (both in the sense of accessed voices and news sources) in kinds of treatment (evaluative direction and style) and in news priorities.

Balance and direction of access

The assessment of evaluative *direction* of media access is complex and often contested (see also Chapters 14 and 17). In politics it usually calls for deployment of a political dimension of the kind already noted (from left to right, or liberal to conservative). Political ideas and sources which are referred to in the media can usually be characterized in such terms (at least by political experts). Sometimes, the associations in content references give clues to direction and intensity. A party or politician is often associated in factual news reports with conditions, persons or events which are either 'positively' or 'negatively' loaded, according to some conventional standard of judgement (corruption, extremism, crime, policy failure are bad, for instance, while prosperity and policy success are good) (see e.g. Hofstetter, 1976).

Beyond positive or negative associations of this kind, reports of third-party praise or criticism can also indicate direction. Criticisms of media on grounds of attributed left or right bias are notoriously unreliable and often politically motivated. Systematic assessment can sometimes deliver quite convincing evidence, where sources, spokespersons, guest speakers or 'experts' can be objectively identified according to political leaning, gender or ethnic identity (e.g. Lichter and Rothman, 1986; Kellner, 1990). Letters published in newspapers can also be analysed in similar ways for similar purposes (Hill, 1981). Without taking account of the *context* and quality of reference, the *amount* of attention to sources may not tell the whole story.

Hegemonic tendencies in media content

Questions about the access for socially marginal voices call for similar kinds of enquiry. The issue is close to another matter – the degree of homogeneity (or 'hegemonic' tendency) of media content (Rachlin, 1988). There is a good deal of evidence that news (in particular) not only tends to focus on a narrow set of problems, especially as defined by governments or other 'elite' or 'official' sources (Paletz and Entman, 1981), but that preferential access is given to the voice of institutional authority. The relative invisibility in media content of lower status or 'unknown' persons and relatively powerless social groups has often been noted. It also seems that the more politically 'extremist' or socially deviant a minority group is, the more likely any access gained is to be on terms set by the 'establishment' and often in a negative context (Paletz and Entman, 1981; Golding and Middleton, 1982; Shoemaker, 1984).

Access and the audience

Two main questions call for attention: the degree to which a given audience, as defined by significant differences such as class, ethnicity, gender, political allegiance or religion, does actually have alternative channels available to it; and the degree to which senders, correspondingly, have effective access to their chosen audience. In practice, these are alternative ways of formulating questions which have already been posed about diversity: this time from the point of view of the would-be receiver, rather than that of the sender, the media system, or of the society. Genuine access for the audience to alternative channels and messages depends not only on the existence of channels, but on their effective distribution, availability and affordability.

Diversity as variety and choice for the audience

According to the 'market/choice' model described earlier (Chapter 11), diversity is essentially a matter of degree of real choice available to the individual 'consumer' of media. This version of the concept is quite central to the problems surrounding media monopoly and it is increasingly relevant to the current expansion in the number of television channels. The principle of freedom of communication presupposes an abundance of channels and choices as desirable conditions of a free and democratic society. Proponents of free market arrangements usually claim that the market, left to itself, will deliver such benefits (Peacock, 1986; Veljanovski, 1989). Critics reply that channel abundance is no guarantee against concentration of ownership or against homogeneity of content, which can result from competition for the same mass audience. The key question for diversity research is whether an increase in channels does actually mean more choice for the individual audience member. This is less easy to answer than it seems.

It is somewhat artificial to maintain the distinction between structure, content and audience (see Figure 11.2) which has been followed until now, although there are obviously separate questions to be asked about degree of choice of channels and choice of content offered by channels. We cannot assume that a larger number of newspaper titles or television channels will offer more variety of content than a system with limited channels (the indications of news duplication mentioned above support this). This is a reason for treating jointly questions of structure and of content, although we need to deal separately with press and broadcasting because of the different kinds of choice offered.

Assessing reader choice

The case of the daily newspaper seems relatively simple to deal with, although it quickly becomes complicated. A potential consumer (reader) is usually located in one place (nation, city or region) with a given set of newspapers at his or her disposal. Diversity (as choice) requires there to be two or more titles to choose from which differ from each other according to some feature which is relevant to the potential reader's interests. The first aspect of this requirement can usually be tested empirically by reference to the number of national, regional or city newspapers. A well-served location (newspaper market), such as a major metropolitan centre, will offer daily city and national titles, together with some other city and regional newspapers. This provides one obvious measure of consumer choice, which can be taken for each 'media market' within a total national market.

The reality of choice offered by different titles cannot be as easily 'read off' from available media market data, although clear differentiation by region and socioeconomic targeting (for advertising as well as editorial purposes) may provide a basis for assessment. Beyond that, differences can usually only be established by some form of content analysis, according to a large number of potentially relevant indicators. Several of these have already been discussed, especially those relating to political or social-cultural differences.

There remains another set of factors which concern the *character* of the newspaper as a product and which are relevant to the appeal to different 'taste-cultures' or market segments based on different life-styles. These refer to matters of presentation, design and style as well as to editorial content. One general dimension is likely to be that of variation in the degree of 'human interest' (Curran et al., 1980) or of 'sensationalism', in its several meanings (see Chapter 15). Crudely, the difference between 'tabloid' (popular, 'boulevard') and 'broadsheet' ('quality') formats may be correlated with these distinctions.

The assessment of daily newspaper diversity is made easier by the limited number of titles usually available in any one place and by the possibility of treating the typical content of each title (channel) as a unity, since the typical reader usually only takes one newspaper at a time. Other media situations are more complex. There may, for instance, be too many (and changeable) magazines, in many different categories, for the same kind of research into content differences to be practicable. In countries with developed media systems, there are normally many hundreds of different periodicals readily available nationally. The diversity of this supply may only be open to rather crude assessment in terms of the distribution across different content categories.

Viewer and listener choice

The task of assessing the choice offered by radio and television channels varies according to the extent of the system and the degree of regional decentralization. The situation of choice for the 'consumer' of broadcasting is also different from that which faces the newspaper reader. At any time, a viewer or listener can usually choose among several channel options ('horizontal diversity' in a time slot), not being confined to the single channel, as with a particular newspaper which has been bought on a certain day.

On the other hand, a newspaper also offers many options at one moment (another version of 'horizontal' diversity), if one treats different articles, news stories or sections as the equivalent of 'programmes' on radio or television. From this point of view, the universe of choice is likely to be much larger with print media, the number of such items in an average newspaper being larger than the number of programmes normally available from a TV or radio receiver. These complications require operational decision-making in any diversity research design. Such decisions will also affect how one calculates the degree of diversity, the kind of result that will be reached from any enquiry and how this should be reported.

Aside from some additional practical obstacles to research which arise from the more fleeting character of television and radio (compared to print), there are conceptual problems about what to regard as *choice*. Are all separately identified programmes equally different and, if not, how different do they have to be for it to count? Do we, for instance, treat a choice of three separate news programmes as offering the same or less choice as three different kinds of programme (e.g. news, a quiz, a serial)? Given the evidence cited above of news replication, three different soap operas might be regarded as offering as much or more choice as three concurrent news bulletins, but this would have to depend on the perspective of the consumer.

Measuring diversity, whether horizontally or vertically, depends on the degree to which we can make valid and reliable distinctions between content categories. Greenberg and Barnett (1971: 90) argue that programmes can be aggregated into categories reflecting the importance placed on them by the audience, and diversity can be defined as differences in programme type provided 'we can specify program types within which we can reasonably believe that variations of quality, advertising, timing, author, · performer, suppliers and degree of competition do not contribute to diversity.' This is a large assumption which would always be difficult to demonstrate.

These conundrums are not easy to solve, except by *ad hoc* operational decisions, but we should bear in mind the frequent warnings about confusing diversity with simple *variety* or with the existence of competition. According to Glasser (1984), variety only offers intra-format diversity – variants of the same cultural product, not genuine cultural diversity of the kind which relates the diversity of what is on offer to some external standard of differentiation in the community or society, as discussed in the preceding sections. As LeDuc (1982) also comments in respect of increased over-air channel choice: 'it resembles the degree of diversity in dining opportunities experienced when a McDonalds restaurant begins business in town already served by a Burger King' (see Sparkes, 1983; Hardenbergh, 1986).

Vertical versus horizontal diversity   The literature on these and related problems is still very thin and mostly relating to the American situation, where consumer choice is often deployed as the main diversity standard in public policy as well as in market logic. Two main aspects of measuring diversity of media consumer choice have been mentioned already (Chapter 11): that of 'vertical diversity' – the number of options offered by a single channel (or a set of channels) over a period of time; and 'horizontal diversity' – which deals with options available to the viewer or listener at any one point in time (Litman, 1979). For instance, if all the available channels offer the same type of programme (e.g. news) in the same time-slot, there may be no real choice (depending on the condition just noted), however varied over time the total offer might be (vertical diversity).

The earliest work in the field appears to be that of Steiner (1952) and, although criticized by Owen (1977), it offers a starting point, which most students of television programme variety have followed. The main Steiner assumptions are:

- There exist meaningful categories called 'programme types' or 'formats'.
- Every broadcast can be assigned to one or other of these types.
- All broadcasts belonging to a given type are perfect substitutes; that is, no listener is made better off by having a choice of two programmes belonging to a given type than he is with only one programme of that type.
- The number of competing broadcasters is small.
- The distribution of tastes is 'skewed' so that there is a large number of consumers who prefer some particular programme type and smaller 'minority taste' groups preferring other types.
- Listeners have no second choice programmes; if their preferred programme type is not available they will not listen at all.
- All programmes have identical production casts and all listeners are worth equal amounts of advertising time.

Steiner's analysis, based on these assumptions, was meant to demonstrate that competition would lead to wasteful duplication of programmes of the same type and neglect of minorities and that improvements could be expected from monopoly or from tight regulative control of the system. While the assumptions listed might not all be accepted now (or then) (especially the third and fourth), it is essential to make some assumptions of this kind in order to carry out research into the diversity of media offer, without having recourse to extremely detailed audience research.

In the United States, the (pre-cable) network system posed a policy problem about the degree of 'real choice' in the sense under discussion. The system also offered a neat set of investigative conditions, which are no longer there. Dominick and Pearce (1976) examined *vertical diversity* of media content for purposes of comparing networks and charting changes over time. They defined diversity as 'an index of the extent to which a few categories dominate prime-time'. They derived their index by assigning prime-time programmes to one of 14 categories and carrying out the following procedure: 'summing the percentage in the top three categories per season and subtracting from 100'. The index could range from zero (all content accountable by three or fewer categories) to 79 (content is equally divided over 14 categories). A low score indicated a restricted range of choice to the audience.

They also measured *homogeneity*, to assess how much the content of one network resembled the content of the other two: 'Mathematically it [the index of homogeneity] is derived by subtracting each network percentage of time per category from the other two and summing the absolute differences. It can range from zero (schedules exactly the same) to 300 (maximum differentiation).' More recently, Wakshlag and Adams (1985) have used an extended category system to show that there has been a sharp decline in variety of prime-time programming between 1950 and 1982.

Litman (1979) applied a different measure of vertical (through time) diversity of prime-time network TV, allocated to nine categories. The method of calculation is not described, but a high coefficient is produced by a greater concentration of programming into a few categories and vice versa. High concentration in this measure is associated both with few programme types and inequality in their sizes. Basically, the index is a measure of *dispersion* of a distribution and is thus appropriate where the relevant standard is one of *equality* (of availability of types of content).

Horizontal diversity was calculated by Litman as follows: for each half-hour of prime-time network programming, the number of differing programme types was counted. This aggregate number was then divided by the number of prime-time half-hours to determine the average number of programme types per prime-time half-hour. This index can range from 1 (perfect imitation) to 3 (perfect diversity). The index was used to show that viewer choice had increased in the USA between 1973 and 1979: 'This increase in diversity means that viewers have a greater menu of TV programs and can more frequently pick their favorite program type rather than settle for second place choices.'

Methodological limitations   These and similar methods can be applied to 'measure' diversity of offer in the current media market place. There are obvious limitations and weaknesses. Aside from major doubts about the extent to which advertiser-supported broadcasting represents a true consumer market (Glasser, 1984), the methods for calculating diversity are based on assumptions which are likely to satisfy neither economists nor humanists (especially, for both, the assumption that all programmes of a given type are perfect substitutes for each other; that is, that the consumer cannot benefit from having a choice of two programmes of the same type or format).

The research methods described are bound to be constrained by the choice of category system. While most attempts to measure choice are based on conventional, industry-derived, categories, there is no overwhelming logic behind the systems. Possibilities and problems in the end often turn on being able to deploy category systems which are both reliable and valid (especially with meaning to the very varied body of 'consumers'). The approaches described can be adapted to apply to numerous media situations. For instance, trends in diversity in popular music have been measured by Peterson and Berger (1975) and by Burnett (1990), using a 'content-free' method, based on the music charts. The method took as a measure of diversity the absolute number of different hits which appeared in the weekly US charts over a period of years. The more *different* number one hits in a year (or in the top 10 or top 100), the more diversity, in the sense of choices available to the average popular music consumer. The method appears to show some systematic variations over long periods which are of interest and open to interpretation.

Underlying the problems referred to is the more general one of assigning values to the choices available. Such measures have to assume that equal value attaches to items within a category (see Greenberg and Barnett, 1971; Levin, 1971; Owen, 1977, 1978). Otherwise differential values, besides format category, have to be assigned. If the latter, we can assign virtually any value we wish. Some of the more obvious options are to weight the choices presented (thus the range of diversity) according to: cost of production; average audience appeal; star performers; cultural merit assigned in some way (see Chapter 21); originality, etc.

It is difficult to deal with programmes which are repeated, since these do not offer the same real choice at successive showings. The more we apply additional criteria in order to weight choice, the more we move away from market choice and towards a situation where diversity has to be defined in terms of some external value or attribute derived from the culture or the supposed needs of the audience.

Audience diversity

Under the heading of 'diversity as choice', several things remain to be said about the audience. In general, we may suppose, according to the theory discussed in Chapter 11, that diversity is best served where audiences are differentiated in composition and actively exercising choice. The matter of audience distinctiveness (homogeneity or heterogeneity) in its composition has already been discussed with reference to reflection and access. What probably matters most is the degree to which there are *distinctive* audiences (or potential media consumer markets) for different kinds of channel or categories of media content (products). There is a continual search by commercial media for new consumer markets for new products and a perennial interest in knowing what the basis might be for differences in demand.

In media research, this interest has been pursued by investigating media 'product images' – how media or content are thought to be perceived by audiences (Ryan and Peterson, 1982) – and by way of audience preferences. The question of diversity has generally been dealt with either in terms of different categories of media supply or in terms of audience preferences and choices. On this second point, research has sought to establish the range of different motives for choice (e.g. for amusement, information, social contact, excitement, involvement, etc.) or, more generally, the bases for (and degree of) *selectivity* which is actually exhibited in media choice behaviour (Rosengren et al., 1985). The more evidence we find of audience selectivity according to some consistent principle, the more we can consider the media public as a whole to show signs of diversity and heterogeneity.

According to extensive research reported by Barwise and Ehrenberg (1988), using indicators such as the extent to which series are followed over time and to which certain programme types are chosen above others, the television audience is very unselective. 'Viewing television' emerges as a generalized form of behaviour, lacking in meaningful structure in terms of content. The different character of print media (especially the fact of individual use, limitations on 'channel-switching' and greater effort required for reading) gives rise to a more differentiated pattern of newspaper and magazine use. Similar conclusions apply to the 'one-off', single-item mass media of phonogram, video, book and film, where there is more evidence of distinctive taste patterns related to format and content differences. It seems that audience diversity is in part an artefact of medium type and social conditions of use.

No end in sight

The concept of diversity is so general and can have so many different formulations and expressions that any conclusion has to be open-ended. However, a number of the issues raised in this chapter are back on the agenda, under other guises, in the chapters which follow.

PART VI
OBJECTIVITY

14
CONCEPTS OF OBJECTIVITY

The trouble with the notion

Objectivity has an ambiguous standing among close observers of news media, for reasons which are not always clear or consistent. For most journalists, the practice of objective reporting – rendering true accounts of events – lies at the heart of their task. It is a professional ideal, in the sense of a goal which cannot be fully attained, requiring the deployment of skill, effort and resources not just by individuals, but by the whole news organization. It is also a very practical guide and instrument in the collection, presentation and even (for the audience) the reception of information. It seems that objectivity is also valued by the news audience for its practical benefits, since it is the key to trustworthiness and reliability and it plays an important part in assessments of performance by the media public (Comstock, 1988; Bogart, 1989).

In the pre-television era, objectivity was often considered an old-fashioned virtue which offered a standard against which the sensationalism and the political bias of popular mass newspapers could be judged: witness its high standing for the American Commission on Freedom of the Press (Hutchins, 1949) and for the British Royal Commission on the Press (RCP, 1949). Since television became established as a main news source, objectivity has become a routine norm of good practice rather than a rare virtue, largely because of the high and privileged status which national television channels have acquired in many countries (Kumar, 1975; Stephens, 1986).

It may therefore seem surprising that there has been so much controversy about the concept and its usage (Hackett, 1984; Entman, 1989; Lichtenberg, 1991). This is less surprising if one considers the obstacles in the way of attaining objectivity in any absolute sense and the alternatives to objectivity which are available and sometimes preferable. Absence of objectivity does not only have to mean inaccuracy and tendentiousness. Research into the views of journalists about their own role shows, for instance, that it may conflict with two other goals – that of playing some active or advocative part in society and that of providing some interpretation of what is going on (Janowitz, 1975; Johnstone et al., 1976; Kocher, 1986).

In part, it is the routinization of the objectivity norm which has attracted the fire of critics, who found the new pretence (as they saw it) of offering undiluted truth about the world more misleading than the old kind of diverse partisanship and propaganda. In their view, it could only provide support for the status quo. Other critics have simply refused to accept that objectivity was really being observed and accused the self-proclaimed objective broadcasters of peddling propaganda, either for the left or for the right, under the guise of neutrality. Glasser (1984), for instance, argued that objectivity is an ideology and itself a form of *bias*: against the watch-dog role of the press; against independent thinking; against genuine responsibility (which would involve taking responsibility for the consequences of reporting). This is a strong claim, but it does at least underline the potential inconsistency between objectivity and independence and diversity.

News research has persistently cast doubt on the possibility of real 'neutrality' in reporting (Gerbner, 1964; Cohen and Young, 1973; Epstein, 1973; Tuchman, 1978; Fishman, 1980). Even supposedly objective news of the highest professional calibre has not escaped attack, when fundamental differences of interests and values are involved. Such situations are usually characterized by a triangular relationship among media, researcher/critic and an 'interested' third party, in which the media claim to be objective, the third party claims it is maligned and the researcher adjudicates on the basis of systematic empirical evidence of performance. In some cases, however, researchers have adopted positions for or against the third-party claim and this has caused 'objectivity' research itself to become controversial and to attract accusations of bias (e.g. Efron, 1971; Anderson and Sharrock, 1980; Harrison, 1985).

The meaning of news objectivity for news people

Setting such problems aside for the moment, along with the naive notion of unambiguous truth, we can piece together a provisional version of objectivity, as a quality of reporting practice, or of news itself, as seen from the perspective of newspeople. Representative of what journalists themselves say about objectivity are the results of an enquiry reported by Boyer (1981), which produced a set of statements about the meaning of objectivity, reducible to six main elements:

- balance and even-handedness in presenting different sides of an issue;
- accuracy and realism of reporting;
- presentation of all main relevant points;
- separation of facts from opinion, but treating opinion as relevant;

- minimizing the influence of the writer's own attitude, opinion or involvement;
- avoiding slant, rancour or devious purpose.

Under one form or another and with varying priorities, these elements recur in most discussions of journalistic objectivity. In essence, it is not so different from objectivity in other contexts such as the law, the human and natural sciences or even military intelligence, where objectivity has similar practical advantages (Phillips, 1977). Roshco (1975) mentions the following benefits of objectivity for journalism and the organization of news. It offers easily employed guidelines for selection and leaves responsibility for content to sources, freeing reporters from the need to acquire expert knowledge. The emphasis on technique rather than substance protects reporters from charges of bias. It also allows interchangeability of reporters for many different kinds of news.

However, each sphere of information work differs in the procedures for attaining objectivity and in the criteria by which performance should be assessed. Some familiar conditions of news reporting set limits to the degree of objectivity which can realistically be expected. There is an enormous volume of potentially relevant information (requiring selection more than collection) which has to be processed under pressure of time. Sources may not readily supply information and there is often intense competition with other journalists for the same information. Information has also to be selected and presented to please consumers and to attract attention, thus emphasizing form more than content. The enterprise takes place in public and under the gaze of interested parties, who may hold the media responsible for consequences of publication.

Such conditions make it difficult for objective news to represent either complete precision (as in science) or unshakeable testimony (as in law). The demands are often divergent (e.g. to be both factual and interesting), but they do not cancel each other out. Objectivity is only one of several attributes of the news product and it may be inconsistent with other qualities (e.g. appeal to the senses, topicality, simplicity, controversiality, etc.), quite apart from evaluative dimensions.

News is typically presented so as to give a summary of the most important points at the start (the 'inverted pyramid' from headline to small print), just as the news medium as a whole is organized to give a clear indication of priorities (by way of relative item prominence, page sequence and time order, headline size, etc.). An objective report is one which is highly factual, in the sense of offering as much detailed and checkable, information as possible. A clear division (of location and definition) is usually observed between fact on the one hand and opinion or interpretation on the other. Wherever possible, reliable sources for information are cited. News has to be *timely,* with the most recent version of effects taking precedence over earlier accounts. It is neutral in tone and form of presentation. It seeks to take up an independent and disinterested position in matters of conflict. Objective news-giving presupposes an absence of personal bias (especially where unacknowledged), self-interest, ulterior motive or service to an advertiser or third party.

Sources of the objectivity norm

Objective news, taking this typical form, owes its origin and a degree of esteem to a disparate set of circumstances (see, e.g., Roshco, 1975; Schudson, 1978, 1982; Schiller, 1979, 1981). Roshco's observation that the (American) press began in two forms – one a reprinting of information from other sources, the other partisan opinion – has a wide application and the rise of modern news media can be viewed as a fusion between these two forms within an independent institution. The objectivity 'problem' is still mainly accounted for by the tension between the two elements. An additional factor at work in the historical development of modern news was the rise of a journalistic *profession*, which has entailed a claim to autonomy, a promise of some ethics of performance and of certain standards of service. It has also been accompanied by training, in which objective practice has become a skill to be learned as well as a virtue to be followed.

Technology has also made its contribution to the rise of the modern form of news objectivity. The invention of the electric telegraph placed a premium on conciseness, clarity and accuracy, as did the subsequent use of the telephone (Shaw, 1961; Carey, 1969). The coming of televised news encouraged the use of film as a different form of objective eye-witness account, to which commentary can be added and which can thus be 'traded' outside its original production context. The tendency of computer-mediated transmission has also been in the direction of precision and factuality. In general, the effect of technology on journalism has been to strengthen its definition as, first of all, a *technique* and, secondly, a particular *format* (and logic), with its own unwritten rules.

More by historical chance than necessity, the development of radio and television in monopolistic or regulated forms has also worked to favour objectivity in the sense described. Neutrality and balance as news conventions, under conditions of restricted access, allow broadcast media more freedom to operate, without upsetting established interests or giving undue leverage to governments. The outcome has been popular both with audiences and with broadcast news journalists themselves. In general, objectivity as a mode of reporting has helped to protect journalists in conditions of political pressure or even danger and has enabled reporting to continue in circumstances of war or conflict. The role of messenger is more secure where his or her neutral status is recognized.

Finally, there are commercial reasons for the rise of objectivity (Schiller, 1981). The more that news information is regarded as a tradeable commodity, the more advantageous it is to offer a 'product' with the widest appeal, causing least offence to potential news distributors, advertising clients or consumers. This has worked in favour of objectivity as outlined and is not in evidence in the world of international news agencies, which have always dealt in a product which seems to be free from local or partisan bias, having some universal, informative, properties.

The features of the objective news product and practice imply an unwritten 'contract' with the presumed beneficiary or consumer of news — the reader, listener, viewer. This 'contract' leads to an expectation that news can be believed, trusted, taken at face value, readily understood, without the need to 'read between the lines'. It is these features of the objective news product, seen in the light of these widely held expectations, which provide the main guidelines for evaluating the quality of media performance in respect of news and information. They offer criteria for distinguishing a (desirable) form of objective news from other (undesirable or out of place) forms of information or knowledge, especially: fiction; propaganda; gossip; ideology. They also distinguish objectivity in general from 'bias'.

Objections to objectivity

The situation is complicated for the researcher (as well as for the normative theorist) by some fundamental objections to the very idea of objectivity which have been levelled by critical theorists (and are sometimes shared by journalists, to judge from Boyer, 1981). The objections fall into two categories: first, that objectivity is impossible and it makes little sense, in consequence, to measure it; secondly, that it is undesirable and should not be treated as a positive performance norm. As Lichtenberg has pointed out, it makes little sense to hold both these views at the same time.

Its impossibility

The impossibility of complete objectivity has been argued on several grounds. One is that the unavoidable process of news *selection* must also entail subjective judgement, of which journalists themselves may be unaware (see Rosten, 1937; White, 1950). Another is that all events and reports of events which are candidates for treatment as news have to be placed in wider frames of reference which give them evaluative meanings (see Chapter 17). Thirdly, the omissions, gaps and silences which are unavoidable may also be eloquent, reflecting implicit (and subjective) judgements about relevance and assumptions about society and its values.

Fourthly, and most broadly, it is quite clear that news is always produced within a context of numerous and powerful external and internal pressures (see Chapter 7), which are almost bound to deflect journalism from any ideal goal of recounting 'truth'. The constraining power of these pressures is strong enough to suggest that journalistic objectivity is a *necessity* rather than a virtue (McQuail, 1986b: 39). Thus one connotation of the general idea of objectivity is of the demands of external reality which cannot be wished away (as when one speaks of 'facing up to reality').

Hackett (1984) refers to *imperatives* which 'unavoidably structure news accounts', under which he includes economic, organizational and technical factors as well as political factors and the influence of news values. Hall (1973) prefers to separate the 'bureaucractic' (organizational and techno-logical) from 'ideological' pressures on news. One might add, as noted above, that the news product is obliged to meet other, 'non-objective', product specifications, especially those related to audience appeal in situations of competition for attention.

Perhaps the most fundamental objection is the view that there *is* no objective reality 'out there' to report on: the best we can expect is no more than different versions of a multifarious set of impressions. No account of reality can be uniquely correct or complete, except in the most trivial instance. Glasser refers to the objective journalist's 'naively empirical view of the world, a belief in the separation of facts and values, a belief in the existence of *a* reality – the reality of empirical facts' (1988: 50). If this were not enough, it also seems that we have no neutral language with which to provide an objective account of reality, even if we accept that this exists.

Its undesirability

The argument for the *undesirability* of objectivity is linked to its impossibility, since it is misleading to offer something which cannot be delivered. Any purportedly objective view of events is likely to privilege one account among several. In turn, more often than not, this will be a version of events which serves the interests of established power, or of whoever finances the news (Shoemaker and Mayfield, 1987). This is not because of conspiracy, but mainly because of the advantage which goes to powerful and efficient sources (Gans, 1979). In short, the privileged version is likely to be closer to their view of the world.

Several of the practices which are intrinsic to objective reporting typically favour the better resourced, better organized and most authoritative interests, since these can offer the promptest and best verification of their versions of events (Sigal, 1973; Roshco, 1975; Gans, 1979). A further objection relates to the practice of *balance*, which calls for equal attention to (usually two opposed) parties in disputes (the even-handed principle), whatever the justice of the case. It treats facts as if they have no moral implication or qualitative dimension beyond their verifiability (Hemánus, 1976).

In general, objectivity is said to elevate impartiality from the status of an instrument to that of an ideal, implicitly devaluing strong belief, partisanship and social solidarity. Critical or engaged journalism is also bound to be undervalued, even if only by implication (thus, the investigative and partisan variants of news described below). The general tendency of objectivity is towards fragmentation, individualization and 'secularization' – the with-drawal from value commitments. In the most critical view of objectivity, the practice is viewed as actively serving, whether willingly or not, the interests of agents of an established order and as reinforcing a consensus which mainly protects power and class interest (Gans, 1979).

These remarks have a bearing on the whole assessment enterprise and have to be taken into account in research which applies objectivity as a norm of performance. Assessment is generally based on the presumption that objectivity is both desirable and possible (up to a point) although difficult to achieve. However, one purpose of research can also be to expose some of the limitations in what purport to be accounts of reality as well as to help uncover the sources of 'distortion' (lack of objectivity). The factors which limit the attainment of objectivity in news content (leaving aside doubts about the very existence of an objective 'reality') can be summarized by referring to Shoemaker and Mayfield's (1987) analysis of theory of news content. They identify four main general factors: the working of media routines for collecting and processing news; the personal attitudes and socialization of journalists; the social and institutional forces working on news; and the efforts of power-holders to exert ideological hegemony.

Non-objective news

The matter is further complicated by the fact that news is not always, or only, intended (or expected by its audience) to conform to the rather austere model of ideal objectivity which has been outlined. There are variants of news practice which follow other conventions, whether through historical survival, cultural variations or simply because of the very diversity of the media and of audience demand. It is not always clear which variant is being offered in any given case, nor what the appropriate criteria of assessment might be.

The 'objective' model of news as useful, reliable information has certainly become predominant, but it has not extinguished some older versions of news especially those related to *human interest, partisanship* and to the *investigative* function of news. Each of these has its own claim to legitimacy and each contradicts one or more features of objective news practice as outlined above.

Human interest and news

News, we are often reminded (e.g. by Darnton, 1975), is still a *narrative* of people and events, with elements of drama, myth and personalization as well as of fact (Hughes, 1940; Morin, 1976; Smith, 1979; Knight and Dean, 1982). These features are embedded in the history (Hughes, 1940) and in the current practice of news (van Dijk, 1983, 1988) and are likely to influence how news is 'read' by its audience and also *why* it is read in the first place. Without narrative appeal and human interest, it is unlikely that news would be widely disseminated or have the same value as a commodity in the news market (Curran et al., 1980). This aspect of news strains against the neutrality, impersonality and adherence to fact, which are so important for the concept of objectivity.

The human interest news tradition is linked with the pejorative notion of 'sensationalism', which usually describes excessive appeal to emotion and the senses. Often this entails dramatic headlines, film or pictures, a focus on personalities, much interest in crime, disaster, sex and violence, all of which may be inconsistent with the norm of neutrally recounting essential facts (see Chapter 15). Such features of this kind can usually be identified in content or presentation, but it is less easy to determine the point at which they go beyond what is necessary to attract and keep audience attention and begin to interfere with the quality of the information offered.

Partisanship and advocacy

The news media are sometimes aligned with a party point of view or take sides on disputed issues. The tradition of press partisanship is as old as those of objectivity and human interest. It draws strong normative support from the values of freedom and diversity. Yet it, too, sits uncomfortably with the notion that objectivity is *the* unique professional ideal and form of practice. The partisan model has itself more than one variant. Seymour-Ure (1974), for instance, indicates three versions of political relationships between the press and its readers: organizational correspondence, where the paper is the organ of a party; the situation of an independent paper which chooses to support the goals of one party or another; and the case of correspondence, often for commercial reasons, between political views in a paper and the dominant views of its readers, arising from social class composition. Each has a different implication for expectations about objectivity.

Partisanship in *comment* on news events, in open *advocacy* of certain viewpoints and in *campaigning* for some goal is easy to recognize and not in itself problematic, since no claim to objectivity is made. Even so, the more these are present, the more difficult it is to maintain the distinction between opinion and fact which the objectivity norm requires. More problematic is the category of 'propaganda', which can also be variously defined, although it always shares with partisanship the characteristic of deliberate bias in a certain direction. The term 'propaganda' may be used in the same sense as advocacy or persuasion, but it is more true to modern usage to follow Jowett and O'Donnell (1986) in treating it as a special form of persuasion which involves attempted manipulation in the interests of the sender (rather than of the receiver) and often, also *concealment* of the real purpose and even of the identity of the originator.

There is another kind of non-objective news reporting, which has been described either as 'unwitting bias' (Golding, 1981) or as 'hidden ideology', which differs from partisanship and propaganda mainly through the absence of any conscious or deliberate intention to take sides. Unwitting bias is especially problematic because it is often embedded in the very practice of objective news reporting. There are varied forms and several different origins, aside from the (unexplicated) personal inclinations and subjective views of newspeople. For instance, normal news collecting and processing routines and reliance on regular sources tend to influence selection in a systematic way. Bias can also stem from the evaluative character of all languages and the unthinking deployment of wider interpretative frames and schemes for telling particular news stories (see Chapter 17).

Investigative news

The investigative tradition of news – exposing scandal, abuse or incompetence – is also hard to reconcile with the objective model, although it, too, has a place in a fuller version of the role of media in society and in audience expectations (Glasser and Ettema, 1991). This news tradition is associated with the idea of the watch-dog, critical or 'Fourth Estate' role, according to which the media are supposed to represent the interests of the general public (Cater, 1964) and to adopt an adversarial stance in relation to government or powerful interests (Rivers and Nyhan, 1973). As described in Chapter 9, it may be a hallmark of an independent editorial policy.

The investigative task is widely acknowledged by journalists and, on one view, it represents the incorporation of the partisan role into objective practice. In general, investigative news is critical in intention and controversial in character, even if objective in manner. It can best be handled in assessment research by applying the distinction between factual (truth) and evaluative aspects of objectivity (see Figure 15.2 below). Investigative reporting is not inconsistent with the larger notion of objectivity, since 'truth' criteria as well as balance and neutral presentation can still be respected.

These remarks are a reminder of the complexity and uncertainty of the task of assessing objectivity, despite the apparent straightforwardness of the unwritten rules and the expectations concerning objective news. In particular, we cannot be sure, from considerations of the news text alone, what the expectations of the audience might be, or what standards of objectivity performance are appropriate in a given case. Decisions about this can only be taken on grounds of contextual knowledge, which makes the application of objectivity as a criterion of performance itself less than fully objective. In practice, most of the research which has been reported has dealt with news channels which do claim to be objective in the sense initially outlined.

The objectivity–bias polarity

It is clear from this discussion that the term 'objectivity' stands opposed to an equally slippery, although simpler, concept, which has most commonly been referred to as 'bias'. This means a consistent tendency to depart from the straight path of objective truth by deviating either to left or right (the word derives from the game of bowls, in which a ball can have an inbuilt tendency to deviate or be made to deviate by a player). In news and information it refers to a systematic tendency to favour (in outcome) one side or position over another. As several critics of the objectivity concept (e.g. Hemánus, 1976) have pointed out, the favoured middle way (between left and right deviations) may itself be a form of bias (in news, though not in bowls) – a choice of one truth above others, which is often neither explicated nor justified. This criticism is valid, at least, where objectivity is thought of as an approximation to absolute truth.

It is hard, however, to see how objectivity can ever be more than relative – a position taken in relation to other positions and established on the balance of available evidence. Much news and related kinds of information is, of its nature, no more than a response to, or reflection of, the claims and doings of established power, which are themselves often bizarre, irrational and certainly not disinterested. There is another sense in which an emphasis on balance as such and on finding the middle way between (often) just two opposed positions can itself give rise to bias. According to Epstein (1973), television news tends to present 'conflicts as disputes between no more than two equally matched sides [tending] . . . to reduce complex issues, which may have a multitude of dimensions, to a simple conflict between protestors (or non-authorities) and authorities' (p. 266). By implication, this denies the relevance of other points of view.

The disputed status of the concepts of objectivity and bias (Hackett, 1984) prevents us from supplying any simple definition of the second term, although it can always be thought of as the *absence* of the attributes of good journalistic practice mentioned above (Roshco, 1975, uses the term to refer to the *subjective* element in an otherwise objective technique). Even so, the deployment of the objectivity norm in research does usually require some specification of how bias can be recognized. The literature reveals a varied choice of indicators and definitions, in keeping with the complexity of the concept.

Efron (1971), for example, writes that political bias is a 'specific type of selective process in a specific political context' and the issue is not one of objective truth or falsity but of 'according preferential status to certain political positions and opinions' (p. 4). Frank (1973) prefers an even more neutral definition of bias as 'selective encoding'. Hofstetter (1976), in his study of the US presidential election campaign, identified four different kinds of bias: as *lies*, 'deliberate, purposeful deception by assertion of untruths'; as *distortion*, when a 'news account is affected by unjustifiable omissions of significant facts, under-emphasis or overemphasis of certain aspects of an event'; as *value assertion*, in the form of ideology, etc. Finally, Hofstetter refers to a *structural* bias of television, as when all three US networks report the same topics in a similar way. However, this is much the same as lack of diversity (for news duplication, see Chapter 13).

Williams (1975) suggests that propositions about bias can come from sender or receiver variables (selective encoding or selective perception) and that they also divide into *cognitive* or *non-cognitive* variables (the latter mainly presentation factors). While most performance assessment research concentrates on selection and presentation, Stevenson and Greene (1980) also emphasize the contribution of the receiver. Their definition of bias is conventional enough: 'the systematic differential treatment of one candidate, one party, one side of an issue over an extended period of time . . . the

	Open	Hidden
Intended	Partisanship	Propaganda
Unintended	Unwitting bias (selectivity)	Ideology

Figure 14.1 *Four types of news bias*

failure to treat all voices equally'. However, they go on to propose that bias is really information in news which is *discrepant* with mental pictures held by the receiver, a discrepancy which evokes an evaluative response, essentially a function of perception. This is particularly relevant for the would-be objective analyst to bear in mind, for what he or she is doing in trying to record bias systematically is actually making predictions about the probability of an evaluative response to features of the news 'text'.

A typology of news bias

For present purposes, a basic differentiation is made between the main varieties of bias in terms of two basic variables: 'hidden' or 'open' on the one hand; and 'intended' or 'unintended' on the other (following Golding, 1981). The cross-classification of these two variables identifies the four main kinds of non-objective news practice which have already been discussed (Figure 14.1). The meaning of these terms has already been explained, but a few words are in order about the categories of content involved and the implications for performance research.

Partisanship This is normally identified in the structure of news media by its form (editorial leading article, opinion column, forum or access slot, letter, paid advertisement). In such cases, the convention is to separate partisan from objective sections – hence the existence of research designed to check on this supposed independence (e.g. Klein and Maccoby, 1954). Sometimes, a channel is openly partisan and one may expect that all elements are likely to be affected by the tendency. However, there are many variants of practice, including one of just separating fact from comment.

Although not strictly 'partisanship', it is probably necessary to treat open campaigning and investigative/critical journalism within this category, since factual and evaluative/directional aspects are often inextricably mixed. Letters to the editor also offer opportunities for editorializing, depending on the policy adopted (Tunstall, 1977b; Renfro, 1979), although it is not easy to know from content alone what this policy is: seeming bias or concerted direction in views expressed in letters may simply represent overwhelming public feeling.

The case of propaganda Hidden and intended bias is more difficult to deal with, partly because the intention *is* concealed. It can often appear in the form of objective news, for instance, as information (or 'disinformation') supplied to news media by spokespersons, public relations sources, interest or pressure groups; or 'pseudo-events' staged to gain media coverage or attract an audience; or as a result of information 'subsidies' (Gandy, 1982) and forms of sponsorship which shape the supply of information in favour of some third party. Since not all players are equal in such games, the results of propagandist efforts do not usually cancel each other out, but may be mutually reinforcing in a certain direction.

The most problematic feature of propaganda, defined like this, is the near impossibility of identifying it in news output in any certain or systematic way. It is often not the channel which is the agent of progaganda, rather some of the messages it carries are instruments for someone else's aims. Sometimes, the presence of propaganda may be signalled by particular presentational devices and uses of language (indicators include prominence and attention exceeding any obvious news value; innuendo; flattering language; non- [or only vaguely] attributed sources); suspicious juxtaposition of items, which associates known propaganda 'targets' with positive or negative contexts. In general the recognition of propagandist intention depends on the adoption of a critical view of the media, such as that taken by Herman and Chomsky (1988) in their analysis of US Government manipulation of news in the interest of national foreign policy objectives.

Unwitting bias Open, but unintentional, bias in the *selection* of topics, events and news angles can usually be recognized as systematic patterns of preferential attention or avoidance which are not justified by any statistical reality, but where there is no reason to suspect propagandist purpose. The most common cause of unwitting bias mentioned in the literature seems to lie with organizational features of the news task – reliance on certain sources, routinization, making assumptions about audiences, etc. (Tuchman, 1978; Fishman, 1980).

Ideology Hidden but unintended bias, embedded in texts, is harder to investigate, partly because (like propaganda) it *is* concealed and can only be uncovered by close interpretation and argument. It cannot easily be demonstrated by content analysis in the way that unwitting bias in *selection* can be demonstrated and it often takes the form of omission or structuring of elements within texts. The essence of 'hidden ideology' is not only the departure in consistent, recurring ways from strict neutrality and accuracy in the telling of news stories, but also the presence of a more or less coherent world view underlying the accounts which are offered. News becomes coloured by a point of view (even if not consciously espoused by the journalist), leans in a certain direction, implicitly takes sides (van Dijk, 1983).

For instance, according to Gans (1979), major American news media have, built into their output, certain 'enduring' values about their own society and the world, often the dominant values of the social milieu of the newsmakers themselves (and perhaps of most of their audience as well). The need for news media to have established and authoritative sources in the society reinforces the tendency towards expressing consensual values. The constant pressure of surrounding society and institutions helps to shape the news in a way which is fundamentally supportive of the established class and power structure, as well as of its political culture. Ethnocentricism about national values and institutions inevitably colours the selection and direction of news and other content which is, in any case, produced for home consumption.

Advertising of products and corporate images is even more likely to be ideological (containing unexplicated value assumptions about society and the world) if not propagandistic (sometimes deliberately concealed) (Pearlin and Rosenberg, 1952; Leymore, 1975; Marquez, 1977; Meadow, 1981; Leiss et al., 1986). While causes and effects are impossible to disentangle, the *direction* of effect (favourable to established norms, values and social power) is in little doubt (Shoemaker and Mayfield, 1987).

Objectivity less obscure

It is to be hoped that this discussion has thrown some light on the ambivalent status of the objectivity concept. Not only is a generally agreed notion of objectivity both supported and attacked, but it is also variably present and absent in different kinds of media content, in ways which are not easy to establish 'objectively'. Moreover, the conventions of objectivity are manipulated and sometimes misused for ulterior purposes, by advertisers, propagandists and all who have an interest in the 'management' of truth, which includes nearly everyone. Whatever the objections to the idea of objectivity and the uncertain degree to which anything like the ideal can be achieved, it is hard to reject Lichtenberg's argument that 'insofar as we aim to understand the world we cannot get along without assuming both the possibility and value of objectivity' (1990: 230). In any case, this is the main justification for giving the topic sustained attention in the chapters which follow.

15
A FRAMEWORK FOR OBJECTIVITY RESEARCH

Westerståhl's model

The most robust conceptual framework for handling objectivity research is probably that developed by Westerståhl (1983) and colleagues (Figure 15.1), who investigated the degree to which Swedish public broadcasting was meeting its legal obligations of impartiality. The research was based on the assumption that impartiality in the news was possible as well as desirable and could be assessed by comparing supposedly neutral broadcast news about controversial matters with other news channels (e.g. newspapers and news agencies). These might either have open partisan biases or just lack the special requirement of impartiality laid on broadcasting. Even so, the framework can accommodate other research, including research based on more critical assumptions about objectivity itself.

The key feature of the scheme is the distinction, already discussed, between the 'cognitive' territory of empirical observation and record and the 'evaluative' field of neutrality and balance in the selection and presentation of news reports. By separating the two, the scheme appears to endorse the contentious view that values and facts can be separated and that value-free

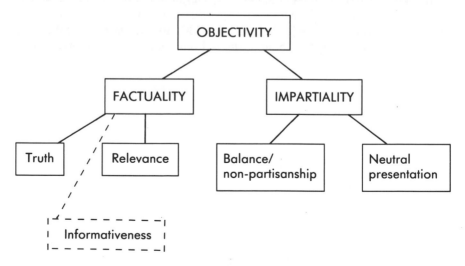

Figure 15.1   *Westerståhl's (1983) objectivity scheme*

observation is possible. However, these assumptions are also built into journalistic work and are routinely made by social scientists and in everyday life. Assessment is difficult unless this division is followed.

The two main terms in the scheme were derived by Westerståhl from Swedish broadcasting law, which avoids, the word 'objectivity'. Rosengren (1980) translates the original Swedish word for factuality as 'matter-of-factness' and offers, as an alternative, the English word 'pertinence'. We may also consider the term 'reality reference' as another possibility. In general, Rosengren views the distinction as representing a cognitive–evaluative dimension. Impartiality refers to all those aspects of news which concern the evaluative direction of news. In the following discussion, the 'cognitive' and 'evaluative' dimensions are dealt with in turn, in terms of key sub-concepts.

Cognitive (information quality) aspects

Factuality and cognate terms

The ultimate criterion of information quality is the potential for audiences to learn about reality. Assessment has been concerned with anything which might affect the amount and quality of comprehension and learning about real events, persons and things (hence the addition of 'informativeness' in Figure 15.1, a topic returned to in the following chapter). The use of the term 'truth' in the first sub-distinction seems to pre-empt the whole enquiry, but here it merely refers to qualities likely to be associated with the *reliability* and *credibility* of accounts – the degree to which different observers might agree on the 'facts', the degree to which reports can be acted on with some confidence, the degree to which they are likely to prove consistent with personal experience.

Our attention is thus directed to several empirically measurable (or indexible) features of news accounts, especially:

- *Factualness*, in the sense of clearly distinguishing fact from opinion, interpretation or comment, backing reports by reference to named sources, avoiding vagueness and redundancy;
- *Accuracy*, a matter of correspondence of report to reality, or to other reliable versions of reality, especially on matters of fact or quantity (numbers, names, places, attributions, times, etc.);
- *Completeness*, or fullness of account, on the assumption that a minimum amount of relevant information is required for understanding.

Some message qualities could be added to this list, especially those which are likely to relate to *readability* and *comprehension* (which are discussed later).

The standard of relevance

Although this seems to be a matter of common sense, it turns out to be a complex and slippery term. The reasons for including it as a criterion are obvious enough: for news to be of value to intended audiences and to the various social processes in which it plays an important part, it has to deal with significant matters of current concern and with what is actually going on. Without relevance in this sense, it would be impossible to have any sensible notion of 'completeness' (since this must require selection according to significance), nor would accuracy and factuality matter very much unless the 'facts' in question are germane to events and to the concerns of the media public.

Relevance is, thus, the key term in assessing the quality of news *selection*. It is a standard which can be applied at different levels in media content: at that of general subject or topic choice (e.g. international v. local news, or crime v. political news); at the level of event or 'story' (some events are more 'newsworthy' than others); within particular 'stories', when selection has to be made among component elements in news editing (e.g. Asp, 1981 who defined a concept of 'internal relevance' as the giving of arguments for or against a controversial decision). Much the same criteria of relevance apply at the first two levels, although at the third (internal relevance), the question of what contributes to adequate *comprehension* on the part of the audience plays an additional role.

What makes the relevance standard most difficult is the problem of establishing the 'significance' of news topics or events. We may take the common-sense view that significance refers to what matters most, what touches people's lives most deeply. However, this leaves open the question of significance for *whom*, about *what* and according to *whose* judgement. The relative significance of the outcome of news selection processes can only be judged by choosing a perspective and making some assumptions.

In practice, relevance judgements are made by news media, on a continuous basis, without agonized introspection, according to established convention and routine, in response to numerous pressures and cues (Hetherington, 1985). Much of this work has been described and analysed within the tradition of 'gatekeeper' research, which has tried to explain systematic patterns in the outcomes of news selection (Shoemaker, 1991). The external 'performance assessor' has a different task, being obliged to identify and apply some independent standard of significance (and thus of relevance) to the news content at hand. The general problem is to find independent sources, or indicators, of 'significance' with which news can be compared.

Alternative sources of relevance criteria

Several possibilities present themselves, each with its own advantages and disadvantages. One is to choose an external absolute authority or standard (for instance, expert judgement or some ideological view). More commonly, reference is made to the empirical (or statistical) 'reality' about which the news gives reports or simply to the news 'agendas' of significant institutions and actors (e.g. parliaments or stock markets). Thirdly, the audience may be looked to for its views on what is interesting or useful to know.

Absolute (normative) standards of relevance   The view that significance
can be judged according to some independent, 'absolute' standard (see
Nordenstreng, 1974) depends upon having faith either in a grand theory or
ideology or on considerable confidence in the judgement of experts. As to
the first, Marxist theory of history might provide a standard of *objective*
relevance, but carries little weight outside the diminishing fold of the faithful.
Comparison with the views of independent experts on what is more or less
significant might seem a more viable option, but these views are likely to
represent a partial and elite view of the world rather than what might
concern the average newspaper reader.

Real world indicators   A no less objective and usable standard would seem
to be offered by independent evidence of the 'real world', in whatever news
terrain might be at issue (politics, crime, economics, sport, etc.). By this
criterion, news is more relevant, the more it corresponds to the reality as
measured by independent records of that reality – in official statistics, other
sources, etc. While this is a component in the common-sense view of
relevance, in practice there is much too much reality to 'reflect' and there are
many good reasons for a skewed correspondence between news and other
versions or records of events (see Chapter 12). Versions of the 'real world' of
everyday life in society are normally mediated through institutional sources
(political, economic, judicial, etc.) which seek to establish (often competing)
priorities and *agendas* which they would like to see in news. This option
deserves some consideration, but is hardly adequate as a total criterion of
relevance.

The audience as guide   Of the remaining possibilities, reference to what
matters to the audience seems to be the most promising empirically and
closest to the common-sense meaning of relevance, to the realities of what
news is, as a 'form of knowledge' (Park, 1940) and also close to the outlook
of most journalists. One US study (Burgoon et al., 1982) found that, in the
view of journalists, the foremost characteristic of 'newsworthiness' is
'consequence' for the audience – what affects readers' lives, what they need
to know, etc. If what is significant is what affects most people's lives most
deeply most often, then it is the people themselves (the media public) who
ought to know. If measures of audience interest or demand are used as the
main criteria of relevance, the outcome is unlikely to correspond with the
views of experts or with 'real world' statistics, or even with any of the various
institutional agendas. Nevertheless, this standard of relevance is readily
applicable, since much is known (or knowable) about audience interests.

Journalistic criteria of relevance

News selection is unlikely to satisfy all these standards and is more likely
simply to reflect journalists' own ideas of what counts as relevant or
'newsworthy'. Some account should, therefore, be taken of professional
journalist criteria of relevance, even though they cannot provide an

independent criterion to apply to the work of journalists themselves. The main factors considered in news selection are likely to be those of *timeliness* or *topicality* and other 'news values' of events (for instance, 'closeness' and 'scale').

In short, we might follow journalism some way and consider that, other things being equal, the 'larger' the event (or topic), the greater the number affected, the more *immediate* its impact (timeliness) and the 'closer' to home (culturally or geographically), the more significance it has and therefore the more relevance. While this view of relevance has its own 'bias' – especially towards the personal and towards the here and now – it also has its own logic and seems to connect well (but not completely) with the logic of audience interest, as noted above (journalists try to predict what audiences will find interesting).

Relevance versus sensationalism

There remains another possibility for relevance research, which is to focus on the *reverse* of what is significant – to measure the incidence of the *trivial* or superficial. The concept of 'sensationalism' comes into play here, usually referring to 'human interest', personalization or other 'entertainment' characteristics of news. The more that news has such features, the more it may be thought to be lacking in 'information value', and thus unlikely to be relevant to information needs, however immediately *interesting* it may be to audiences. While this critical view is based on a value judgement, there is firmer ground for the supposition that, in general, information about celebrities and individuals has less utility or application value than information about concrete conditions and events close to hand.

We are increasingly led to conclude that there are a number of equally valid standards of relevance, and thus that there is an inevitable tension between 'pure' objectivity and diversity, as performance criteria, since diversity places a value on different ways of looking at the world as well as on a wide range of reference.

Evaluative (impartiality) aspects

The second main element of the objectivity concept, as identified by Westerståhl (see Figure 15.1), that of impartiality, is evidently a quality prized by audiences as well as in the clauses of broadcasting policy documents and journalistic codes of practice. Even so, its recognition and analysis is not always easy especially because it calls for a study of values embedded in news and because of the variable purpose and good faith of different news providers. The more that 'propaganda' (intentional, but concealed, bias) or 'ideology' are suspected to be present, the more likely we are to need methods which can deal with *latent* meanings and the less easy it may be to generalize. The main issue in impartiality research is whether or not news texts tend systematically to favour one side over another in controversial or disputed matters – to lead the receiver consistently in a certain direction. The sub-criteria of *balance* and *neutrality* essentially divide the problem into two questions of evaluation: these have to do either with *selection* and balance; or with the form and *manner of presentation* – the means by which positive or negative responses may be evoked, whatever the 'facts' presented, or the balance between them (Rosengren, 1980).

Impartiality requires the reporter (or news channel) to maintain a distance, not to take sides in matters where there are two or more points of view or different valuations. What constitutes such neutrality and the permitted deviations from it are themselves largely matters of convention and consensus. Some very 'negative' events do not usually allow alternative value positions (for instance, natural disasters, serious crimes, aggressive war, terrorism, torture). However, most potentially newsworthy events are not of this kind. News media are expected to reckon with alternative evaluations and interests, with the diversity of audiences, and with the need to do justice to the complexity of a reality in which divergent values and points of view have a place.

Balance

The 'balance' component of the impartiality concept refers mainly to matters of *selection* or *omission* in respect either of facts which may imply values or of expressions of points of view on the supposed 'facts' by the parties involved. The requirements of balanced reporting can be understood in different ways, depending mainly on the number, relevance and status of the parties involved in an issue or event. It can be taken to require either *equal* attention to the main protagonists (e.g. management and unions in an industrial dispute or each contending political party in an election campaign) or attention proportionate to the varying significance of the actor's involvement in an event (there are normally minor as well as major actors). Attention can be balanced in terms of measurable space or time in news, but it also involves questions of relative prominence and of the context and 'quality' of attention. All publicity is not good publicity.

Neutrality

The line between balance and neutrality of presentation is an uncertain one, but the second refers mainly to the use of potentially evaluative words, images and frames of reference and also of different styles. When assessing neutrality, we look for *connotation* rather than *denotation* (as in the case of balance). Assessing non-neutrality in presentation entails some reference to likely impact on the audience and to how content might be perceived and interpreted. According to Westerståhl, 'Neutral presentation implies that the report not be composed in such a way that the reporter is shown to identify with, or repudiate, the subject of the report' (1983: 420). Thus it applies only to pure news reports and not to commentary, where taking sides is permissible.

CRITERIA FOR ASSESSMENT

		Cognitive	Evaluative
TO BE ASSESSED	Presentation	Truth	Neutrality
	Selection	Relevance	Balance

Figure 15.2 *Dimensions of news assessment*

For some assessment purposes (for instance, in determining whether public broadcasting follows rules of neutrality), we may only need to decide whether content is impartial or not, without needing to take account of the specific *direction* of any apparent bias. Whatever the resulting balance, any evaluation is a departure from pure objectivity in the sense of factuality and neutrality. The two main components of the objectivity concept – factuality and impartiality – are independent of each other and often mutually inconsistent.

There are many ways in which supposedly factual or objective accounts can be tendentious, but the principal means involve: language (use of words and phrases with positive or negative connotations); visual/aural forms (camera angles, music, image juxtaposition etc., as described, for instance, in Tuchman, 1978); contextualization and structure of event accounts which can activate positive or negative responses and images. Within the conventions of objective news, there can be quite large variations in style of performance, which may affect presentation and interpretation.

This discussion can be concluded and, in part, summarized by reference to Rosengren (1980), who reorganized the main components of the objectivity scheme which has been discussed, in terms of two dimensions or dichotomies, one of *cognition versus evaluation* and the other separating *selection* from *presentation*. The result is shown in Figure 15.2.

The strategies and methods for assessing objectivity described in the following chapter can be conveniently grouped according to this four-fold division. We can also, in the light of this discussion, expand the initial framework for objectivity analysis given in Figure 15.1 as a way of summarizing the tasks for research (Figure 15.3).

Objectivity is always relative

It is important to stress that both 'news performance' and its assessment take place in cultural settings which define and limit both. Ideas of what is fair and reasonable in the way of objectivity may vary from one society to another and even from one theme or issue to another, depending on the overall balance of view in the society. The idea of impartiality as an ideal is itself an ideological message as well as a cultural principle, characteristic of Western

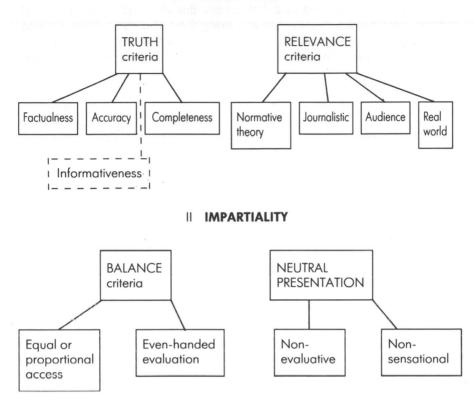

I FACTUALITY

TRUTH criteria
- Factualness
- Accuracy
- Completeness

Informativeness

RELEVANCE criteria
- Normative theory
- Journalistic
- Audience
- Real world

II IMPARTIALITY

BALANCE criteria
- Equal or proportional access
- Even-handed evaluation

NEUTRAL PRESENTATION
- Non-evaluative
- Non-sensational

Figure 15.3 *Dimensions and criteria of factuality and impartiality*

society (see Glasser, 1988). But it is also subject to limits set by popular feeling and national self-interest.

According to Rosengren (1980), 'news reporting in a country must be partial in a way reflecting the basic values and actual sympathies of the population. The reason is simply that otherwise the credibility of the media would disappear.' Problems can arise for media in trying to be impartial about evil crime, abuse of state power, a national enemy, etc. The problem for media assessment in such cases is not one of measuring evaluative *direction*, but of knowing where these limits to objectivity are set and of deciding what can reasonably be expected of news media, when impartiality requirements conflict with popular sentiment. News media which do their best to be objective meet the severest test when they have to deal with very sensitive issues involving either national interest or strong public feelings or both together, as in the case of war (see Chapter 18).

Finally, we should not lose sight of the fact that 'news' is not simply facts, but a special form of knowledge (Park, 1940), which is inextricably compounded of information, myth, fable and morality. Unfortunately (or not) the performance of news is rarely judged (by its critics and researchers) against any other standard than that of objective information. Audiences, of course, take a much broader view, making their own choices and seeking and judging their own satisfactions. In turn, this is the main reason why the providers of news and their performance critics will never see eye to eye.

16
MEASURING OBJECTIVITY: NEWS AS INFORMATION

The factual component of objective performance

Factualness, accuracy and *completeness* are the three most essential aspects of information quality in news. They are closely inter-related, but the keystone of the three is the first, since accuracy and completeness can only be investigated in news texts once basic facts have been identified. In the absence of an agreed general definition, but according to news convention, facts can be considered as self-contained units of information in any account which claims to report on actual events or situations. A 'fact' is clearly different from a subjective opinion or a comment and it should, in principle, be verifiable by reference to reliable sources or to other independent accounts.

Factualness

For purposes of research into factualness, an operational decision has to be made about which textual elements in a news account to treat as facts. One option is to divide the whole text into a series of units of analysis, each comprising a self-contained factual statement (or reference) or, alternatively, a self-contained 'main point' in the larger sequence of a news 'story' or item. An alternative is to identify all informative references which are precise enough to be checked (for instance, name, time, age, place, date, etc.). The verbal (and to some extent, visual) text of radio or television news can be treated in essentially the same way.

There are different reasons for investigating factualness, within the scope of objectivity research. One is to check whether the principle of separation of facts from comment is being observed. For this purpose, elements of text can be identified as 'fact', 'comment/opinion' or 'mixed'. A second main motive is to assess the reliability of reporting, given the importance of accuracy in the journalistic canon. Thirdly, degree of factualness is also a general indicator of the degree of informativeness, according to the definition of information as 'uncertainty reduction'. In general, the more facts, the less uncertainty.

The fragmenting effect of this approach may, however, fail to do justice to the 'information value' of a complete news account. The more that statements of fact are related to each other in some logical way, the more a news account may be thought to be informative (and vice versa). A text made up of isolated items of fact (as in some news agency files) is likely to have a lower informative potential than a worked out news 'story'. More sensitive measures are needed and especially ones which might apply to visual texts (Watt and Krull, 1974).

Information value Asp (1981) developed a measure of 'information value' (or 'informativity') of news reporting on a given controversial issue, based on three different indicators of news information, having first established a universe of relevant points in news reports on the issue. The measures were of: 'density' – the proportion of all relevant points given; 'breadth' – the number of *different* points as a proportion of the total possible; and 'depth' – the number of facts and motives accompanying and helping to explain the basic points. The main 'information value' index was obtained by multiplying the density score by the breadth score. While this method is very labour-intensive, it is reassuring to learn from Asp that the index correlates highly with the amount of space given by different newspapers to the issue (although not with amount of time in radio or TV news). For some purposes, a simple measure of news volume may thus serve as an indicator of informativeness.

Readability This measure of information 'richness' is akin to its opposite – the measure of redundancy. News texts with a relatively low incidence of facts are likely to have a high degree of redundancy and to convey little information. However, they are, in general, easier to read and to understand (see below). The 'cloze' procedure, developed by Taylor (1953), originally for the purpose of comparing the readability of different styles of writing, is the most familiar method for measuring redundancy. It requires an experiment in which a reader has to substitute words for systematically omitted words, the ease of substitution being a measure of ease of reading, but also of low information potential. The denser the information supplied, the harder the task of filling gaps. The method of measuring redundancy is very laborious and is only likely to be used in case studies or for generally characterizing some regular news channels (Stempel, 1981). On its own, factualness may not merit high esteem as an attribute of news since the relative significance of facts cannot be taken into account, nor, for the reasons noted, is information 'density' any guarantee of communication effectiveness (Smith 1984).

Checkability An aspect of factualness which is also open to indexation is the degree to which the 'facts' offered are (in principle) 'checkable' (as noted above), or supported by a named source and relevant supporting evidence. The higher the proportion of verifiable units of information in a text, the more factual it may be considered.

Accuracy

The measurement of accuracy has long been of interest to journalist educators, since so much store is set by accuracy as a quality of news reports (Charnley, 1936; Shapiro, 1989). Accuracy also matters a lot to subjects of news reports, whose reputation or interest might be adversely affected by the publication of incorrect information. Thirdly, accuracy is related to the question of the credibility of news media for their audiences, since reports perceived to be inaccurate on one point may not be believed on others.

Verification of facts against a 'reality' record   One investigative strategy is to check points in a text against an external, reliable, version of the same information (or with the original source). There are too many possible kinds of error to apply a uniform approach. Blankenberg (1970), for instance, listed 14 categories of error, including: omission; under- and over-emphasis; misspelling; faulty headlines; misquotes; incorrect ages, names, dates, etc. The *quality* of the version of events against which to check accuracy of facts can also be problematic. Official reports or statistics are often highly regarded, but they are limited by delay in their appearance and lack of comparability with the news report form (they are also compiled for quite different purposes). Many events of public significance may have no complete or independent record (but see below).

For this reason, *other media* are often used for comparison in place of official records, especially: prestige newspapers (papers of record); original news agency material; factual compilations from several such media (e.g. *Keesings Archives, US News and World Report*). The choice is based on the assumption that these sources are likely to be reliable, relatively complete and also *impartial*. In addition, a set of *different* news reports of the same event can provide a reasonable version of the *universe* of relevant known facts. However, 'media of record' are also selective, subject to human error and not immune from bias. The variable status of sources and the variable news-making power of 'event-definers' also undermines the basic assumption of this strategy, since it presumes that 'authoritative' views of reality are more reliable (Molotch and Lester, 1974).

Validity may only be achievable in limited topic areas (e.g. Ryan and Owen, 1977 on 'social issues') or where a particular kind of error is being investigated. Such conditions allow more account to be taken of context and more use of expert judgement, as in the case of science news (Johnson, 1963; Tankard and Ryan, 1974; Ryan, 1979). Any procedure for checking against external evidence is bound to be time-consuming and some events leave no definite record apart from the news itself. Where the external checks have been applied, a high incidence of error in news reports has been revealed, albeit of minor kinds. As with factualness, it is hard to distinguish objectively according to the *significance* of any error. Trivial errors in trivial facts are usually the easiest to identify but may not be related to inaccuracy on significant matters.

Source or subject perception of accuracy   A second strategy for investigating accuracy is to check with persons or organizations which are the subjects or sources of news (e.g. Berry, 1967; Scanlon, 1969; Meyer, 1988; Bell, 1991). Use of this method has indicated that, while *most* errors are trivial, the ones perceived to be most significant by those directly affected are more often matters of difference of interpretation or of alleged misrepresentation, than of indubitable fact (much evidence of perceived error surfaces regularly in newspaper letter columns). Tillinghast (1983) found that most such errors (those claimed by sources or subjects) are also disputed by the reporters concerned. This points to the uncertain boundary between questions of 'cognitive' correctness and questions of partiality or evaluation. Often the perception of inaccuracy by either the subject in news reporting or the 'reader' of the text is really a response to unacceptable evaluative implications (Meyer, 1988).

If this is so, it is doubtful if accuracy measures can take us very far, although the degree of care about detail can be useful in discriminating among media channels. For instance, McQuail (1977) compared different newspaper accounts of the same stories on the same days in terms of the equivalent sets of facts and figures offered. The rather high degree of inter-media difference which emerged said more about the different possibilities of presenting factual information than about the accuracy performance of the newspapers. Even so, some qualitative assessment of accuracy is possible, especially when small differences can be shown to be systematic and cumulative, or where one or other channel deviates widely from an inter-channel average or consensus.

Eye-witness comparisons   There is a complex variant of research which has been developed as a general strategy for recording the way in which news media 'construct' their own reality, especially as a result of their distinctive working procedures. An early classic was the study by Lang and Lang (1953) of the television reporting of the supposedly triumphal return of General McArthur to New York, after his dismissal from supreme command in Korea. News commentaries on the event were compared with observations made by informants located at the points of television coverage along the procession route. The results showed that the news followed more the lines of a script written in advance than the 'reality' of what was going on. The situation was 'defined' in advance, effectively 'pre-structured' by the media, the news report conforming to what has subsequently been called a 'media logic' (Altheide and Snow, 1979).

The same strategy (comparing eye-witness with media accounts of an event) was applied (by Halloran et al., 1970) to investigate the way in which the media reported another major public event (an anti-Vietnam War demonstration in London) which had also been extensively *pre-defined* (by the media and by authorities). The results confirmed that media may be more influenced by their own organizational (and technical) logic and the logic of the 'story' or 'script', based on earlier events, than by actual 'reality' as it occurs.

Audience assessment of accuracy A further possibility is to ask the audience to rate news media according to perceived degree of accuracy (Lawrence and Grey, 1969; Heffner, 1973; Fedler and Counts, 1981; Salman and Lee, 1983). This requires decisions about *who* to ask about *what* (for instance, the general public about all media or readers about their own paper, or some special public about special topics). The method produces results which are often crude and probably tell us more about the general attitude of the public on a particular topic than about media accuracy.

However, *comparisons* can be made among media and over time. An American example is provided by the results of a major national survey of opinion and the media conducted for Time/Mirror (Gallup Organization, 1986). The question asked was whether news organizations generally 'get the facts straight', or were often 'inaccurate', producing a split of 55 per cent to 34 per cent respectively. Among six main criteria of media performance (including fairness, patriotism, independence), this was, nevertheless, the criterion on which the media received the most positive rating. Different media were shown to vary a good deal in the degree to which they were perceived as accurate.

A British survey of reader attitudes (Royal Commission on the Press, 1977) asked for views on the factual correctness of several categories of newspaper, the results suggesting a stable pattern of assessment and expectation, with 'papers of record' perceived as more accurate by their respective sets of readers than were popular papers by their readers. Significantly, perhaps, the lowest accuracy rating was received by the local evening paper, which usually deals with events closest to the personal experience of readers. Whatever the doubts about audience response as a tool of evaluation, it is clear that the public places a high value on accuracy (see, e.g., Burgoon et al., 1981).

Credibility We are approaching the question of general *credibility* of media, which has been much investigated (Shaw, 1973; Lee, 1978; Gantz, 1981; Gaziano and McGrath, 1987a, b; Carter and Greenberg, 1965), especially with a view to comparing television and the newspaper press (Bogart, 1989: 242–248). According to an extended series of surveys by the Roper Organization in the United States, television moved far ahead of newspapers in ratings of 'believability' between the 1950s and the 1980s. While *perceptions* of accuracy (Wilson and Howard, 1978; Kocher and Shaw, 1981) no doubt play a part in the attribution of 'believability' (Robinson and Kohut, 1988), the research literature suggests that, in general, credibility has most to do with trust in the *source* on grounds of its fairness, good faith and lack of bias; in other words, it belongs more to the impartiality than to the factuality component of objectivity. Credibility of media is not necessarily well correlated with measured informativeness (Robinson and Levy, 1986; Bogart, 1989).

'Internal' accuracy   There are several other aspects of accuracy measurement which are not covered by the three main approaches outlined. An example is the question of *internal* accuracy of reports, especially the consistency of the relation between the headline and the substance of the story which follows. This was mentioned by the American Commission on Freedom of the Press (Hutchins, 1947) as a dimension of responsible performance and it is especially important in the light of evidence that a significant proportion of news stories are only known by their headlines. One assessment method is to classify headlines as 'accurate', 'irrelevant' or 'misleading' when compared to the text beneath them (as in Marquez, 1980).

Completeness

The matter of *completeness* or fullness of news accounts can be investigated in much the same way as can accuracy. It is usually thought to be a precondition of proper understanding of news, and the media generally promise completeness in the sense of a full range of information about significant events of the day (though not completeness of account about each news event). Completeness, thus has two aspects: *internal* completeness (all the essential facts of a given story) and *external* (all the essential stories, which may be measured in much the same way as diversity or relevance).

There is a third dimension which may sometimes be relevant – that of cumulative completeness over a long-running story. News media are sometimes criticized for not 'finishing' stories and they have no obligation to do so. Typical media content research designs (often based on samples of issues rather than continuous periods) are not well adapted to dealing with this question. The appropriate standard for assessment is also elusive, since there is rarely an 'extra-media' standard of completeness available. On the one hand, total reporting would be impossible and unnecessary; on the other, no information at all on certain aspects or events might be thought too little. The appropriate point between these extremes cannot be located without considering criteria of *relevance* (see below).

Reference to event records   While it is rare to find any absolute standard by which to judge completeness or fullness, something like a complete record may sometimes be available: for instance, in the record of proceedings of a parliament; a press conference; by working from some source text (such as a party election programme) to a media report. This may work in comparing newspaper texts with the written text of record or source, although it is hardly likely to work for television, when alternative reporting teams film the same event, which itself leaves no unique or independent *visual* record (Tiemens et al., 1988).

Fullness/range of coverage The investigation of completeness in the sense of the range of coverage of different types of news topics or events, or of detail within some topic area, can proceed by routine content analysis of samples of media content, in terms of any comprehensive set of news categories (e.g. McQuail, 1977; Curran et al., 1980). The approach helps to identify systematic patterns of imbalance or omission in respect of certain news topics, sources, references, etc., and it allows some (superficial) conclusions about relative performance.

Enquiry into omissions and gaps in coverage of particular topic areas is probably best represented in the literature by research into international news coverage (e.g. Gerbner and Marvanyi, 1977; Golding and Elliott, 1979; Womack, 1981; Adams, 1982). The usual method is the same as for diversity research: a pattern of news content distribution is compared with a 'real-world' distribution (e.g. of countries and populations). Political communication campaigns have also been studied for evidence of completeness in covering party programmes (e.g. Danielson and Adams, 1961; Graber, 1976a). The external standards for assessing completeness have mainly been found in public documentary records or in official statistics relating to the topic area.

Harvey and Stone (1969) used a historical standard – the main known 'facts' of a crisis – in comparing the fullness of news coverage by US national newspaper front pages and network television. They found rather high percentage coverage and little difference between media or channels. Another research example involved listing the (16) main issues from a government proposal and examining different newspapers for their proportionate attention to the total universe so established (Sullivan, 1985). In general, 'agenda-setting' research produces evidence concerning the range of media attention (see below and p. 163 above).

Other media channels can also serve as a quasi-independent standard (as with accuracy research). McQuail (1977) compiled a total inventory of all 'main points' on a given event, derived from all national daily newspapers under study and calculated the proportionate share of each title in reporting the complete set, producing a 'completeness' score for each paper. The results were summed up over a number of events to give cumulated scores for different newspapers. Several of the studies referred to earlier in connection with diversity of reflection of social reality are also, implicitly, studies of relative completeness (e.g. Graber, 1980a on crime news; Glasgow Media Group, 1976, on industrial relations).

Quantitative adequacy It is virtually impossible to find any objective criterion of what would be a *sufficient* amount of information, either generally or in a given case. The question has, however, been approached by way of surveys of the audience, although other terms are used (e.g.

'thoroughness', 'depth', 'fullness of coverage'). Research tends to reproduce stereotyped features of different media and to reveal little about actual performance (e.g. Royal Commission on the Press, 1977). In comparative ratings of media, newspapers have always scored more highly than television on questions about 'fullness' and 'depth' of coverage (Bogart, 1989), logically enough, since they do have more space available. There is some scope for detailed case studies of audience response on particular topics or issues.

Information delivery and news comprehension

There is a wider aspect of the adequacy of news quantity. Very broadly, the supply of news has increased very much, while the time available to attend to it has remained roughly constant. This simple logic of the information society (van Cuilenburg, 1987), as well as other evidence of saturation (Hicks, 1981) on the part of the audience, suggests that the appropriate criterion should be, not so much completeness of information available, as the effectiveness of information delivery on key topics to key groups – broadly, the degree of achieved or potential 'informativeness'.

The very large subject of news comprehension can only be touched upon. The origins of 'readability' research go back to the 1920s, focusing then on the stylistic qualities of written prose which would make for ease of reading and understanding. The first readability measure was designed by Flesch (1948). As with subsequent methods, this took account of various aspects of texts in order to establish potential 'ease of reading'. The main factors were: use of difficult words; length of sentences; aspects of personalization and human interest. Later researchers (e.g. Trenaman, 1967) established that such factors as concreteness of reference and personalization aided comprehension and recall of various kinds of media. There have been many studies of learning from, and understanding of, television news (e.g. Neuman, 1976; Berry and Clifford, 1982; Reese, 1984; Bernard and Coldevin, 1985; Findahl and Hoijer, 1985; Davis and Robinson, 1986; Woodall, 1986; Gurevitch and Levy, 1986; Gunter, 1987a), mainly concerned with the relation between attributes of news messages and learning effects.

The findings are complex, but leave us with the broad conclusion that attributes of 'personalization' (human interest), 'concreteness' and vivid 'visual presentation' are the message (content) factors most predictive of audience comprehension and recall. Although research is well advanced in methods of *message* analysis, the same cautionary lesson has been repeated through several decades – that factors of audience interest, attention and capacity to understand (education and prior knowledge) are more important for effective communication than are content variables. Another cautionary message, relevant to performance assessment, is that factors such as personalization, ease of vocabulary and vivid display, which are sometimes criticized as 'sensationalizing', 'trivializing' (see Chapter 17) or as interfering with true informative purpose, can be powerful aids to comprehension.

'Relevance' aspects of objective performance

Relevance is important to objectivity because even the most accurate facts are valueless if they are trivial, dated, uninteresting or beside the point. At issue is the central matter of news *selection*. According to the discussion in Chapter 15, relevance has primarily to be assessed in terms of the correspondence between what is offered to the audience and some independent standard of significance. Aside from the question of 'intra-textual' relevance (choice of text elements within one 'story'), there are three main foci of enquiry: the distribution of topics/news categories; the relative attention to particular events; and the picture of 'reality' offered overall in a given universe of content. These three can be measured on the 'media side' without great difficulty and in similar ways.

There are larger obstacles to finding appropriate and comparable 'extra-media content' indicators for assessing the degree of correspondence between message and a relevant reality. According to the earlier discussion (Chapter 15), such indicators can take any of several forms. One would be an 'ideal' or norm-based distribution, possibly derived from views of experts on what ought to be reported. Secondly, journalism's own professional criteria of news value may be deployed. A third possibility is to refer to the interests, preferences or opinions of the relevant media public (audience). Finally, some measures of external reality can be obtained by reference to the 'agendas' supplied by key institutional actors in the society. None of these, for reasons already noted, can offer a fully objective version of reality.

In interpreting findings about news performance, we have also to keep in mind that daily news is essentially a continuing guide to, and summary of, recent or current events and items of immediately useful information. It is produced under strong 'pressure of events', under conditions of intense competition with other media, which have their own versions of the day's agenda and from which it is difficult for any one medium to stray. News has also to meet quite restricting 'product specifications' which are built into the news form and embedded in the normal expectations of audiences. It is a perishable commodity which has to be sold continuously to a fickle set of customers. Much of the criticism of media on grounds of irrelevance stems from the gap between expectations of critics and the routine imperatives of news production.

Indicators of relevance in news

News selection and presentation is normally guided by the wish to help readers or listeners to grasp the essentials of events. The main question at issue is whether the choices made by news compilers are indeed adequate to the needs of the audience. In seeking to assess relevance from this point of view we have to assume that we can indeed 'read off' from content the journalistic judgements of relevance which were built into the selection and composition decisions of news media. The relative *salience* given to different topics or to event accounts in the news according to space, time or prominence is usually assumed to be an indicator of degree of imputed relevance. Traditional methods of content analysis allow us to pick up these cues. The usual procedures call for a measure of space/time allocation as between chosen categories of topic, actor, type of event, etc.

There are additional clues to salience, as early content analysts noted (Bush, 1960), since presentation and location in the newspaper usually indicate the relative priority which is *intended*: front, upper or right-hand page position as well as headline treatment and photographic illustration are the most common indicators. Primacy in order of presentation in radio and television news bulletins, as well as amount of time given, serve a similar purpose. There is evidence that such indicators of significance are also good predictors of actual audience attention to news items (e.g. McCombs and Mauro, 1988). The problem remains of finding independent standards of significance for assessing journalistic judgements of what is relevant for the audience to know. In order to go beyond these empirical indicators, we need to look in more detail at the other sources of relevance criteria introduced in Chapter 15.

Normative approaches to assessing relevance

Normative expectations about the needs which news information is supposed to meet in society provide one potential source of criteria. These may claim to specify 'objective' needs, but they are essentially subjective, often based on criticism of media shortcomings and on a commitment to some theory of media functions in a democratic society. Nordenstreng (1974), for example, explored the possibility of basing television news selection on a consistent 'informational policy', in which criteria of external objective significance might be deployed, but ended with more modest suggestions for separating decisions about the 'real significance' of news events from decisions about form or presentation. He also recommended providing more background commentary to explain the significance and make sense of the news.

In general, most normative approaches do tend to end up by simply favouring conventional categories of 'heavy' or 'serious' news about politics, economics and world events and news which have a high component of 'background' information. News of this kind is supposed, *in the long term*, to relate to things which affect more people's lives more deeply. In theory, such information might, eventually, help people to change or control their circumstances. This view of relevance is essentially a view from political theory in which significance is closely related to power. It is not likely to coincide with criteria of relevance derived from commercial or audience-attracting aims of media. It does, however, find an echo in the professional aspirations of some journalists, especially those with 'prestige' assignments (e.g. political and foreign desks) and those close to established social institutions.

Where *experts* have been asked to rate events or stories for their significance, the results generally reproduce similar conventional assumptions about what is important, or they reflect the priorities of news media themselves (Davis and Robinson, 1986; Vilanilam, 1989). It is not too surprising that Davis and Robinson (1986) should have found that the 'relevance' of US and British television news (among many other factors), as rated by experts on a five-point scale, proved to be a 'poor predictor of comprehension' (p. 208), since relevance was defined as 'importance to society', rather than importance to viewers. This underlines the potentially large gap between objectively assessed importance and what people subjectively find interesting.

Requirements for democracy The media have often been criticized because of their alleged failure to serve the needs of informed political participation. For example, the report of the first British Royal Commission on the Press (1949), which benefited from a detailed content analysis, concluded (para. 572): 'In our opinion, the newspapers, with few exceptions, fail to supply the electorate with adequate materials for sound political judgement.' Some subsequent supportive evidence for this view has been collected by way of tests of 'the knowledge gap hypothesis' (Gaziano, 1983), according to which differential exposure to media results in differential levels of knowledge, leading to structured inequalities in the distribution of information in society. Those sectors of a population which are relatively less exposed to informative media become functionally more ignorant. In democracies, this is thought to lead either to dangerous populism or to low levels of participation and to elite domination.

Most tests of the knowledge gap hypothesis (conducted in the United States) have assumed that television offers less, and less relevant, information than print media and that those more dependent on television for news are relatively disadvantaged. Clarke and Fredin (1978) argued, for example, that certain kinds of knowledge (the basis for making a rational choice between political alternatives) constitute the minimum conditions for informed citizenship. The 'mobilizing information' identified by Lemert (1989) might be an example of what counts as relevant from this point of view (see Chapter 9).

The rise of television as a primary medium for political campaigning has added to vocal public complaints that politics has been 'trivialized' to the level of a beauty contest or horse race and is no longer a major learning experience for citizens. Research into campaign coverage (e.g. Danielson and Adams, 1961; Graber, 1971; Adams, 1983) has shown a consistent tendency for television, especially, to pay more attention to (politically) superficial matters (personalities; 'horse race' aspects; mud-slinging; entertainment) than to substantive coverage of issues and policies.

There are obvious reasons why television might be less inclined to perform well in offering politically relevant information (in this sense) than the newspaper, as several studies have shown (Clarke and Ruggels, 1970; Robinson, 1972). Clarke and Fredin (1978) define possession of political information in terms of the ability to give reasons for favouring or rejecting political alternatives and show (by way of surveys) that reliance on television has a 'suppressing' rather than an 'enabling' effect in this respect (the knowledge gap, once more). According to critics, then, the media, in pursuit of their own ends, offer superficial content, irrelevant to political choice and, in so doing, they devalue the political institution. Their priorities, it is argued, owe more to 'media logic' (Altheide's phrase) than to political logic (Mazzoleni, 1987).

Sensationalism and human interest as problems 'Human interest' has been measured in several different ways. Curran et al. (1980), for instance, simply treat as 'human interest', any press content dealing with show business, crime, sex scandal and gossip, celebrities, etc. While rules can be made for classifying by theme or topic, this definition does not easily allow for the case of serious categories of news (e.g. politics) which may also (possibly for good reason) be treated in a 'human interest' manner.

An alternative approach to this aspect of relevance assessment is to measure 'sensationalism' as an attribute of all news, whatever the category (e.g. Tannenbaum and Lynch, 1960, 1962; Lynch et al., 1967; Lynch, 1968; Pasadeos, 1984; Pasadeos and Renfro, 1988) by giving attention to elements of personalism, drama, excitement, etc. (see Chapter 17). While attention to *personalities,* as such, is not necessarily *ir*relevant, the logic of this approach supposes that a near-exclusive attention to personal matters is diversionary and trivializing. Aside from diverting attention *from* what is of supposed *real* significance (serious things that impinge on the material experience of many people), concentration on human interest and sensation is said to exaggerate the importance of individual actions in world events (Ostgaard, 1965), and to reduce the will and capacity of people to act *on* real problems. It also appears, from studies of audience behaviour and from the 'knowledge gap' research mentioned above (Genova and Greenberg, 1979; Palmgreen, 1979), that it is the less well-off who are differentially supplied with the less relevant (more 'human interest') content and the better-off who also have a better supply of more 'nourishing' news (Curran et al., 1980).

Professional judgement as source of relevance criteria

It is questionable to assess media performance by the standards of journalism itself, but it makes sense to take some account of what news selectors think they are doing. In principle, an 'outside' investigator can also independently apply journalistic criteria to the news outcome. The pattern revealed by content analysis is only an aggregated version of the result of many individual decisions, rather than a clear indication of what journalists and editors really think about relevance. Much research, under the label of 'gatekeeping', has sought to describe and explain the systematic features of decision-making (Carter, 1958; Shoemaker, 1991). However, the results have shed little light on what news selectors generally regard as 'relevant', because so many other factors influence decisions (especially subjective ideas of what will interest an audience, ideas about topicality, the particular policy or persona of the news medium, the pressure of time and topicality).

News selection Participant observation of journalists at work has helped to chart the complexity of news decision-making, especially under great pressure of time. A detailed set of case studies of British newspapers and television illustrates this. Hetherington (1985) described how his own experience as an editor had led him to devise a 'seismic scale' of news value, comprising: significance; drama; surprise; personalities; sex; scandal; numbers; proximity. The components of 'significance' for most British media, he describes as: 'events or decisions which may affect the world's peace, the prosperity or welfare of people in Britain and abroad and the environment in which we live'. In his view this perspective puts an emphasis on continuity and harmony of the liberal democractic system, usually supports the status quo, occasionally attends to reform and is always somewhat parochial about British national interests.

Hetherington concluded that significance as interpreted by journalists has always tended towards 'sociocentrism' – the reinforcement of established society, upholding of law and order, gradualist reform (1985: 12). He concludes that journalists, consciously or not 'base their choice and treatment of news on two criteria (i) what is the political, social, economic and human importance of the event? And (ii) will it interest, excite and entertain our audience?' He claims that the first takes precedence over the second, but this is unlikely to be a universal rule. Cross-national evidence (e.g. Golding and Elliott, 1979; Gaunt, 1990) suggests that much the same factors play a similar role in different media systems.

According to Gans (1979), 'story importance' (as distinct from its potential interest) was judged by journalists according to four main dimensions: rank in government (or other hierarchies); impact on the nation and the national interest; impact on large numbers of people; significance for past and future (e.g. 'scoops' or 'record-breaking' events). Story 'importance' may also have a self-fulfilling character. Thus, Galtung and Ruge (1965) proposed that news events (or topics) already 'in the news', *ceteribus paribus*, have a higher chance of *remaining* in the news (following a similar notion of what counts as relevant).

News values The same authors concluded that certain news values, especially those which emphasize the 'personal', 'elite' and the 'negative' also influence decisions about news. Peterson (1979, 1981), looking at *input* by journalists rather than at output in content, found much confirmation of the Galtung and Ruge hypotheses. From interviews with journalists on *The Times* of London, using hypothetical news events, she concluded that the 'results suggest strongly that news criteria shape a picture of the world's events characterised by erratic, dramatic and uncomplicated surprise, by negative or conflictual events involving elite nations and persons.' The more this is true, the more it implies that relevance is determined by internal (organizational) considerations. There is a good deal of evidence as well as dispute concerning the allegation that media pay too much attention to 'bad news' (Gieber, 1955; Haskins, 1981; Haskins and Miller, 1984; Stone and Grusin, 1984).

'Significance' versus 'interest' as factors in judgement   A guide to what journalists think 'news' consists of, based on a survey of US press journalists, underlines an important distinction between significance and *interest* (Burgoon et al., 1982). First of all (41 per cent response), factors to do with *consequences* of events (things which affect the lives of readers) are mentioned. Secondly (32 per cent) come factors of *interest* (unusual, entertaining, talking point). Thirdly, at 17 per cent comes *timeliness*, followed by *proximity* and *prominence*, at 5 and 2 per cent. From this point of view, it would seem that the main components of relevance cut across conventional categories of content as used by producers or by most content analysts.

The approach to measuring relevance in terms of the relative prominence of certain conventional news *categories* (rather than characteristics of content or of actual events) is further undermined. In general, it also looks as if the conceptual distinction between 'importance' and 'interest' may not be much observed in day-to-day practice (what is important is just assumed to be interesting and vice versa). Nor is the distinction easy to sustain in any formal analysis.

However, support for drawing on professional journalistic judgements of significance, in assessing performance, can be derived from surveys of journalist and editor opinion which compare what editors think important with three other indications: what they think audiences actually want; what is actually offered as news priorities; what audiences say they want (e.g. Bogart, 1979; Ogan and Lafky, 1983). The evidence suggests that journalists do have a view of significance which differs from the priorities 'inscribed' in output, or from the immediate interests of audiences.

The audience as a guide to relevance assessment

Most journalists think that whatever affects and interests the public should have most influence on news selection. For performance assessment, the main requirement is to have a scale of news interests based on the views of the audience, which can be applied to what the media actually do offer. One method is to measure newspaper 'page traffic' (by readers) to discover what news items or kinds of content are looked at, with what degree of interest. Comparable measures of interest (relative attention or recall) can be taken for radio and television news bulletins, item by item (Robinson and Levy, 1986). The results can be processed to show relative interest in different topics and types of content, according to any chosen category system.

An American press example (Lehman, 1984) involved asking 1,200 readers about 36,000 items on sampled pages in two media markets. The results showed that an average of 35 per cent of all items were read, with a range of 22–51 per cent for 18 categories. High-scoring categories were: news summaries, 51 per cent; personal advice columns, 47 per cent; crime, 48 per cent; war, rebellions, 44 per cent. Environmental news and general interest took 36 per cent. Low-scoring categories were: unsigned editorial, 27 per cent; sport and government actions, 30 per cent. The results obviously depend on the events in any period sampled. British data derived in a similar way (Curran et al., 1980) have seemed to show a consistent, across the board, reader preference for 'human interest' subjects over hard news.

Another survey (Burgoon et al., 1982) asked readers to say which item they looked at in 'today's paper' with particular interest, using the copy as an aid to recall. The results divided roughly equally between national news stories (30 per cent) and state/local news (31 per cent), with 23 per cent mentioning international news items. A much simpler, but more dubious method (because so general and subject to 'social desirability'), is to ask about interest in given *types* of news. A British example of reader research (Royal Commission on the Press, 1977) reported that a high 49 per cent were interested in news about what the government is doing in Britain, followed by 27 per cent interested in foreign news. However, interest in news about local and regional matters was even higher, at 58 per cent. This seems to confirm the view that perceived relevance is closely related to actual *proximity*.

What readers or viewers notice and recall or say they find interesting is likely to be affected by *placement* in papers or bulletins (see above). Conventionally, more prominence is given to 'significant' political or international items, tending to increase the 'score' of these categories in audience ratings of interest, relevance or attention-giving. While reader (or viewer) interest can be charted in several ways, the results vary according to the methods used and the questions asked. McGrath (1980) showed, in addition, that the factors which seem best to explain audience attention vary from one subject area to another. In relation to government stories, headline size was the best predictor of interest, while for stories about people it was degree of human interest; for sport news it was the factor of length.

There are several other ways of assessing relevance for readers and viewers. For instance, members of the public can be asked which events they consider important during a previous year, as did Ogan and Lafky (1983), with a view to comparing the audience's perception of news values with that of media decision-makers. Respondents ($N = 196$) mentioned 1,258 events, nearly 100 of them different. The results appeared to show a higher audience rating for major international and national events than conventional news decisions make allowance for. This conflicts with a more commonly heard view that responsible journalism has to struggle against the more 'trivial' interests of their audiences.

Another divergent example of a research approach is Weaver's (1979) proposal to assess people's information needs by asking, not what items people read, but what they would *miss*. These do not mean the same thing. Weaver's more general argument is that conventional measures of audience needs/interests are too strongly shaped by what is currently on offer and readily available. Consequently, reference to the audience will not necessarily produce an independent assessment of relevance. Such alternative methods of assessing the relevance of news in terms of correspondence with empirical measures of audience interest imply a standard of 'consumer sovereignty' which conflicts with some claims of journalistic professionalism, as well as with the 'absolutist' or expert approaches discussed at the outset. Most evidence (especially where it relates to more 'responsible' media) does confirm a mismatch between supply and demand for serious and background news and analysis, reflecting the conflict between professional judgements of relevance (as a sign of significance) and the apparent 'immediate gratification-seeking' of news audiences (Levy, 1978).

In general, it has to be concluded that any audience-based approach to assessing performance in terms of relevance is subject to several limitations. Different methods of research (and forms of questioning) can produce quite different results and thus different versions of what the audience expects. Secondly, the results of audience research always reflect current media practice to some degree and are, consequently, not fully independent of actual performance. Thirdly, there remains an unresolvable conflict between the professional viewpoint which claims autonomy of judgement about selection and the pressure to please an audience by giving them what they appear to want.

'Real world' indicators and institutional agendas

The path to establishing relevance by comparing media priorities with actual events ('real world' priorities) has been followed in several studies. For example, Behr and Iyengar (1985) collected 'indicators of current conditions' in each issue area studied. These indicators were drawn mainly from economic statistics and from (US) presidential addresses to the nation. They concluded, after an analysis of a six-year period, that network TV news is partially determined by real world conditions and events and then goes on to influence the public opinion agenda. Erbring et al. (1980) used similar methods with similar results, although most research casts doubt on the degree to which media attention correlates with 'reality' (Funkhouser, 1973). 'Real world' tests of selection bias (see Chapter 17) can also serve as indicators of relevance (e.g. crime statistics; industrial dispute statistics). However, we cannot assume that there is a knowable empirical reality 'out there', or that the news media ought simply to 'reflect' this in a quantitatively proportional way (see Chapter 12). There are always alternative standards by which the 'real world' can be assessed (Rosengren, 1980).

Divergent audience realities   In any case, any total audience is always differentiated according to their experience of reality and potential information needs and interests (especially by reference to life-cycle and socioeconomic position). Different media can also be differentially relevant for different purposes. Gollin (1982) has empirically identified five main 'social roles' for which a newspaper might be relevant as: family member; citizen or voter; worker; consumer; user of leisure time. It would be impossible to say, in general, which of these was more salient, yet each leads to a somewhat different notion of relevance.

When the British Press Commission (1977) looked at attitudes of community 'influentials' to the press (in business, politics, education, etc.), they found significantly different expectations and judgements (from those of the general public), reflecting their special professional and political information requirements. Any special public or set of relevant 'opinion leaders' can be regarded as providing an independent standard of relevance. Research into audience 'uses and gratifications' has also opened the way to possible divisions of the audience according to different news interest, which can serve a similar purpose (e.g. Levy, 1978; McLeod et al., 1982; Wenner, 1985).

Institutional agendas The study of media influence, under the heading of 'agenda-setting' (Becker, 1982; and p. 163 above) has provided, as a by-product, another means of assessing the relevance of news, if the standard of what is relevant is defined in terms of priorities (e.g. among issues or topics) which are set outside the media. Agenda-setting research has mainly sought to test the proposition that priorities found in media (as measured by space and prominence) will shape the priorities of public (or audience) opinion. The related proposition that media priorities reflect those set by politicians (or other agencies seeking to influence the public) has also been investigated. Leaving aside the question of *direction* of influence, on which there is little agreement, the data from such research yield two alternative and simple tests of relevance: media are more relevant where their priorities are closer to those of politicians (or other opinion leaders); or more relevant where they are close to those of the public.

Mass communication, crisis and risk

A different route to assessing informational performance of mass media is to study critical situations and events when the media are very much depended on, rather than looking at the separate dimensions of performance on their own. In times of war, civil disturbance, disaster or crisis (and more routinely at elections), there is a heightened awareness of the role of the media and most of the factors discussed here will be important. There is a growing literature on these questions (see Scanlon, 1961; Walters et al., 1989; Nacos, 1990), which deploys various criteria of media performance, but especially: the speed and accuracy of information transmission; the diversity of sources drawn on (to reduce reliance on official spokespersons and chance of news manipulation); and the adequacy of advance warnings given by the media.

A related object of enquiry has been the performance of the media in giving information about long-term risks on a wide range of matters, ranging from health to crime (e.g. Friedman, 1981; Freimuth et al., 1984; Singer and

Endreny, 1987). Singer and Endreny generally indict the media for paying undue attention to the very serious and very rare hazards and very little to everyday and continuing *risks*, which do not have the same news value as disaster and crisis.

Diversity of relevance

It is clear that there are quite a few different and independent sets of criteria, and thus measures of relevance, which can be sensibly applied to actual news on offer. However, there is no single objective way of choosing between the different criteria and any choice will have to be supported by arguments for its particular merits. The problem for the media themselves is less one of making relevant selections than of oversupply of potential news and also the problem of being faced with multiple, inconsistent and only partly predictable audience requirements. A common response in these circumstances is to offer 'something for everyone', a practice which inevitably 'dilutes' the seeming relevance for any single interest or point of view, according to any one standard. In a sense, *diversity* of offer is likely to be incompatible with any notion of systematic or consistent relevance.

For reasons of convenience and clarity, this chapter has dealt almost exclusively with *cognitive* aspects of news information. For purposes of close examination, facts have been illegitimately separated from values and dimensions of performance disaggregated from each other in an abstract way. The following chapter tries to redress the balance by looking at value dimensions of media information, but it needs to be said that an exclusive attention to the criteria of assessment discussed in this chapter would largely fail to capture the nature of mass media information. The media respond to complex events in complex ways and are used by different interests for quite diverse purposes.

17
MEASURING OBJECTIVITY: THE EVALUATIVE DIMENSION OF NEWS

News as values

It is hard to overstate the degree to which all news information is bound to be an expression, reflection and outcome of values as well as a recital of facts, although the balance between the two varies a good deal. In general, however, 'news is values' for three main reasons. First, the sources of news, in any of the senses identified earlier, are usually pursuing some value goal of their own. Secondly, the media and news producers are also influenced by their values, however much these are kept in check. Thirdly, the audience for whom news is produced and selected (according to 'news values'), not only looks for information, but also needs to make sense of the world in evaluative terms. They (we) want to know if things are getting better or worse, are better here than there, want to see praise or blame apportioned and want to follow the doings of heroes and villains. The evaluative frameworks deployed by media and audiences are often more pervasive, enduring and powerful than any cognitive schemes. The attempt to cope with this situation in assessment research has been guided by the notion of impartiality.

The impartiality component of objective news performance

The idea of 'impartiality' is a complex mixture of several elements, which can be found under different names, including even-handedness, neutrality, fairness, non-partisanship. Or it can be recognized by what it is not, especially 'bias', 'slant', tendentiousness, etc. A choice has been made to deal with it under two main headings: *balance,* which refers to the selection and substance of news; and the other concerned with *neutral* presentation (see Figure 15.3). The two are not, even so, easy to distinguish either in research practice or in the *perceptions* of an audience. In the investigation of evaluative direction, we should bear in mind that there are different types of bias (see Chapter 14) and the form taken by value direction will vary from one type to another, as will the methods which are appropriate. In general, the more 'open' kinds of bias ('unwitting' and partisanship) are more easily dealt with by way of face-value classification and statistical methods, while 'hidden bias' (ideology and propaganda) may call for more depth of qualitative analysis and more interpretation and argument.

Balance

Most research into balance or its absence has followed a fairly standard pattern. Relevant content is first identified for analysis by channel and format (news item, editorial, letter, etc.). Within items, smaller units of analysis may be located in different ways: as shots (in TV); as units of continuous speech; as 'main points' of a news story; as units of information (facts); as statements, sentences or even words. This 'unitization' opens the way for characterizing news accounts in terms of the degree of space/time given to one or other 'side', interest, viewpoint, etc., leading to precise measures of tendency in terms of balance of attention between the relevant positions. Decisions about which positions, actors or perspectives are relevant have to be taken case by case.

Important to any interpretation of results will be the initial choice of a criterion of balance and the selection of a universe of content and of items to study. Balance can be determined either according to the *internal* balance within news story/item (or whole programme in the case of television documentary) or, alternatively, over a range of items and programmes (thus over time). Balance may also be assessed either 'horizontally' (across different media at one point in time) or 'vertically' (one or several media over an extended time period).

While the approach described is usually sufficient to establish the basic 'facts' of balance in a news text or universe of texts (or in a single media channel over time), further refinements are possible which extend the range of this research model, although usually with reduced reliability. For instance, account can be taken of conventions of news make-up (as noted earlier), according to which relative prominence and rank order, linkage, sequence, etc., can be interpreted as implying direction and valuation. Impartiality, in the sense of balance, would call for even-handed allocation in texts as between the relevant sides, actors or interests. Also relevant to balance may be the topics of news with which actors are associated, especially where negative or positive value is implied (topics may vary in this respect).

In essence, the model relies on the assumption that cognitive references (all 'facts', real world objects and events) are given meaning and thus an implied evaluative direction (positive, neutral, negative) in two main ways: first, as an aspect of *selection*, by their relative prominence and the degree of attention received; secondly, as an aspect of *evaluative direction by association*, direct or indirect, with indicators of value or favourability in language (verbal or visual), e.g. the 'grammar' of network news analysed by Frank (1973) or by overall context, which can have a positive or negative implication or connotation.

There is a quantitative aspect to both: what counts is the overall balance of attention to relevant objects (*ceteribus paribus*, more attention equals more positive), plus any excess of positive over negative indicators of evaluation, or vice versa. The logic of assessment calls for separate attention to these two factors, since they can and often do vary independently, although they often overlap. Entman (1989) adds two other indicators of what he calls 'slant': the inclusion of specific criticism (or praise); and 'perspective' – essentially the degree to which a *diversity of sources* is drawn on (in general, the fewer sources, the more likely that an interpretation in one direction is being favoured; Shoemaker, 1983).

Balance in election campaigns

The prototypical situation for applying balance analysis has been that of news reporting of democratic elections, where the opposing sides are easy to identify and where there are clear criteria of assessment (balance = equal or proportional representation of parties or candidates). There are usually expectations (albeit variably) of fair treatment and great potential significance is attributed to access (see also Chapter 13). The history of research into media balance in elections pre-dates the second World War. Lazarsfeld et al. (1944), for instance, compared press and radio coverage of candidates Roosevelt and Wilkie in the 1940 presidential election and found that the media '*centred*' on Roosevelt by a margin of 3 : 2 (in quantitative terms), but they *favoured* Wilkie by a margin of 2 : 1, illustrating the independence of measures of *degree* and of *direction* of attention, as noted above.

A large number of studies followed, prominent amongst them Klein and Maccoby's (1954) research into newspaper bias in the 1952 US election, especially into the relation between the editorial stand of newspapers and the content of their news reports. They defined bias as the 'existence of a *differential*, larger than could be expected by chance alone, between the front page coverage allotted the two candidates by the two sets of papers (supporting Eisenhower or Stevenson)'. Here 'differential' was measured by 18 variables, including aspects of prominence, language, quotes, photos and biased remarks.

A heightened level of political controversy in the United States in the 1960s and the enhanced role and status of the supposedly objective network TV news led to renewed research, sometimes of a polemical nature (e.g. Efron, 1971; Cirino, 1971; Weaver, 1972; Meadow, 1973; Stevenson and Shaw, 1973; Paletz and Elson, 1976). Representative of this phase is Hofstetter's (1976) careful analysis of the network news coverage of the 1972 election campaign, for possible bias in attention to the presidential candidates, McGovern and Nixon. Balance was assessed in terms of amount and kind of attention, choice of topics, coverage of policies, linkages of candidates to other groups and interests and any possible evaluative associations. Little evidence of any tendency to favour one or other was found, nor any differential political bias by the three networks.

Patterson and McClure's (1976) study of network news in the same election, however, reached a different conclusion, reporting that network news disadvantaged McGovern, especially by neglecting his policy positions and personal qualities for leadership. While he received about the same attention as Nixon in these respects, the result was said to be relatively unfair to the *contender* for office (as opposed to the incumbent). Referring to other studies, Comstock et al. (1978) decide that any 'bias' that might be imputed was more due to campaign strategies deliberately adopted by the candidates rather than by the media coverage as such. Clancy and Robinson (1988) looked in great detail at the balance of attention to Reagan and Mondale in the 1984 campaign, computing the precise number of seconds on several dimensions of coverage, according to whether the candidates received a 'bad' or a 'good' press. On matters of candidate quality, Reagan received 7,230 seconds of 'bad press' and Mondale only 1,050, while on 'horse-race' stories, the balance was reversed at 1,200 : 5,880.

It is clearly difficult to reconcile the claim for precise numerical balance in these terms with the expectation that news will faithfully reflect a *reality* in which the candidates, as well as their policies and their chances of success, are very likely to merit (or for other reasons actually receive) varying evaluations. The 'real world' has no obligation to be statistically fair. *Relevance* criteria are also unlikely to coincide precisely with the norm of balance. The real significance (by whatever criterion) of what candidates do or say and their potential interest to audiences, are not likely to coincide.

The studies cited illustrate well the limitations of precise quantitative measures for reaching conclusions about 'bias' and also the tenuousness of arguments and interpretations based on *omission*. The stop-watch measure of balance in output only takes one to a certain point. It reflects the concerns of interested 'senders', rather than any rational weighing of likely consequences of balance or imbalance. Unless audience reach (and, if possible, response) is also taken into account – thus factors of timing and format, which determine how much of what kind of message is likely to reach how many and what kind of viewer – amount of media attention is limited as an indicator of media performance. Nor can time/space measures reveal much without reference to the context and the specifics of actual content.

The attempt to assess the balance of direction in treatment of political figures, in or out of elections, is also often vitiated by the 'intervention' of other factors, especially 'real world' events (good or bad) in which political figures are implicated (for instance, the Iran hostage crisis and Carter's electoral fortunes, as analysed by Entman, 1989). The requirements of the media system itself for certain kinds of stories and certain kinds of sources also intervene to make absolute balance an unrealistic expectation.

Evaluative direction in news accounts

There are many matters of political controversy, besides elections or party politics, where news has to deal with alternative positions and opposed sides (or multiple parties to an event). These issues include nuclear power, industrial relations, abortion, crime and punishment, international conflicts, armaments and defence, all subjects which have been represented in research into impartiality. The norm generally applied in such issues is based on the widespread public expectation of 'fairness' in presenting alternative points of view which, in turn, is often interpreted as requiring strict neutrality.

However, there are events (e.g. a terrorist outrage on innocent bystanders) where such strong emotions are aroused that neutrality is not even an acceptable option (Hemánus, 1976). In practice, the expectation of neutrality is relative and can even be reversed, where fundamental values are at stake. Comstock et al. (1978) make a similar point in relation to television coverage of the Vietnam War, which was extraordinarily balanced according to the evidence they discuss. They write: ' "Balanced" coverage would include an equal weight of pro- and anti-administration content; but this might not be "fair" – a concept which would vary with views of the war' (Comstock et al., 1978: 50).

The aims of analysis are much the same in most such controversies: to identify the direction and strength of tendencies in news reports, which can in the end be reduced to a positive or negative sum, for or against one position or the other. The most widely used method (aside from identifying obvious 'slant' in supposedly neutral accounts) is to judge whether reported actions, events or other associated facts are likely to reflect favourably or unfavourably on one side, position or party to the controversial issue. It is a method which requires speculation of a common-sense kind on the likely impression made on an average audience. Westerståhl (1983) applied the approach in order to assess the neutrality of Swedish broadcasting in covering the Vietnam War (and other issues). He gives examples of items of news 'favourable' to Vietnam as: support given by the civilian population; release of prisoners; willingness to negotiate; successful military action. Items 'unfavourable' to the Vietnamese cause include: low morale; murder of civilians; no desire for peace.

The numerical sum of negative and positive items, assessed in this way, constituted a scale along which different media channels and different objects of reporting could be compared in terms of the implicit direction of reporting. Clearly, the mathematical 'middle point' along such a scale will be an arbitrary outcome (depending on the specific channels and content chosen and the criteria applied for judging value implications) and not an absolute standard. However, the method serves quite well for comparative and relative assessment.

In various versions, it has been widely used; for example, for comparing the CBS and NBC coverage of US Vietnam War policy (Russo, 1971); for assessing the treatment of ethnic minorities (Hartman and Husband, 1974; van Dijk, 1991); for assessing the balance of news treatment of workers and management in disputes (McQuail, 1977); in comparing news images of Israel and the Arab countries (e.g. Rikardsson, 1978); for assessing the German media treatment of the 1973 oil crisis (Kepplinger and Roth, 1979); in analysing media coverage of nuclear energy (Westerståhl and Andersson, 1991). In an adapted form, it has been used for comparing US media treatment of elections in El Salvador and Nicaragua (Herman, 1985), where 'supportive' and 'non-supportive' aspects of news were cited. Shoemaker (1984) also used the approach to compare differential media treatment of 'established' and 'marginal' minority groups.

Reasonable degrees of reliability seem to be attainable in assigning positive or negative value to news, although these judgements must presuppose some broad consensus about what is 'good' or 'bad'. However, it is clear from the research that many elements of news reports cannot be classified as either positive or negative, so that an assessment of overall balance or tendency may often depend on a rather small proportion of the total volume of relevant news information (cf. the research by Lichter and Rothman, 1986). The results *ought* also to reflect a considerable element of 'reality' input (thus not just media 'bias') if the news really is independent and objective. Thus, *unsuccessful* participants in events (e.g. Carter in Iran, or the US in Vietnam), or those with negative roles (e.g. unions in strikes), or various kinds of victim, are likely, in the nature of the case, to come out 'badly' (in a negative light) according to such measures, without their being any intended, or even avoidable, *bias* on the part of the news media.

We are dealing rather with a predictor of *effect on audiences*, than with a measure of intention by the sender. However, where (as Westerståhl reported), different media channels do deviate sharply from each other in reporting the *same* event, we have some control of the 'reality' component and there is *prima facie* evidence of conscious editorial choice on the part of news media to favour a particular side as well as of prediction of effect. What is presumably happening is *differential selection* of (and possibly differential prominence for) positive and negative aspects, sometimes out of policy, sometimes by chance or as a result of organizational factors.

External tests of balance in coverage

It is theoretically possible to apply *external* and independent standards of 'truth' or reality to what is found in news reports, for instance by way of official or judicial reports of events such as riots and civil disturbances, but this is unusual. Another possibility is to measure supposed media bias on a controversial matter against an external standard of truth furnished by 'experts'. Lichter and Rothman (1986), for instance, looked at the issue of nuclear power and claimed to show a pronounced 'anti-nuclear' bias by the *New York Times* and network news, compared to opinion held by the relevant scientific community. However, even in this case, 83 per cent of 486 newspaper stories were classified as 'neutral/balanced'. Some of the theory and evidence discussed in Chapter 12, in respect of 'distortion' of social reality, is also relevant to this point (see Rosengren, 1980).

Source bias

A frequent element in impartiality analysis is a count and classification of *sources*, referred to or cited, according to side or perspective on an issue. In general, the balance norm calls for an equal or proportionate reference to sources of similar standing, on similar terms. These conditions are rarely achieved, because of varying power and status of groups (sides) in disputes. Most studies show more attention to official, more authoritative, sources or more attention to the 'voices' with the best organization and resources.

It is not surprising that Donohue et al. (1985) found, in their Minnesota community study, that the powerful are more satisfied with the media coverage they receive than are less-resourced groups. Because of possible association with negative events, it is not necessarily beneficial to be cited. For instance, in British industrial relations reporting, research has shown there to be a tendency for union spokespersons to have higher 'visibility' than management in disputes (e.g. McQuail, 1977), but also to be often associated with strikes portrayed as harming the public. The possible contribution of management to the causing of strikes was implicitly underplayed, as a result of their low profile in news reports (see Fiske, 1987). Kellner (1990) comments on the invisibility of labour in TV news and on the fact that the networks have business reporters but no labour reporters.

In some cases, the very absence of certain sources may indicate a one-sided definition of an issue or will predictably lead to one-sided reporting (Wulfmeyer, 1983b). Giffard's (1989) study of media reporting of the US withdrawal from UNESCO in 1984 depends heavily on evidence of the differential use of sources by American media. Most news came from the main American news agencies, whose reports were overwhelmingly hostile to UNESCO in thematic content, the news agencies themselves obtaining the bulk of their attributed statements from the US government (also hostile to UNESCO). The result in media content predictably reproduced the anti-UNESCO imbalance, even though there were enough alternative reports and positions available for source 'balance' to have been achieved on the withdrawal issue, had this been wanted (see also Preston et al., 1989, for similar conclusions).

The effects of over-reliance by US media on State Department information about Central America (Herman and Chomsky, 1988) and about other incidents closely related to national foreign policy concerns have also been detailed (e.g. the manipulation of the media after the shooting down of the Korean airliner in 1983; Herman, 1986). The nature of what is conventionally acceptable as sources for news limits the range of diversity (Brown et al., 1987), and sometimes it is virtually impossible to balance sources acceptably.

In some categories of event with a high immediate impact (e.g. a nuclear accident or a military action), it is first impressions which may shape public response to, and definition of, an event and 'expert' and official sources may inevitably play a disproportionate role (Walters et al., 1989). Use of *unattributed* sources may, in itself, be taken as an indication of lack of objectivity, partly because this breaks with the normal rules of evidence and is one way of introducing, or allowing in, partisan views (Shoemaker, 1983;

Wulfmeyer, 1983b). It also tends to disadvantage the less powerful, who are less able either to deploy (or to object to), this form of source support (Shoemaker, 1984).

Semantic and discourse bias

There has been much interest in the differential use of language as an indicator of underlying meaning, direction or ideology (and thus of bias). It is assumed that evaluative direction is always implicit in the choice of words and phrases in any kind of text, and that such direction is open to decoding (examples of approaches include Lasswell et al., 1952; Osgood et al., 1957; Graber, 1976a; Edelman, 1977; Porter, 1983; Bennett and Edelman, 1985; Geis, 1987; Manoff and Schudson, 1987; Edelman, 1988; van Dijk, 1988, 1991). Analysis of language use can be applied to reveal the precise nature of intended 'bias' or partisanship or to uncover unintended direction or 'slant'. Methods of analysis vary from the common sense to the arcane, but all share an assumption that any culture organizes meaning and allocates values, by means of symbols, in a consistent way so that what counts as positive or negative can be readily deciphered by those who share the culture (the relevant language or 'interpretative' community).

A simple method adopted by the Glasgow Media Group (1985) in their study of television coverage of the Falklands War involved making an inventory of the words used in TV news to report the sinking of an Argentine cruiser, the *Belgrano* and the loss of a British destroyer, the *Sheffield*. They found that, in the former case, the word 'killed' or 'killing' only appeared once in 249 separate statements in the news (implicitly modifying the gravity of what was a controversial action). In the *Sheffield* case, a much 'harder' terminology was used to refer to the Argentine deed, with much more frequent use of death and 'killing' word equivalents. A somewhat similar analysis was applied by van Dijk (1991) to reports of racial disturbances in Britain.

More systematic and elaborate methods have been based on Osgood and colleagues' (1957) work on the evaluative structure of texts and language usage. This approach depends on having some independent empirical evidence of the evaluative direction and intensity of commonly used terms, as these are usually interpreted by users of the language. The method of 'evaluative assertion analysis' (see Holsti, 1969) was developed to measure evaluative direction and intensity of meaning in texts. It has recently been revived and converted for computer-aided application by van Cuilenburg et al. (1986).

In order to apply the method, texts are divided into units of analysis ('nuclear' sentences) and three main verbal elements are identified: attitude objects (references to persons, things, etc., which are objects of evaluation); words (usually adjectival or adverbial) referred to as having 'common meaning' – thus whose evaluative direction (and relative intensity) will be widely understood in the language community (e.g. 'evil' and 'unreliable' are both negative in direction, but the former more so than the latter); and 'connectors' – language parts which supply the *linkages* between attitude objects and common meaning terms, thus establishing calculable patterns of evaluative direction.

Complete texts can be rendered in terms of directional scores for any attitude object referred to and also for the whole complex of evaluative relations between attitude objects. This step reveals 'networks' of attraction and dislike. The method has been variously applied (e.g. Westley and Higsbie, 1963; Lynch and Effendi, 1964; Holsti, 1969; Kanno, 1972), although its labour intensiveness has, in the pre-computer age, been a major drawback (but see van Cuilenburg et al., 1986 for a partial solution). Variants of this approach can be found in Geis (1982, 1987) or by way of Stevenson's Q-sort (see Holsti, 1969).

Evaluative structures (frames) of meaning

Related to such methods are approaches which characterize reports according to larger evaluative frameworks, 'referential structures', 'definitions of situations' or 'themes'. Various such framing devices may be derived from an analysis of ideology, narrative forms, from the nature of news discourse itself (e.g. Schudson, 1982; van Dijk, 1983, 1991), or from the conventions and practices of news organizations (Bell, 1991). Altheide (1985) and Altheide and Snow (1979), for instance, have argued that news is 'packaged' in standardized formats each with typical 'codes' for presentation which tell the receiver how to 'read' stories. The Glasgow Media Group (1976) make a similar claim.

There are many variants of method for recognizing such structuring devices, but they all share the assumption that meaning and evaluative direction are likely to be differentially influenced by the wider context (of other information and opinion) in which event reports are placed, however factual or balanced the event report itself. Such research also makes (unspoken) appeal to the notion of 'common meaning' as applied to definitions of news events. However, some theorists would put more emphasis on the possibilities of differential decoding and on the chance to apply an 'opposition' reading (Hartley, 1982). In other words, while a ready-made interpretation (a 'preferred meaning') may be 'offered', the offer may well be declined if it fails to match the situation and disposition of the receiver.

There are numerous examples of the shaping of news within larger frames of interpretation. Halloran et al. (1970) showed that news of an anti-Vietnam War demonstration in London in 1968 was shaped in actual reporting by advance definitions of the event as violent, confrontational and involving foreign 'agitators'. The news accounts were 'pre-structured' by certain 'news angles' which derived more from the culture of the news media and the climate of the times than from the specific reality of the event.

Both Hartman and Husband (1974) and van Dijk (1991) analysed reporting of 'race relations' in terms of dominant news themes, which tended to define the very presence of 'immigrants' as 'problematic' for the host society. McQuail (1977) used a thematic classification of various categories of news (international; social welfare; industrial relations) in order to assess evaluative tendencies in content. Giffard (1989) analysed coverage of the withdrawal from UNESCO in terms of 189 themes, ultimately reduced to three categories: pro-UNESCO; anti-UNESCO; and future-orientated. The approach sometimes draws on the notion of a news 'angle' or 'peg' which is likely to influence selection and shape treatment (Roshco, 1975). It is linked to the wider questions of news values and relevance.

Sometimes very broad scenarios or schemas (another analogy from drama, implying that news is 'scripted' or framed in advance – see Axelrod, 1973) are invoked, such as those of 'cold war', 'energy crisis', 'environmental disaster', 'world terrorism', etc. When such frameworks are deployed, objective practice, in the sense of balance or impartiality on matters of fact, is bound to have much more limited scope and cannot secure neutrality of overall tendency, since this is likely to be governed by definitions embedded into schemas. Journalistic judgements about what is relevant (which, theoretically, should increase objectivity) are also likely to be guided by such frameworks of meaning. What is relevant within one overall definition may not be so in any other sense or in an alternative schema.

'Preferred reading' in news

For similar reasons, much critical theory and research on news (see, e.g., Hartley, 1982) sees news practice as inescapably ideological and tendentious, with balance itself serving only to emphasize what Hall has termed a 'preferred reading', or an interpretation preferred by the source (usually favourable to the established social order). If balance in the news is the balance of the 'powers that be' then it is likely to have a conservative tendency, however unintended. The essence of the case is that news (and objectivity) ultimately rests on an assumed consensus (the sociocentrism mentioned by Hetherington, 1985) about the legitimacy of the established order and about national and institutional interests.

News practices, especially those which serve to define the range of issues and what is relevant to them, inevitably legitimize certain sources and actors and stigmatize others. They also invoke common meanings and often operate to close off oppositional or deviant perspectives on events (Davis and Walton, 1983). The discourse of news is structured in a way which discourages diversity of interpretation, even when formally open and balanced. However, there can be significant variations in the degree to which news storytelling is open or closed (Schlesinger et al., 1983).

Neutral presentation

Several of the methods for assessing the balance of direction also touch on aspects of presentation (for instance, matters of placement, relative prominence, headlining, choice of words, etc.). There is, nevertheless, scope for separate analysis. In general, irrespective of who might or might not benefit, objectivity requires that reporting be dispassionate, cool, restrained and careful. By that measure, all forms of sensationalism, use of loaded words, emotionalism or 'colour' in presentation are departures from neutrality and objectivity.

Sensationalism

There have been a number of attempts at systematic measurement of sensationalism, for instance by Tannenbaum and Lynch (1960, 1962; Lynch, 1968). Aspects of sensationalism have also been included as attributes of news stories in research on news comprehension (Robinson and Levy, 1986). In the end, 'sensationalism' often comes down to a high degree of personalization, emotionalism and dramatization in content. It also entails distinctive forms of presentation designed to gain audience attention: use of large headlines, photographic illustration, much film material, sound and dramatic music, etc.

Formats and visuals in TV news

Aside from the view that visual devices designed primarily to catch attention are incompatible with strictly neutral reporting, it has also been argued (with some supporting evidence) that visual elements in TV news are often irrelevant to, or diversionary from, the essence of a news story as told in words (e.g. Katz et al., 1977). If so, visual elements can distract attention from, or interfere with, 'learning' from the verbal text of news, which may itself remain 'neutral' in form. The increasing use of a 'happy news' format in television, in which presenters chat with each other, has also been suspected of reducing the information value of news (Dominick et al., 1975).

Even so, news has to attract and interest an audience in order to communicate at all, and most of the presentation features which have been mentioned seem likely to contribute to this end, especially under conditions of competition for audience attention. The ideal of total presentation neutrality is only likely to be reached under monopoly channel conditions or in cases where highly motivated (and relatively small) audiences are being addressed.

Aside from the matter of strongly coloured and value-laden words and phrases in news texts, especially in print and broadcast headlines, the analysis of presentational devices is little developed (but see Lichty and Bailey, 1978). Most researchers into the presentational 'bias' of television news would agree that as much account has to be taken of pictures, sound effects, captions, logos, etc. as of words. Research teams, such as the Glasgow Media Group (1980, 1985), have tried pragmatically to do so, but so far there is no agreement on what a relevant 'grammar' of television news film would be like (Frank, 1973; Adams, 1978).

Analyses of news stories usually develop as *ad hoc* interpretations of presentation (e.g. Davis and Walton, 1983, on the Moro abduction story). It is quite clear that selection, sequence and interaction of visual and auditory content in television are usually planned with an intention of conveying a particular meaning and, therefore, with a potential for biasing the interpretation of the viewer. One of the few clear conclusions which Davis and Walton (1983) were able to draw from their extensive analysis of television news is the low degree of *iconicity* of visuals – meaning that visuals rarely convey images of the reality which is being described in verbal texts and that they are usually ambiguous.

Television news style is only beginning to be analysed in detail. Nimmo and Combs (1985), for instance, distinguished four journalistic styles in television news: the 'popular/sensational'; the 'elitist/factual'; the 'ignorant/ didactic' (treating the audience as ignorant); and the 'pluralist' (treating the audience as very diverse). Only the second of these really conforms to the objective mode.

Especial attention has focused on camera angles, timing, distance and shot framing as devices for conveying meaning (Tiemens, 1970; Frank, 1973; Mandell and Shaw, 1973; Zettl, 1973; Tuchman, 1978; Kepplinger, 1983). Tiemens et al. (1988) concluded from a detailed analysis of visuals in reporting by five TV sources of Jackson's 1984 Democratic convention speech that each version was a different experience for the viewer and also different from the actual speech as it occurred. By implication, there was no objective mediated version, but also no way of reliably assessing any bias in intention.

Stereotypes, juxtaposition and linkages

Numerous other possibilities exist for features of presentation to influence interpretation. Brief mention can be made of two such: stereotyping and linking/juxtaposition. The use of stereotypes has long been observed and sometimes investigated in relation to bias (e.g. Merrill, 1965). Individuals, groups or nations are often treated in news according to simplified and recurrent attributes, which may have positive or negative associations, but are neither neutral nor likely to correspond with a particular reality. The stereotype may be used for economy or ease of communication, but its use always carries risks of loss of neutrality and can have a biasing effect.

News media frequently link things together: different aspects of a single news event; different stories in the same news bulletin or page area; different actors in relation to a single event or issue, etc. Often this is in the interest of establishing unity or cohesion in situations of diversity or uncertainty. Sometimes it helps to establish a particular mood (e.g. of alarm or crisis, which may serve the self-interest of the news media). It also stems from the practice of employing certain kinds of news discourse or narrative structure which can reinforce certain overall schemes of interpretation (Graber, 1976b).

Juxtaposition (either by association or contrast) of items on newspaper pages (or film montage) can also alter the apparent meaning of separate elements of news texts. A study of psychological propaganda in the Chilean press before the military overthrow and murder of President Allende in 1973 showed a tendency to associate left-wing political activity with gruesome crime, by way of juxtaposing reports on the page. The intention was, apparently, to promote a climate of alarm and horror which would undermine the government (Durán and Urzúa, 1978).

The audience view of balance and neutrality

If objectivity (or its absence) is ultimately significant because of its probable or actual effect on audiences, there would seem to be scope for audience research on several of the questions discussed. Much attention has been paid to the general question of *credibility*, a quality which is related to accuracy as well as to perceived independence and neutrality of the news offered (see Chapter 16). Certainly, there is no shortage of methods for enquiring into how the audience evaluates media presentation or for assessing perceptions and possible effects of bias in media content.

In the early days of research into persuasion and propaganda, for instance, the question of whether it was better to present 'both sides' of an argument rather than one in order to achieve some persuasive purpose was investigated. At issue was the possibility that 'bias' (even when used with good intentions) might always be counter-productive, because it would undermine credibility. However, the news situation differs from that of planned persuasion and the findings are not likely to be interchangeable. In general, research into the effect of bias has to be of a quasi-experimental or intensive nature, yielding results concerning *particular* content and events (see Halloran et al., 1970). The findings have usually lent more support to the school of audience resistance, 'differential decoding' and unpredictability of effect than to those who fear the direct effects of biased news.

In respect of 'believability' (credibility) of news, audience research does not typically show much potential for discriminating among particular channels or sources. For instance, Robinson and Kohut (1988) report ratings of 'believability' for a number of US news 'sources' (persons as well as specific programmes and channels), showing that such ratings vary within a rather narrow range. On a scale of zero (low) to 4 (high), the Macneil/Lehrer News Hour came second, with a score of 3.22 and *USA Today* was in eleventh place with 2.94 (only Ronald Reagan and the sensationalist weekly, *The National Enquirer* received lower scores).

The British Royal Commission on the Press (1977) study of attitudes to newspapers also showed little variation in attribution of 'fairness' to the main national newspapers despite large differences in measured 'sensationalism' and in type of readership. But the attribution of 'fairness' was not overwhelming. The same seems true of the United States media, to judge from the Times/Mirror survey (Gallup Organization, 1986). According to this, only 34 per cent agreed that news organizations are 'fair to all sides in presenting political and social issues'. On the other hand, Comstock (1988) discounts the view that there is deep or growing public lack of confidence in the media. The public is simply inclined to see bias where it disagrees.

While audience research can yield quite reliable evidence from detailed studies of news reporting of particular events, it does not help to settle any general questions about whether news reporting really is balanced or neutral according to the various standards discussed. Nor is such research usually sensitive enough to be able to link particular features of presentation with variable response and interpretation by the audience. Actual effects and perceptions of content are both too strongly shaped by 'audience' factors to give a clear indication of any inbuilt tendency of media messages. Even so, the considerable volume of evidence showing limited media effect, audience 'independence', and apparent failure by the audience to discriminate among media is a caution against over-interpreting fine distinctions which may be established by content analysis.

Ifs and buts

Objectivity itself can only be assessed, with varying degrees of approximation, by way of indicators. All the research procedures described call for value judgements about priorities, criteria of performance and choice of indicators. The 'objective assessment of objectivity' is only possible within severe limits set by another set of values (our own or those we adopt). Aside from value judgements, decisions have to be made in research, often according to rule of thumb, common sense, skill, art of argument, much as in the news itself.

The findings never speak for themselves and always need interpretation. The enormous number and diversity of media texts, even in the category of news and information, makes it impossible to have full knowledge of format or context or of all the many definitions and meanings which may be in force. In addition to these limitations, it seems that perceptions of 'bias', especially on the part of interested parties, often operate independently of evidence and, in particular, are often not shared by the relevant media public, which can often be as blind to what seems shameless partisanship as it is inclined to see partisanship where none is intended. Conclusions drawn from subtle measures of media partiality in news texts have to be treated with caution.

PART VII
MASS MEDIA, ORDER AND SOCIAL CONTROL

18
MEDIA AND THE MAINTENANCE OF PUBLIC ORDER

Concepts of order and their assessment

The point of departure for this section is a broad concept of 'order' in the sense of the principle (and value) of social cohesion and social harmony: whatever has to do with the binding together of society, the interdependence of its members, the organization of their activities, the shared awareness of belonging and of a common identity in group, community and society. Within this wide scope, we can also distinguish between the social and the cultural domains, even if the boundary is rarely clear or fixed. The chapters which follow in this part are concerned with the social domain, leaving issues of the media and culture for subsequent attention. For present purposes, social order will be dealt with as having to do either with control (relations of power and compliance) or with solidarity (mutual attachment and cooperation), while matters of culture have to do with meanings and symbols.

Both functionalist and critical theories of mass communication have associated the working of mass media with social order. The first attributes to mass media the 'function' (or hidden purpose) of securing the continuity of a given social order, maintaining control, establishing a broad consensus of values, integrating activities, anchoring individuals and groups in society (e.g. Wright, 1960). Critical theory has often involved a view of mass media as controlled by powerful class elites which impose their dominant meanings on the many and use the media to marginalize and delegitimize opposition (Hall, 1977). The differences are more of interpretation than of disagreement about the underlying process. A more fundamental alternative points to the possibilities for individuals and groups actively to create their own social order out of materials made available from mass media. Whatever the choice of theory, no evaluation can be made without first determining *whose* order might be sustained or disrupted by mass media: that of society, of ruling elites or what individuals choose to construct for themselves.

In most societies, social institutions exert a 'bias' in favour of 'normality' and of social harmony, with which 'good order' is usually identified. This bias favours the existing hierarchy of social status and of economic reward. There is also a 'bias' in socially approved values towards cooperation rather than conflict. A consensus on some 'fundamental values' of the society is usually presumed (though it does not go completely unchallenged). This establishes the point of balance or 'middle ground' (Kumar, 1975), which the main mass media are constrained or expected to occupy and which is also the bench mark for much evaluation of performance. Often, the result has been to highlight those aspects of the media which appear *disruptive* of the established order – especially representations of conflict and violence, 'bad news', deviance, discontent, crime, scandal, etc. Critical theory has to be invoked to expose the conservative and social control exercised by the established mass media (e.g. Kellner, 1990).

While the question of *effects* of mass communication lies outside the scope of this study, much of the evidence about media performance in respect of social order has been collected in the context of research on effects. Two concepts have been central: 'socialization' and 'cultivation'. There is no agreed definition of either, but the former refers to the teaching or learning of values and patterns of behaviour, as these are symbolically portrayed in mass media and variably rewarded and punished.

'Cultivation' (analysis) was coined within the research project of Gerbner and colleagues (see Signorielli and Morgan, 1990) to refer to the process whereby systematic representations of reality in television content provide 'lessons about reality' which are learned differentially more by those most exposed to media content. According to Signorielli and Morgan, cultivation is not a one-way effect process but a 'continual, dynamic, ongoing process of interaction among messages and contexts' (1990: 19). Some doubts about the concept and the reality of the process have been expressed by Gunter and Wober (1988).

Because of disagreements about the effects of mass media, issues concerning media performance in relation to 'good order' have come to be defined according to either a critical or a conservative perspective. The difference in perspective may also be expressed as a choice between that of the controllers and the controlled – in crude terms 'them' or 'us' – those with more power and those with less. In discussing the assessment of performance in terms of order, it should be kept in mind that other criteria – of freedom, diversity and objectivity – remain 'in force', and are also applicable to many of the cases discussed in the following pages.

There is another division which flows in part from this difference of perspective, but is empirically independent of it: that between the controlling and the solidaristic aspects of order. The latter derives from the principle of voluntary cooperation and shared interests of sub-groups in society. Order, from this point of view, is associated with mutuality, balance, self-determination. Standing against a unitary view of a consensual good order in a nation state there are alternative perspectives which have in

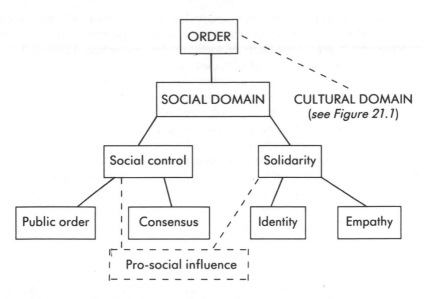

Figure 18.1 *Social order: framework for performance research*

common a resistance to control from above, although there may be large variations of purpose and values.

A framework for performance research

In line with these remarks, the framework introduced in Figure 6.4 above can be extended and used to guide research strategies and choice of performance indicators (Figure 18.1).

Under the overall heading of 'order', the first sub-principle (of the social domain), that of *control,* can, in its turn, be treated according to two main aspects – one relating to overt matters of maintaining *public order* here and now, the second to the building maintenance of a longer term *consensus*, a matter of indirect social control by managing the 'symbol system'. The line which separates the two is uncertain, but the main issues for assessment can be separated adequately enough.

The principle of *solidarity* can be treated either as a matter of sub-group identity and cohesion or as relating to empathy, fellow feeling and the construction of a shared 'moral order' (with a possible third, 'pro-social', concept to be kept in mind, which also has links with social control). The principles of 'control' and 'solidarity' each have two dimensions – one more to do with a structural dimension (public order and identity respectively) and a second which is more 'cultural' (consensus and empathy).

Divergent expectations concerning social control

Because of conflicts which undermine any absolute consensus on dominant values, expectations concerning the proper role of the mass media are often unclear and divergent. The media are widely expected to avoid undermining established authority, but they are also expected to promote innovation and change and to reflect the shifts of social norms and values. Free media are also expected to take a critical attitude to the exercise of political power and it is not easy to set limits to this critical spirit. In any case, the principle of freedom of expression, as well as the expectations of access, diversity and objectivity which have been outlined, can bring media into potential conflict with forces of the established social order and upholders of dominant values. For these reasons, research has also followed alternative lines, sometimes guided by established authority, sometimes by its critics.

Another distinction can be made: between situations where the security and integrity of the state and the maintenance of basic order are at issue and those which involve individual crime, violence or simply deviance from conventional standards of behaviour. In the former case, there is often strong pressure on mass media to support the 'powers that be', under conditions of diminished freedom and sometimes of fissures in the social consensus. On the second kind of issue, there is usually an unspoken consensus on the values of law and order, but much uncertainty about how far the media should accept responsibility for helping in the routine 'policing' of the norms and values of society. In both situations it is difficult to define the proper role of the media and to name appropriate standards of performance for the different mass media.

Three main categories of event have given rise to questions concerning public order in the first sense: international conflicts, where states have been involved in limited wars and where questions of patriotism have arisen (thus the loyalty of the media to the state or to the 'national interest'); cases of public disorder or unrest, involving localized loss of control by police or established authority; terrorist activities, involving violence against agencies of the state. These are discussed in sequence, followed by questions relating to individual crime and violence.

Limited war situations and the mass media

The European process of decolonialization or American actions to oppose world communism or to protect hemisphere interests have given rise to situations where free media have been exposed to severe strains. Early examples of the first were Britain in Suez and Central Africa, and France in North Africa and Indo-China. Of these events, only the Suez conflict seems to have raised any question about media loyalty, but there was no systematic media research. The more recent Falklands conflict (1982) led to much more controversy and a good deal of research. The United States has been involved in several limited engagements, apart from the Vietnam War: Lebanon (1982), Grenada (1984), the Persian Gulf (1988 and 1989) and Panama (1989). The most recent case, that of the 1991 Gulf War, has already generated both controversy and research into the role of the media (see Chapter 10). The terrain indicated has uncertain boundaries with other matters where state security and media may be inter-related (e.g. matters of defence secrecy or of intervention by agents of government in other countries).

The most characteristic and media-relevant features of these otherwise diverse events are as follows:

- A vital national interest, as determined by the government of the day, is at stake, involving matters of life and death and of national prestige.
- A significant degree of controversy about the legitimacy of state action is present.
- A strong interest is shown by the authorities in managing the flow of information and in keeping some matters secret.
- The events have high salience and there is considerable public interest and demand for news (hence a potential conflict with the interest of authorities).
- Immediate consequences are felt outside the national territory and by non-participants, so that world attention is also involved.

Aside from the scale and intensity of events themselves, the main differences from a total war situation have been the absence of full control over media, the lack of total consensus (in public opinion) about the threat posed by an 'enemy' and/or about the legitimacy of war aims. The short-term and manageable character of the conflict is an additional feature (the option of avoiding or concluding military commitment has usually been available). It is clear that the media are subject, under such conditions, to conflicting normative expectations, as well as to conflicting pressures. The mass media, in their normal operation, tend to be rooted in a nexus of unexplicated attachment to the 'national interest' and to values of patriotism. The nature of this attachment leads us to expect some 'pro-national' bias in the news as a matter of course (e.g. Hallin, 1986). But the media are also widely credited with a role of neutral reporter and of 'watch-dog' on behalf of citizens, in whose name war is being waged.

Under these circumstances, assessment is likely to be guided by divergent standards and expectations, but with particular reference to the following: the degree to which support is given to the official view of national interest; the degree of dedication of the media to informing their audience, despite official restrictions or disapproval; and the degree to which opposing views are reported and a balance of evaluation on controversial issues maintained. These three criteria between them represent approximately the views of supporters and opponents of military action plus the 'consensus' needs for an adequate flow of reliable information to the public in the interests of opinion formation and reducing anxiety.

Although the Vietnam War fitted the problematic conditions stated above and lasted almost ten years, it appears to have stimulated relatively little in the way of systematic assessment of media coverage, apart from studies of supposed 'bias' in network news set in the context of competitive elections (where the war was only one issue, e.g. Efron, 1971; Russo, 1971; Hofstetter, 1976). The commonly expressed view that television coverage undermined the will to fight was not really substantiated by critical research (but see Braestrup, 1977). The myth that the war was brought home to the US public has also been exposed (Hallin, 1986). The opposed hypotheses that mass media had either fomented the war or brought it to a premature end have never really been tested.

In retrospect, it seems that the war, which grew unobtrusively and dragged on so long, did not impinge strongly enough on public consciousness as an event to become unmanageable for routine media coverage, except when it was associated with domestic unrest (Gitlin, 1980). The military also seemed to reach new heights of public relations and news management achievements. According to Comstock and colleagues' assessment (1978: 49–52), on the basis of somewhat limited evidence concerning television, the tone of network television coverage at crucial times was rather neutral and balanced, neither very positive or negative to the war policies of the administration.

The legitimacy of the Vietnam War seems also to have been insufficiently challenged by politicians at home at the time, its level of violence was apparently 'acceptable' to the American public and it was far enough away not to disturb unduly relations between media and government or military authorities. According to Paletz and Entman (1981), the media tended only to voice opposition to the war as a reflection of what a section of the established elite was already expressing. By the time evidence of anti-war bias in the media was produced (Lefever, 1976), the war had already become unpopular.

According to Gitlin (1980), as the war lost legitimacy, anti-war activity became respectable. Within the general shift in political momentum, the media then helped to frame the respectable opposition as an explicit alternative. All this is very different from an undermining of the patriotic cause. By contrast, a comparatively minor event like the Grenada invasion of 1984, where temporary media silence was imposed, seems to have led to a good deal more media *angst* about manipulation by government.

The British conflict with Argentina in 1982, though also negligible in scale by comparison with Vietnam and, by most assessments, more broadly supported at home for its short duration, led to much examination of the role of the media (Glasgow Media Group, 1985; Harris, 1983; Morrison and Tumber, 1988). This attention was stimulated partly by the public disagreement between the government and broadcasting authorities over the alleged failure to support the national 'war effort' and partly by media irritation at heavy-handed efforts to manage the flow of news about the engagement. The controversy which ensued suggests that the wrong lessons may have been drawn by the British authorities from the Vietnam example – with emphasis on secrecy and on news management, leading to reduced credibility and increased anxiety.

Whatever the causes of greater concern for or by the media, most research was designed to test both the official view that the media failed to support the war and also the opposed view that media were either uncritically patriotic or hamstrung by censorship. The content analysis by Morrison and Tumber (1988) of press and television news included indicators of: how far a committed (to Britain) or a neutral position was adopted in accounts of particular events; how far Argentinian (thus 'enemy') sources and points of view were reported; how far (and how) opposition or divisions in public opinion at home were reported; how the media reacted to official attempts at news management (or disinformation).

Television news received most research attention since it was the main object of criticism and also carried formal obligations to be neutral and balanced. There seems to have been an underlying, if unexplicated, presupposition that broadcasting, because of its public service status, had a duty to be 'patriotic'. In practice, the relative neutrality of TV and radio probably made them seem less patriotic than a rather jingoistic press. The short war also provided an opportunity to assess public evaluation of the role of the media. Most results (e.g. Morrison and Tumber, 1988) have testified to a predominant public satisfaction with media coverage and also to a general preference for balanced and diverse information and points of view, even though a large majority of the public supported the patriotic cause. Research largely acquitted the British media of excessive subservience to official policy, although the media as a whole were by no means even-handed between Britain and Argentina (Glasgow Media Group, 1985). An unusual feature of this particular conflict is that the authorities had almost total physical control over all reports and the media could not be blamed for the many deficiencies in reporting.

Control of information may not be so unusual in a limited war, as the more recent experience of the 'Gulf War' showed, at least not when the war is being pursued by what are effectively the main (Anglo-American) 'media powers'. The case of the Gulf War has not yet been fully examined, but it seems to have been characterized by an unusual degree of patriotic, even militaristic, media fervour in the belligerent countries. One British survey of a local audience response (Shaw and Carr-Hill, 1991) found that 33 per cent of respondents criticized television for 'glorifying war too much'. The case was unusual in media terms for the coalescing of several 'news frames', including those of oil and energy, 'unjust military aggression', patriotism, possibly 'dangers of Arab fundamentalism', 'threats to Israel'. Such a combination might be expected to fuel media symbolic aggression and even xenophobia.

On many specific issues of international conflict, the media have been examined and shown to be routinely inclined to follow, if not always openly to support, the official line of their national government, military or foreign ministry (cf. Glasgow Media Group, 1985; Herman and Chomsky, 1988; McNair, 1988). The media generally operate within a frame of interpretation which is likely to be that of the 'home government' and also shared by the majority of the audience. They may also have little choice of sides, where key sources of information are under the control of authorities and opportunities for alternative access to media channels are scarce. Despite this basic 'set', of support or conformity, there is always some room for alternative performance and the conclusion is never foregone.

Civil disturbance

Domestic unrest and localized violence have recurred sporadically in many Western countries since the 1960s, often raising questions about the role of the media. There are divergent interpretations, one proposing that media have stimulated, encouraged and helped to spread riotous behaviour, another that media have been too compliant with authorities in helping to conceal or misrepresent civil unrest and in so doing have served conservative political ends. The media have, on occasion, been commended for vividly reporting and even for encouraging (another country's) civil disorder, as in Prague in 1968 or Peking and Berlin in 1989. The *direction* of comment in the media performance thus depends on the perspective adopted by an observer and on the (political) definition of the events.

There is inevitably much diversity about the occasions of civil unrest which have generated controversy. Two variables play most part in the definition of events: the degree of *politicization* (and of challenge to the legitimate political order) involved; and the degree of *violence* against authorities and property. The more of both, the more inclination on the part of established authority to limit media freedom to report, the more alarm is heard about the effects of reporting and the more difficulty for the media in applying the normal routines of 'objective' reporting. The more of both elements, the more difficult it is also to find agreed standards of performance to apply in assessment.

Critics of the established order are usually more concerned with standing up for media freedom and they also object when the media supply definitions of civil unrest which are over-supportive of the official point of view, lending justification to forcible suppression. The main events which have yielded research evidence have been: the collective urban violence in the US in the mid-1960s, often related to racial divisions; similar outbreaks in England in the 1980s (Tumber, 1982; Murdock, 1984; van Dijk, 1991); political unrest and public demonstrations involving clashes with police or army (relating, for example, to civil liberties or to the Vietnam War); major strikes involving physical confrontation (as in the British miners' strike of 1983–84); communal violence over religion, language differences, etc. (Northern Ireland provides a prime example); finally, seemingly unmotivated large-scale 'hooliganism' by the young (e.g. Cohen, 1972).

The norms for media performance vary according to the nature of the case and local conditions. There seem to be at least two widely held views, both inside and outside the media, which cover all five cases: first, that media *ought* to report such happenings fully and fairly, because of the public 'need to know'; secondly, that their reporting should not itself contribute to illegal behaviour (see Baker and Ball, 1969: 221). These norms may, however, come into conflict with each other (with no rules for precedence) and they are not easy to translate into performance indicators.

The main inconsistency stems from the common view that 'undue' or 'incorrect' media representation of violent events may itself stimulate violence (an extension of the same logic leads authorities to impose media blackouts in situations of endemic conflict). The authorities (especially those on the spot) have often claimed that the presence of TV cameras can provoke violence for reasons of publicity or exhibitionism, can help to spread it from one locality to another (by 'contagion') or can amplify incidents beyond their real significance, thus also amplifying their real consequences in undermining the forces of law and order (Shapiro and Williams, 1984).

Critical perspectives have indicated more diverse propositions (since the issue for critics is not usually the maintenance of the order *per se*), but especially the possibility that media: 'take the side of' authorities and either minimize the contribution of police or army in instigating violence (the case of a 'police riot') or exaggerate the violence of supposed rioters; subordinate reports of the political or protest aims of demonstrations to reports of violence which may be only incidental, but which have higher news value; and use the occasion of unrest in ways which create 'moral panics' or which stigmatize minorities and sub-groups, irrespective of causes, facts or the true significance of events.

The design of assessment research will obviously vary according to the propositions chosen. However, research has usually to be retrospective, based on documents, content analysis and interviews after the event, with a view to reconstructing the role of the media. This is how the Kerner Commission, for instance, dealt with charges against the media in relation to the 1967 Detroit riots. They looked, in particular, for systematic evidence of sensationalism or 'misinformation' in newspaper and TV accounts at the time. In the event, they found insufficient evidence to substantiate any principal charge that the media *contributed* to disorder. Research following the British riots in 1981 came to similar conclusions (Tumber, 1982).

If there is a 'media effect', according to Singer (1970), it is more likely to occur by media *drawing attention* to incidents (e.g. of racial or other causes of tension) which might be a cause of riot behaviour, or by giving *advance notice* of possible occurrences of violence (e.g. giving times and places, a sort of 'mobilizing information' of a less benign kind than usually intended, see Chapter 9). Both of these, however, seem to belong to the media's legitimate informative task. The suppression of news, which authorities would often like to see (Paletz and Dunn, 1969; Slater and McCombs, 1969) can itself be a cause of disorder or it can facilitate counter-violence by forces of 'law and order'.

From the perspective of those who become involved in legitimate challenges to the social order, there may be as much to complain of as there is for conservative or for critical observers. Gitlin's (1980) account of the relation between media and the student protest movement against the Vietnam War convincingly describes ways in which the media did tend to have a distorting effect on the protest movement: a tendency ultimately counter-productive to the aims of the movement and not especially conducive to an orderly process of protest. According to Gitlin, the general effect of media coverage, itself courted by the movement, was to exaggerate militancy and to promote celebrated leaders (cf. Halloran et al., 1970). The media, he wrote, 'unintentionally helped polarize the society between revolutionism and embattled reaction' (Gitlin, 1980: 196).

Whatever the particular outcome, the impression remains that the media do have considerable capacity to define the nature of events, under conditions of upheaval and uncertainty, even if they are ultimately on the side of moderation and the established order (if only because of the access advantages and the opportunity to define events which goes with power in society; Lester, 1973; Molotch and Lester, 1974).

An unusual chance to plan research into the media interaction with civil disturbance was exploited by Halloran et al. (1970) at the time of a 1968 anti-war protest meeting in London. Their study of the advance organization of coverage, the event itself, the coverage of it on television and in newspapers and the audience reaction to coverage, concluded that the media contributed to an advance definition of a major event as likely to involve violent confrontation stimulated by revolutionary (and alien) leaders. When the violence failed to materialize on any large scale, the media made the most of what did happen in order to fulfil the definition of the event they had themselves set up. The main charge sustained against the media was that their conduct was guided by their own predefinition of the situation, their 'media logic' and organizational requirements, rather than by the demands of objective reporting of events as they happened.

As in other similar cases, we are left with the impression that the media do not have power to cause any disorder which is not already latent in the situation and that their self-interest in news of disorder diverges both from the aims of authorities and from the intentions of the disturbers of the peace, except perhaps in the most extreme cases (e.g. in Northern Ireland, where the authorities may be unequivocally supported, or in circumstances where the 'good guys' revolt against oppression, as in Peking in 1989, Prague in 1968, Bucharest in 1989, etc.).

The degree of legitimacy (attributed or assumed) of those who threaten the peace, and the degree of legitimacy of methods used by, or against, them are both relevant to media coverage and to the choice of standards for assessment. There is no hard and fast rule, but, in general, legitimacy can be claimed for civil disturbance where the aim is to redress some known and considerable grievance, or where a deep political division is present. Cases of anti-war protest, major strikes, political or civil rights demonstrations, etc. have been credited with some legitimacy and media, consequently, have been more free to keep a distance from authorities.

'Illegitimate' forms of civil disturbance include violent rioting for no clear purpose beyond enjoyment (soccer hooliganism, etc.) or crime (e.g. looting). In these cases, the media are more likely to side with the forces of law and order, within the limits of norms of 'truth' and 'balance' (even if these are not always observed; Cohen, 1972). As in the case of war, and for similar reasons, the degree of public support for any unrest and disturbance plays a *de facto* role in forging the conventional norms for media performance.

The case of terrorism

There is a long history of public acts at once violent and political that have attracted the term 'terrorism' (see Schmid and de Graaf, 1982), but since the 1960s the term has acquired a somewhat special meaning in the discourse of Western news media and in the framing and labelling of certain news events. 'Terrorism' has become a familiar kind of news story and almost a separate genre of television and print fiction (Schlesinger et al., 1983; Alali and Eke, 1991). Terrorism is designed by its perpetrators to disturb the social order and the media are implicated with these aims, whether wittingly or unwittingly.

What 'terrorism', as a news reference, actually means is less easy to say with precision. The term is loosely and variably applied by sources of news, often with ideological purpose and as a code word to indicate a certain category of event (Kelly and Mitchell, 1981; Dowling, 1986; Delli Carpini and Williams, 1987; Weimann, 1987; Simmons, 1991). It may, for example, be used by interested parties in order to delegitimize a nationalist group or any rebel or resistance movement which uses violent methods. The media rarely label violence carried out by states as terrorist, especially where a friendly state is involved.

In general, the word 'terrorists' refers to members of a violent dissident *group* (rather than to individual criminals), often specified by known circumstances, such as the IRA in Britain, the Red Army Faction in Germany, the ETA in Spain, the Italian Red Brigade, etc. (Paletz et al., 1982). Thus terrorism is what such groups do, providing some consistency of meaning for the term. Schmid and de Graaf (1982) asked journalists to give their definitions of the term and uncovered 27 different versions. The main recurring elements seem to yield a definition of terrorism much as follows: 'Acts of extreme and wanton violence and illegality undertaken for political ends by opponents of established authority in order to exert influence, directly on authorities or, indirectly, by creating a climate of public fear and shock, often entailing innocent victims.'

The security services and supporters of 'official' points of view have sometimes emphasized the possibility of TV helping terrorists (Atwater, 1987) and the need to enrol the media in the propaganda war against terrorism, despite the fact that the above definition clearly places the media 'on the side of' the victims. The media have been said to give a platform (the 'oxygen of publicity'), as well as legitimacy, to some political aims of terrorism. They may undermine, by criticism, the police and other forces of order and fail to convey the enormity of terrorist acts. By simply reporting events they may encourage terrorism by way of contagion or imitation and collaborate with terrorist strategies which include the demoralization of the public (Alali and Eke, 1991).

These complaints are not all consistent, but together they add up to a case for censorship or manipulation (in the 'public interest') and, at the very least, may have a 'chilling' effect on reporting. They also offer guidelines for a programme of critical assessment of the news media. Account has to be taken, however, of positive entries on the balance sheet, even from the official perspective. For instance, the media can give 'terrorists' a bad name, provide a peaceful forum for grievances, diminish the level of terror and panic by information and generally collaborate with the forces of law and order (Elliott, 1977b; Kelly and Mitchell, 1981; Paletz et al., 1982; Curtis, 1984; Scanlon, 1989).

There are other perspectives on terrorism besides the official 'war against terrorism' view. Schlesinger et al. (1983) distinguish three such perspectives: an 'alternative' view, which offers a balanced assessment of the terms of debate, more recognition of possible legitimacy and of the coerciveness of the state; a 'populist' perspective, which puts the needs for law and order above legality (thus supporting 'official terrorism' and psychological warfare); an 'oppositional' view, which effectively supports violence as a means of last resort against an oppressive system. The position of most established media is, generally, 'on the side of' authorities, adopting the official definition of events as a matter of course. This makes less plausible the complaints that the media foment terrorism even if counter-insurgency strategies will sometimes conflict with journalistic norms and with media logic. The self-interests of media organizations are certainly not co-extensive with those of counter-terrorist agencies.

There is little evidence to show that the media *do* serve the interests of terrorists (although plausible instances can be cited). Evidence would be hard to come by, especially evidence of effects on the terrorists themselves. The charge of contagion or imitation effects from media has also not been substantiated (Phillips, 1980), although both Schmid and de Graaf (1982) and Kelly and Mitchell (1981) have argued that the media had probably increased terroristic activities. Picard (1991) has dismissed the evidence for contagion as both pseudo-scientific and threatening to media freedom. Media have been blamed for 'sensationalizing' accounts (Bennett, 1982; Weimann, 1983; Atwater, 1987), as well as for underestimating the horror of terrorist outrages. Detailed, objective, reporting may, incidentally, offer a platform for the views of 'terrorists'. However, it looks as if the media could never satisfy their critics on such emotive issues.

From different standpoints, critical research into media coverage (Herman, 1982; Davis and Walton, 1983; Schlesinger, 1990) seems more to challenge than to sustain the official perspective on the role and effects of media. For instance, Paletz et al. (1982) looked at US TV network coverage of political terrorist groups and concluded that the effect of coverage was to magnify the importance of left-wing anti-state terrorism and underestimate right-wing and state terrorism, thus largely supporting an official US view of the 'terrorist menace' in the world. News of terrorism almost always comes from government (or related) sources, objectives are rarely explained or justified, terrorists are identified with criminal violence or threats to national security (Simmons, 1991). Other researchers support the view that news media often allow themselves to be used as an instrument of propaganda and of crisis management by forces of law and order.

The means for assessing the evaluative direction of news about terrorism are not essentially different from those already discussed in relation to 'information quality', balance and presentation. This means looking especially at the amount and direction of reporting, applying measures of 'sensationalism', recording sources, analysing language and pictures, assessing frames of reference and interpretations offered, recording the degree and kind of explanation of events (Alali and Eke, 1991).

The normal rules of 'fairness' probably do not apply in the same degree to those who set themselves outside the protection of public opinion as well as of the law. It is not at all clear what the norms of fairness might be in such cases, and it has been established (Schmid and de Graaf, 1982: 150–171) that media themselves have widely adopted various rules and forms of self-censorship, with a view to assisting the authorities in particular cases. This means that information about terrorism is often constructed differently from other news.

Different TV formats can 'behave' differently in their representation of terrorism. Schlesinger et al. (1983), for instance, introduced concepts of 'open' or 'closed' reporting, differentiating between news reports which give single or multiple perspectives. In general, news bulletin formats are more closed and 'tighter' than current affairs or documentaries. A second distinction between 'tight' and 'loose' formats distinguishes between programmes which lead to a single, unambiguous, *preferred*, interpretation and those which include alternative values, ambiguities, contradications and unresolved loose ends. These are useful tools for assessing the degree to which media follow 'official' lines and for uncovering the ways in which they may deviate. A further advance by the same researchers was to apply the same concepts, albeit in an illustrative rather than systematic way, to televised drama dealing with terrorism. They uncovered a range of treatments, deviating from 'official' viewpoints and from 'propaganda' models, at least on British TV in the early 1980s.

Communication values give way to power

The kinds of content discussed in this chapter all relate to matters of great sensitivity in society – potentially matters of life and death and, arguably, occasions when the collective security of the society is at stake. As a result, values which seem more fundamental than those which normally guide and protect public communication may be invoked. Whether or not circumstances actually justify the overriding of communication values can only be decided after the event, since media operate in the immediate present, often under pressure from those who have power to impose their value priorities. Because of these circumstances, dispassionate application of measures of media performance is usually impossible in the 'heat of the moment' and assessment belongs to history.

19
POLICING THE SYMBOLIC ENVIRONMENT

An intermediate zone of control

In the 'space' which lies between the clearly motivated wish to implement control from above, following lines of institutional power (as in the cases of war, riot, insurrection or terrorism described in Chapter 18) there are, as noted earlier, many diverse expectations from mass media which are related in some way to their perceived role as potential agents of socialization and legitimation. This area of performance is too large to explore in detail, but it is now a commonplace to think of the mass media as having the power to encourage or discourage individual behaviour as well as wider social patterns and values, by example or by symbolic reward and punishment.

The media are often held accountable for their sins of omission as well as commission, far beyond what any conclusive evidence has shown them capable of achieving. On the other hand, such evidence may never be available and the onus of proof tends to lie more with the media than with their critics. Generally, the pressures from society in such matters are an unwelcome, but unavoidable, fact of life for the media. The more they are *mass* media, the stronger the pressure to respond to claims for more conformity to higher (or just conventional) standards of conduct and morality and to offer messages of a 'pro-social' and 'positive' kind, especially where the protection and development of children is at stake.

Regulations for broadcasting in many countries (including the transnational Television Directive of the European Community) often dictate what is acceptable or not acceptable, especially in matters of sexuality and violence, but in quite a few other normative areas (see Chapter 5). On the whole, these rules (whether voluntary or not) have been taken over or adapted from earlier codes and rules for the cinema. Aside from the need to comply with legal or agreed standards and the irksome nature of many pressures from the surrounding society, there are genuine problems for some media in responding to the expectations described. Often these conflict with claims to freedom of publication, perhaps less often with the imperatives of creativity and artistic integrity.

Media, crime and violence

Not surprisingly, a number of the issues discussed in relation to terrorism (Chapter 18) also arise in respect of 'civil' crime and violence as shown or reported in the mass media. In fact, the 'law and order' framework which has been applied to terrorism is an adapted version of that developed over a longer period to apply to crime, violence and law enforcement. The main elements of expectation, or criticism, relating to media (e.g. DeFleur, 1970; Comstock et al., 1978) ultimately presuppose that the media may increase real crime and violence by way of several intermediate processes, especially by 'glamorizing' crime and its rewards, demonstrating the effectiveness of violence as a means to some (possibly admired) end, distorting the true nature and incidence of crime and violence or by teaching techniques of crime. The media may also desensitize people to the reality of violence and even stimulate its imitation. While there are some well-founded reverse expectations (media fictional violence may reduce real violence), these have never been used as a justification for giving more media attention to crime and violence.

Mass media as perceived cause of crime

The whole question of the *effects* of media portrayals of crime and violence falls outside the scope of this discussion. The results of research into media effects provide few unambiguous guidelines for the media to follow, beyond what common sense might suggest (Comstock et al., 1978). Even so, assessment in this matter, from the perspective of *social control* is ultimately shaped by considerations of effect (see Baker and Ball, 1969; Gunter, 1985). There are also other perspectives, in which more attention is paid to the emotionally disturbing effects of portrayals of violence, or simply their offence to good taste.

Aside from the question of possible effect, there are other parallels with the question of terrorism. Fictional and non-fiction content (and variations of genre and format within each) also need to be distinguished. There is little doubt that the media have generally 'sided' with law enforcement and against crime and violence. The long-standing (and still powerful) convention which rules that fictional crime 'shall not pay' still largely holds, as does the tendency for law enforcers to be given popular heroic status. There is also tension, however, between such routine, stereotypical, support for social order and the 'media logic' of giving the audience what it really does seem to want. This includes a large diet of crime and violence (whether rewarded or disapproved), a taste which does not coincide very closely with the goals of law enforcers.

Images of crime

As to the quality of what the media offer, there has been much attention to both news and fiction. Research into crime in the news (e.g. Davis, 1952; Baker and Ball, 1969; Roshier, 1973; Dimmick, 1974; Graber, 1980b; Jaehnig et al., 1981; O'Keefe and Reid-Nash, 1987) has looked at the amount and type of crime reported, the relation between crime in the news and crime in the relevant statistics and the degree of 'sensationalism' in crime reporting. These foci imply certain performance norms for news content, from the perspective of law enforcement and social control, especially: crime should not be over-sensationalized in reporting; reported crime should broadly reflect actual crime in amount and type. These norms recognize a legitimate public interest in having reliable information about disorder in society, but also that crime news is a commodity whose (audience) market value may be higher than its value according to other criteria: relevance, accuracy, concern about effect, real significance, etc.

There is little difficulty in measuring, by the normal methods of content analysis, the degree of attention paid to crime news, or in classifying it in ways which allow comparison with crime statistics. Most research shows that patterns of crime as reported do deviate from statistics, usually by an over-emphasis on crimes against the person and by neglect of 'white-collar' crime (Graber, 1980b). This is thought to reflect the influence of 'newsworthiness' criteria, human interest and of the ways in which crime comes to the attention of the media (Fishman, 1980). Different media channels are also shown to vary in how they perform in relation to crime. National media systems can also vary. It has been shown, for instance, that Canadian (CBC) news was less inclined to show aggressive content than American TV networks (Singer, 1970).

Apart from the assessment of market demand, there are few widely accepted independent norms for deciding what amount and kind of attention would be 'better' or 'worse', although Graber (1979) suggests a criterion of 'significance' (which would give higher weight to 'white-collar' crime) and most researchers deploy the standard of crime statistics as a measure of crime 'reality'. In practice, reporting is shaped more by the way the system of law enforcement works at the key moments of the crime process (discovery – pursuit – capture – trial – sentence) than by the publication of crime *statistics* as such, which may be a doubtful 'reality' criterion anyway (Chibnall, 1977; Fishman, 1980).

Measuring media violence

The question of *violence* as such in news is much more complex, because it occurs and is reported in so many forms (not always 'criminal' ones; see Baker and Ball, 1969). A choice of assessment perspectives is usually available, since representation of violence in news ranges from its supposedly legitimate use by authorities (police, armies, etc.) to individual acts of resistance and may also include violence associated with natural disaster, traffic accidents, plus cruelty and inhumanity of many other kinds. The analysis of violence in fiction presents an even larger problem of recognition and it is fiction (especially on television) which has attracted by far the most attention.

The 'amount' of violence on television has been measured in many different ways (e.g. Head, 1954; Baker and Ball, 1969; Dominick and Pearce, 1976; Gerbner and Gross, 1976), but most basically in terms of the average number of violent incidents (or behaviours) per programme or per hour, usually with some attention to other variables of type of violence and context. The numerous options for measurement have been critically assessed by Comstock et al. (1978) and Gunter (1985), among others. It is clear that all such indicators are to some degree arbitrary and cannot claim to offer unequivocal and objective 'measures' of violence in content. Gunter (1985) makes a convincing claim for the view that content measures need to be weighted in some way according to audience perceptions of the differential significance of representations of violence. Nevertheless, such indicators are useful for tracking trends over time and for approximate comparison between different channels and time periods. Generally, they have shown that the incidence of fictional crime on television is high (although higher in the USA than in Europe) and far exceeding what could be considered a true reflection of the real world incidence, however this might be assessed.

A longitudinal research project which has some claim to primacy in this field, the 'violence profile' of Gerbner and co-workers (1976, etc.) has supported the view that the most important result of exposure to violence is less the direct stimulus to behaviour than the long-term, repeated, 'lessons' which are received about power in society and about the relative risks run by members of different classes and groups. The main alleged lessons of US TV include the following: life is dangerous (possibly short) for the ethnic minority urban poor and for women; non-white and foreigners are more violent than white Americans; 'good guys' are as violent as bad guys; violence may be a legitimate means to desirable ends. There may be some validity in these 'lessons', but they can have distorting, self-fulfilling, consequences. This long term 'drip-drip' formulation of the effect of television has been challenged by Greenberg (1988), who suggests that a 'drenching' effect of a single, highly significant portrayal may be more important. This tends to undermine objections against media representation of violence based only on quantitative content data.

In order to draw any conclusion about long-term socializing effects, it is necessary to go beyond the classifying and counting of violent acts on the screen and to make some qualitative assessment which takes account of who does what to whom, why and with what reward or punishment. The assessment of fictional content in the terrain of crime and violence is now immensely varied and complex in method, but several conclusions with normative implications can be singled out (see especially Comstock et al., 1978; Gunter, 1985, for evidence). For example, it makes a difference whether violence is symbolically *rewarded* or *punished* and whether it is perpetrated by the 'good' or 'bad' characters. The more realistic, contemporary and near to home the violence, the more potential there is for impact and disturbance. The more stylized and conventional the genre in which violence has a part, the less impact it has. Violent acts which are gratuitous, in terms of plot, and visibly and needlessly cruel to victims are more disturbing than motivated and 'sanitized' acts. While many such variables can be reliably 'read-off' from the content as seen on the screen (or in other text forms), the *values* implied by content are not easy to extrapolate without close qualitative analysis (Lee, 1988).

Norms for portraying violence

The norms most commonly deployed to guide research have not changed greatly since the early 1930s (the Payne Fund studies of Blumer et al.), although there is now more recognition of the danger of stigmatizing marginal or ethnic minority groups (as in the role of perpetrator of crime and violence). There has also been more sensitivity to the implications of fictional violence carried out against women (Zillman and Bryant, 1982; Preston, 1990). A probable increase over time in the visibility and realism of media violence has led to an interest in the degree of explicitness and 'sensationalism'. The results of pressures on media, from minority interests especially (Montgomery, 1989) may have led content to be less socially realistic as well as less prejudicial.

The assessment of performance in relation to violence in media can usefully draw on evidence of public attitudes (see Gunter, 1985). There is often vocal criticism of screen violence, but such criticism is also often imprecise in its focus, internally inconsistent and usually insufficiently discriminating to make it more than a blunt political or advocacy weapon (Comstock, 1988). Often the most vocal majority in respect of television violence is neither the intended nor the actual audience of this kind of content. There is no shortage, however, of codes of practice designed for the guidance of programme-makers or of official guardians which can also be used by researchers. Such guidelines are usually blunt instruments, reflecting the tastes, preferences and prejudices of their compilers, but at their best they can incorporate lessons from theory and research and make some provision for creative integrity (e.g. Broadcasting Standards Council, 1989).

These brief references to what is now a vast literature cannot convey all the relevant lessons for assessing performance. While it is clear that standards and criteria chosen will always embody personal tastes and values, there are some specific lessons, based on research, which could be applied to help decide whether actual practice in the portrayal of violence and crime is more or less acceptable.

Socialization and consensus

Views of the part played by mass media in maintaining social consensus have generally been split along a now familiar fissure: a conservative tendency regards modern popular media as undermining traditional values and social controls; while a critical tendency interprets much news and entertainment as a powerful means of social control, favourable to the values of the national culture and the dominant social order. In brief, the reigning *media consensus* has been characterized either as overly liberal or leftist or as conservative, depending on the view of the critic. Analysis of media institutions and their activities has generally supported the view that the underlying logic of commercial and of publicly controlled media will lead them to sustain, rather than undermine, consensus (e.g. Gans, 1979; Olien et al., 1983). There are usually more readers, viewers and listeners (not to mention advertisers) who will be offended rather than attracted by positive representations of deviant or unconventional behaviour. However, the 'lesson' on behalf of conformity is more often implicit than explicit, occurring by omission rather than active propaganda (Breed, 1958).

It is widely presumed that the mass media, in their entertainment function at least, have no mandate to undermine established values, and that when commercial self-interest may pull in this direction (for instance, through the market demand for pornographic content), some restraining force may be legitimately exercised by 'society'. On the whole, the onus is on the media to justify any significant departure from conventional norms, although there may be an acceptable defence in the claim to be following changing standards and social mores.

The cultivation process

Centrally at issue is the maintenance of a social and normative order, by way of informal socialization through mass media. Most accounts of this process (e.g. in Baker and Ball, 1969) posit a considerable, long-term and consistent flow of messages from the media, as in the 'message system' described by Gerbner et al. (1982), which 'cultivates' a 'mainstream' set of outlooks, assumptions and beliefs about society (Signorielli and Morgan, 1990). The audience is also usually assumed to be rather dependent (however much voluntarily) on the media as a source of ideas, information and impressions.

This model of media as an instrument of social conformity is thought to work in quite a simple way. The 'stories' which the media tell (in news as well as fiction) comprise a large universe of social morality plays in which good qualities and good deeds are rewarded, while undesirable or wicked things are symbolically punished. The claimed effectiveness of the process lies in the consistency of the tales, their attractiveness and interest, their seeming relevance, truth and also their connection with everyday experience and with the other morality lessons learnt in the institutional contexts of home, school, church, workplace, etc.

Symbolic reward and punishment

Symbolic rewarding is accomplished in several familiar ways, but especially by identifying heroes, villains and neutral characters and associating them with character traits, beliefs or kinds of behaviour. Much the same may occur in news accounts of real world events, with the added possibility of taking positions and associating news accounts with particular perspectives (e.g. the 'public good', consumer interest, the needs of industry, the nation, forces of justice, a minority need, or whatever).

Symbolic punishment is achieved in much the same way, with a tendency to label or stigmatize certain activities or traits as anti-social, deviant or undesirable, sometimes explicitly, sometimes by way of unspoken assumptions and the framing of news accounts (see Chapter 17). To a large extent, the essentially ideological effect is achieved by way of taking for granted the *normality* of current social arrangements across a wide terrain. Whatever is normal requires no explanation or justification, while whatever seems to challenge normality is suspect. Among the more significant 'normal' or 'natural' (Fiske, 1987) arrangements taken for granted by Western mass media (in news and much fiction and entertainment) include: marriage and the nuclear family; heterosexual love; traditional role divisions between men and women; large inequalities of property and income; the work ethic; free market principles in economic matters; parliamentary democracy; great poverty of the Third World; vast defence establishments which cannot be dismantled, etc.

Conformity and deviance

This summary version of a complex process and of its most probable outcomes shows the general line sustained by research, of which there is a vast amount, much of it going back to the early days of media content analysis (see Holsti, 1969). There are many early studies which demonstrated various kinds of reflection and support for dominant social values in media content (Arnheim, 1944; Berelson and Salter, 1946; McGranahan and Wayne, 1948; Head, 1954; Albrecht, 1956; Breed, 1958; DeFleur, 1964). More recent work has been dominated by the major enquiries of Gerbner and colleagues (Signorielli and Morgan, 1990) and the work of Comstock et al. (1978), Greenberg and Atkin (1980) and Gunter (1986, 1987b), but there is almost no limit to the number of studies which deal with the media treatment of salient social values and attitudes in ways relevant to consensus maintenance (Cantor, 1979, 1980).

In the economic sphere, for instance, research into media treatment of welfare claimants (Golding and Middleton, 1982) reveals the social stigmatization of reliance on welfare. Much research concerning media and industrial relations has indicated a predominant bias against any disruption of the normal production process or anything which might upset the established balance of economic rewards in society (Glasgow Media Group, 1976, 1980). Both examples indicate scope for an alternative media process – that of developing social empathy (see Chapter 20) – and the crisis years of the early 1980s, perhaps, produced more evidence of media recognition of the needs of society's victims. In general, we are reminded again of the extent to which news is inevitably normative, offering a series of lessons in morality, as well as information about current events.

The research literature on gender roles and family life continues to multiply (cf. Durkin, 1985; Signorielli, 1985; Gunter, 1986), with signs of an increase in media recognition (if not yet advocacy) of equality between sexes (e.g. G.J. Robinson, 1983) and of diversity of family arrangements and roles, even of variety of sexual orientation as legitimate (Berry, 1988). In general, there has been a shift in media presentation from a strong normative control tendency towards one of increased solidarity with minorities and with once 'deviant' groups (although remaining in some degree stigmatized). This can apply, for instance, to single parents, homosexuals, the mentally ill, followers of various alternative life-styles, and immigrant labouring groups distinctive by colour or religion (Winick, 1978). The media seem belatedly and partially to follow leading social trends, although they may still be ahead of the majority of their audiences. Despite progress, sexism and racism are likely to remain high on the agenda of performance assessment research.

These remarks point to the inextricable relationship between changes in the overall balance of direction of social norms and values on the one hand and changes in media structure and content on the other. There is a case for continuous research to monitor the state of the predominant 'consensus', as it is represented in the media. The basic processes of reflection and dissemination which relate media to social change are likely to remain much the same, but the balance of forces may be quite variable from place to place and case to case and the content of the symbolically represented moral order can never be fully predicted.

Questions of taste and morality

The research approaches described are largely based on expectations that media will have *effects* either of a conformist or a destabilizing kind and thus performance standards are based on instrumental reasoning. It is not so much what is offered which is open to objection, as the potential consequences for which media can be held accountable. There remains another approach to the question of performance, in which the supposed *intrinsic* moral or cultural quality of the content itself becomes the object of assessment. Performance may be directly measured according to the degree to which its outcome in *content* deviates from what are widely accepted standards of taste or decency. Usually such deviations will have no positive aspect or theoretical defenders (although not everyone will find the same features objectionable or in the same degree).

The definition of what is culturally offensive ('non-cultural' or 'uncultured') is often itself very culture-specific and thus variable, although on some matters (such as certain kinds of pornography or explicit sexuality there may be wide cross-cultural agreement). The history of film and television provides numerous examples of attempts to specify, investigate and proscribe several features of media content regarded as objectionable and contrary to the conventional standards of taste, public decency, morality or behaviour generally. It is the protection of the young and supposedly vulnerable which has stimulated most regulation, although offence against adult codes of morality and ideas of propriety has played its part. In the nature of things, the standards by which culturally disapproved traits are assessed are continually changing over time, just as they vary between cultures.

Standards applied often vary from one medium to another, partly because of historical chance (e.g. the power of Catholic forces for morality in the USA in the 1930s with reference to films), partly as a reflection of the varying probability of exposure to media on the part of vulnerable groups. Television is still the medium most subject to content controls relating to propriety because of its open availability to children in the home, while print media remain the least under control. It would seem that, in general, what is broadcast on television is considered to have the character of *public* display and thus to attract normative controls similar to those which apply to behaviour in public places (in such matters as sex, language, blasphemy, cleanliness, aggression, etc.).

Issues of proscribed ('non-cultural') content

The list of potential causes of offence to taste and social mores can be very long and seems to be growing rather than shrinking, despite a supposed relaxation of standards. A full guide for an assessor's task (more or less equal here to the role of censor) cannot be given, only an indication of the main headings and possible indicators which could be applied to recognize undesirable elements of performance, from this point of view.

Representation of sex   In the dominant cultures of many societies there are conventions about the representation of sexual behaviour, ranging from the extremely prudish and repressive to the liberal, in the matter of what is in good or bad 'taste'. This refers mainly to the representation in media of all kinds of normal sexual behaviour, from holding hands to full intercourse and to degrees of nakedness displayed. It is quite possible for researchers to record the incidence of such portrayals in detail, as Greenberg has done (Greenberg et al., 1981a; Greenberg and D'Alessio, 1985) although the assessment standard applied (where the threshold of acceptability is located) has to be determined for each society and case. There is even more inter-cultural variation about whether unconventional sex (e.g. homosexuality) is culturally acceptable in its representation, but its incidence in media content is open to observation. Most unanimity is found in cultural proscriptions relating to the most widely disapproved forms of deviance such as incest and abuse of children, rape, bestiality, sadomasochism.

While content analysis designed to identify overt sexual behaviour presents no real difficulty, there are often hidden understandings and shades of meaning which complicate the issue of what to regard as 'non-cultural'. In particular, attention is often directed to the imputed *motive* for portrayal or the possible motive of the receiver. More sensitive codes of practice (e.g. that of the Broadcasting Standards Council, 1989) recognize that the portrayal of almost any kind of sexual behaviour or scene may sometimes be required as an intrinsic part of the plot (in the case of fiction), for artistic integrity or as an aspect of documentary truth.

It is 'gratuitous' sexual portrayal (for its own sake, or for reasons of sensationalism) which is usually frowned upon by guardians of moral cultural taste, although ideas of what counts as such are notoriously divergent. Some kinds of sexual display or representation may be considered as 'artistic', a legitimate provision for an adult minority, or as having a positive erotic value.

Violence   The same basic principles tend to apply. The use of violence often offends against social norms and its depiction against cultural norms (unless specifically legitimated, as in war or law enforcement). Representation of violence usually steps above the threshold of the culturally acceptable (although the threshold is set very differently in different cultures) when it is: deemed too explicit; shocking; sadistic; connected with sex and/ or applied to women, children and animals; is frequent and gratuitous (McCormack, 1980; Brannigan and Goldenberg, 1987; Einsiedel, 1988).

As with sex, some forms of violence are sub-culturally valued, as in the martial arts, boxing, actual war or counter-terrorist action. Because of strong policy interest the research apparatus for assessing the portrayal of violence in all forms is very well developed (e.g. Howitt and Cumberbatch, 1975; Gunter, 1985). The general sensitivity about *suicide*, as well as fear of imitative behaviour, can make this form of self-violence a particular object of cultural concern.

Commercialism in media content   The degree to which 'commercialism' as such is regarded as culturally dubious is extremely variable. Disdain for commerce has several tangled and inconsistent roots – in religion, art, socialist politics, aristocratic values (Leiss et al., 1986). Whatever the reasons, several societies do put strict limits to the extent of commercial financing and on 'commercial content' and nearly all countries have self-policing arrangements for advertising practice, in recognition of beliefs about the power of advertising and its potential for misuse (and also because of the wish to protect the image and good name of advertising).

Where commerce as such is culturally problematic, the relevant indicators of commercialism are fairly clear: the relative frequency or total amount of actual advertising content; the practice of commercial sponsorship, where it clearly affects the communication content; covert advertising by displaying products and brandnames; merchandising strategies, etc. Less visible to the normal media user or the analyst, but often equally frowned upon, are tendencies to blur the difference between advertising and non-advertising matter. Subliminal advertising, whether evidenced or not, is also disapproved. (It is forbidden for instance, by the European Television Directive.) In general, most penalized are tendencies for the aims of the advertiser to subvert the purposes of communication (whether as information, entertainment, education or art). For some, the main objection is simply to the promotion of 'consumerism', viewed as a negative cultural trait. This objection is sometimes made against television game shows and games of chance in which large prizes can be won, although it might also be laid against all advertising.

Beyond the measures directed against advertising as such there are many different regulations about what it is in good taste to advertise on what medium. Aside from potentially dangerous substances, like alcohol and tobacco, the rules concern mainly taboo areas related to sex, death, sickness, violence, drugs and medicine. Advertising communication has less freedom in these matters than normal communication.

Blasphemy and bad language Content offensive to religious believers is often subject to formal and informal control and regarded as culturally unacceptable, but there are wider proscriptions against swearing and cursing. The objectionable kinds of content are various, ranging from 'taking the name of the Lord in vain' to irreverent or scurrilous portrayals of religious themes and figures. The latter may precisely comprise a minor cultural genre, thus defying any simple identification of what is 'against the rules' in any given place, time or medium. Most cultures also have their own rules for what counts as culturally acceptable or unacceptable use of language in public. Most kinds of swearing and cursing are readily recognizable, although, as with sex and violence, there are distinctions to be made between 'gratuitous' use of bad language and cases where plot and setting may justify it.

Other causes of cultural offence These may include intrusion on privacy, gossip and scandal. Codes of good media practice usually legislate on this matter, but lines are especially hard to draw, and potential offence hard to recognize without ambiguity.

Harmful stereotyping, or symbolic abuse, of minorities is another sensitive area. The definition of potential 'victims' varies and changes as do standards of what might be permitted, but the aim is often to protect ethnic minorities and other vulnerable groups, such as the mentally ill, disabled, etc. There is a growing demand, especially in the United States, for the outlawing of uses of language which are not 'politically correct', for instance denigratory phrases in which the word 'black' or cognate terms appear (such as 'denigratory').

There is a changing 'list' of undesirable social behaviours which, though often quite common practices, it is widely thought should not receive any implicit support from the media, including such things as cruelty to animals, smoking, drinking, drug-taking, harming the environment, etc. Various types of personal behaviour can also be regarded as 'gross' or in bad taste: spitting, over-eating, bodily functions, drunkenness, etc. The portrayal of these, depending on context, may also give rise to proscriptive norms and enter into the question of performance.

Absence of consensus

The kinds of media performance dealt with in this chapter cover a very wide range, from matters of life and death and the very foundations of a society to what seem trivial and ephemeral matters of taste and social mores. They are only connected by having a potential to arouse negative public response or by having attracted the attention of critics who have invoked some version of the 'public interest'. In other words, they are all matters which belong within the public sphere and all have some connection with a public role attributed to the media, as carriers of the culture, embodiment of a collective social identity. This point is not weakened by the fact that almost all the matters raised are contested in some degree. The absence of consensus in modern societies does not seem to prevent most of us from reacting to the media as if there ought to be one.

20
SOLIDARITY AND SOCIAL IDENTITY

Media and solidarity

As far as the media are concerned, the voluntaristic principle of social order, as indicated in Figure 18.1, refers to three main things. First, it refers to support from media for the aspirations and identities of sub-groups in society, either by positive representation or by way of opportunities for access and self-communication (Rubin, 1980). Social and cultural minorities are likely to be involved in shared experiences, in which information and cultural support from the media may be helpful. The term 'identity' can serve as a summary label for this important terrain of media performance.

Secondly, the solidaristic principle refers, in general, to all those aspects of mass media performance which involve the symbolic extension of sympathy to individuals or groups in trouble or need as well as to the public recognition of shared risks, sorrows and hardships, which reminds people of their common humanity. This includes the reporting of distant hardships, disasters and injustice. It relates, thus, to whatever serves to link private and local experience (of media audiences) to global circumstances and conditions elsewhere (the term 'empathy' refers to these matters). Thirdly, the solidaristic principle can refer to some media processes which have been labelled 'pro-social' – generally to content which might reinforce 'positive' social values: good behaviour, care for others, community involvement, etc. This recognizes that much media content is supportive of, rather than threatening to, society. However, much of what is usually referred to as 'pro-social' belongs also to the domain of social control (however gentle) and to socialization, thus overlapping with the questions discussed in Chapter 19.

Mass media and social identity

There is no absolute distinction between the process of mass media support for a dominant 'consensus' and the process whereby alternative, minority, identities and sets of values can be supported by communication (if rarely by *mass* media). Where the line is drawn depends mainly on the perspective and values of an observer – one person's social control is another's cohesion. The continuity between the two is illustrated by considering the matter of *identity*. It is clear that mass media contribute to establishing an awareness of *national* identity under (normal) circumstances, where media audiences belong to a national society and where the boundaries of audience and of nationality often coincide. There are almost insoluble problems in defining precisely what is meant by a 'national identity' (Schlesinger, 1987, 1990). Generally, the term refers to a collective property of a society which is widely recognized and personally significant to many. Its key ingredient seems to be a sense of belonging to a particular collectivity with shared attributes (of place, language, culture) and a sense of exclusivity.

There are several means by which national identities are promoted by the media. The media employ the language and deploy symbols of the nation, with frequent substantive reference to the national life. The media also often adopt the role of representative of, or apologist for, the nation and constantly presume a 'national interest', which is shared with the reader/listener/viewer. The 'inscribed reader' (see Sparks and Campbell, 1987) of most national media *is* someone with the appropriate national identity and constant reiteration and presumption reinforces this identification. This is most evident in news, where the name of the nation (or its capital city) is often used as a short-hand term to denote complex interests or single home country agencies of diverse kinds – diplomats, football teams, business firms.

The 'national' identification is likely to be invoked, on behalf of the audience member, more frequently than other collective identifications which are potentially available. These can include, for example, social class, religion, gender, ethnicity, which cut across national identity boundaries. There can also be identifications of a supra-national kind, such as the world, Europe, the West, Third World, etc., which do occasionally figure as *alternatives* to national identification. The relative incidence of national versus other identifications in media content (fiction or reality) is open to investigation, if these ideas are accepted. In some circumstances, the degree to which content is imported rather than home produced may give a crude indication of this feature of media performance (see Chapter 22).

The number of possible conditions of minority identity and group attachment is very large and few have been studied in any depth (at least not with reference to mass media). Questions of communication are, nevertheless, bound up with most minority situations. Four main questions recur, concerning the following:

- the possibilities for a minority group to communicate *internally* and thus to become conscious of shared interests and identity and to organize for its own needs, or on its own behalf;
- the possibilities for a minority group to have access into the main (national) mass media to speak directly *to* the wider society, on its own terms;
- the possibility for the group to be itself effectively *reached* by the communications media of the wider society;
- the *quality* of representation of the minority in the main national mass media.

These questions can be looked at in relation to four different kinds of minority identification, about which some research has been done: counter-cultures; ethnic minorities; gender; locality.

Counter-cultures and the media

The term 'counter-culture' was coined in the 1960s (Roszak, 1968) to refer to a wide range of new social movements and alternative life-styles, which were seen as deviant or dissident in relation to an increasingly bureaucratic, consumerist, militaristic society. The social phenomenon of 'alternative' ways of life was not new, but it was more exposed to view in an age of mass communication. There was an interest in how such counter-cultures (based on diverse philosophies) would cope with (or without) mass media. There was also speculation about the positive ways in which new means of communication might be applied to the development of alternative social forms (Enzensberger, 1970). Closer to the present purpose, a number of studies were made of the communications developed by members of different 'counter-cultural' groups (e.g. Downing, 1984; Wilson and Gutierrez, 1985).

No general conclusion can be drawn, but it is clear that varied forms of publication, ranging from printed sheets to pirate radio, have helped minorities to achieve some of their aims in respect of the first of the four questions posed above – those of self-organization and identity. In the nature of many counter-cultural groupings, there was no call for access to established media and no wish to be reached by the wider society. There was also little interest for many of the groups in how they would be presented to a wider society, from which they had withdrawn and little good was to be expected from such representation. Research into sub-cultures and deviance (e.g. Cohen, 1972; Hall et al., 1978; Shoemaker, 1983) confirmed this last supposition.

Ethnic minorities and the media

The variety of ethnic minority situations and communication-relevant needs is almost as great as that just discussed, although there is a much longer tradition of research and more of it to draw upon (e.g. Greenberg et al., 1981b; Wilson and Gutierrez, 1985; Fielder and Tipton, 1986; Greenberg, 1986). The communication needs and expectations of ethnic minorities depend on several main variables, especially the degree of actual cultural distinctiveness and isolation, the degree to which a group wants political and cultural autonomy or, on the other hand, integration into a 'host society'. The level of economic strength of a minority usually plays a decisive part in determining actual minority media provision.

Almost all ethnic minorities need and expect sympathetic treatment in established mass media and would like to be able to speak, on their own terms, to the majority, by way of established mass media. The groups that most want autonomy do not usually want to be reached by dominant media and want their own exclusive channels. Those that want integration, or just treatment on equal terms with the majority (e.g. most African or Hispanic Americans, or many economic immigrants all over the world), are less likely to require their own media or to object to incorporation into normal majority audiences. Assessment of actual media situations and of media performance has to depend on a diagnosis of the particular needs of the particular minority.

Women and mass media

While most research on this topic has related to stereotyping of gender roles (Dominick and Rauch, 1971; Busby, 1975; Tuchman et al., 1978; Greenberg and Atkin, 1980; Seggar and Hafen, 1981; Durkin, 1985; Gunter, 1986, 1987b; Thoveron, 1986) or work opportunities in media (e.g. Butler and Paisley, 1980; Gallagher, 1981), there is scope for enquiry into some other aspects of the case, if women are viewed as constituting a minority social group, with distinctive social and economic objectives and thus with communication needs relating to identity and self-organization (Cantor and Jones, 1983; Dervin et al., 1989). As to the first question listed above, women as a social group (or category) seem to be unusually well provided with their own channels, ranging from many campaigning feminist publications to very large circulation national magazines, which are directed towards female readers (and often edited by women). In addition, many general newspapers provide special sections through which the voice of women's interests, outlook and claim can reach the wider society. The seeming richness of provision does, however, conceal some equally obvious deficiencies.

First, while there are many 'micro-media' serving the 'cells' of the active feminist movement, the reach is probably very limited and, therefore, also the real opportunity to raise consciousness amongst women in support of their identity and interests. Secondly, the seeming abundance of media for women is largely accounted for by the key role of the woman as a consumer (of media as well as of other goods and services) and as 'gatekeeper' of many household budgets. The apparent richness reflects more the self-interest of advertisers than the degree of service to women as a minority group.

This does not mean that commercially well-supported content produced for women is unable to serve some objectives of maintaining identity and pursuing some emancipatory ends, although it is likely that political edge will be dulled by commercial purpose. This is a matter for empirical assessment in each case (see Ferguson, 1983). Thirdly, there is little sign, so far, of access for women as a minority as such having extended to radio and television – seemingly few channels for women and little special access programming.

The deficiencies mentioned are open to investigation by research into media structure, content and audiences. It is clear that, as with the case of ethnic minority identification, there is a variable aspiration on the part of women themselves to be treated as having a separate identity (rather than real equality and recognition) and this would have to be taken into account in setting appropriate standards for performance by media in terms of structure and content.

Local media and local identity

Locality has kept its significance as a principle of media structure and thus scope for local identification via media remains. The reasons have less to do with the great importance of the local place for people themselves than with the commercial significance of the various local markets, in which local media serve as vehicles for advertising as well as being local products. Whatever the reasons, there has been a good deal of interest in the relation between local community identification and the vitality of local communities on the one hand and the existence of local media and their quality of performance, on the other.

Of the four questions relevant for minorities posed above, the most salient is that which relates to having an independent and adequate local media provision. Since local media usually serve to supplement national or regional media, the question of access to, or representation in, national media does not usually arise. However, the standards appropriate to assessing local media performance should take into account the media alternatives which are available (McCombs and Winter, 1981). The earliest substantial enquiry into the quality of local media provision and a landmark for later research was that of Janowitz (1952). This was inspired by sociological theory concerning the decline or survival of community life in large urban environments. Janowitz tested several propositions about (commercial) urban community newspapers, especially the view that they serve many unanticipated social needs, that they help to maintain local consensus, contribute to family and social cohesion and link individual communication to society-wide communication.

His research into content, audience and publishers provided evidence to sustain his hypotheses. He showed, in particular, that there was a strong correlation between attachment to the community and loyal readership of the local press, that local newspapers avoided controversy, sensation and 'bad news', that they served as enforcers of a local order and were perceived, by readers and non-readers alike, to be non-commercial, non-partisan and essential aids to local social life.

Subsequent research has followed very similar lines with similar results, often emphasizing the triangular relationship between: attachment to local place; audience attachment to local media; quality of local service provided by media (see Edelstein and Larsen, 1960; Bogart and Orenstein, 1965; Jackson, 1971; Ghiglione, 1973; McCombs, 1983; Stamm, 1985). The variable of local attachment has been measured in different ways, sometimes objectively in terms of length of residence and intensity of local ties, sometimes subjectively in terms of feelings of liking and perception of the place as home or as neighbourly (Janowitz, 1952).

Assessment has generally involved studies of content (e.g. Duncan, 1952;

Brander and Sistruk, 1966; Cox and Morgan, 1974; Wulfmeyer, 1982; Kariel and Rosenvall, 1983; Franklin and Murphy, 1991) or of questions of local ownership (Stempel, 1973; Roberts and Dickson, 1984). Janowitz had shown that non-local (chain) ownership was likely to be associated with a lower degree of community orientation, a less personalized and intimate news coverage and more sensationalism. Olien et al. (1983), following a different line of analysis, found that non-local (out-of-state) ownership was likely to lead to less attention to issues of significant local controversy and thus to less public involvement. Stone (1987) reported a good deal of inconsistency in the impact of type of ownership on the quality of local news performance (see also Chapter 9). Lemert (1989) discusses 'Afghanistanism' in local media: the tendency to give much critical attention to far-away issues and ignore conflicts close to home.

The most commonly applied measures of content as indicators of quality of local media performance have been as follows:

- the relative attention to local news and issues;
- the use of own news-gathering staff;
- the degree of attention to matters of local controversy, to criticism and different opinions (Murphy, 1976; Franklin and Murphy, 1991);
- the taking of editorial stands on matters of local controversy;
- advance information about, and coverage of, local activities;
- relative attention to 'positive' local news (as against crime, sensation, disorder news: Jackson, 1971; Stone et al., 1987);
- giving support to local interests in conflicts with external bodies (e.g. over investment, environment, jobs, etc.);
- giving support to local business;
- the extent to which local or regional media are *distinctive* in their general content (thus supporting diversity) (Donohue and Glasser, 1978; Hynds, 1982; Morgan, 1986).

These potential indicators are not all consistent, especially those relating to consensus and to conflict. This is another reminder that cohesion and control may be two sides of the same coin and that the question of who benefits from local cohesion has to be taken into account in setting criteria (Hankins, 1988).

Local media *audience* research has, aside from the question of reach and use, dealt mainly with subjective attachment to media and evaluation of local provision (Greenberg, 1964; Jackson, 1982). Attitudes to local competition or monopoly have also been looked at. Attachment can be assessed either according to degree of media use or by direct questions about the perceived significance of local media (Wulfmeyer, 1983a). Burgoon et al. (1980, 1983b) identified a significant 'local awareness' factor in audience evaluations of media functions. This mainly involved an expectation of provision of useful local information. Gollin and Macht (1986) tried to assess readers' 'feelings of personal attachment' to local papers, by rating according to 'closeness to the newspaper', 'reliance' and 'identification'.

There has been research in the tradition of media 'uses and gratifications' which has testified to the potentially key role of media in 'connecting' individuals to their social environment (Katz et al., 1973), but little dealing specifically with *local* media (an exception is Brown, 1978). Stone et al. (1987), citing Stempel (1973) and McGrath and Gaziano (1986), says there is little audience awareness of who owns the media. Audience research has never given much support to concerns about reduced competition (e.g. Bigman, 1955), perhaps indirectly telling us that local media are not, after all, so vital for local identity in the cases studied.

Solidarity: the empathy factor

The central idea is that the mass media can help individuals to feel attached to the wider community and society and to share in its collective life, on the basis of sympathetic fellow-feeling, especially for others in difficulties of various kinds. The media help by providing information about problems and also by offering sympathetic assessments which invite understanding and help. In their study of attitudes and values of American journalists, Weaver and Wilhoit (1986) discovered a strong 'image of altruism', which they say has a long history in the profession (Christians, 1986). According to their evidence, the single most important component of journalists' job satisfaction, outstripping 'job security' was 'helping people'. Gans (1979), in a more incidental way, confirms this.

A wide recognition of this media 'function' has also been demonstrated by studies of the motivations of audiences for attending to various kinds of media content, especially documentary and realistic drama. Expressions of this attitude can be found, for instance, in endorsements of the view that television news: 'helps me to understand the problems of others', 'makes me feel sad', or 'makes me feel my life is not so bad after all' (McQuail et al., 1972: 160).

McGuire's (1974) theoretical discussion of psychological motivations for the use of media identifies this phenomenon under the heading of 'affiliation' theories. He writes, 'the affiliative concepts stress that aspect of human motivation that drives the person to establish with other people connections that are characterized by mutual helpfulness and reciprocal positive affect.' He describes them as theories which 'focus on altruism and cooperativeness' (1974: 188). In a later overview, Wenner (1985) emphasized the 'affective' function of mass media.

Another origin for the idea of 'empathy' derives from research into the harmful effects of the media, against which the notion of 'pro-social effects' was countered (Poulos et al., 1975; Lee, 1988). Television companies went to some trouble to point to the amount of 'pro-social' messages in their content. Lee, for instance, in research for CBS, identified three main features of the 'pro-social': altruistic actions, like sharing, cooperating, helping; affective behaviours such as showing affection, emotion, empathy or sympathy; control over negative predispositions. In this research, the single most frequent category (out of 10) of 'pro-social' behaviour was that of showing sympathy or empathy. Feshbach (1988) offers a clarification of empathy as a social psychological behaviour. She says it is 'a shared emotional response between the viewer and the viewed – between subject and object in an interaction . . . [It] is a basic ingredient of social understanding and social harmony . . . the opposite of egocentricism' (1988: 262). Applied to the television experience, 'Empathy entails the capacity to assume another's perspective, a skill that involves an act of imagination.'

There is no easy line to draw between media content which lends itself to this form of engagement between audiences and their social environment and content which has a binding or socially controlling effect. The expression of sympathy for individuals and groups in society can also have an effect of reinforcing the social order. Arguments for more 'pro-social' or empathic content are often arguments for socialization to the norms of society rather than pleas for lessons in altruism. However, we are not usually in a position to assess empathic or controlling *effects* (though both can, in principle, be measured). For purposes of performance assessment, we would need only to be able to recognize the relevant features of media content. These turn out to be varied and quite extensive.

It is convenient to consider the question in terms of three main kinds of potential 'beneficiary' of empathic tendencies in the media: individual victims; larger groups in the national society who may be victims of social conditions or of disasters; the disadvantaged and victimized abroad. The media frequently offer sympathy to a wide range of individuals and groups who have suffered in some way, often as if speaking 'on behalf of' the society or community and as if inviting their audiences to join in the expression of sympathy or understanding. The more routine and formal examples are to be found where well-known personalities or prominent citizens suffer some tragedy, accident, injury, loss or bereavement. Major disasters, with large loss of life (e.g. boat, train or crowd accidents) are also occasions for displays of media empathy.

The media formats in which the collective expression of empathy appear are varied, including especially: news background; documentary and docudrama; realistic fiction (e.g. 'soap opera'); editorial comments; letters to newspapers; appeals for support, fund-raising efforts and media campaigns on behalf of groups in need; advertising in the media; attention to spokespersons in chat shows and magazines. The list could be longer. The categories of problem which can receive sympathetic attention are also numerous, including: all kinds of illness and disability; homelessness and poverty; old age; social isolation; drug addiction; racial discrimination; imprisonment and prison conditons; experience of rape; child and sexual abuse; homophobia. It is clear from this brief list that a 'social desirability' factor is also likely to operate and to be reflected in the distribution of empathic attention by media.

It is possible, on this basis, to discriminate, within content, in terms of the way in which empathy is 'allocated'. Although the *degree* of empathy is hard to measure (except by space/time to the category), there is usually a recognizable difference between the amount and/or kind (thus the quality) of empathy directed towards different categories of victim. Those who enjoy sympathy, by large consensus (e.g. society's own 'heroes' in trouble, widows of servicemen, helpless children, homeless families, young victims of illness, etc.) usually receive more attention than those whose condition might either be considered deserved or even self-inflicted.

These include, for instance, drug addicts, convicted criminals, the supposedly idle and feckless, victims of AIDS, immigrants, the mentally ill, unemployed, homosexuals, sometimes also women victims of rape or battering. Clearly, both the distribution of sympathy and the nature of the consensus do vary from place to place and time to time and may themselves be the outcome of long-term trends of media treatment (see Golding and Middleton, 1982; Shoemaker, 1984). Nevertheless, it should be possible to assess the degree to which media do allocate sympathy and understanding as between more and less 'popular' or 'deserving' causes. The latter would constitute a more 'pure type' of empathy, the former often just a routine reaffirmation of consensual values.

The methods of research available are much the same as those described earlier for dealing with representations of minorities and access, together with those methods which allow an assessment of evaluative direction. In general, an appropriate research design would involve identifying space/ time given to a problem, together with measures of the balance of evaluation of victims. The degree of social marginality or consensual valuation of groups, might, for the reasons given, also need to be taken into account (although a measure independent of media treatment might be hard to find). However, some assessment on the basis of known social attitudes can be made. Shoemaker (1984), for instance, found it possible to distinguish between minority advocacy groups according to whether they were established and 'socially central' or marginal, even deviant.

The international dimension of media empathy

The general principles outlined apply in a similar way to wider aspects of human solidarity. While fellow-feeling towards other nations and cultures and their problems is usually regarded by the media as more 'optional' than is sympathy for deserving victims at home, there has probably been an increased awareness of the interdependence of national societies and of their shared global fate, now ecologically as well as economically and politically. There has been increasing pressure on the mass media (themselves subject to internationalizing tendencies) to play a part in these developments, since they are believed to be influential in the formation of public awareness and opinion.

At issue here is less the *adequacy* of provision of information about global events than the *quality* of attention, especially the *affective* quality of sympathetic understanding, as described above and also the consistency of attention. The key question concerns the extent to which the media might contribute to better understanding of problems in the world and to an extension of fellow-feeling beyond the boundaries of the home country, own race, religion, etc. The 1978 UNESCO Mass Media Declaration provided a useful base for research by restating some principles of media performance in international affairs.

The Declaration speaks against all incitement to war, hatred of other nations, aggression, racism, and asks for 'positive discrimination' on behalf of the oppressed and an informed attitude to problems of poverty and underdevelopment. A Finnish research project (Holopainen, 1987) sought to evaluate several prominent newspapers according to these principles by way of intensive qualitative examination of large numbers of articles. While labour-intensive, this may be the only way to deal with assessment on such broad criteria.

Otherwise, there has been much research attention to the international flow of news (e.g. McBride, 1980; Adams, 1982; Boyd-Barrett, 1985; Kivikuru and Varis, 1985; Mowlana, 1985; Larson, 1986), often from a perspective which is critical of many ethnocentric and negative aspects of international news. Work in the tradition of peace research (e.g. Varis, 1986) has also done much to put the issue of media and international solidarity on the research agenda. The appropriate research methods usually call for an adaptation of existing types of content analysis and attention to certain recurring news issues and events, especially the following:

Issues of peace and disarmament, within the context of international conflict. Accuracy of information aside, media reporting can be more or less positive towards efforts by either 'side' towards a goal of less war, or risk of war, emphasizing, or not, the benefits of disarmament (Rubin and Cunningham, 1983; Varis, 1986).

The general matter of 'images' of foreign countries, especially those which have been historically regarded as hostile or culturally alien or inferior (Sreberny-Mohammadi, 1984; Albritton and Manheim, 1985; McDonald, 1985; Dorman and Farhang, 1987; Perry, 1987; McNair, 1988). The more the balance of 'positive' over 'negative' representations, references and contexts, the more content is likely to contribute to empathy. Adequate treatment of this matter requires more than just attention to 'hard news'. A lot may turn on coverage in sport, human interest and cultural contexts and, of course, in fictional portrayals, plots and settings.

Reference to disasters and emergencies abroad (earthquake, famine, flood, etc.) (Adams, 1986). In general, the more attention, the more positive the likely effect (despite the risk of creating an image of 'disaster-proneness'). Emphasis on cooperation in aid-giving and some positive features of the victims or recipients of aid can be helpful. The more that victims are able to speak for themselves, the more likely it is that media reports help bridge a cultural gap and influence attitudes.

Reference to refugee and migratory movements. These may need separate attention because they usually have a dual or ambiguous character: establishing sympathy for minority groups forced to flee, but often activating negative images of national majorities or regimes (or fears of immigration) (van Dijk, 1991). A relevant dimension may be the degree to which the issue is dealt with as a human tragedy or a political conflict.

Economic relations between the developed and developing world and 'Third World' economic news in general. Degree of attention to Third World economic problems, dependency and the inequality of relations (especially from their point of view) is itself an indicator of potential empathy. More detailed qualitative indicators can also be thought of, for instance reports of positive developments and 'good news'.

The general treatment of *relevant institutions and agencies,* including UNESCO bodies, international charities, etc. which have the task of putting empathy into action. The media can contribute to more or less recognition, and positive (or negative) images, of such bodies (Roach, 1982; Giffard, 1989; Preston et al., 1989).

Reports of ecological problems. This can also be dealt with from a more or less internationalist perspective, emphasizing (or not) elements of shared risk and shared costs of ecological repair.

Media follow rather than lead

The evidence discussed in this chapter and in Part VII as a whole reminds us yet again of the great potential and severe limitations of the mass media. There is a latent power to advance collective ends and humanitarian goals, but it is very sporadically and selectively exercised. This is not a random effect, but the result of two factors: one is the primacy of media organizational goals, another the fact that media are generally instruments, not instigators, of other social forces. They are not primary social actors.

PART VIII
MEDIA AND CULTURE

21
QUESTIONS OF CULTURE AND MASS COMMUNICATION

Protecting cultural quality

MEDIA AND CULTURE

21
QUESTIONS OF CULTURE AND MASS COMMUNICATION

Protecting cultural quality

In a wider view, everything discussed so far counts as 'media culture'. For the most part, however, public interest claims have been limited to certain aspects and types of 'culture', or according to limited perspectives. Privileged treatment and protection is often given to certain kinds of media content which are thought to have implications for the wider cultural life of a society. As noted already (Chapter 5), many broadcasting regulations give attention to the 'cultural' task of television and radio, often by encouraging or requiring a minimum degree of educational programming as well as of programming which is home produced and/or in the language of the country (Shaughnessy and Cobo, 1990; Blumler, 1992).

Some other categories of content are also singled out for protection, in the name of the 'public interest', especially those which relate to arts, crafts and customs of the nation or its component regions and to what is generally thought to be a worthy part of human 'cultural heritage', more broadly conceived. Often the special cultural needs of children and of various religious and minority groups are given special attention. While non-broadcasting media are rarely regulated in the same way, normative discussion of their performance often follows similar lines.

These remarks imply a broad distinction between the many symbolic ways in which cultures are expressed and the general culture of a society, in the anthropological sense of all human actions and artefacts. Only the former (which are directly matters of communication) are strictly relevant to media performance, but the line cannot be too sharply maintained, since the significance attributed to the symbolic representation of culture stems ultimately from the fuller sense of the term. There is another distinction which is often found in the terminology of those who reflect on media performance: that between the value attached to 'high' culture, usually as allocated by institutional elites, and the value which is attached to any authentic cultural expression of a people, irrespective of aesthetic or artistic value. Both types of the cultural value have been invoked as justification for claims on public interest grounds.

There are three main reasons why the social value attached to culture leads to a concern with the performance of the mass media. One is because the media produce and disseminate cultural *texts* – works which may be seen as having some intrinsic cultural value. Secondly, the media may be important channels for the public communication activities of other *cultural institutions* (especially those to do with the arts and education). Thirdly, the media can have *effects* (positive or negative) on the cultural 'environment' of individuals as well as on personal taste, customs and ways of behaving. The media are also important for participation in cultural activities and for national or regional identity. The multiplicity of possible connections between mass media and cultural life rules out any possibility of having a single blueprint for a comprehensive assessment of cultural performance of the media. Even so, we should be able to identify a set of relevant *content* criteria and indicators for enquiring into performance standards.

Culture and society: fragmentation and relativism

The underlying reasons for cultural policies are less easy to unearth. The culture of any society involves a structured set of preferences for: certain *forms* of expression; particular *meanings*; certain *ways* of doing things. In the (notional) early, 'organic', form of society (if the first generation of anthropologists is to be believed), there was likely to be a more or less agreed and consistent hierarchy of values indicating *what* ought to be said and done, in respect of the main contingencies of human experience. A shared set of values indicated *how* things should be done – the customs and conventions of regular activities, from ways of eating to the organization of politics and economics. Culture is the most fundamental attribute of any society or community, defined as a bounded set of individuals, sharing the same space and having a common history and sense of identity. Culture always involves a set of selection criteria (prescriptions and rules for their application) and is itself fundamentally and inescapably normative.

This is a highly schematic and ideal-typical view of the 'original' relationship between culture and society. It does not coincide very closely with the present-day reality on two main points. First, no modern society is characterized by a single culture, in the sense described: having an agreed hierarchy of values and a single set of preferences, which remain stable over time. Secondly, 'culture' and society have become, to a large extent, detached from each other, in the sense that there is no longer a one-to-one relationship between a configuration of symbolic practices and prescriptions and a social collectivity. The spatial boundaries of society and of a domain of culture now rarely coincide if only because culture changes more rapidly than society and is not spatially limited. There are often numerous competing or alternative cultural options and sub-cultures, available across space and time, undermining the old dependence on the culture of one's own 'tribe', region or nation. This is certainly true for what count as 'modern societies'.

For these reasons, the criteria which are applied to 'cultural' performance of the media are often dated and difficult to define. They are also often fragmentary and inconsistent, based on divergent principles and claims. It is now rare to find any attempt to apply a 'unitary' standard of what would be in the public interest in the way of culture, although it is not inconceivable, where a single creed or ideology predominates (the unitary type of public interest theory).

Principles of cultural policy for the media

Despite the obsolescence of the unitary paradigm of culture and society, the view that a society should protect and advance its own symbolic culture still survives and is expressed in discourse on cultural policy by reference to four main principles: of hierarchy; equality; identity; taste and morality.

Hierarchy The principle of hierarchy of cultural quality and values leads to discrimination according to standards of intrinsic educational, scientific, aesthetic or artistic merit (usually as determined by professional or social elites). While there is less certainty than in the past about which standards to apply, the general idea of a hierarchy in matters of cultural quality has largely survived, certainly in the form of many 'official' justifications for public protection of, or subsidy for, culture, education and the arts. Tradition, inertia, consensus and powerful cultural institutions all help to sustain the idea that valid distinctions and gradations of cultural quality can be made.

Equality (equity) The principle of fairness, democracy and rights of citizenship all lend support to the view that cultural goods should be equitably distributed and that there should be chances for the many to share in a valued common cultural heritage. This applies especially to educational and information provision, since the mass media are, in principle, an important means by which initial gaps and deficiencies of 'cultural capital' (Bourdieu, 1986) can be rectified. Equity also calls for the 'message' of symbolic culture to be fair and non-discriminatory, free, for example, from negative stereotypes of race, belief or social condition.

Cultural identity However loose the connection may have become between culture and society, there usually remains a core set of cultural features which are thought to identify a human grouping, especially one which has a clear location in space and time, such as a nation, ethnic or religious minority. Culture, in this sense, expresses a consciousness of belonging to a place, a period and a community of others. Culture helps individuals to find or create personal meaning in experience and a shared sense of locality and belonging. What matters most in this respect are language (and all that is stored and carried in language from the past) and symbols of place, especially of nation and region, but also of the immediately local space and whatever marks it out as distinctive and familiar.

Taste and morality The fourth principle has to do with rules and conventions for public social intercourse. It mainly applies to matters of speech and behaviour in public places and is usually known by terms such as 'good taste', 'decency', or even 'manners'. At issue is conformity, or offence, to the local sense of what is 'right' and 'proper'. Culturally acceptable behaviour in the sense meant here – of decency, decorum and civilization – is expected of everyone, whatever their estate and is also expected of the mass media in their capacity as public channels of communication. The principle does presume a degree of *conformity* to norms and correct *forms* of social intercourse. It is assumed that we can identify certain cultural forms as more deviant, disapproved or 'uncultured'. These matters have, for the most part, been dealt with in Chapter 19, under the heading of 'Questions of taste and morality'.

Agents and claimants

The privileging of whatever is identified as of symbolic cultural value has to be initiated or supported by some specific interest, group or agency in society and usually involves reference to some version of the 'public interest'. It is always, in one sense, a political matter, implying an allocation of preference or resources. Identifying the agents of cultural claims helps to establish the range of relevant criteria of cultural quality which apply in a particular time and place. The following headings cover the most likely 'agents of preference'.

Cultural institutions The most likely instigators and supporters of cultural policies for media belong to familiar cultural institutions, especially those connected with education, the arts and sciences (schools, universities, galleries, libraries, museums, arts and sciences councils and foundations, etc.). All of the principles named can help to provide legitimacy for the 'preference claims' made by such institutions, although the idea of hierarchy of aesthetic value may be most prominent.

Cultural industries Businesses and industries related to production, exhibition and distribution in the arts, education and sciences (production companies, publishers, dealers, etc.) also have an interest in these matters. Individual artists and cultural workers will also, of course, make claims on behalf of artistic culture and for its proper representation in media output. The principle of cultural identity often helps to support claims for cultural subsidy or protection.

Political interests A distinct set of political interests and agents (although there is much overlapping) often advocate policies for the expression of national, regional or local autonomy, or for the cultural rights and protection of minorities. For these 'advocates', cultural benefits often have important symbolic value in a broader strategy for a place, people or cause. What usually matters is the *identity* of the culture rather than its specific *content* and quality. Politicians are most likely to press claims of cultural policy on grounds of the equity principle noted above.

Pressure groups There is a broad range of organized cultural advocates concerned more with the *forms* of culture and behaviour, especially with morals, manners, decency, language. They usually include a diverse set of religious, and/or conservative voices, often with a broad base of public support for some of their aims, especially keeping the media 'clean and decent'. However, amongst them are also to be found critics of media commercialism and voices which speak up against stereotyping, racism and sexism.

Pressure groups are more likely to define what they are *against* and what they want banned or controlled, rather than what they positively value. However, they may also advocate positive kinds of culture: content which will reinforce conventional (and 'pro-social') values of social behaviour and morality, or the values of their own way of life. Such pressure groups have been active and often effective in achieving codes of decency and forms of censorship in theatre, film and broadcasting. They can also be influential in securing 'positive discrimination' for minorities in media content (Montgomery, 1989).

From cultural politics to performance criteria

The advocates of higher cultural standards and proponents of cultural policies are very disparate, although their appeals often overlap and reinforce each other. In any case, the main actors and advocates in the field of media cultural politics have, between them, set an agenda of concerns which offers a pragmatic guide to the main questions for performance research and to relevant criteria of assessment. Four broad categories of media content or types of performance have attracted attention, under the rubric of 'culture', and between them provide a framework for media cultural performance assessment.

The categories are largely defined according to the four principles named above and comprise: education and scientific content, as conventionally understood; artistic content – written, pictorial and performed; any content that may have to do with 'cultural identity', where cultural value derives from provenance and from reference to local place; matters of taste, decency and morals (already dealt with). It is less easy to place these concerns in the theoretical framework presented earlier (see Figure 18.1 above), where the 'cultural domain' is separated out from that of the social. The conceptual distinctions which have been introduced do not entirely match those chosen

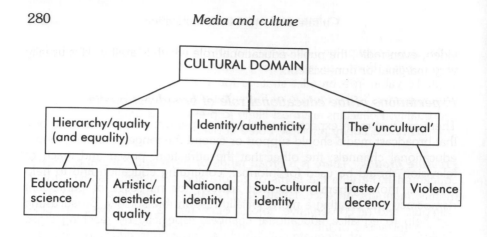

Figure 21.1 *The main component criteria of the media cultural domain*

for practical purposes. But the following schematic version may serve to bring the theory and practice of assessment in better relation to each other (Figure 21.1).

In the rest of this chapter, attention is given to describing empirical indicators of media performance in respect of education and of artistic culture.

Culture as education and science content in mass media

Here, the main issue for performance assessment is the extent to which the media provide channels and access, first, for informal education and information and, secondly, for more formal educational provision which is linked to educational institutions. A public interest may be attributed to the wider dissemination of what is otherwise considered to be specialist or expert knowledge. The expectation that mass media should play a part in a process of public education varies in strength from place to place and from medium to medium. The print media generally fulfil the expectation by responding to market demand for educational and science material. Sometimes supply is indirectly subsidized by cultural institutions, sometimes cultural and educational content is cross-subsidized by more 'commercial' activities or undertaken for purposes of prestige or chosen policy.

In practice, in respect of informal as well as formal educational provision, most attention has been paid to the general public educational role of broadcasting (and television in particular). This is especially true where broadcasting has been run as a public service; quite strong and specific requirements about providing educational content are to be found in most instruments of licensing and regulation of broadcasting. For other media, music, film,

video, even radio, the public educational role which is attributed is usually
very marginal or non-existent.

Expectations of the educational role of broadcast media

There are two main expectations relevant to performance assessment: one
that broadcast media should support or extend the range of existing formal
educational channels; the other that the attraction, power and reach of
television should be used for informal, continuing education and to help
create a more generally informed society, for purposes of participant
democracy and creating a more socially responsible society. Broadcasting
can help to equalize educational chances, especially by reaching those
denied chances of adequate childhood participation in education. It is this
second principle (contribution to informal public education) which is most
relevant.

Assessment has to take account of the tension between this potential
educational role and the normal goals and operating conditions of a medium
such as television. While the television medium may seem ideally suited to
the task of continuing public education, it is usually financially unprofitable
to carry it out, under conditions of audience choice and competition, and
not easy to carry out effectively for the same reasons. The typical audience
demand for educational content on television is generally rather weak
(compared to that for entertainment and news) and very fragmented
because of the range of potential interests and of topics for treatment.

In respect of television the main performance criterion is the *amount and
kind* of educational content offered, bearing in mind the interests and
capacities of audiences likely to be reached. Secondly, there is the question
of the intrinsic *quality* of what is offered, as judged against 'educational'
criteria. Thirdly, there is the question of actual *reach* and the devices
employed to achieve it (favourable scheduling, publicity, good presentation,
production values, etc.).

Quantitative assessment

The assessment of the *amount* of educational content depends, as usual, on
having an appropriate category system and on being able to allocate content
to categories according to consistent principles. Although most broadcasters
in Europe, within public service regimes, do render an account of their
educational provision (and have developed a common category system for
this purpose: the EBU 'ESCORT' system), the obstacles to reaching a
reliable measure of educational content are considerable.

The existence of national rules requiring a proportion (or quota) of such
content may even add to the problem, since this often leads to manipulation
of superficial features of content or presentation to give the appearance of
filling quotas. Alternatively, a genuine wish to reach a large audience can
produce a *reverse* tendency: educational purpose is concealed within
'entertainment' formats (for instance, as quizzes or competitive games, or in

the guise of 'docudrama') and programmes may then cease to 'qualify' in the appropriate cultural accounting system.

The potential diversity of format and of content makes it extremely difficult to draw boundary lines, except rather arbitrarily, or on an *ad hoc* basis. While some formats may clearly qualify as popular education and science, there are many more which are likely to defy easy classification. These include, especially: certain documentaries and current affairs programming; dramatizations of historical events; nature and travel programmes, which can be 'scientific' or just entertainment; 'how to do it' programmes which can have an equally wide range. There are several ambiguous content categories which might well qualify as educational, although their primary classification looks quite different, for instance religion, crime or sport.

While an accounting of television programming according to the educational principle is quite feasible in principle, in practice it is almost impossible to secure agreement between an organizational (internal) and an independent (external) classification or to ensure comparability between different media channels or across time and place. If the perceptions of the audience are also introduced in order to identify what should be counted as educational or culturally informative, consistent classification would clearly become impossible. There is no reason to believe that the general audience deploys a more clear or consistent content category system than do media providers.

Qualitative assessment

Assessment of the (informational) *quality* of what is offered as (popular) educational provision is even more difficult and has not often been attempted (but see the early broadcasting research of Joseph Trenaman, 1967). Although there may be agreement (amongst experts at least) on general criteria of quality, the interpretation of actual cases is likely to involve much subjectivity and be extremely labour-intensive. Two main kinds of criteria are, in principle, available. One relates to the 'information value' of content, the second to form and presentation. Information value of educational content is related to truth qualities of the kind discussed in respect of news (Chapter 16).

Value is attached to the amount of factual information (density of information), to its relevance, seriousness of purpose, good faith and originality. Guidelines for assessing content can also be found in the 'scientific credentials', expertise and authority of presenters and sources. An implicit distinction is often deployed which separates systematic, useful knowledge from information which just satisfies curiosity (of the 'Trivial Pursuits' variety). While the distinction looks obvious enough in common-sense terms, it is not easy to use in practice.

A second set of criteria mainly relates to presentation formats and style, especially the degree of 'superficiality' or 'sensationalism' of informational programming. In practice, these often boil down to the presence or absence of culturally 'negative' features: the use of show business techniques, fast pace, sensationalism, gimmicks to arouse attention, appeals to emotion, personalization, etc. These features are thought to be diversionary from educational goals and associated with superficiality and triviality, even if they may be chosen for purposes of effective communication and appeal. The difficulties of classification are illustrated by the quiz-show format, which can vary considerably in its educational value, but which cannot automatically be excluded from consideration.

The two sets of criteria are likely to be correlated (educationally 'shallow' content going with sensationalist or superficial format, and vice versa) whether from 'good' motives or 'bad'. The practical value of these two kinds of criteria for performance assessment is uncertain. While we might, with their help, be able to distinguish a feature about sex and satanism in suburban cemeteries from a programme on the life and work of Charles Darwin, there will be many more uncertain cases.

There are other factors which can help to indicate relative informational quality. These include the question of whether a programme is new or old, shown for the first time or repeated, original or derivative, commercially sponsored or not, made with a high or a low budget. Each of these has some potential for discriminating between one media offering and another. While detailed investigation of every case might produce a fairly reliable ranking of specific examples, systematic performance assessment of any large body of output probably has to depend on simple dichotomies of the following kind: 'heavy' versus 'light' information; much or little use of entertainment presentation features; high or low personification, etc.

Reaching the audience

The evaluation of the timing and audience reach of educational programming is simple, compared to the difficulties just discussed, although it too depends on being able to categorize content reliably. Audience figures should give precise numbers to performance in terms of *delivering* educational content. Scheduling can be a test of good faith, if nothing else, on the assumption that peak-hour timing is evidence of serious educational commitment. Guidelines for cultural and educational provision may contain requirements that such offer be made at times when the intended audience (the general public usually) is likely to be reached (thus not in the early hours of the morning or very late at night).

Audience size figures alone are not enough, since an *inappropriate* audience (e.g. of small children) may be no better than no audience and a small, but appropriate, audience may be better than a large, but inappropriate, one. One of the built-in limitations of planning for cultural/educational purpose is at work here – it is possible to require the supply, but not the demand (from the public). Assessment has at least to take note of this limitation. There remains the whole question of actual or potential communication effectiveness, which was raised in relation to news (Chapter 16), but which goes beyond the scope of this discussion.

Assessing artistic cultural provision

The main public interest goals relating to artistic cultural provision in mass media concern support for traditional cultural values for their own sake and, secondly, the wish to disseminate the acknowledged cultural goods of a society more widely and equitably – helping all to share in the cultural heritage (thus the two principles of Hierarchy and Equality introduced above). The popular media may be the only effective means for bringing some of the arts (for instance, opera, ballet, classical music and drama, art photography or film) to the wider public. They can also serve generally as a 'gateway' for awareness of all the arts. Mass media (music recording, television, film, etc.) can also be regarded as significant contemporary art forms in their own right and essential to the development of the living arts.

Cultural policy for the arts is thus directed not only to securing channels for reaching people with artistic cultural experience of accredited value, beyond the distribution capacity of traditional cultural institutions, but also seeks to encourage the creative potential of modern media. Television is especially relevant because of its many modes and formats, its responsiveness to public policy aims and its great reach. As with educational content, assessment usually calls for a quantitative and qualitative accounting of the representation of aesthetically and culturally valued content in media channels. However, the identification of relevant content is made more difficult by lack of agreement on criteria of cultural quality.

'High' versus 'low' culture

In the early years of media research and of the study of popular culture, attempts were often made to distinguish both qualitatively and quantitatively between 'good' and 'bad' in mass media culture. Much of this effort was inspired by the long, bitter and confused debate over 'mass culture' (e.g. Rosenberg and White, 1957). Protagonists in this debate were moved by quite diverse motives and concerns. One source was an aesthetic aversion to the banality of much popular culture, in whatever form, and an attempt, in reaction, to establish and defend absolute cultural values. Another was a traditional conservative fear of the uneducated mass – more social and moral than aesthetic in motivation. This resulted, especially, in a blanket condemnation of all forms of mass culture, in effect of most of what appealed to the working class.

On the other hand, there were radical and socialist critics who interpreted mass culture as the cultural arm of manipulative capitalism (generally the Frankfurt School position) and also democrats and populists of various persuasions who wanted to save the working class from themselves (and from commercial exploitation) or to stand up, variously, for the dignity, the right to choose or the essential nobility of ordinary working people (Hoggart, 1957; Williams, 1958). According to Williams, there was no such thing as the masses, only ways of seeing people as masses, and the same thought can be applied to the 'culture of the masses'.

Most of the empirical research carried out according to the terms of mass culture debate (e.g. Wilensky's, 1964, attempt to relate cultural taste in media use to occupational background) offers little help to the present-day student of media performance (but see Neuman, 1982). Little progress was made in objectively identifying variations in cultural 'quality' of media content. Conventional, hierarchical and class-related (and thus self-fulfilling) standards were generally applied. Wilensky's attempt at definition indicates the limits reached within this tradition:

> 'High culture' will refer to two characteristics of the product: (i) it is created by, or under the supervision of a cultural elite operating within some aesthetic, literary or scientific tradition . . . (ii) critical standards independent of the consumer of the product are systematically applied to it . . . 'Mass culture' will refer to cultural products manufactured solely for the mass market. Associated characteristics, not intrinsic to the definition are *standardization* of product and *mass behavior* in use. (Wilensky, 1964: 176)

Bourdieu (1986) has demonstrated the systematic connection between socioeconomic class position and cultural preferences, if evidence were needed. The connection established implies that cultural taste is primarily the manifestation of values learnt and transmitted by way of the class system. If nothing else, this is a warning that any discriminating criteria we apply to actual cultural artefacts and performances may do no more than embody and express the dominant values of a class society. Cultural choice behaviour is also predominantly a reflection of the differential possession of 'cultural capital', as distributed through the education and occupational system and thus a reflection of class position (Bourdieu, 1986). Alternatively, media cultural choice may simply be an artefact of a particular media distribution system and of habitual audience behaviour patterns (Barwise and Ehrenberg, 1988).

There is no escaping facts of this kind, which are bound to cast doubt on any attempt to make an objective assessment of the 'artistic cultural' quality of what the media offer. In class societies, 'high marks' are more likely to be given to what conforms to conventional middle-class standards of quality: usually to artists and works which are established in the traditional or academic canon of national and international classics and to genres and forms in which these classics have appeared – opera, ballet, symphonies, plays, novels, etc. Correspondingly, lower cultural 'marks' will go to whatever appears on channels with a mass or working-class following and to what appeals to the many, the less educated or sometimes just the young (like many forms of popular music). Many conventional criteria of assessment have a built-in bias which associates 'high' quality with minority (elite) appeal and low quality with wide popularity, sometimes with potential justification, but not usually sufficient for reliable assessment to be possible.

Ways around the impasse

There are, nevertheless, other ways of distinguishing between media products according to cultural quality. It is particularly important to be able to discriminate among content which does not have an established place in the traditional hierarchy of culture. Increasingly, the mass media (especially television) are an original source, or a principal channel, of new or old arts and have to be evaluated in their own terms, according to new criteria. It is also important to find ways of recognizing which is original and new in substance and in forms of expression (both types of media and genres), without being limited by ideas of quality which are legitimated by the dominant art institutions and by the 'academy'. Thirdly, we should be more aware of social qualities (e.g. pro-social and empathic) and of their opposite – meanness, denigration, social ignorance and insensitivity in fiction especially.

There is a clear need to apply multiple and overlapping (often inconsistent) criteria of quality. Aside from conformity to conventional notions of established culture, we can consider quality in terms of: innovation and originality; intrinsic moral or political values, both in content and in respect of the communicative relationship between author/performer and receiver; expressions of folk traditions. The last mentioned often have virtues of distinctive form and local provenance, simplicity and integrity, vital participation in performance. Even correlates of market success – thus popularity itself – should not be ruled out as indicators of quality.

There follow suggestions of dimensions and indicators which might be applied to media content, with some (though very variable) expectations of reliable results. While the possibilities are described as if for use in indexing the cultural quality of media supply and for comparisons across channels or over time, the same approach could serve to assess actual and potential audience demand or patterns of actual 'consumption' (thus indexing the cultural 'taste' of sectors of the public). This is emphatically not a coherent framework for a programme of quality assessment, but rather a 'shopping list' of possibilities from which a motivated selection would have to be made.

Dimensions and indicators of cultural quality

Space for 'high' culture

• The allocation of time/space to the artistic forms and genres conventionally associated with traditional culture: ballet, opera, tragic drama,
   symphony concerts, recitals, etc. These may also include serializations of
   past literary classics or historical dramatizations.
• Incidence of actual works recognizably belonging to the canon of
   established art and culture.
• Incidence of content *about* established art and culture in the form of
   publicity, reviews, commentary, instruction, etc.
• Value patterns in other content (e.g. fiction or news) relating to traditional

art and culture. Methods of value analysis in texts have now been developed to allow almost any chosen value (ideal quality or preferred form of conduct or goal) to be identified and quantified (see Holsti, 1969; Cheesebro, 1982). The 'cultural indicators' tradition of enquiry (Signorielli and Morgan, 1990) can also offer a methodological base for assessing the incidence and weight, in media content, of particular values about art and culture.

The standard of originality

Direct or indirect indicators of originality include the following:

- Novelty in the sense of first-time showing/appearance. The content of television channels can, for instance, be scored according to the number of starts of new series or one-off productions in any of the relevant genres (especially drama, film, music). In fact, the *cahiers des charges* of some French television channels have specific requirements for the amount of new programming, along these lines.
- Controversiality and unconventionality. Content which does not fit conventional form and genre categories of the traditional arts or of popular culture is, by one definition, original and can be identified in this way. Associated qualities of content which may be attributed on the basis of content analysis or audience reaction (unusually low or divergent ratings; high rates of letter or telephone complaints) include: ambiguity; obscurity; disturbance; stridency; critical attitude to social convention or 'sacred cows'. Following this line of thought, satire, or even just humour, in various forms, is often thought to have cultural merit. Media professional judgement might be enlisted in applying this criterion.
- Minority appeal as such. The *fact* of minority appeal, as known after the event, is likely to be one consequence of originality (because this, in its turn, can imply unfamiliarity, unconventionality, an experimental character – the qualities just discussed). Minority appeal (low qualitative or quantitative rating) is equally (or more) likely to index: orientation to a small or exclusive group; artistic failure; popular rejection; failure of publicity; poor scheduling. On its own, it is an uncertain test of quality, but worth noting.

Criteria of social morality or political value

While the relevant qualities are bound to be varied and to require a motivated choice, several commonly invoked dimensions of cultural quality are as follows. They are based on diverse theoretical positions, but all share a notion of art and culture as having a serious purpose and potential for enlarging experience and a capacity to cope with real human experience. They can only provide a provisional orientation to devising tests of quality.

- Reality reference. Direct reference in theme or setting to the probable real-life circumstances of the audience or the society can be reckoned as a cultural virtue and is open to empirical indexation. The quality of realism or naturalism stands opposed to some features of mass culture which are often criticized, especially as fantasy, escapism, triviality, etc. Reality reference is often associated with seriousness of purpose, though it need not be so.

- Political or moral commitment. Content with a value-directed (from whatever point of view), didactic, socially critical or propagandist purpose can usually be recognized. Its cultural 'virtue' can obviously be open to question in any given case, but the general quality indicated sets it apart from mindless entertainment. Allocation to this category can be made according to stated intention or informed judgement (or formal content analysis methods, such as evaluative assertion analysis – van Cuilenburg et al., 1986).
- Purpose to communicate. A similar, but broader criterion recognizes all content which has a 'message' from an author, which seeks honestly to say something or express some genuine experience, emotion or point of view. This might be used as an approximate reverse test to identify mass-produced, routine, stereotyped, superficial, 'slick', commercial drama.
- Pro-social content. Recognition can be given to popular content, with entertainment values and no artistic pretensions, which tries (often as a subsidiary purpose) to increase social awareness, understanding and empathy or to reduce and counter negative and discriminatory stereotypes. There is no easy path to recognition.

Production values and professional quality

- Cost of production. In general, quality has to be paid for and the financial cost of production, even if its does not necessarily buy quality, can be used as an index of commitment to quality.
- Professional or technical excellence. A more direct assessment of production quality, separate from content, can be derived by reference to expert professional judgement (Blumler and Nossiter, 1991). Independent assessment may also be based on reviews in other media or gaining of prizes and awards (see Blumler et al., 1986).
- Degree of stardom. The relative fame of artists, directors, actors, performers, etc., in whatever kind of cultural content, while no guarantee of quality, is likely to be a correlate of commitment to quality and achieved success.

Folk art and crafts

For reasons noted briefly above, a separate category of cultural performance should be reserved to recognize content which does not belong to conventionally established 'high art' genres or to commercial popular culture, but does have a folk character (whether modern or traditional). The most likely candidate categories will be in performance of music, dance and song, but may also include folk-tales and some historical works. In non-Western cultures, the category is likely to be much broader and larger, including film and drama.

Commercial criteria of success

Although there is often thought to be a fundamental conflict between cultural values and commercialism (as many of the criteria suggested illustrate), there is a case for taking account of success in the market. Great popularity, fame and frequent repetition and reference in media texts, place some media products above the normal run and may given them ultimately a form of classic or cult status which is evidence of quality beyond what can be manipulated by publicity or artificial promotion. Objective indexation is readily achieved, by reference to best-seller lists, charts, ratings, box-office returns, opinion polls, etc. Measures of success can also take account of survival value over time and the cumulative success of some classics (Dickens, Verdi, etc.).

These various indicators of 'artistic-cultural' performance are obviously not all equally appropriate to all purposes, nor can they all be given the same weight (some are mutually quite inconsistent). Nevertheless, it is evident that there are quite a few possibilities for cultural assessment of a range of different content forms and media types.

Multiple paths to assessment

These suggestions are not exhaustive. They generally call for rather detailed specification of content attributes, and thus much work. Of course, they can be followed on a selective, sample basis. They leave open at least two other possibilities of assessing the general cultural quality of complete media services (see, e.g., Blumler et al., 1986; Ishikawa and Muramatsu, 1991). In particular, the question of *diversity* of overall offer can be investigated, in a number of different ways, using a small number of the indicators described. There are also a number of possibilities of basing ratings of 'intrinsic' quality on the assessments of audiences, since it has been demonstrated that audience assessments of *quality* are made independently of ratings of popularity (Leggatt, 1991). In other words, people can distinguish between what they recognize as intrinsically 'good' and what they personally like more of more of the time (what provides immediate satisfaction). This opens up many possibilities.

22
CULTURAL IDENTITY AND AUTONOMY: WHOSE MEDIA CULTURE?

Political tests of media cultural performance

The preceding discussion has been based on the assumption that there are some standards of cultural quality, according to which media performance can be rated. If this assumption is not accepted (all 'culture' being assumed to be equal, or no discrimination feasible), or if it is held that subjective judgements of quality cannot be empirically used, then little can be done to assess artistic/aesthetic performance, according to the terms of this project. However, when we turn to the notion of media culture as an attribute, expression or reflection of the culture of a set of *people*, we appear to be on surer empirical ground. Culture, or its symbols and artefacts, can then be considered, in effect, as a form of *property*. The issue then becomes *whose* culture (not *what quality* of culture) is being offered (or received).

Uncertainty about identity

According to at least one critical and eloquent voice, the sure ground is indeed more apparent than real, because of conceptual weakness, inconsistency and vagueness in almost all of the key terms which figure in the discussion, especially those which refer to 'social identity' and its relation with communication (see Schlesinger, 1987). Moreover, just as in the discussion of social control, the basis in evidence (and even theory) about any *effect* from mass media on cultural identity (or any cultural effects) is very weak or contestable.

Nevertheless, in the relevant communication research and policy literature, problems concerning cultural identity have been posed and often answered with little hesitation, largely because they are guided by political rather than intellectual concerns. This applies, for instance, to the wish to protect and foster the supposedly shared cultural heritage and identity of Europe. It is also true of the efforts made, in and around UNESCO, to defend the cultural interests of the Third World from international cultural 'invasion' or worse. At another level, there are efforts made on behalf of language-based cultures, for instance to protect a francophone or latin cultural 'space' (Mattelart, 1984). Many national polities seek to protect and defend their own national culture in the communication sphere and, within states, political forces make a plea for communication policies which respect and advance regional and local integration and identity.

Claims made on the media

A very similar policy line is pursued at each level of social organization (from global to local), making assumptions about the nature and significance of the link between mass communication and the culture of people or place. It may not matter too much for performance assessment that concepts are unclear or assumptions made without evidence, as long as the demands in relation to media are loud and unambiguous enough.

In any case, there does seem to be a certain degree of pragmatic coherence about the *basis* for the claims as well as about the content of the claims (essentially asking for more local content). One of the key normative terms is that of the 'right to communicate' (Fisher, 1982) and another is that of 'cultural autonomy'. In its broadest meaning, the second term implies the right of people (whether collectively defined in social or spatial terms) to the means to express and enjoy their 'own culture', in the sense of a 'symbolic' or communication environment which they can recognize as their own, which serves their self-determined needs, or which they have produced for themselves. A long tradition of sociological theory has underpinned the value of having a consciousness of identity and belonging to a shared community of place (Nisbet, 1967; Meyrowitz, 1985). Loss of cultural distinctiveness is thought to contribute to a weakened sense of personal identity and increased *anomie* and rootlessness (thus reduced social integration).

The long age of nationalism (Anderson, 1983) is not yet over and may even be acquiring a new impetus as East Europe and the Soviet Union take up where they left off in mid-century or earlier. Whatever the real or perceived bases for having a sense of cultural distinctiveness, the strong claim to cultural autonomy by people or groups is often a compelling 'social fact'. It is not equally compelling in every case and perhaps the supposed 'European' identity is one rather weak example (see Schlesinger, 1987), given the uncertain self-recognition by Europeans of the European label and the other cultures to which most 'Europeans' already belong (i.e. the identity of nation and region).

The success of claims to cultural autonomy usually depends on having good potential access to media channels and content which in some way correspond with the values, experience and outlook of receivers. In effect, this is the same as a claim to a particular kind of reflective media diversity. The obverse is the claim to protection from an oversupply (however defined) of content which originates outside the boundaries of the culture and society of the receiver. It is clear that such claims rest on the assumption that relevant groups of 'receivers' do have distinctive sets of values and also have a pre-existing sense of cultural identity. In the normative discussions at the several different levels mentioned, three main kinds of issue have been discussed with reference to mass media: that of international flow of media and its effect; the survival or not of sub-national identities at regional or local level; and the question of the potential for communicative autonomy for sub-cultural groups based on criteria other than place.

Transnationalization of media

The working out of the issue of nationalism in relation to modern mass communication has taken a number of forms. Transnationalization was slow to be defined as a cultural problem because mass media were, from the start, organized on a national basis: media served their own (national) society first and usually reinforced the idea and reality of nationalism. Before the Second World War, it was also regarded as normal that great powers should try to disseminate their culture and religion in the wake of armies and trade. International flow of media content was, until mid-century, generally only seen as problematic in the context of competing ideologies and nation states – a matter of international politics rather than culture.

This limited definition of the problem was altered after the Second World War by several circumstances: the much increased international flow of media content; the even more dominant position of the United States in this flow (Tunstall, 1977a); the independence and nationalist movements of former colonies; and the global competition between the ideologies of communism and capitalism fought out in debates about international communication flow in UNESCO and other forums (McPhail, 1981).

Cultural imbalance and invasion

The case of First and Third World imbalance in communication flow has been extensively debated since the mid-1970s, often with reference to the concepts of 'cultural imperialism' or 'cultural dependency' (Dorfman and Mattelart, 1975; Boyd-Barrett, 1977; Mattelart, 1984; Varis, 1984; Kivikuru and Varis, 1985; Mowlana, 1985; Tomlinson, 1991). The essential point has been to apply the standard of autonomy or dependency to the predominant flows of media content of all kinds (news, film and TV programmes) from the developing world into the nascent media systems of developing countries, with potentially damaging impact on their autonomous cultural and political development. During this same period, a seminal study by Tunstall (1977a) under the title *The Media are American* claimed that most of the modern mass media (especially film, press and television) were essentially inter-national in form and format, if not in actual product.

More recently, as noted, another expression of the same issue has arisen in the context of the expansion of European television systems and increased cross-frontier broadcasting (e.g. Thomsen, 1989). These develop-ments have been regarded as posing a cultural problem on three main counts (e.g. Pragnell, 1985): the inhibition of home-based audiovisual cultural industries of European countries (especially *vis-à-vis* America); the potential undermining of the capacity of smaller countries to maintain their own cultural and language autonomy; the possible dilution and homogenization of media culture in Europe, especially through a process of 'Americanization'. In response to this perceived problem, the European Television Directive (see Chapter 5) has recommended, for instance, that a majority of programming should consist of European production.

The key question for performance assessment in respect of culture has often been the degree to which media systems serving specific national cultures have become 'internationalized', penetrated by cultural products of 'foreign' origin, or external to the national culture. Attempts to answer this question either for the Third World or for Europe (Varis, 1984; Pragnell, 1985; Sepstrup, 1989; De Bens et al., 1992) have usually made a distinction between an imported media product, thus a product first made in and for another national society, and a domestic (and supposedly more 'authentic') one. The balance between the two has been taken as the main measure of 'transnationalization'.

Television has been the most common focus of attention (but also the cinema) because of the widespread economic dependence of many television systems on imported programming or formats. The first results of the enquiries mentioned have demonstrated the high degree to which poorer or smaller countries are, indeed, reliant on foreign content to operate their media, their television diet being correspondingly 'poorer', according to the criterion of 'cultural autonomy'. Concern has been accentuated by the increasing tendency for media products to become significant economic as well as cultural goods. Arguments about 'protection' of home cultural producers and 'quotas' of imports have to rely on the crude distinctions of product origin which have been mentioned.

Varieties of transnationalization

The facts of 'cultural dependency' and the reasons for this condition have by now been quite well established (e.g. Mowlana, 1985), although theory and methods of research have been queried. Apart from some real technical problems in reliably establishing the categories of imported and exported television content (e.g. Schlesinger, 1986), there is the problem of dealing with transnational *formats* (as distinct from actual products). Much television and other media content has been effectively *internationalized* in terms of genre or format, even when it is locally produced. Typical of such 'international formats' are quizzes, game shows, many soap operas, telenovellas, and other dramatic fiction genres, the news itself, sporting events, chat shows, etc. Many 'home-produced' programmes may use international settings or stars or be explicitly made as 'home' versions of 'foreign' shows. The implication is that home-produced culture is not necessarily more culturally 'autonomous' than the imported product. Aside from this, several of the larger European countries routinely dub foreign (mainly American) films and series into the home language, creating another intermediate category of symbolic culture. This particular problem has been accentuated by the trend toward transnational co-productions, especially of dramatic fiction serials.

In addition, the real cultural *impact* of imports has never been investigated, only assumed and little account is taken in the export–import studies of actual and relative audience reception. Sepstrup (1989a, b) has helped to clarify the broader conceptual and empirical questions by distinguishing different kinds of transnational flow and three levels of impact of cultural imports from beyond one's own frontiers. The main kinds of flow are:

- *national*: what is offered within a national system by way of the domestic media channels and the share of imports offered;
- *bilateral*: what is offered in one system and received across the frontier directly (e.g. from USA by Canada, from Britain by Ireland, from Germany by Holland);
- *multilateral*: what is offered internationally for reception in many countries; for instance, much of what is offered by pan-European satellite and cable systems in Europe, or by the international distribution of US films or popular music.

As to levels of cultural impact, Sepstrup invites us to consider separately research evidence concerning: what is *supplied*; what is actually *received* by audiences; what cultural *effects* are produced.

Cultural profit and loss

These ideas provide us with some essential tools for evaluating the performance of media systems in terms of cultural autonomy, leaving us free to decide for ourselves whether cultural imports are necessarily as bad as they are painted in the political discussions. It cannot be assumed that all transnationalization is bad (certainly not equally for everyone), nor without cultural compensations (quite apart from great uncertainties about actual impact). A trans-border flow of symbolic culture (meanings and values) has been an essential ingredient of human progress, according to most histories of human kind.

Often the political definition of cultural problems involves the assumption that imported culture is either intrinsically less good (often for the kind of reasons discussed above in relation to mass culture and aesthetic quality) or is less good because it is second best, the result of forced choices imposed on poorer importers of 'second-hand' media products. The proposition of inferiority of imports can be tested according to two different principles: one that of *quality*; the other that of *diversity* or (system) *openness*. On the matter of artistic quality, we can refer to the alternative quality criteria already discussed.

There is no general reason why imported television content has to be culturally inferior, according to several of the quality standards introduced in Chapter 21. It is clear, for instance, that some small, but relatively wealthy European national television systems (e.g. those of Sweden or Holland) use their resources to buy from their European neighbours expensively produced and/or culturally 'high-quality' programmes, which they cannot make for themselves. The import costs of much content of this kind is not prohibitive, especially compared to the prices asked for content likely to attract high audiences, such as coverage of major sporting events. Obviously, the rating of resulting system 'performance' will depend on whose views are asked: the sport and entertainment-loving public or cultural and political elites.

Autonomy versus diversity

For the same reasons, the relatively few imports that make their way into United States network television are more likely than not to raise the cultural level of national supply (and increase its diversity), according to some of the educational and aesthetic quality criteria discussed above (even if the upgrading is not popularly appreciated). In any case, it is doubtful if the evident 'cultural autonomy' of American television, in itself, contributes a great deal to the quality of the system, however defined. Aside from the particular criteria of quality applied, such a degree of autonomy entails limited competition and limited programme diversity.

Following this line of thinking, transnationalization can be thought of as leading to more cultural diversity, the more it leads to wider spread in the sources from which programmes are derived. This diversity can be viewed in a positive light, although, in some cases, it would have to be weighed against the view that low-cost, poorer or Third World systems are disadvantaged culturally by a dependence on American or Western supplies of television content.

The growing phenomenon of programming which is deliberately multi-national or international in format or appeal – games, contests, news programmes, exchanges of reporting, etc. – suggests that cultural diversity as a result of diversity of origin may decline as the 'product' is homogenized to maximize wider market appeal and to minimize cultural difference and distance. Nevertheless, it is clear that, especially under conditions of balanced economic relationships between nations, internationalization can have a 'virtuous' side and 'cultural autonomy' a negative aspect (where it implies cultural isolation).

The message as effect?

The negative *effects* of limited cultural autonomy (actual impact on cultures) remain unproven and largely untested (and are likely to remain so). It is, however, worth entertaining the possibility that, to paraphrase McLuhan, the 'media may be the message'. The very arrival and diffusion of a medium like television, with all its technological and cultural baggage, irrespective of precise content, is already a major effect in itself. It is plausible to suppose that, at the very least, it carries powerful messages of modernization and secularization and reduces the chances of any receiving culture following its own traditional or self-chosen cultural path into the future. The more one inclines to this view, the less it matters that particular content effects can scarcely ever be measured.

Research and its outcomes

The methods for enquiry into television provision, along the lines indicated by Sepstrup (1989b), appear to be relatively straightforward, although he warns against pitfalls and points to many anomalies in the research that has been done. The essential requirement is to be able to identify the country of origin of content and to have reasonable audience data. Neither are without problems. The 'origin' of content, for instance, can be variously defined according to source of finance, authorship, nationality of performers and location of action. There can often be complex co-production arrangements which defy simple classification. The adoption in 'home production' of borrowed and adapted programme formats is probably impossible to deal with satisfactorily, except by way of rather crude (or refined but subjective) categories which identify 'universal' formats.

The main findings of research concerning the early period of transnationalization of European television, which are reviewed by Sepstrup (1989a, b), tell us quite a lot about what has been happening during the 1980s. In brief, a rather stable 75 per cent or so of television output in Western Europe has been home-produced (with much inter-country and inter-channel variation). A little more than half the imports have been from the USA, largely concentrated in drama and series, thus not an overwhelming degree of 'Americanization' of supply. The first indications derived from relating supply to consumption suggest that the European viewer's average diet of television tends to over-represent imports, largely because the imported categories are popular ones (see also De Bens et al., 1992). The pattern is likely to change, as commercial channels proliferate and gain audience share. Most of all, we need to keep in mind Sepstrup's warning that a European *average* does not mean a great deal and that each national (and cultural) situation needs to be assessed separately.

Global images

Much attention has been paid to the negative consequences, for the Third World countries, of their portrayal as unstable and disaster stricken (Galtung and Ruge, 1965; Sreberny-Mohammadi, 1984; Stevenson and Shaw, 1984; Kivikuru and Varis, 1985) or simply as invisible and insignificant (Said, 1981; Riffe and Shaw, 1982; Wilhoit and Weaver, 1983; Belkaoui, 1987). In general, the standard methods of content analysis can produce basic findings on apparent images of foreign countries in news and other media content.

A most elaborate scheme for analysing the structure and global flow of television was developed and applied by geographers in the Cambridge

International Flows Project (Gould et al., 1984). Their method was to code the national television output (or a sample thereof) of certain countries according to a complex multiple coding frame which involved assessing content in detail according to programme types (in 44 categories), themes, settings, topics and values, as well as according to country of origin. This allowed them to present not only a profile of national origin of all output and types of output, but also to characterize and compare the imports from particular (other country) sources in terms of all other variables. The researchers had a particular concern with the representation of other countries and cultures in what is offered by way of television. For purposes of cultural exchange analysis, the authors developed a set of 32 sub-categories of world culture types (e.g. East European, Saharan, North American, Japanese culture) and eight main types.

Of special relevance here is their way of assessing the extent to which other cultures (especially small and weak ones) can 'speak for themselves' in what is transmitted elsewhere (Gould et al., 1984: T108). They look in detail at such matters under the heading 'cultural exchange' and distinguish programme content according to whether: it is made 'at home' and about the native culture for consumption at home; or made at home about another culture for home consumption; or made by and about a particular culture but seen abroad (e.g. an American documentary about an American issue shown in Sweden); or made by one country about a second country for showing in a third country (e.g. a British documentary about Africa shown in Sweden). The potential complexity of cultural experience from television as well of the degrees of cultural 'autonomy' or integrity which may be involved is evident from these examples. Although the task of measurement can be handled by way of such categories, the interpretation of cultural implications is likely to be speculative.

Cultural identity in media content

The question of cultural identity does not have to be examined only in negative or *deficit* terms. Within the body of what is self-produced or shown 'at home', there are likely to be relevant variations according to the principle of representing the national culture or offering opportunities for recognition and identification to individual viewers. We can look for clear and positive representations of the 'authentic' culture of people or place.

National identity

For example, certain kinds of media content can be thought of as rather formally expressing national identity: by way of attention to significant ceremonials and events – royal, parliamentary or state occasions, ceremonies which express national identity and values, remembrance of war dead, national heroes, holidays and religious festivals, centenaries and so forth. Preferential access for such matters (including national participation in international sporting events), especially by way of special television coverage may, other things being equal, be taken as a sign of active engagement by the media with the national culture.

More informally, media coverage can also be beneficially 'cultural' in the sense under discussion, by paying attention to culturally unique or characteristic sports, pastimes and activities (e.g. cricket in England; ice-skating in Holland; carnival in Belgium; beer festivals in Germany and so on). A further indicator of positive cultural identification in content is the use of familiar national historic locations and symbolic places for programming. Certain traditional themes, stories, genres and myths may also be indicators of cultural specificity (American westerns, Soviet revolutionary themes, Japanese samurai drama, British war films, Chinese kung-fu movies, etc.), even if many have become international property.

Locality and identification

There are many ways in which national symbols can be displayed and the symbolic identity of the culture potentially reinforced. The same methods and strategy can also be adapted for analysing the cultural composition of media provision, in terms of *regional* or other relevant sub-cultural identifications (Hagerstrand, 1986). Aside from the question of identification with the region as such, we can suppose that the more that distinctive local places and their ways of life are represented within national output, the more potential also for media to contribute to cultural identity. Imported content, even when (or precisely because) it is internationalized is usually distinguished by lack of real local colour.

The basic question for local identity is much the same as that raised above in respect of representation of the country's own national culture (and similar to the general matter of diversity): do media provide content which reflects or expresses the cultural environment of component minorities and social categories? The categories chosen as relevant can be regionally or sub-nationally defined, sometimes in terms of language, custom, religion, etc. Or they may be defined in terms of social class, speech (accent), life-style (a particular milieu, for instance), demographic category (age group, gender), or location (attention to city or region within a country). In practice such questions are complicated by the reality of different levels of media provision. We *can* ask such questions about the content of national media, but overall assessment depends on the extent to which national provision is complemented by an adequate and diverse local media provision (which has been discussed earlier, Chapter 13).

Minority identity

The question of how far media systems offer special (and adequate) provision for minorities and sub-cultures has also been addressed under the heading of 'solidarity' and little more need be said. At issue in the present context is the specificity of what the media offer, in terms of the visibility of many sub-cultures or distinctive minorities. Much of the available evidence suggests that many sub-groups are relatively invisible in the normal run of media content and they do not have their own kinds of access. Sometimes this reflects marginal or low status in society, sometimes aspects of the 'media culture' and organization, which lead to relative neglect.

An example of the latter is the under-representation of the old, especially on television, but probably in other media. Gunter and Wober (1988) report some findings concerning US television which showed a 2 per cent representation of over 65s in television shows, compared to a 10 per cent share of the American population. Probably many social or cultural minority categories (the poor, unemployed, migrant workers, sick, etc.) would also be under-represented and for similar reasons – lack of interest to advertisers, lack of any intrinsic glamour or audience appeal. The limits of what can reasonably or realistically be expected from media are soon reached.

Measurement possibilities

The discussion in this chapter and Chapter 21 has been wide ranging, but it can be summarized in terms of a few possible strategies for research. In general, these involve first defining a universe of cultural provision (or cultural reception) and, secondly, applying a set of criteria, chosen from amongst those which have been described. In practice, television has received most attention, being the most culturally relevant and dominant mass medium and the one most subject to normative surveillance. However, the same logic can be applied to the cinema, or popular fiction, or comic books for children, for example.

The assessment process requires a value choice and an assumption (from a given performance perspective) that some things are better than others: home-made better than foreign; established classics of literature better than ephemeral popular favourites; good taste better than bad taste; education better than entertainment; reality better than fantasy; heterogeneity better than homogeneity; live shows better than recorded; original programmes better than re-runs; 'deep' content better than superficial; suitable for children better than unsuitable; non-commercial better than commercial; local and regional better than national and international; provision for specific minorities better than something designed for everyone, etc. This leads to two main kinds of research procedure.

One approach calls for the identification of a set of categories, based on such values, of *subject* matter or content which are then applied to units of content (programmes, films, time of output, print volume, etc.). The relative incidence of the different kinds of content leads to an assessment (for instance, a large proportion of 'high culture' formats or of 'own production' leads to a more favourable cultural rating). The second approach requires value preferences to be converted into qualitative dimensions or variables which can be applied to any body of content or form of presentation (for instance, degree of 'localness' of plot or setting, occupational or gender roles portrayed, ethnic composition of characters). Content is then assessed in multiple ways, cutting across the separate component items or media services.

The alternative approaches have different uses and advantages. The first is obviously simpler, and suitable for the approximate ranking of different channels and services according to a few basic criteria of cultural performance in any of the three main areas indicated – that of education; artistic/cultural quality; identity content. Most kinds of media content can be characterized as 'positive', 'negative' or 'neutral', on chosen dimensions, by such means. The more detailed approach by multiple qualitative assessment of items of content is inevitably more labour-intensive and more likely to be ambiguous in outcome. But it is also potentially more discriminating and more sensitive to nuances of cultural judgement.

There are other ways of doing such work, since the range of methods of qualitative analysis is continually widening and becoming more sophisticated. Complex structuralist and semiological approaches can potentially offer subtle (but often more subjective) readings of media texts, according to any conceivable dimension of evaluation. Methods for the ethnographic study of audiences and of reception processes add to the potential capacity for research (Ang, 1990; Jensen, 1991). In general, these approaches require a very close focus on single problems of representation and on particular genres, or even single case studies of a media text. However, they are likely to take us beyond the scope of this project and beyond the reach of what systematic social science methods can achieve.

PART IX
IN CONCLUSION

23
CHANGING MEDIA, CHANGING MORES: IMPLICATIONS FOR ASSESSMENT

Striking a balance

This account of media performance issues and assessment has looked back over several decades and is witness, at the very least, to a steady increase in the amount and competence of research and in the range of matters which have been addressed. Even so, the growth and diversification of the mass media has far outstripped the capacity of research to cope with potential demand. There are many blank spaces on the 'map' of media performance issues and the agenda grows longer rather than shorter, as the importance of mass media for many social and political processes increases.

Most research has been fuelled by sporadic public inquiries, by minority vocal criticism on particular issues or by the parallel growth of 'communication science' and 'media studies' into whose terrain issues of performance have come to fall. A reader of this book may be struck by the fact that the normative approaches followed by 'society', by media critics or by researchers are very selective and largely ignore much of what the mass media are actually doing most of the time, which is to entertain, divert and catch the eye for no particularly noble purpose or even for no purpose at all. The media, it is said, are 'not just any other business', but the business they are in is more likely to be 'show business' than serving the general welfare in any other way.

The bias of the book cannot now be denied or undone. It reflects a large and probably unbridgeable gap between the norms and expectations concerning public benefit from the media, on the one hand, and the realities on the other. If one accepts these in-built limitations, it might seem that the media do not emerge too badly from the assessment process. This would mean accepting great variability of quality, persistent and systematic biases of omission and commission, pervasive ethnocentricity, stereotyping and submission to the constraints of routine and organization. Even so, the media probably turn out, from this review of research, as more fair and informative and less mean-spirited and socially insensitive than their more severe critics have alleged. Nor should this verdict be altogether surprising, given the degree of professional commitment to quality which exists in the media and the external pressures and sound commercial reasons which often promote or reward 'good' performance.

It is doubtful if a verdict of this kind will satisfy critics of the media institution or restore confidence in it as a bastion of independence and enlightenment. In practice, this means that no balance of evaluation can ever be struck and assessment has to be a continuing process. It also implies a need to look again at the body of normative theory relating to media which provided the starting point for this enquiry. If many of its prescriptions are unrealizable or simply mythical, then it may well have to be regarded as more ideology than theory, as critics have already claimed. For the time being, it is not easy to displace. In any case, the interim assessment just offered has no great authority and certainly does not stand for all places and times. It makes sense, therefore, to conclude this book with an informed glance forwards at the emerging media conditions and their implications for performance. This calls for some account to be taken, as well, of changes taking place in society which affect the media and of public expectations concerning them.

Looking ahead to the information age

Despite the lack of precision concerning the broad concept of the much-heralded 'information society', the essence of the idea can be readily summarized. Melody (1990: 26–27) describes information societies as having become 'dependent upon complex electronic information and communication networks and which allocate a major portion of their resources to information and communication activities'. It is the centrality of, and dependence upon, communication and information which matter. Opinion seems more or less equally divided on the net benefits or costs of the 'informalization' of society, but few doubt its inevitability. Although the mass media are only a small part of the whole information complex, they are deeply implicated with this key feature of social change.

It is now equally a commonplace to point to the 'globalization' of almost all aspects of human activity, but it seems to apply especially to the transmission of information and of culture across formerly closed or restricted national frontiers. Time and distance are no longer the critical limiting factors on communication (Ferguson, 1990). The effects of globalization on the mass media are all-pervasive: in the contents of news, the forms and genres of media fiction entertainment, the definitions of markets and audiences, the structures of ownership and the contours of pressures on the media.

A feature of the times which may be less fundamental and enduring, but no less immediately relevant to the media is a renewed belief in the merits of the free market as a principle for governing social arrangements. It has received an additional impetus from the decline and fall of communism in Europe. The spirit of the times is no longer favourable to large public monopolies of the kind which have dominated telecommunications and broadcasting. The fashionable rhetoric invokes the principles of consumer choice and entrepreneurial freedom in the interests of diversity, innovation and greater liberty (Fowler and Brenner, 1983; Veljanovski, 1989).

Privatization of economic activity has been matched, according to some sociologists, by privatization of social life (and for a good deal longer). Former collectivist and communal social forms are said to have given way to individualist, consumerist and privatized ways of living. These changes have been in about equal degree hailed as liberating or bemoaned as alienating and isolating (the 'lonely crowd' syndrome). Associated with social privatization there is a seeming weakening of the hold of older structures of political and social control and participation (political parties, churches, family) which provided 'cement' for society and guidance for individuals.

In sociocultural matters we are told of the rise of what has been called a 'post-modern' society and culture (Harvey, 1989). The new theory seems to be appropriate to a privatized 'information society' which is driven by consumerist market forces. The concept of post-modernity is complex and also obscure, but it has a relevance for the present theme. Its political implication is that the 'Enlightenment project' of continuous and rational social progress has drawn to an end, especially in respect of applying legal-bureaucratic means to achieve socially planned, collective ends.

As a sociocultural philosophy, post-modernism stands opposed to the traditional notion of fixed and hierarchical cultural values and beliefs. It is favourable to forms of culture which are transient, superficial, appealing to sense rather than reason. Post-modern culture is volatile, illogical, kaleidoscopic, inventive, hedonistic. It has certainly more affinity with the newer, audiovisual media than with print media. While post-modernism may be little more than a fashionable version of liberal and secular thinking, without deep or coherent philosophical foundations, it does seem to express some significant features of current social consciousness and it finds a resonance in the popular mass media, especially television and music. Like the other changes mentioned, post-modernization has been greeted with ambivalence and a degree of scepticism.

Changes in the communications media

The key changes in the mass media are easier to identify. Most obvious is the sheer increase in volume of media output: more kinds of media; more channels; more words, pictures, images produced and distributed at an exponential rate (even if not proportionately more 'consumed'). A main cause of this growth lies in the efficiency of new distribution and production technologies which reduce costs and increase the attractiveness of communication services and media products. As far as the *mass* media are concerned, the most striking fact has been the rise of television to a pre-eminent position as a media institution of global significance, complementing the print media and radio but 'outranking' them by some criteria: certainly by measures of reach and popularity and possibly also in terms of public prestige and credibility.

Advances in cable and satellite technology have largely removed the technical scarcity caused by limited transmission range and wavelength interference. This has allowed more access to television and radio channels for suppliers of information and culture, as well as more apparent choice for receivers. While not yet accountable as 'mass media', the interactive electronic media, in various forms, have opened up a very large potential for quite different kinds of information provision and exchange, especially the possibilities for individual access to a very large amount and range of electronic media services. The changes have been summarized in terms of a shift from 'allocutory' media forms (centre–periphery mass dissemination media) to 'consultative' and 'interactive' types of communication relationship and information flow (Bordewijk and van Kaam, 1986; McQuail, 1986a).

The technical possibility (in some degree realized) of greater media 'abundance' has a good many implications for the traditional media institutions of the nation state. They are now less confined within national frontiers and less under the control of the national political system. Not only technical changes, but also international agreements (on standards, content regulations, rights to communicate, intellectual property and more) and transnational media business arrangements (multinational multimedia companies and vertical integrations of activities) make the media more and more international in character.

Coincident with the growth of international media industries, based on global corporate ownership, transnational markets and production arrangements, we see evidence of an international 'media culture', which can be recognized by way of similar professional standards worldwide, as well as in universal content forms, genres and the actual substance of communication. This is true not only of radio (especially music and news) and television, but also of newspapers, books and magazines, where stories, authors, marketing strategies, fashions and trends are no longer restricted by a particular language or national culture. Internationalization of culture has brought with it an inextricable and worldwide 'intertextuality' of the main mass media of books, newspapers, phonogram, film, television, radio, magazines. They overlap, reinforce and feed on each other in content and commercial as well as technical arrangements.

This very large terrain can be summed up in terms of a few main trends affecting the media, which help to specify the implications for public interest theory and future research, as follows: expansion; interactivity; globalization; commercialization. The essence of the first three terms has already been described and each of them is closely connected with the main social trends described earlier. The fourth media trend mentioned – commercialization – is a consequence both of expansion and of the deregulatory and privatizing trends already noted. It shows itself in greater reliance on advertising and sponsorship, declining public ownership and control of media, conglomeration, trends to populist, audience-maximizing strategies (see Murdock, 1990).

Such changes reflect more than just a changing fashion in economic and political thinking or the technical challenge to older forms of public regulation. More fundamentally, they derive from the steady growth in the economic and industrial significance of mass communication. This has led to an irreversible increase in the relative economic/industrial status of media industries and a correlative reduction in the power of national governments to regulate and control them. More 'commercialization', in the sense of any move away from public financing, planned development or subsidy and towards free market financing, in now inevitable in some form or another, although its consequences on content and culture remain uncertain and controversial. The relative decline in public service broadcasting in Europe is one of the most striking aspects of commercialization (Rowland and Tracey, 1990; Euromedia Research Group, 1992; Siune and Truetzschler, 1992). This 'commercializing' and deregulatory trend is not without its eloquent critics (Levin, 1986; Melody, 1990; Curran, 1991; Keane, 1991; Blumler, 1992), but its impact on the media is considerable.

There are related changes in media organizational structure. Two in particular have implications for the quality of media performance and, potentially, for the public interest: first, the now familiar *convergence* between different 'modes' of communication, which were once separated by differences of technology, of purpose and of regulatory regime; secondly, the *fragmentation* and functional disaggregation of different organizational activities: ownership, management, production, editorial, distribution, research. An obvious example is the trend for European television channels (especially those distributed by cable or satellite and under commercial management) to produce less of their own content. Organizational fragmentation may be accompanied by increasing vertical integration of *ownership* of different phases of production. It is also often associated with increasing *audience* fragmentation.

The separating out of organizational tasks which until now have usually been performed 'under one roof' by a single organization takes varied forms and has several causes, not least the process of commercialization itself. These structural trends are being reinforced by the development of multimedia companies whose business logic can indicate varied and ever-changing forms of management and organization. One result is that it is no longer so easy to identify a media *originator* (what used to be called the 'mass communicator') who has full responsibility for public performance or who might, in principle, be held accountable to 'society', according to public interest criteria.

The public interest in an information age

If these assessments of social and media change are correct, then they have implications for the demands which might be made on the media on behalf of society or by citizens in some collective capacity. If we wish to retain the notion of a 'public interest' as sketched at the outset, we need to adapt its expression to change media conditions. The consequences of the changes described are unclear and possibly inconsistent. There are some grounds for supposing there to be more, rather than less, need for control or supervision by society – a strengthening of the public interest concept. This, for instance, is Melody's (1990: 29) conclusion in respect of communications policy: 'In the information society, policy direction will become more important. Therefore it is essential that it be informed and that it encompass the broad public interest.' He adds, 'In the information society, access to information and communication would appear to be the most essentially public utility' (p. 31). In changing times, there may be more reason than ever to strengthen a potentially unifying social institution which seems to be flourishing – that of public communications in its varied forms. The need for mechanisms of countervailing power against private and vested interests is unlikely to have diminished as a result of any of the changes mentioned above.

On the other hand, a strong case has also been made for the view that public intervention in communication should be avoided or reduced for several reasons. Free markets and competition can stimulate innovation and development of new technology (not to mention the matter of 'consumer sovereignty'). The basis of legitimacy for earlier forms of control and regulation of communication has been undermined by technological changes and by internationalization. In a post-modern society, the required normative consensus may be too weak to sustain any consistent intervention. What counts as being 'in the public interest' is less self-evident than it used to be and there is less agreement on what counts as the 'good of society', or even on what arrangements will best secure the 'basic communication values' sketched in Chapter 6.

While this fundamental difference of view cannot be resolved in any objective way, it is clear that there has been, *de facto*, a general shift in the balance of normative approaches to mass media. Certain concerns are *less salient* in public debate about the media, while others seem to have endured, with some new issues merging. The greater 'media abundance' has diminished concern at the possible shortage of diverse information adequate for modern democracies. Public guarantees of universal provision of service, of the kind which justified early broadcasting and telecommunication monopolies, seem less necessary even if one accepts that abundance does not necessarily lead to more freedom, access or real choice. In the cultural sphere, similar conclusions have been drawn. The expansion of media industries of all kinds and the rise in consumer prosperity has reduced the pressure to subsidize (socially valued) cultural production and consumption on 'public interest' grounds. This applies especially when we can no longer state clear and widely agreed standards of cultural quality. Although there is still life in the demands that media avoid harm to the young and vulnerable, especially through violence and pornography, the claim of a direct, causal connection between media and behaviour has lost credibility. The evidence has not sustained the main charge, although social pressures have done much to ensure a degree of media restraint.

A revised agenda of public interest concerns

Despite these comments, there has, if anything, been an increase in the variety of means for implementing policy about a widening range of issues. These issues include: the public responsibilities of telecommunication providers; the choice and implementation of technical standards; copyright; advertising standards; rights of reply; international obligations; party political interests; cultural content; monopoly and cross-ownership; journalistic standards; privacy; pornography and many other matters. The very forces of growth and internationalization have generated much new normative thinking and many new forms of regulation.

There has been a shift of focus from predominantly *negative* concerns about mass media to the many potential benefits of the communication 'revolution'. The new worry is that these will be wasted or unfairly distributed as a result of lack of reduced public control or because of the free play of global market forces. Logically, in an 'information society', the 'public interest', however defined, is more likely to lie in securing the *benefits* of information and communication than in preventing *harm* from communication.

In the light of these remarks, it is possible to redraw the map of relevant issues for normative media theory, without having to stray very far from the core values which guided earlier mass communication research. Often it is a matter of reformulating 'old' issues in the light of changed circumstances and of setting different priorities. The new 'agenda' can be described under three main headings: one relating to freedom and democracy, a second to social equality in the information age and a third to questions of social order and culture.

Issues of freedom and democracy Two issues may now require special attention: one concerning the communication conditions for healthy democratic politics; another the possibilities for the independence and creativity of those who work in media production. In this content, 'healthy' democratic politics needs no new definition, since it continues to refer to active and *informed* debate on current issues of significance, in which a *diversity* of viewpoints is expressed and taken note of, and in which a majority of citizens is involved, be it only as spectators or listeners. From this point of view, public communication is held to address its audience in the role of citizen rather than consumer; the second cannot be substituted for the first. This topic goes far beyond the scope of the present discussion, but the (old) mass media have been linked with a potential 'decline of democracy', as just defined (Picard, 1985b; Neuman, 1986; Entman, 1989; Kellner, 1990; Curran, 1991; Keane, 1991), and especially with reduced participation and relatively low levels of popular knowledge and understanding. The complexity of the world increases and the demands on popular understanding continually increase, while more and more diversion and entertainment clogs channels of public communication.

The conditions for an informed democracy still depend to a large extent on mass media, at a time when increased competition makes it harder for them to give privileged attention to world affairs or to the routine details of domestic politics, let alone to the interests and views of powerless minorities. The typical logic of competitive mass media is to offer selective, often 'sensationalized', and very summary, news and opinions (the US phenomenon of 'tabloid TV' is symptomatic). It is not the 'fault' of the media that politics and world affairs are not the most attractive consumer commodities on the media market. Nevertheless, the chances of the mass media contributing to informed debate and citizen involvement seem to diminish rather than to grow and the 'new media' are not yet sufficiently developed to make up the deficiency.

The issue of editorial independence and producer creativity is not new, but it too has been highlighted by current trends in media structure and organization. Concentration of media industries is increasing at the same time as the scope for public service broadcasting is being reduced. A process of global vertical integration leads to large software media companies being taken over by large electronic hardware companies or sometimes by trading companies which have no prior media history at all (Murdock, 1990). These media 'software' companies have already grown by horizontal integration, absorbing other companies as they grow, crossing the boundaries of existing media. Often the most vulnerable to takeover are successful local or specialized media, which may also be the media which are the most innovative and responsive to their publics.

These trends inevitably impinge on 'editorial' or 'creative' freedom, reducing the scope for autonomy, or just putting a brake on imagination, creativity, risk-taking. Increasingly, content for new cable and satellite television channels is produced by independent production companies which often make programmes to order, following specifications influenced by advertisers, sponsors, managers. The producers are not likely to have the resources to allow much scope for risky experiments, creative freedom or independent editorial judgement in documentary or news programming.

In the end, the problem of creativity and editorial independence overlaps with that of loss of political depth and diversity just described and largely for the same reasons. The different media are converging on each other, as they compete for much the same market. The media market, in general, is tending towards global product standardization, under pressure from the same economic logic. Of course, there is bound to be innovation and 'turnover of product', but this is not the same as allowing more scope for creativity and editorial independence.

Equality issues The problems under this heading which remain or increase, according to widely current public interest criteria, concern, especially, the widening (or narrowing) *information* and *cultural* gaps in most societies and difficulties of *access* on equal terms to the main channels of communication for minority and opposition voices. While there is almost certainly *more* information and 'culture' (of all kinds) readily available in most developed media systems now than in the past, the actual *distribution* does not seem to be any more equitable. One of the promises of an 'information society' is surely greater equity in relation to the central 'good' of such a society, for reasons of efficiency as well as justice.

Two main forces are at work, one affecting production (software), the other delivery (hardware plus money). On the production side, the relatively small demand (in mass market terms) for high-quality (rare and expensive) culture and information often does not justify continuous investment in its production, on the part of commercial firms. The task tends to be unequally borne by a shrinking public (or subsidized) sector. Otherwise, high-quality content can only be provided for small, high-income, markets. The distribution problem arises partly from the fact that, by definition, the potential audience markets are small and the domestic technology required to benefit from specialist supplies is often beyond the reach of average-income households.

The era of universal distribution of high-quality services is giving way to one of widening gaps in real chances of access to these, even if total supply and potential availability rises. Beyond basic services, there are considerable potential and actual sources of inequality. The minimum cost for an average household of participating in the basic range of media already represents a large share of its budget (Golding, 1990). In the end, cultural and informational inequality is caused by social and economic inequality (rather than vice versa), but the communication media have a real potential for helping to equalize the quality of life in a modern society. In the market logic of the emerging media landscape, high-quality and specialist provision will be available at a premium to select groups of 'consumers', while the majority will be served with low-cost products to suit an average taste and larger demand. The promise of abundance based on new technology is real enough, but it will not be automatically realized on the basis of technology and business alone.

The second 'equality' problem, that of *access* to media channels as *senders*, should also, in theory, be soluble via the multiplication of channels and the proliferation of new kinds of media. Unfortunately for the optimists, these trends have led to a higher commercial price and value being placed on media access (for senders), especially where these reach larger audiences. For minorities which do receive access, the result has, if anything, been an even greater degree of marginalization, through exclusion from the mass media.

Issues of order and culture   Competition between many channels for the same more or less constant audience is likely to increase media 'sensation-alism' (to use the old term), with its many, largely negative, implications for the cultural and informational quality of the performance of the media (Blumler, 1992). Ethical standards of the media are likely to be placed under severe strain, where these conflict with commercial goals. The bonds of trust, affection and habit between audiences and their favoured media are almost certainly going to be weaker, as new channels continually emerge and then disappear and there is a constant pressure (or incentive) to shift attention from one channel to another.

The whole notion of having some attachment or loyalty to a newspaper or a broadcasting organization, even of a purely habitual kind, is becoming anachronistic. There will be many more different audiences and 'sets' of viewers or readers, constantly recomposing along lines of taste and consumption patterns. Media use is more individuated (than ever). Even national media systems, in some cases, will no longer be able to claim the attention of their natural domestic publics as cross-border reception grows and internationalization of content increases.

The likely 'public interest' in 'culture' has also changed rather than disappeared, even in this 'post-modern' era, with less emphasis on traditional standards of intellectual or artistic quality and more on *authenticity* and on relevance to national, regional or group *identity*. The international communication debate which used to refer mainly to relations of imbalance and dependency between First and Third Worlds now also affects relations between countries *within* the First World (for instance, among European countries or between USA and a European country) and also within national societies, where a powerful metropolitan culture increasingly dominates regional, local and minority cultures.

The alternative points made about changing normative theory can be summarized in Figure 23.1.

The degree to which the media trends described above should be considered problematic or not for society depends on local circumstances, on the perspective adopted and is a matter for debate, for claim and counter-claim. Despite the pessimistic tone of these remarks, it is arguable that the expanded, internationalized, less bureaucratic and less centralized media have already played a positive role in increasing global awareness of issues of conflict, the environment and North–South divisions. An 'information society', in a shrinking world, *can* be a more informed society and a more creative, politically active, more culturally diverse society. However, the main path to this goal is still by way of the means of public communication (the mass media) rather than technologically mediated interpersonal communication.

Fading issues	Enduring and new issues
Universal provision of basic service	Bridging information and culture gaps
Mass manipulation and propaganda	Securing political involvement
Portrayal of violence and crime	Maintaining creativity, independence and diversity
Mass (low taste) culture	Social solidarity and minority rights
	Cultural autonomy and identity

Figure 23.1 *Changing normative concerns about mass media*

Adapting media performance assessment

If the reformulation of issues for public concern, brought about by changes in media and in society, does follow the lines sketched above, there remains a long agenda of items for enquiry. The *mass* media – those that regularly reached large majorities with similar information and culture – will continue to play a critical role in the public life of societies for a long time to come, even though they are much affected by the changes described.

Research into the public role of the media has to come to terms with these changes. The model widely deployed in the past was that of a *national media system*, in which citizens were largely dependent on the same, relatively limited, supply of news and culture which was distributed from a centralized metropolitan centre. The content and service provision of major channels could be studied at source, usually by sampling a limited and homogeneous output. The results could also be readily treated as a guide to the overall quality of provision for the public or society as a whole.

It looks as if this model will no longer serve. The correspondence between the typical fare offered by a few dominant media and what actually reaches the media consumer has become weaker. Earlier media conditions of mass press and national or network television produced a much stronger and more predictable connection between media supply and consumption, partly because there were fewer other options. A fair degree of homogeneity of 'media environment', within the lines drawn according to geography and socioeconomic circumstances, could be counted on.

Current changes in media and society have reduced the homogeneity and consistency of audience experience, along with its predictability. The multiplication of radio and television channels is the most obvious factor but there are many other sources of information: free newspapers and magazines, teletext, information on personal computer software, personal stores of recorded information and culture on disc and tape, which can be called on. Family, local neighbourhood, place of education, workplace,

OLD MODEL

Limited supply → Homogeneous → Passive mass → Undifferentiated
content   audience   reception/effect

NEW MODEL

Many different → Diverse   →   Fragmented → Varied and
sources   channels and   and active   unpredictable
                 contents   users/audience reception/effect

Figure 23.2 *Old and new media assessment models compared*

leisure group, advertising and public relations industries are each adding to the volume and diversity of supply, often aided by desk-top publishing.

Increasingly, both supply and reception cross national frontiers. While, according to measures of *time use*, a few national media channels still predominate in the 'intake' of information and culture for most people, there is a growing share which cannot be accounted for in this way. Nor can predominance in terms of duration of attention and share of 'media time' necessarily be equated with *significance* for receivers or society. While the mass media remain and are crucial for some purposes, for others they are relatively less significant. The implication of these comments can be summarized by comparing a typical 'old' and an emerging 'new' media research model (Figure 23.2).

It follows that we can no longer rely so much on research into the *content* of main national media channels to tell us about the quality of informational and cultural experience in a society, looked at from the point of view of the public interest. The problem has become, first of all, one of scale and complexity; secondly, one of assigning relative significance to the multiplicity of media supply. There are too many possible channels and sources to analyse and their relative salience is too variable and hard to assess.

Different research strategies and designs are needed, following two main lines of change: more attention to *structures* of provision and more attention to *audience* and reception. By definition, the quality of 'media performance' is most easy to assess by reference to the *content* (in the widest sense) of what is offered but, logically, there can really be a 'public interest' only in what *reaches* the public and might have consequences for public life.

This means that we need to know more about the audience and the conditions of reception. We cannot assume that what is received is co-extensive with what is sent or that its meaning will be understood as intended by its sender (Swanson, 1987; Ang, 1990; Jensen, 1991). The mass distribution model is simply out of date, too much modified by new ways of producing and receiving. A further implication of change is that it makes less sense to treat one medium at a time, except for purposes of a particular case study (for instance, into the effect of losing or gaining a channel in a particular system). Multimedia analysis of content and reception is now needed more than ever.

A shift in balance of attention from print to audiovisual media is also called for. Performance research has hardly caught up with the rise of video and sound recording, in respect of methods of analysis. Many of the problem definitions and research approaches are still rooted in a print culture and the ways of thinking about research are shaped by rational-informational models appropriate to 'linear' print media. Without progress on this, performance assessment will, increasingly, have a ritual character and be irrelevant to key features of public experience.

Focusing on audience reception and response The alternative is to view media performance in terms of what given audiences *receive* or attend to, irrespective of the source or channel. The logic of such an approach, assuming a typically multimedia audience experience, is that sampling of content (as received) can take the individual audience member as the basis for selection. A relevant universe of content for performance assessment is arrived at by this route and profiles of different sub-audiences can also be established. This approach can yield an assessment of performance at the point of *delivery* (reception) of information or culture. The typical audience fare can be accounted in terms of local or national origin and according to the balance of different kinds of content.

The balance of evaluation research moves closer to the audience, whose response can be used as a measure of performance success. Such research need not only inventorize reception, attention and interest. Qualitative research can be targeted on performance qualities which are of particular relevance: for instance, on audience *perceptions* of diversity, independence, accessibility, comprehensibility, relevance, trust, etc.

One reason for adopting a more audience-centred approach lies in the growth of consultative and interactive modes of communication made possible by new technology and the 'new media' generally. Even if these media remain for long a minority preserve, mass media use has already been pushed in the same direction by the wide diffusion of means of sound and video recording. The 'personalized' mass media diet is no longer a fanciful notion.

Case studies The performance research field already offers many examples of evaluative case studies directed towards key events or topics. Even so, there has been some bias against the method because of the limits to its ability to generalize. It may now be time to discriminate in favour of case studies. Broad generalization, like universal attention to media supply, is an increasingly unrealistic goal, given the scale of the task and the multiplicity of media experience. Only case studies can deal with the complexities involved in looking at structure, content and audience together.

Cross-national, cross-system comparisons The decline in the typical 'national' monopoly of media attention patterns has a number of implications, aside from the fact that quality of media performance in one country directly affects quality of reception in another (which has long been the case). The increasing similarity of media systems in different countries (globalization again) makes it more feasible and instructive to make comparisons between different national experiences. The degree and nature of similarity and difference can provide a guide to what is going on and shed light on other possibilities for media arrangements. The situation in one country can also be taken as a benchmark for assessing performance in another. Media transnationalization can really only be studied by way of transnational research designs.

Performance assessment options

Contradictory trends have been noted in the definition of the public role of the mass media: on the one hand, it is increasingly left to chance and to the market; on the other hand, it is regarded as too important to suffer benign neglect. It is probably safe to conclude, nevertheless, that direct and large-scale public intervention in media performance, on grounds of public policy becomes less rather than more likely, even if regulation of structures continues. In place of direct control, we are likely to see more reliance on self-regulation and on the informal effects of public or pressure group demands.

This has general implications for media performance research. It is no longer appropriate, if it ever was, to see it as a tool of social control and media engineering: as if expected to produce blueprints for an ideal system, or to monitor and evaluate the working of a defective system. This version of the research role inevitably identified the activity of assessment with that of the regulator and planner on the one hand, or the critic on the other, often with an illusory sense of competence and superior rectitude. Research was often conceived as a means of advancing some dominant value, in the spirit of the unitary type of 'public interest' theory described in Chapter 3. In place of this version of the performance research task, different branches of assessment research can be envisaged, as growing out of the basic stock described in this book. Three such are likely to flourish (none entirely new, but each growing more strongly than in the past): a professional/ organizational self-assessment variant; a public debate model; and a concession/monitoring model.

The professional/organizational variant of assessment

The first of the three needs little explanation. The research tradition is already rich in contributions from the media institution itself, especially as a result of more professionalization, greater corporate responsibility (and awareness of public relations), sometimes in response to public pressure. Research for the purposes of the media industry has sometimes yielded results of wider public relevance. It is quite likely that increasingly competitive conditions will lead to relatively more research by and for the media themselves which is orientated to coping with pressures from the political environment as well as from public opinion. The more that self-regulation replaces government regulation, the more demands are likely to be heard for media responsibility and accountability.

The public debate model

This can be understood in terms of the concept of public interest chosen for emphasis at the outset – a version in which open criticism and active debate in the public sphere of society continually lays claims against the media, seeks to influence public policy and keeps issues of media quality and performance before the public eye. It has been a consistent theme of this book that there are many criteria and variations of media condition which can be claimed as being 'in the public interest'. All claims have to be argued and justified. The chief task, and also benefit, of media performance research should be to provide the *information* which can inform public or policy choices. It is no longer feasible simply to invoke an absolute value or an authority which can establish some desired condition and police subsequent performance.

The concession/monitoring model

Finally, while public policy and regulation of communication appears generally to have adopted a lower profile, especially as the newer electronic media 'come of age', it has been widely remarked that there has never been a more active time for media policy and for regulation or re-regulation. This is partly a response to innovation and expansion, but it also reflects the increasing economic and sociopolitical importance of communication in society, requiring legal frameworks and definitions for new types of social and economic relationship.

Valuable concessions and franchises to operate media services (sometimes under natural monopoly conditions) are also increasingly being allocated according to general conditions of adequate service to the public. These conditions may be more loosely formulated than were older public relations and may be directed more towards structure than conduct and performance, but they still need precise statement and they imply accountability and thus the possibility of monitoring performance. Performance in the future is, in general, more likely to be tested in law courts or some other adjudicatory forum, rather than embodied in statutes or left to the discretion of highly placed 'insider' decision-makers. It is this potential which provides the scope for growth of the third branch of performance research.

Information for guidance and accountability

In an 'information society', it is appropriate that there should be a continuous flow of information about all aspects of public communication.

Communication research itself is quintessentially an informational activity since it produces information about information. This should be collected in a scientific way, according to clear and coherent criteria if it is to be of use in the politics of communication arrangements. Ultimately, the purpose of this book has been to advance this cause, and indirectly the 'public good', however this may be defined by an enlightened and active public.

Knowledge without action is not enough and in the end the only action which can advance the wider public interest promised by the 'communications revolution' has to be taken by the media themselves. This means that useful information about performance has also to take account of realities of media industries and media professional aspirations. A good deal of what has passed for performance assessment in the past has been well intentioned but unrealistic in what is expected from mass media seeking to serve general audiences and very disparate purposes. It has also often been unduly directed, or limited, by what conventional methods of media research (especially content analysis) allow. The 'administrative-critical' branch of research identified at the outset has to be more innovative as well as more realistic.

REFERENCES

Adams, W.C. (1978) 'Visual Analysis of Newscasts: Issues in Social Science Research', in W.C. Adams and F. Schreibman (eds), *Television Network News: Issues in Content Research*, pp. 155–173. Washington, DC: George Washington University.

Adams, W.C. (ed.) (1982) *Television Coverage of International Affairs*. Norwood, NJ: Ablex.

Adams W.C. (ed.) (1983) *Television Coverage of the 1980 Presidential Campaign*. Norwood, NJ: Ablex.

Adams, W.C. (1986) 'Whose Lives Count? TV Coverage of Natural Disasters', *Journal of Communication* 36(2): 113–122.

Adams, W.C. and F. Schreibman (eds) (1978) *Television Network News: Issues in Content Research*. Washington, DC: George Washington University.

Alali, A.O. and K.K. Eke (eds) (1991) *Media Coverage of Terrorism*. Newbury Park, CA: Sage.

Albert, P. (1990) *La Presse Française*. Paris: La Documentation Française.

Albrecht, M.C. (1956) 'Does Literature Reflect Common Values?' *American Sociological Review* 21(6): 722–729.

Albritton, R.B. and J.B. Manheim (1985) 'Public Relations for the Third World', *Journal of Communication* 35(1): 43–49.

Altheide, D.L. (1982) 'Three-in-One News: Network Coverage of Iran', *Journalism Quarterly* 59: 482–486.

Altheide, D.L. (1985) *Media Power*. Newbury Park, CA: Sage.

Altheide, D.L. and R.P. Snow (1979) *Media Logic*. Beverly Hills, CA: Sage.

Altschull, J.H. (1984) *Agents of Power*. New York: Longman.

Anderson, B. (1983) *Imagined Communities: Reflections on the Origins and Spread of Nationalism*. London: Verso.

Anderson, D. and W.W. Sharrock (1980) 'Biassing the News: Technical Issues in Media Studies', in G.C. Wilhoit and H. de Bock (eds), *Mass Communication Review Yearbook*, vol. 1. Beverly Hills, CA: Sage.

Anderson, H.A. (1977) 'An Empirical Investigation of What Social Responsibility Means', *Journalism Quarterly* 54: 33–39.

Andren, N. (1968) 'Sweden: State Support for Political Parties in Sweden', *Scandinavian Political Studies*, 3. New York: Columbia University Press.

Ang, I. (1990) 'Culture and Communication: Towards an Ethnographic Critique of Media Consumption', *European Journal of Communication* 5(2/3): 239–260.

Annan, N. (1977) *Report of the Committee on Broadcasting*. London: HMSO.

Applebaum, L. and J. Hébert (1982) *Federal Cultural Policy Review Committee*. Ottawa: Information Services.

Arnheim, R. (1944) 'The World of the Daytime Serial', in P.F. Lazarsfeld (ed.), *Radio Research 1942–3*, pp. 507–548. New York: Duell, Sloan and Pearce.

Asp, K. (1981) 'Mass Media as Molders of Opinion and Suppliers of Information', in C. Wilhoit and C. Whitney (eds), *Mass Communication Review Year Book*, vol. 2, pp. 332–354. Beverly Hills, CA: Sage.

Atkin, C., J.K. Burgoon and M. Burgoon (1983) 'How Journalists Perceive the Reading Audience', *Newspaper Research Journal* 4(2): 51–63.

Atwater, T. (1987) 'Network Evening News Coverage of the TWA Hostage Crisis', *Journalism Quarterly* 64: 520–525.

Atwater, T. and F. Fico (1986) 'Source Reliance and Use in Reporting State Government: A Study of Print and Broadcast Practices', *Newspaper Research Journal* 8(1): 53–61.

Axelrod, R. (1973) 'Schema Theory: An Information Processing Model of Perception and Cognition', *American Political Science Review* 67: 1248–1266.

Baer, W.S., H. Geller, J.A. Grundfest and J.B. Possner (1974) *Concentration of Mass Media Ownership: Assessing the State of Current Knowledge.* Santa Monica, CA: Rand Corporation.

Baerns, B. (1987) 'Journalism versus Public Relations in the Federal Republic of Germany', in D.L. Paletz (ed.), *Political Communication Research*, pp. 88–107. Norwood, NJ: Ablex.

Bagdikian, B.H. (1985) 'The U.S. Media: Supermarket or Assembly Line?', *Journal of Communication* 35(3): 97–109.

Bagdikian, B.H. (1988) *The Media Monopoly*, 2nd edn. Boston: Beacon Press.

Baker, S. and S. Ball (1969) *Mass Media and Violence*. Staff Report No. 9 to the Kerner Commission. Washington, DC: GPO.

Baldridge, P.D. (1967) 'Group and Non-Group Owner Programming: A Comparative Analysis', *Journal of Broadcasting* 11(2): 125–130.

Banfield, F.C. (1955) 'Note on Conceptual Scheme', in F. Banfield and M. Meyersohn (eds), *Politics, Planning and the Public Interest*, pp. 326–334. New York: Free Press.

Bantz, C.R., R.L. Price and J.E. Townsend (1981) 'Community Leaders' Perceptions of Access and Fairness', *Journal of Broadcasting* 25(1): 81–86.

Barkin, S.M. and M. Gurevitch (1991) 'Out of Work and on the Air: TV News of Unemployment', in R.K. Avery and D. Eason (eds), *Critical Perspectives on Media and Society*, pp. 303–328. New York: Guilford Press.

Barnett, S.R. (1980) 'Media Monopoly and the Law', *Journal of Communication* 30(1): 72–80.

Barron, J.A. (1972) *Freedom of the Press for Whom? The Right of Access to Mass Media.* Bloomingdale, IN: University of Indiana Press.

Barrow, R.L. (1968) 'The Equal Opportunities and Fairness Doctrines in Broadcasting: Pillars in the Forum of Democracy', *Cincinnati Law Review* 37(3): 447–557.

Barry, B. (1965) *Political Argument.* New York: Humanities Press.

Barvis, G.L. (1980) 'The Newspaper Preservation Act: A Retrospective Analysis', *Newspaper Research Journal* 1(2): 27–38.

Barwise, P. and A. Ehrenberg (1988) *Television and its Audience.* London: Sage.

Batscha, R.M. (1975) *Foreign Affairs News and the Broadcast Journalist.* New York: Praeger.

Bauer, R.A. (1958) 'The Communicator and the Audience', *Journal of Conflict Resolution* 2(1): 67–77.

Bazelon, D.L. (1982) 'The First Amendment and the "New Media". New Directions in Regulating Telecommunications', in D.L. Brenner and W.L. Rivers (eds), *Free But Regulated: Conflicting Traditions in Media Law*, pp. 52–63. Ames, IA: Iowa State University Press.

Becker, L.B. (1977) 'Foreign Policy and Press Performance', *Journalism Quarterly* 54: 364–368.

Becker, L.B. (1982) 'The Mass Media and Citizen Assessment of Issue Importance', in C. Whitney and E. Wartella (eds), *Mass Communication Review Year Book*, vol. 3, pp. 521–536. Beverly Hills, CA: Sage.

Becker, L.B., R. Beam and J. Russial (1978) 'Correlates of Daily Newspaper Performance in New England', *Journalism Quarterly* 55: 100–108.

Behr, R.L. and S. Iyengar (1985) 'Television News, Real World Cues, and Changes in the Public Agenda', *Public Opinion Quarterly* 49: 38–57.

Belkaoui, J.M. (1987) 'Images of Arabs and Israelis in the Prestige Press, 1966–1974', *Journalism Quarterly* 55: 732–738, 799.

Bell, A. (1991) *The Language of News Media.* Oxford: Blackwell.

Bennett, J.R. (1982) 'Page One Sensationalism and the Libyan "Hit Team" ', *Newspaper Research Journal* 4(1): 34–38.

Bennett, W.L. (1990) 'Towards a Theory of Press–State Relations in the United States', *Journal of Communication* 40(2): 103–125.

Bennett, W.L. and M. Edelman (1985) 'Toward a New Political Narrative', *Journal of Communication* 35(3): 156–171.

Berelson, B. and P. Salter (1946) 'Majority and Minority Americans', *Public Opinion Quarterly* 10(2): 168–190.

Berkowitz, D. (1987) 'TV News Sources and News Channels: A Study in Agenda Building', *Journalism Quarterly* 64: 508–513.

Bernard, R.M. and G.O. Coldevin (1985) 'Effects of Recap Strategies on Television News Recall and Retention', *Journal of Broadcasting* 29(4): 407–419.

Berry, C. and B. Clifford (1982) 'Professional Journalists, Amateur Psychologists: How Well Does TV News Communicate?' *EBU Review* 33: 13–19.

Berry, F.C. (1967) 'A Study of Accuracy in Local News Stories of Three Dailies', *Journalism Quarterly* 44: 482–490.

Berry, G.L. (1988) 'Multicultural Role Portrayals on Television as a Social Psychological Issue', in S. Oskamp (ed.), *Television as a Social Issue*, pp. 88–102. Newbury Park, CA: Sage.

Bigman, S.K. (1948) 'Rivals in Conformity: A Study of Two Competing Dailies', *Journalism Quarterly* 25: 127–131.

Bigman, S.K. (1955) 'Public Reactions to Death of a Daily', *Journalism Quarterly* 32: 267–276.

Blackman, J.A. and H.A. Hornstein (1977) 'Newscasts and the Social Actuary', *Public Opinion Quarterly* 41(3): 295–313.

Blackwood, R.E. and J.A. Smith (1983) 'The Content of News Photos: Roles Portrayed by Men and Women', *Journalism Quarterly* 60: 710–714.

Blanchard, M.A. (1977) 'The Hutchins Commission, the Press and the Responsibility Concept', *Journalism Monographs* 49.

Blanchard, M.A. (1986) *Exporting the First Amendment: The Press–Government Crusade of 1945–1952*. New York: Longman.

Blankenberg, W. (1970) 'News Accuracy: Some Findings on the Meaning of the Term', *Journalism Quarterly* 47: 375–386.

Blumer, H. (1939) 'The Crowd, the Public and the Mass', in A.M. Lee (ed.), *New Outline of the Principles of Sociology*, pp. 185–189. New York: Barnes and Noble.

Blumer, H. and P.M. Hauser (1933) *Movies, Delinquency and Crime*. New York: Macmillan.

Blumler, J.G. (1969) 'Producers' Attitudes towards the TV Coverage of an Election', in P. Halmos (ed.), *The Sociology of Mass Media Communicators*, pp. 85–115. Sociological Review Monographs, 13. Keele: University of Keele.

Blumler, J.G. (ed.) (1983) *Communicating to Voters: TV in the First European Parliamentary Elections*. London: Sage.

Blumler, J.G. (ed.) (1992) *Television and the Public Interest*. London: Sage.

Blumler, J.G., M. Brynin and T. Nossiter (1986) 'Broadcasting Finance and Programme Quality', *European Journal of Communication* 1(3): 343–364.

Blumler, J.G., B. Franklin, D. Mercer and B. Tutt (1990) 'Monitoring the Public Experiment in Televising the Proceedings of the House of Commons', in *Review of the Experiment in Televising the Proceedings of the House*, pp. 8–67 (265–I). London: HMSO.

Blumler, J.G. and D. McQuail (1968) *Television in Politics*. London: Faber and Faber.

Blumler, J.G. and T. Nossiter (eds) (1991) *Broadcasting Finance and Transition*. New York: Oxford University Press.

Bogart, L. (1979) 'Editorial Ideals, Editorial Illusions', *Journal of Communication* 29(2): 11–21.

Bogart, L. (1989) *Press and Public*, 2nd edn. Hillsdale, NJ: LEA.

Bogart, L. and F.E. Orenstein (1965) 'Mass Media and the Community Identity in an Interurban Setting', *Journalism Quarterly* 42: 179–188.

Bollinger, L. (1976) 'Freedom of the Press and Public Access: Toward a Theory of Partial Regulation of the Mass Media', *University of Michigan Law Review* 1.

Bonbright, J.C. (1961) *Principles of Public Utility Rules*. New York: Columbia University Press.

Bordewijk, J.L. and B. van Kaam (1986) 'Towards a New Classification of Tele-information Services', *Intermedia* 14(1): 11–21.

Borstel, G.H. (1956) 'Ownership, Competition and Comment in 20 Small Dailies', *Journalism Quarterly* 33: 220–222.

Bourdieu, P. (1986) *Distinction: A Social Critique of the Judgement of Taste*. London: Routledge.

Bowers, D.R. (1967) 'A Report on Activity by Publishers in Directing Newsroom Decisions', *Journalism Quarterly* 44: 43–52.

Boyd-Barrett, O. (1977) 'Media Imperialism', in J. Curran, M. Gurevitch and J. Woollacott (eds), *Mass Communication and Society*. pp. 116–134. London: Arnold.

Boyd-Barrett, O. (1985) 'News Agencies: Political Constraints and Market Opportunities', in U. Kivikuru and T. Varis (eds), *Approaches to International Communication*, pp. 67–94. Helsinki: UNESCO Commission.

Boyer, J.H. (1981) 'How Editors View Objectivity', *Journalism Quarterly*, 58: 24–28.

Braestrup, P. (1977) *Big Story*. Boulder, CO: Westview Press.

Brander, L. and T. Sistruk (1966) 'The Newspaper: Molder and Mirror of Community Values?', *Journalism Quarterly* 43: 497–504.

Brannigan, A. and S. Goldenberg (1987) 'The Study of Aggressive Pornography', *Critical Studies in Mass Communication* 4: 262–283.

Breed, W. (1955) 'Social Control in the Newsroom: A Functional Analysis', *Social Forces* 37: 109–116.

Breed, W. (1958) 'Mass Communication and Socio-Cultural Integration', *Social Forces* 53: 326–335.

Breitling, R. (1980) 'The Concept of Pluralism', in S. Ehrlich and G. Wootton (eds), *Three Faces of Pluralism*, pp. 1–19. Farnborough: Gower.

Brennan, T.J. (1989) 'The Fairness Doctrine as Public Policy', *Journal of Broadcasting* 33(4): 419–440.

Brenner, D.L. and W.L. Rivers (1982) *Free But Regulated: Conflicting Traditions in Media Law*. Ames, IA: Iowa State University Press.

Briggs, A. (1961) *The History of Broadcasting in the United Kingdom*. London: Oxford University Press.

Broadcasting Standards Council (1989) *A Code of Practice*. London: British Standards Council.

Brown, J.D., C.R. Bybee, S.T. Wearden and D.M. Straughan (1987) 'Invisible Power: Newspaper News Sources and the Limits of Diversity', *Journalism Quarterly* 64: 45–54.

Brown, J.R. (1978) *Characteristics of Local Media Audiences*. Farnborough: Saxon House.

Browne, D. (1989) *Comparing Broadcasting*. Ames, IA: Iowa State University Press.

Browning, N., D. Grierson and H.H. Howard (1984) 'Effects of a Conglomerate Takeover on a Newspaper's Coverage of the Knoxville World's Fair: A Case Study', *Newspaper Research Journal* 6(1): 30–38.

Budd, R.W. (1964) 'Attention Score: A Device for Measuring News "Play" ', *Journalism Quarterly* 41: 259–262.

Burgoon, J.K. et al. (1980) 'Evaluations of Newspaper and Television Coverage of Local, National, and World News', *Newspaper Research Journal* 2(1): 4–11.

Burgoon, J.K., M. Burgoon and C.L. Atkin (1982) *The World of the News*. New York: Newspaper Advertising Bureau Inc.

Burgoon, J.K., M. Burgoon and M. Wilkinson (1983a) 'Dimensions of Content Readership in 10 Newspaper Markets', *Journalism Quarterly* 60: 74–80.

Burgoon, J.K., J.M. Bernstein and M. Burgoon (1983b) 'Public and Journalist Perceptions of Newspaper Functions', *Newspaper Research Journal* 5(1): 77–90.

Burgoon, M., J.K. Burgoon and M. Wilkinson (1981) 'Newspaper Image and Evaluation', *Journalism Quarterly* 58: 411–419, 433.

Burnett, R. (1990) *Concentration in the International Phonogram Industry*. Gothenburg: University of Gothenburg.

Burns, T. (1977) *The BBC: Public Service and Private World*. London: Macmillan.

Busby, L.J. (1975) 'Sex Role Research in Mass Media', *Journal of Communication* 24(4): 107–131.

Bush, C.R. (1960) 'Content and *Mise en Valeur*': Attention as Effect', *Journalism Quarterly* 37: 435–437.

Busterna, J.C. (1987) 'Improving Editorial and Economic Competition with a Modified Newspaper Preservation Act', *Newspaper Research Journal* 8(4): 71–84.

Busterna, J.C. (1988a) 'Competitive Effects of Newspaper Chain "Deep Pockets" ', *Newspaper Research Journal* 10(1): 61–72.

Busterna, J.C. (1988b) 'Concentration and the Industrial Organization Model', in R.G. Picard, M. McCombs, J.P. Winter and S. Lacy (eds), *Press Concentration and Monopoly*, pp. 35–53. Norwood, NJ: Ablex.

Butler, M. and W.J. Paisley (eds) (1980) *Women and the Mass Media*. New York: Human Science Press.

Butsch, R. and L.M. Glennon (1983) 'Social Class: Frequency Trends in Domestic Situation Comedy, 1946–1978', *Journal of Broadcasting* 27(1): 77–81.

Calcutt Committee (1990) *Report of the Calcutt Committee*. London: HMSO.

Cantor, M.G. (1971) *The Hollywood Television Producer*. New York: Basic Books.

Cantor, M.G. (1979) 'The Politics of Popular Drama', *Communication Research* 6(4): 387–406.

Cantor, M.G. (1980) *Prime Time TV*. Beverly Hills, CA: Sage.

Cantor, M.G. and E. Jones (1983) 'Creating Fiction for Women', *Communication Research* 10(1): 111–137.

Carey, J. (1969) 'The Communications Revolution and the Professional Communicator', in P. Halmos (ed.), *The Sociology of Mass Media Communicators*, pp. 23–38. Keele: University of Keele.

Carey, J. (1989) *Communication as Culture*. Boston: Unwin Hyman.

Carnegie Commission on the Future of Public Broadcasting (1978) *The Public Trust*. New York: Bantam.

Carroll, G.R. (1987) *Publish and Perish: The Organizational Ecology of Newspaper Industries*. Greenwood, CT: JAI Press.

Carter, R.E. (1958) 'Newspaper "Gatekeepers" and the Sources of News', *Public Opinion Quarterly* 22(2): 133–144.

Carter, R.E. and B. Greenberg (1965) 'Newspapers and Television: Which Do You Believe?', *Journalism Quarterly* 42: 29–34.

Cass, R.A. (1981) *Revolution in the Wasteland: Value and Diversity in Television*. Charlottesville, VA: University Press of Virginia.

Cassata, M. and T. Skill (1983) *Life on Daytime Television*. Norwood, NJ: Ablex.

Cater, D. (1964) *The Fourth Branch of Government*. New York: Random House.

Chafee, Z. (1947) *Government and Mass Communications: A Report from the Commission on Freedom of the Press*. Chicago: University of Chicago Press.

Chaffee, S.H. (1981) 'Mass Media Effects: New Research Perspectives', in C. Wilhoit and H. de Bock (eds), *Mass Communication Review Yearbook*, vol. 2, pp. 77–108. Beverly Hills, CA: Sage.

Chaffee, S.H. and D.G. Wilson (1977) 'Media Rich, Media Poor: Two Studies of Diversity in Agenda-Holding', *Journalism Quarterly* 54: 466–476.

Chamberlin, B.F. and C.J. Brown (eds) (1982) *The First Amendment Reconsidered: New Perspectives on the Meaning of Freedom of Speech and the Press*. White Plains, NY: Longman.

Charnley, M.V. (1936) 'Preliminary Notes on a Study of Newspaper Accuracy', *Journalism Quarterly* 13(2): 394–400.

Cheesebro, J.W. (1982) 'Communication, Values and Popular TV Series', in H. Newcomb (ed.), *Television: the Critical View*, pp. 8–46. New York: Oxford University Press.

Chibnall, S. (1977) *Law and Order News*. London: Tavistock.

Chittick, W.O. (1970) *State Department, Press and Pressure Groups*. New York: Wiley.

Christians, C.G. (1986) 'Reporting and the Oppressed', in D. Elliot (ed.), *Responsible Journalism*, pp. 109–130. Beverly Hills, CA: Sage.

Christians, C.G. and K.B. Rotzell (1983) *Media Ethics: Cases and Moral Reasoning*. New York: Longman.

Cirino, R. (1971) *Don't Blame the People: How the News Media Use Bias, Distortion and Censorship to Manipulate Public Opinion*. New York: Random House.

Clancy, M. and M.J. Robinson (1988) 'The Media in Campaign "84": General Election Coverage', *Public Opinion* Dec/Jan.: 49–54, 59.

Clarke, P. and S.H. Evans (1980) ' "All in a Day's Work": Reporters Covering Congressional Campaigns', *Journal of Communication* 30(4): 112–121.

Clarke, P. and E. Fredin (1978) 'Newspapers, Television and Political Reasoning', *Public Opinion Quarterly* 42(2): 143–160.

Clarke, P. and L. Ruggels (1970) 'Preferences Amongst News Media for Coverage of Public Affairs', *Journalism Quarterly* 47: 464–471.

Cohen, B. (1963) *The Press and Foreign Policy*. Princeton, NJ: Princeton University Press.

Cohen, S. (1972) *Folk Devils and Moral Panics*, London: McGibbon and Kee.

Cohen, S. and J. Young (eds) (1973) *The Manufacture of News*. London: Constable.

Cole, B. and M. Oettinger (1978) *Reluctant Regulators: The FCC and the Broadcast Audience*. Reading, MA: Addison-Wesley.

Compaine, B.M., C.H. Sterling, T. Guback and J.K. Noble (1982) *Who Owns the Media?: Concentration of Ownership in the Mass Communications Industry*. White Plains, NY: Knowledge Industry Publications.

Comstock, G. (1988) 'Today's Audience, Tomorrow's Media', in O. Oskamp (ed.), *Television as a Social Issue*, pp. 324–345. Newbury Park, CA: Sage.

Comstock, G. (1989) *The Evolution of American Television*. Newbury Park, CA: Sage.

Comstock, G., S. Chaffee, N. Katzman, M. McCombs and D. Roberts (eds) (1978) *Television and Human Behavior*. New York: Columbia University Press.

Comstock, G. and R.E. Cobbey (1976) 'Watching the Watchdogs', in W. Adams and F. Schreibman (eds), *Televison Network News*, pp. 46–63. Washington, DC: George Washington University.

Cony, E.R. (1953) 'Conflict–Cooperation Content of Five American Dailies', *Journalism Quarterly* 30: 15–22.

Corry, J. (1980) *TV News and the Dominant Culture*. Washington, DC: Media Institute.

Cox, H. and D. Morgan (1974) *City Politics and the Press*. Cambridge: Cambridge University Press.

Cranford, R.J. (1960) 'Regional News Coverage in US Dailies', *Journalism Quarterly* 37: 69–74.

Cuilenburg, J.J. van (1987) 'The Information Society: Some Trends and Implications', *European Journal of Communication* 2(1): 105–121.

Cuilenburg, J.J. van, J. de Ridder and J. Kleinnijenhuis (1986) 'A Theory of Evaluative Discourse', *European Journal of Communication* 1(1): 65–96.

Culbertson, H.M. (1979) 'The Neutral and Participant Perspectives – What Do They Mean?', *Newspaper Research Journal* 1(1): 60–72.

Culbertson, H.M. (1983) 'Three Perspectives on American Journalism', *Journalism Monographs* 83.

Curran, J. (1978) 'Advertising and the Press', in J. Curran (ed.), *The British Press*, pp. 229–267. London: Macmillan.

Curran, J. (1991) 'Mass Media and Democracy: A Reappraisal', in J. Curran and M. Gurevitch (eds), *Mass Media and Society*, pp. 82–117. London: Arnold.

Curran, J., A. Douglas and G. Whannel (1980) 'The Political Economy of Human Interest Stories', in A. Smith (ed.), *Newspapers and Democracy*, pp. 288–316. Cambridge, MA: MIT Press.

Curran, J. and J. Seaton (1988) *Power Without Responsibility: The Press and Broadcasting in Britain*, 3rd edn. London: Routledge.

Curtis, L. (1984) *The Propaganda War: The British Press and Northern Ireland*. London: Pluto Press.

Cutlip, S. (1954) 'Content and Flow of AP News from Trunk to TTS to Reader', *Journalism Quarterly* 31: 441–452.

Dahl, R.A. (1967) *Pluralist Democracy in the US: Conflict and Consent*. Chicago: Rand McNally.

Dahlgren, P. (1988) 'What is the Meaning of This? Viewers' Plural Sense-making of TV News', *Media, Culture and Society* 10: 285–301.

Danielson, W.A. and J.B. Adams (1961) 'Completeness of Press Coverage of the 1960 Campaign', *Journalism Quarterly* 38: 441–452.

Darnton, R. (1975) 'Writing News and Telling Stories', *Daedalus* Spring: 175–194.

Davey, K.D. (1970) *The Uncertain Mirror*. Report, Vol. 1 of Special Senate Committee on Mass Media, Ottawa.

Davis, D.K. and J.P. Robinson (1986) 'News Story Attributes and Comprehension', in J.P. Robinson and M. Levy (eds), *The Main Source*, pp. 179–210. Newbury Park, CA: Sage.

Davis, F.J. (1952) 'Crime News in Colorado Newspapers', *American Journal of Sociology* 57: 225–230.

Davis, H. and P. Walton (1983) *Language, Image, Media*. Oxford: Basil Blackwell.

De Bens, E., M. Kelly and M. Bakke (1992) 'Television Content: The Dallasification of Culture', in K. Siune and W. Truetzschler (eds), *The Dynamics of Media Politics*, pp. 75–100. London: Sage.

DeFleur, M. (1964) 'Occupational Roles as Portrayed on Television', *Public Opinion Quarterly* 28: 57–64.

DeFleur, M. (1970) *Theories of Mass Communication*, 2nd edn. New York: David McKay.

Delli Carpini, M.X. and B.A. Williams (1987) 'Television and Terrorism', *Western Political Quarterly* 40: 45–64.

Demers, D.P. and D.B. Wackman (1988) 'Effect of Chain Ownership on Newspaper Management Goals', *Newspaper Research Journal* 9(2): 59–68.

De Mott, J. (1980) 'Newspaper Ethics and Managing Editors: The Evolution of APME's Code', *Newspaper Research Journal* 1(3): 75–84.

Dennis, E.E. (1986) 'Social Responsibility, Representation and Reality', in D. Elliot (ed.), *Responsible Journalism*, pp. 99–108. Beverly Hills, CA: Sage.

Dennis, E.E. (1989) *Reshaping the Media: Mass Communication in an Information Age*. Newbury Park, CA: Sage.

Dennis, E.E. et al. (1991) *The Media at War*. New York: Gannett Foundation.

Dervin, B., L. Grossberg, B.J. O'Keefe and E. Wartella (eds) (1989) *Rethinking Communication*, 2 vols. Newbury Park, CA: Sage.

Desmond, R.W. (1947) 'Of a Free and Responsible Press', *Journalism Quarterly* 24: 188–192.

Dijk, T.A. van (1983) 'Discourse Analysis: Its Development and Application to the Structure of News', *Journal of Communication* 33(2): 20–43.

Dijk, T. van (1988) *News as Discourse*. Hillsdale, NJ: LEA.

Dijk, T. van (1991) *Racism and the Press*. London: Routledge.

Dimmick, J. (1974) 'The Gatekeeper: An Uncertain Theory', *Journalism Monographs* 37.

Dimmick, J. and P. Coit (1982) 'Levels of Analysis in Mass Media Decision Making', *Communication Research* 9(1): 3–32.

Dizier, B.S. (1986) 'Editorial Page Editors and Endorsements: Chain-Owned vs. Independent Newspapers', *Newspaper Research Journal* 8(1): 63–68.

Dominick, J.R. (1977) 'Geographic Bias in National Television News', *Journal of Communication* 27: 94–99.

Dominick, J.R. and M.C. Pearce (1976) 'Trends in Network Prime-Time Programming, 1953–1974', *Journal of Communication* 26(1): 70–80.

Dominick, J.R. and G. Rauch (1971) 'The Image of Women in Network TV Commercials', *Journal of Broadcasting* 6: 259–265.

Dominick, J.R., A. Wurtzel and G. Lometti (1975) 'Television Journalism vs. Show Business: A Content Analysis of Eyewitness News', *Journalism Quarterly* 52: 213–218.

Donohue, T.R. and T.L. Glasser (1978) 'Homogeneity in Coverage of Connecticut Newspapers', *Journalism Quarterly* 55: 592–596.

Donohue, T.R., C.N. Olien and P.J. Tichenor (1985) 'Reporting Conflict by Pluralism, Newspaper Type and Ownership', *Journalism Quarterly* 62: 489–499, 507.

Donsbach, W. (1981) 'Legitimacy through Competence Rather than Value Judgements: The Concept of Journalistic Professionalization Reconsidered', *Gazette* 27: 46–67.

Donsbach, W. (1991) 'Exposure to Political Content in Newspapers', *European Journal of Communication* 6(2): 155–186.

Dorfman, A. and A. Mattelart (1975) *How to Read Donald Duck: Imperialist Ideology in the Disney Comic*. New York: International General.

Dorman, W.A. and M. Farhang (1987) *The U.S. Press and Iran*. Berkeley, CA: University of California Press.

Douglas, S., N. Pecora and T. Guback (1985) 'Work, Workers and the Workplace: Is Local Newspaper Coverage Adequate?' *Journalism Quarterly* 62: 855–860.

Dowling, R.E. (1986) 'Terrorism and the Media: A Rhetorical Genre', *Journal of Communication* 36(1): 12–24.

Downing, J. (1984) *Radical Media*. Boston, MA: South End Press.

Downs, A. (1962) 'The Public Interest: Its Meaning in a Democracy', *Social Research* 29(1): 1–36.

Dreier, P. (1982) 'The Position of the Press in the US Power Structure', *Social Problems* 29(3): 298–310.

Duncan, C.T. (1952) 'How the Weekly Press Covers News of Local Government', *Journalism Quarterly* 29: 281–293.

Durán, C. and P. Urzúa (1978) 'On the Ideological Role of *El Mercurio* in Chilean Society', *Latin American Research Unit (LARU)*, 11(3): 46–64.

Durkheim, E. (1947) *The Division of Labour in Society*, translated by George Simpson. Glencoe, IL: Free Press.

Durkin, K. (1985) *Television, Sex Roles and Children*. Milton Keynes: Open University Press.

Dye, L. and P.J. Ziegler (1982) *American Politics in the Media Age*. Belmont, CA: Wadsworth.

Edelman, M.J. (1977) *Political Language: Words that Succeed and Politics that Fail*. New York: Academic Press.

Edelman, M.J. (1988) *Constructing the Political Spectacle*. Chicago: University of Chicago Press.

Edelstein, A.S. and O.N. Larsen (1960) 'The Weekly Press' Contribution to a Sense of Urban Community', *Journalism Quarterly* 37: 489–498.

Efron, E. (1971) *The News Twisters*. Los Angeles: Nash Publishing.

Einsiedel, E.F. (1988) 'The British, Canadian and US Pornography Commissions and their Use of the Social Sciences', *Journal of Communication* 38(2): 108–121.

Einsiedel, E.F. and J.P. Winter (1983) 'Public Attitudes on Media Ownership: Demographic and Attitudinal Correlates', *Journalism Quarterly* 60(1): 87–92.

Elliott, D. (ed.) (1986) *Responsible Journalism*. Beverly Hills, CA: Sage.

Elliott, P. (1972) *The Making of a Television Series*. London: Constable.

Elliott, P. (1977a) 'Media Organizations and Occupations', in J. Curran et al. (eds), *Mass Communication and Society*, pp. 142–173. London: Arnold.

Elliott, P. (1977b) 'Reporting Northern Ireland', in *Ethnicity and Mass Media*, pp. 263–373. Paris: UNESCO.

Emerson, T.I. (1963) 'Towards a General Theory of the First Amendment', *Yale Law Journal* 72: 877–954.

Emerson, T.I. (1970) *The System of Freedom of Expression*. New York: Random House.

Engwall, L. (1978) *Newspapers as Organizations*. Farnborough, Hants: Saxon House.

Entman, R.M. (1985) 'Newspaper Competition and First Amendment Ideals: Does Monopoly Matter?' *Journal of Communication* 35(3): 147–165.

Entman, R.M. (1989) *Democracy Without Citizens: Media and the Decay of American Politics*. New York: Oxford University Press.

Enzensberger, H.M. (1970) 'Constituents of a Theory of the Media', *New Left Review* 64: 13–36.

Epstein, L.K. (1973) *News from Nowhere*. New York: Random House.

Erbring, L., E.N. Goldenberg and A.H. Miller (1980) 'Front-Page News and Real World News: A New Look at Agenda-Setting', *American Journal of Political Sciences* 24: 16–49.

Ericson, R.V., P.M. Baranek and J.B.L. Chan (1987) *Vizualizing Deviance*. Toronto: University of Toronto Press.

Ernst, M.L. (1946) *The First Freedom*. New York: Macmillan.

Ettema, J. and C. Whitney (eds) (1982) *Individuals in Mass Media Organizations*. Beverly Hills, CA: Sage.

Euromedia Research Group (1992) *The Media in Western Europe*. London: Sage.

Evans, H. (1983) *Good Times, Bad Times*. London: Coronet.

Farace, V. and L. Donohew (1965) 'Mass Communication in National Social Systems', *Journalism Quarterly* 42: 253–261.

Febvre, L. and H.J. Martin (1984) *The Coming of the Book*. London: Verso.

Federal Communication Commission (1946) *'Blue Book': Public Service Responsibilities of Broadcasting Licensees*. Washington, DC.

Fedler, F. (1973) 'The Media and Minority Groups: A Study of Adequacy of Access', *Journalism Quarterly* 50: 109–117.

Fedler, F. and T. Counts (1981) 'Variations in Attribution Affect Readers' Evaluations of Stories', *Newspaper Research Journal* 2(3): 25–34.

Fedler, F., T. Counts and L.F. Stephens (1982) 'Newspaper Endorsements and Voter Behavior in the 1980 Presidential Election', *Newspaper Research Journal* 4(1): 3–11.

Fedler, F. and D. Jordan (1982) 'How Emphasis on People Affects Coverage of Crime', *Journalism Quarterly* 59: 474–478.

Ferguson, M. (1983) *Forever Feminine: Women's Magazines and the Cult of Femininity*. London: Heinemann.

Ferguson, M. (ed.) (1990) *Public Communication: the New Imperatives*. London: Sage.

Ferguson, M. (1991) 'Politics, Culture and Technology: The Holy Trinity of Canadian Broadcasting', in J. Blumler and T. Nossiter (eds), *Broadcasting Finance in Transition*, pp. 158–187. New York: Oxford University Press.

Feshbach, N.D. (1988) 'Television and the Development of Empathy', in O. Oskamp (ed.) *Television as a Social Issue*, pp. 211–269. Newbury Park, CA: Sage.

Fielder, V.D. and L.P. Tipton (1986) *Minorities and Newspapers. A Survey of Readership Research*. Southbridge, MA: ASNE.

Fielder, V.D. and H.D. Weaver (1982) 'Public Opinion on Investigative Reporting', *Newspaper Research Journal* 3(2): 54–62.

Findahl, O. and B. Hoijer (1985) 'Some Characteristics of News Memory and Comprehension', *Journal of Broadcasting* 29(4): 379–396.

Fisher, D. (1982) *The Right to Communicate: A Status Report*. Paris: UNESCO.

Fishman, M. (1980) *Manufacturing the News*. Austin, TX: University of Texas Press.

Fiske, J. (1987) *Television Culture*. London: Methuen.

Fjaestad, B. and P.G. Holmlov (1976) 'The Journalist's View', *Journal of Communication* 26(4): 108–114.

Flesch, R. (1948) 'A New Readability Yardstick', *Journal of Applied Psychology* 32: 221–233.

Fletcher, F. (1981) *The Newspaper and Public Affairs*, Research Studies vol. 7. Ottawa: Royal Commission on Newspapers.

Foote, J.S. (1989) *Opposition Access to Network Television 1969–1988*. San Francisco: ICA.

Foote, J.S. and M.E. Steele (1986) 'Degree of Conformity in Lead Stories in Early Evening Network T.V. Newscasts', *Journalism Quarterly* 63: 19–23.

Fowler, J.S. and S.W. Showalte (1974) 'Evening Network News Selection: Confirmation of News Judgement', *Journalism Quarterly* 51: 212–215.

Fowler, M.S. (1982) 'The Public's Interest', *Communication and the Law* 4: 51–58.

Fowler, M.S. and D.L. Brenner (1983) 'A Marketplace Approach to Broadcast Regulation', in E. Wartella et al. (eds), *Mass Communication Review Yearbook*, vol. 4, pp. 645–695. Beverly Hills, CA: Sage.

Fowler, R.M. (1965) *Report of the Committee on Broadcasting*. Ottawa: Queen's Printer.

Frank, R.S. (1973) *Message Dimensions of Television News*. Lexington, MA: Lexington Books.

Franklin, B. and D. Murphy (1991) *What News? The Market, Politics and the Local Press*. London: Routledge.

Franzwa, H.H. (1974) 'Working Women in Fact and Fiction', *Journal of Communication* 24(2): 104–109.

References

Freimuth, V.S., R.H. Greenberg, J. De Witt and R.M. Romano (1984) 'Covering Cancer: Newspapers and the Public Interest', *Journal of Communication* 34(1): 62–73.

Friedman, S.M. (1981) 'Blueprint for Breakdown: Three Mile Island and the Media', *Journal of Communication* 31(3): 116–128.

Funkhouser, G.R. (1973) 'Trends in Media Coverage of the Issues of the 60s', *Journalism Quarterly* 50: 533–538.

Gallagher, M. (1981) *Unequal Opportunities: The Case of Women and the Media.* Paris: UNESCO.

Gallup Organization (1986) *The People and the Press: A Times Mirror Investigation of Public Attitudes toward the News Media.* Los Angeles: Times Mirror.

Galtung, J. and M. Ruge (1965) The Structure of Foreign News. *Journal of Peace Research* 1: 64–90.

Gandy, O.H. (1982) *Beyond Agenda Setting.* Norwood, NJ: Ablex.

Gans, H.J. (1979) *Deciding What's News.* New York: Free Press.

Gantz, W. (1981) 'The Influence of Researcher Methods on Television and Newspaper News Credibility Evaluations', *Journal of Broadcasting* 25(2): 155–169.

Garnham, N. (1986) 'The Media and the Public Sphere', in P. Golding et al. (eds), *Communicating Politics*, pp. 37–54. Leicester: Leicester University Press.

Gaunt, P. (1990) *Choosing the News.* Westport, CT: Greenwood Press.

Gaziano, C. (1983) 'The Knowledge Gap: An Analytic Review of Media Effects', *Communication Review* 10(4): 447–486.

Gaziano, C. (1989) 'Chain Newspaper Homogeneity and Presidential Endorsements, 1971–1988', *Journalism Quarterly* 66(4): 836–845.

Gaziano, C. and K. McGrath (1987a) 'Segments of the Public Most Critical of Newspapers' Credibility: A Psychographic Analysis', *Newspaper Research Journal* 8(4): 1–18

Gaziano, C. and K. McGrath (1987b) 'Newspaper Credibility and Relationships of Newspaper Journalists to Communities', *Journalism Quarterly* 64: 317–328.

Geis, M.L. (1982) *The Language of Television Advertising.* New York: Academic Press.

Geis, M.L. (1987) *The Language of Politics.* Berlin: Springer Verlag.

Genova, B.K.L. and B.S. Greenberg (1979) 'Interests in News and the Knowledge Gap', *Public Opinion Quarterly* 43(1): 79–91.

Gerbner, G. (1964) 'Ideological Perspectives and Political Tendencies in News Reporting', *Journalism Quarterly* 41: 495–508.

Gerbner, G. (1969) 'Institutional Pressures on Mass Communicators', in P. Halmos (ed.), *The Sociology of Mass Communicators*, pp. 205–248. Keele: University of Keele.

Gerbner, G. (1988) *Violence and Terrorism in the Mass Media.* Report on Mass Communication 102. Paris: UNESCO.

Gerbner, G., M.J. Beeck, S. Jeffres-Fox and N. Signorielli (1978) 'Cultural Indicators Violence Profile No. 9', *Journal of Communication* 28(4): 176–207.

Gerbner, G. and L. Gross (1976) 'Living with Television: The Violence Profile', *Journal of Communication* 26(2): 173–199.

Gerbner, G. and G. Marvanyi (1977) 'The Many Worlds of the World's Press', *Journal of Communication* 27(1): 52–66.

Gerbner, G., N. Signorielli and M. Morgan (1982) 'Charting the Mainstream: Television's Contributions to Political Orientation', *Journal of Communication* 32(2): 100–127.

Ghiglione, L. (ed.) (1973) *Evaluating the Press: The New England Daily Newspaper Survey.* Southbridge, MA: ASNE.

Ghiglione, L. (1984) *The Buying and Selling of America's Newspapers.* Indianapolis, IN: R.J. Berg.

Gieber, W. (1955) 'Do Newspapers Overplay "Negative" News?' *Journalism Quarterly* 32: 311–318.

Gieber, W. and W. Johnson (1961) 'The City Hall Beat: A Study of Reporter and Source Roles', *Journalism Quarterly* 38: 289–297.

Giffard, A. (1989) *Unesco and the Media.* New York: Longman.

Gitlin, T. (1980) *The Whole World is Watching.* Berkeley, CA: University of California Press.

Glasgow Media Group (1976) *Bad News*. London: Routledge and Kegan Paul.

Glasgow Media Group (1980) *More Bad News*. London: Routledge and Kegan Paul.

Glasgow Media Group (1985) *War and Peace News*. London: Routledge and Kegan Paul.

Glasser, T.L. (1984) 'Competition and Diversity among Radio Formats: Legal and Structural Issues', *Journal of Broadcasting* 28(2): 127–142.

Glasser, T.L. (1986) 'Press Responsibility and First Amendment Values', in D. Elliott (ed.), *Responsible Journalism*, pp. 81–89. Beverly Hills, CA: Sage.

Glasser, T.L. (1988) 'Objectivity Precludes Responsibility', in R.E. Hiebert and C. Reuss (eds), *Impact of Mass Media: Current Issues*, pp. 44–51. White Plains, NY: Longman.

Glasser, T.L. and J. Ettema (1991) 'Investigative Reporting and the Moral Order', in R.K. Avery and D. Easons (eds), *Critical Perspectives on Media and Society*, pp. 203–255. New York: Guilford Press.

Goldenberg, E. (1976) *Making the Papers: the Access of Resource Poor Groups to the Metropolitan Press*. Lexington, MA: Lexington Books.

Golding, P. (1981) 'The Missing Dimension – News Media and the Management of Social Change', in E. Katz and T. Szescko (eds), *Mass Media and Social Change*, pp. 63–81. London: Sage.

Golding, P. (1990) 'Political Communication and Citizenship', in M.F. Ferguson (ed.), *Public Communication*, pp. 84–100. London: Sage.

Golding, P. and P. Elliott (1979) *Making the News*. London: Longman.

Golding, P. and S. Middleton (1982) *Press and Public Attitudes to Poverty*. Oxford: Martin Robertson.

Gollin, A. (1982) 'The Newspaper in Readers' Minds'. Research Report. New York: Newspaper Advertising Bureau Inc.

Gollin, A. and M.L. Macht (1986) 'Readers Rate their Daily Newspaper'. Research Report. New York: Newspaper Advertising Bureau Inc.

Goodwin, H.E. (1983) *Groping for Ethics in Journalism*. Ames, IA: Iowa State University Press.

Gormley, W.T. (1977) 'How Cross-Ownership Affects News-Gathering', *Columbia Journalism Review* May/June: 38–43.

Gormley, W.T. (1980) 'An Evaluation of the FCC's Cross-Ownership Policy', *Policy Analysis* 6: 61–83.

Gothberg, J.A. (1983) 'Newspaper Subsidies in Sweden Pose No Danger, its Editors Feel', *Journalism Quarterly* 60: 629–634.

Gould, P., J. Johnson and G. Chapman (1984) *The Structure of Television*. London: Pion.

Gouldner, A. (1976) *The Dialectic of Science and Technology*. London: Macmillan.

Graber, D.A. (1971) 'The Press as Opinion Resource During the 1968 Presidential Campaign', *Public Opinion Quarterly* 35(2): 168–182.

Graber, D.A. (1976a) 'Press and TV as Opinion Resources in Presidential Campaigns', *Public Opinion Quarterly* 40(3): 285–303.

Graber, D.A. (1976b) *Verbal Behavior in Politics*. Urbana, IL: University of Illinois Press.

Graber, D.A. (1979) 'Is Crime News Coverage Excessive?', *Journal of Communication* 29(3): 81–92.

Graber, D.A. (1980a) *The Mass Media and American Politics*. Washington, DC: Congressional Quality Press.

Graber, D.A. (1980b) *Crime News and the Public*. New York: Praeger.

Greenberg, B.S. (1964) 'Community Press as Perceived by its Editors and Readers', *Journalism Quarterly* 41: 437–444.

Greenberg, B.S. (1986) 'Minorities and the Mass Media', in J. Bryant and D. Zillman (eds), *Perspectives on Media Effects*. Hillsdale, NJ: LEA.

Greenberg, B.S. (1988) 'Some Uncommon TV Images and the Drench Hypothesis', in O. Oskamp (ed.), *Television as a Social Issue*, pp. 88–102. Newbury Park, CA: Sage.

Greenberg, B.S. and C.K. Atkin (1980) *Life on Television: Content Analyses of U.S. T.V. Drama*. Norwood, NJ: Ablex.

Greenberg, G.S., R. Abelman, and K. Neuendorf (1981a) 'Sex in the Soap Operas: Afternoon Delight', *Journal of Communication* 3: 83–96.

Greenberg, B.S., M. Burgoon, J. Burgoon and F. Korzenny (1981b) *Mexican Americans and the Mass Media*. Norwood, NJ: Ablex.

Greenberg, B.S. and D. D'Alessio (1985) 'Quantity and Quality of Sex in the Soaps', *Journal of Broadcasting* 29(3): 309–321.

Greenberg, E. and H. Barnett (1971) 'T.V. Program Diversity: New Evidence and Old Theory', *American Economic Review* 61(2): 89–93.

Grotta, G.L. (1971) 'Consolidation of Newspapers: What Happens to the Consumer?' *Journalism Quarterly* 48: 245–250.

Grunig, J.E. (1976) 'Organizations and Public Relations: Testing a Communications Theory', *Journalism Monographs* 46.

Gunter, B. (1985) *Dimension of Television Violence*. Aldershot: Gower.

Gunter, B. (1986) *Television and Sex Role Stereotyping*. London: John Libbey.

Gunter, B. (1987a) *Poor Reception: Misunderstanding and Forgetting Broadcast News*. Hillsdale, NJ: Lawrence Erlbaum.

Gunter, B. (1987b) *Behind and in Front of the Small Screen: TV's Involvement with Family Life*. London: John Libbey.

Gunter, B. and J.M. Wober (1988) *Violence on Television: What Viewers Think*. London: John Libbey.

Gurevitch, M. and M. Levy (1986) 'Information and Meaning: Audience Explanations of Social Issues', in M. Robinson and M. Levy (eds), *The Main Source*, pp. 159–175. Beverly Hills, CA: Sage.

Gustafsson, K.E. and S. Hadenius (1976) *Swedish Media Policy*. Stockholm: Swedish Institute.

Habermas, J. (1989) *The Structural Transformation of the Public Sphere*. Cambridge: Polity Press.

Hachten, W.A. (1963) 'The Press as Reporter and Critic of Government', *Journalism Quarterly* 40: 12–18.

Hachten, W.A. (1981) *The World News Prism: Changing Media, Clashing Ideologies*. Ames, IA: Iowa State University Press.

Hackett, R.A. (1984) 'Decline of a Paradigm? Bias and Objectivity in News Media Studies', *Critical Studies in Mass Communication* 1: 229–259.

Hadenius, S. (1983) 'The Rise and Fall of the Swedish Party Press', *Communication Research* 10: 287–310.

Hadenius, S. (1992) 'Vulnerable Values in a Changing Political and Media System', in J. Blumler (ed.), *Television and the Public Interest*, pp. 112–130. London: Sage.

Hagerstrand, T. (1986) 'Decentralization and Radio Broadcasting', *European Journal of Communication* 1(2): 7–26.

Haiman, F.S. (1987) *Citizen Access to the Media: A Cross-cultural Analysis of Four Democratic Societies*. Evanston, IL: Northwestern University Research Monographs.

Hale, F.D. (1978) 'Press Releases vs. Newspaper Coverage of California Supreme Court Decisions', *Journalism Quarterly* 55: 696–702.

Hale, F.D. (1988) 'Editorial Diversity and Concentration', in R. Picard, M. McCombs, J.P. Winter and S. Lacy (eds), *Press Concentration and Monopoly*, pp. 161–176. Norwood, NJ: Ablex.

Hall, S. (1973) 'The Determination of News Photos', in S. Cohen and J. Young (eds), *The Manufacture of News*, pp. 176–190. London: Constable.

Hall, S. (1977) 'Culture, the Media and the Ideological Effect', in J. Curran, M. Gurevitch and J. Woollacott (eds), *Mass Communication and Society*, pp. 315–348. London: Arnold.

Hall, S. (1980) 'Coding and Encoding in the Television Discourse', in S. Hall, D. Hobson, A. Lowe and P. Willis (eds), *Culture, Media, Language*, pp. 128–138. London: Hutchinson.

Hall, S., J. Clarke, C. Critcher and B. Roberts (1978) *Policing the Crisis*. London: Macmillan.

Hallin, D. (1986) *The 'Uncensored' War: the Media and Vietnam*. New York: Oxford University Press.

Halloran, J. (ed.) (1976) *Race as News*. Paris: UNESCO.

Halloran, J.D., P. Elliott and G. Murdock (1970) *Communications and Demonstrations*. Harmondsworth: Penguin.

Hankins, S.R. (1988) 'Freedom and Constraint in Objective Local News Coverage', *Newspaper Research Journal* 9(4): 85–98.

Hardenbergh, M. (1986) 'Promise vs. Performance: Four Public Access Channels in Connecticut, a Case Study', *Mass Communication Review* 13(1–3): 32–39.

Hardt, H. (1979) *Social Theories of the Press*. Beverly Hills, CA: Sage.

Harris, R. (1983) *Gotcha!: The Media, the Government and the Falklands Crisis*. London: Faber.

Harrison, M. (1985) *Television News: Whose Bias?* Hermitage: Policy Journals.

Hartley, J. (1982) *Understanding News*. London: Methuen.

Hartman, P. and C. Husband (1974) *Racism and Mass Media*. London: Davis Poynter.

Harvey, D. (1989) *The Condition of Postmodernity*. Oxford: Basil Blackwell.

Harvey, R.F. and V.A. Stone (1969) 'Television and Newspaper Front-Page Coverage of a Major News Story', *Journal of Communication* 19(2): 181–188.

Haskins, J.B. (1981) 'The Trouble with Bad News', *Newspaper Research Journal* 2(2): 3–16.

Haskins, J.B. and M.M. Miller (1984) 'The Effects of Bad News and Good News on a Newspaper's Image', *Journalism Quarterly* 61: 3–13, 65.

Head, S.W. (1954) 'Content Analysis of Television Drama Programs', *Quarterly Journal of Film and Radio* 9: 175–194.

Heffner, B. (1973) 'Communicatory Accuracy: Four Experiments', *Journalism Monographs* 30.

Held, V. (1970) *The Public Interest and Individual Interests*. New York: Basic Books.

Hemánus, P. (1976) 'Objectivity in News Transmission', *Journal of Communication* 26(4): 102–107.

Herman, E.S. (1982) *The Real Terror Network: Terrorism Fact and Propaganda*. Boston, MA: South End Press.

Herman, E.S. (1985) 'Diversity of News: "Marginalizing" the Opposition', *Journal of Communication* 35(3): 135–146.

Herman, E.S. (1986) 'Gatekeeper versus Propaganda Models', in P. Golding et al. (eds), *Communicating Politics*, pp. 171–196. Leicester: University of Leicester Press.

Herman, E.S. and N. Chomsky (1988) *Manufacturing Consent*. New York: Pantheon Books.

Hess, J.D. (1966) 'An Inquiry into the Meaning of "Social Responsibility" ', *Journalism Quarterly* 43: 325–327.

Hess, S. (1984) *The Government/Press Connection*. Washington, DC: Brookings Institution.

Hetherington, A. (1985) *News, Newspapers and Television*. London: Macmillan.

Hicks, R.G. (1981) 'How Much News is Enough?' *Newspaper Research Journal* 2(2): 58–67.

Hicks, R.G. and J.S. Featherston (1978) 'Duplication of Newspaper Content in Contrasting Ownership', *Journalism Quarterly* 55: 549–554.

Hill, D.B. (1981) 'Letter Opinion on ERA: A Test of the Newspaper Bias Hypothesis', *Public Opinion Quarterly* 45(3): 384–392.

Hirsch, F. and D. Gordon (1975) *Newspaper Money*. London: Hutchinson.

Hirsch, M. (1976) 'The Sins of Sears are not News in Chicago', *Columbia Journalism Review* 15(July): 29–30.

Hirsch, P.M. (1977) 'Occupational, Organizational and Institutional Models in Mass Communication Research' in Hirsch, P.M. (ed.), *Strategies for Communication Research*, pp. 13–42. Beverly Hills, CA: Sage.

Hocking, W.E. (1947) *Freedom of the Press: A Framework of Principle*. Chicago: University of Chicago Press.

Hodges, L.W. (1986) 'Defining Press Responsibility: A Functional Approach', in D. Elliott (ed.), *Responsible Journalism*, pp. 13–31. Beverly Hills, CA: Sage.

Hoffman-Riem, W. (1987) 'National Identity and Cultural Values: Broadcasting Safeguards', *Journal of Broadcasting* 31(1): 57–72.

Hoffman-Riem, W. (1992) 'Protecting Vulnerable Values in the German Broadcasting Order', in J.G. Blumler (ed.), *Television and the Public Interest*, pp. 43–60. London: Sage.

Hofstetter, C.R. (1976) *Bias in the News: Network Television Coverage of the 1972 Election Campaign*. Columbus, OH: Ohio State University Press.

Hoggart, R. (1957) *The Uses of Literacy*. London: Chatto and Windus.

Hollstein, M. (1978) 'Government and the Press: The Question of Subsidies', *Journal of Communication* 28(4): 46–53.

Holmes, D. (1986) *Governing the Press: Media Freedom in the U.S. and Great Britain*. Boulder, CO: Westview Press.

Holmes, S. (1990) 'Liberal Constraints on Private Power', in J. Lichtenberg (ed.), *Mass Media and Democracy*, pp. 21–65.

Holopainen, V. (ed.) (1987) *Case Studies in International Norms and Journalism*. Tampere: University of Tampere Department of Mass Communication and Journalism.

Holsti, O. (1969) *Content Analysis for the Social Sciences and Humanities*. Reading, MA: Addison-Wesley.

Holz-Bacha, C. (1991) 'The Road to Commercialization: From Public Monopoly to a Dual Broadcasting System in Germany', *European Journal of Communication* 6(2): 223–233.

Homet, R.S., Jr (1979) *Politics, Cultures and Communication: European vs. American Approaches to Communication Policymaking*. New York: Praeger.

Hopple, G.W. (1982) 'International News Coverage in Two Elite Newspapers', *Journal of Communication* 32(1): 61–74.

Horton, P.C. (ed.) (1978) *Third World and Press Freedom*. New York: Praeger.

Hoskins, C. and S.M. McFadyen (1989) 'TV in the New Broadcasting Environment: Public Policy Lessons from the Canadian Experience', *European Journal of Communication* 4(2): 173–190.

Howitt, D. and G. Cumberbatch (1975) *Mass Media, Violence and Society*. New York: John Wiley.

Hughes, H.M. (1940) *News and the Human Interest Story*. Chicago: Chicago University Press.

Hulten, O. (1984) *Mass Media and State Support in Sweden*. Stockholm: Sweden Books.

Hulteng, J. (1969) 'Public Conceptions of Influences on Editorial Page Views', *Journalism Quarterly* 46: 362–364.

Hutchins, R. (1947) *A Free and Responsible Press: Commission on Freedom of the Press*. Chicago: University of Chicago Press.

Hynds, E.C. (1982) 'How Distinctive are South, Southern Newspapers Today?', *Newspaper Research Journal* 3(2): 32–37.

Ickes, H.L. (1939) *America's House of Lords: An Inquiry into the Freedom of the Press*. New York: Harcourt, Brace.

Immerwahr, J. and J. Doble (1982) 'Public Attitudes toward Freedom of the Press', *Public Opinion Quarterly* 46(2): 177–187.

Ishikawa, S. and Y. Muramatsu (1991) 'Quality Assessment of Broadcast Programming', *Studies of Broadcasting* 27: 207–220.

Iyengar, S. and D.R. Kinder (1987) *News that Matters: Television and American Opinion*. Chicago: University of Chicago Press.

Jacklin, P. (1978) 'Representative Diversity', *Journal of Communication* 28(2): 85–88.

Jackson, I. (1971) *The Provincial Press and the Community*. Manchester: Manchester University Press.

Jackson, K.M. (1982) 'Local Community Orientations of Suburban Newspaper Subscribers', *Newspaper Research Journal* 3(3): 52–59. See also 2(3): 42–49.

Jaehnig, S., M. Fico and D.H. Weaver (1981) 'Crime Reporting', *Journal of Communication* 32(1): 88–96.

Jaffe, D.L. (1989) 'Development of a Conformity Index to Assess Network TV News', *Journalism Quarterly* 66(3): 662–669.

Jamieson, K.H. and K.K. Campbell (1983) *The Interplay of Influence: Mass Media and their Publics in News, Advertising, Politics*. Belmont, CA: Wadsworth.

Janowitz, M. (1952) *The Community Press in an Urban Setting*. Glencoe, IL: Free Press.

Janowitz, M. (1975) 'Professional Models in Journalism: The Gatekeeper and the Advocate', *Journalism Quarterly* 52: 618–626.

Jansen, S.C. (1988) *Censorship*. New York: Oxford University Press.

Jansen, S.C., J. Leftwitch and J.R. Dasin (eds) (1982) *Press Control Around the World*. New York: Praeger.

Jensen, K.B. (1991) 'When is Meaning? Communication Theory, Pragmatism and Mass Reception', in J. Anderson (ed.), *Communication Yearbook 14*, pp. 3–32. Newbury Park, CA: Sage.

Johnson, K.G. (1963) 'Dimensions of Judgment of Science News Stories', *Journalism Quarterly* 40: 315–322.

Johnson, N. (1987) 'Regulating American Style', *Intermedia* 15(4/5): 31–33.

Johnstone, J. (1976) 'Organizational Constraints on Newswork', *Journalism Quarterly* 53: 5–13.

Johnstone, J.W.C., E.J. Slavski and W.W. Bowman (1976) *The News People*. Urbana, IL: University of Illinois Press.

Jones, J.C. (1980) *Mass Media Codes of Ethics and Councils: A Comparative International Study on Professional Standards*. Paris: UNESCO.

de Jong, A.S. and B.J. Bates (1991) 'Channel Diversity in Cable TV', *Journal of Broadcasting* 35(2): 159–166.

Jowett, G. and V. O'Donnell (1986) *Propaganda and Persuasion*. Beverly Hills, CA: Sage.

Kalven, H. (1967) 'Broadcasting, Public Policy and the First Amendment', *Journal of Law and Economics* 10: 15–30.

Kanno, A. (1972) *Evaluative Encoding of the New York Times and London Times during Selected African Crises*. Ann Arbor, MI: Microfilms.

Kariel, H.G. and L.A. Rosenvall (1981) 'Analyzing News Origin Profiles of Canadian Daily Newspaper', *Journalism Quarterly* 58: 254–259.

Kariel, H.G. and L.A. Rosenvall (1983) 'Cultural Affinity Displayed in Canadian Daily Newspapers', *Journalism Quarterly* 60: 431–436.

Katz, E., H. Adoni and P. Parness (1977) 'Remembering the News – What the Picture adds to Recall', *Journalism Quarterly* 54: 231–239.

Katz, E., M. Gurevitch and H. Haas (1973) 'On the Use of Mass Media for Important Things', *American Sociological Review* 28: 164–181.

Katz, E. and G. Wedell (1977) *Broadcasting in the Third World*. Cambridge, MA: Harvard University Press.

Keane, J. (1991) *The Media and Democracy*. Cambridge: Polity Press.

Kelley, D. and R. Donway (1990) 'Liberalism and Free Speech', in J. Lichtenberg (ed.), *Democracy and the Mass Media*, pp. 66–101. Cambridge: Cambridge University Press.

Kellner, D. (1990) *Television and the Crisis of Democracy*. Boulder, CO: Westview Press.

Kellner, P. and R.M. Worcester (1982) 'Electoral Perceptions of Media Stances' in R. Worcester and M. Harrop (eds), *Political Communication*, pp. 47–63. London: Allen and Unwin.

Kelly, M. and T. Mitchell (1981) 'TV and National Terrorism in the Western Elite Press', *Political Communication and Persuasion* 1: 269–296.

Kent, T. (1981) *Royal Commission on Newspapers Report*. Ottawa: Canadian Government Publishing Centre.

Kepplinger, H.M (1983) 'Visual Biases in Television Campaign Coverage', in F. Wartella, C. Whitney and S. Windahl (eds), *Mass Communication Review Yearbook*, vol. 4, pp. 391–405. Beverly Hills, CA: Sage.

Kepplinger, H.M. and H. Roth (1979) 'Creating a Crisis: German Mass Media and the Oil Supply in 1973–4', *Public Opinion Quarterly* 43: 285–296.

Kerner Commission (1969) *National Commission on the Causes and Prevention of Violence*. Washington, DC: GPO.

Kerrick, J.S., T.A. Anderson and L.B. Swales (1964) 'Balance and the Writer's Attitude in News Stories and Editorials', *Journalism Quarterly* 41: 207–215.

Kivikuru, U. and T. Varis (1985) *Approaches to International Communication*. Helsinki: Finnish National UNESCO Commission.

Klein, M.W. and N. Maccoby (1954) 'Newspaper Objectivity in the 1952 Campaign', *Journalism Quarterly* 31: 285–296.

Kleinsteuber, H. and U. Sonnenberg (1990) 'Beyond Public Service and Private Profit:

International Experience with Non-Commercial Local Radio', *European Journal of Communication* 5(1): 87–106.

Knight, G. and T. Dean (1982) 'Myth and the Structure of News', *Journal of Communication* 32(2): 144–161.

Knutson, A.L. (1948) 'The Commission vs. the Press', *Public Opinion Quarterly* 12(1): 130–135.

Kocher, D.J. and E.F. Shaw (1981) 'Newspaper Inaccuracies and Reader Perception of Bias', *Journalism Quarterly* 58: 471–474.

Kocher, R. (1986) 'Bloodhounds or Missionaries: Role Definitions of German and British Journalists', *European Journal of Communication* 1(1): 43–64.

Kornhauser, W. (1960) *The Politics of Mass Society*. London: Routledge and Kegan Paul.

Krugman, D.M. and L.N. Reid (1980) 'The "Public Interest" as Defined by FCC Policy Makers', *Journal of Broadcasting* 24(3): 311–325.

Kumar, C. (1975) 'Holding the Middle Ground', *Sociology* 9(3): 67–88.

Lacy, S. (1987) 'The Effects of Intracity Competition on Daily Newspaper Content', *Journalism Quarterly* 64: 281–290.

Lacy, S. and D. Matusik (1984) 'Dependence on Organization and Beat Sources for Story Ideas: A Case Study of Four Newspapers', *Newspaper Research Journal* 5(2): 9–16.

Lahav, P. (ed.) (1985) *Press Law in Modern Democracies*. London: Longman.

Lambeth, E. (1986) *Committed Journalism: An Ethic for the Profession*. Bloomington, IN: Indiana University Press.

Lang, K. and G.E. Lang (1953) 'The Unique Perspective of Television and its Effect', *American Sociological Review* 18(1): 103–112.

Larson, J.F. (1984) *Television's Window on the World: International Affairs Coverage of the U.S. Networks*. Norwood, NJ: Ablex.

Larson, J.F. (1986) 'Television and U.S. Foreign Policy: The Case of the Iran Hostage Crisis', *Journal of Communication* 36(4): 108–136.

Lasswell, H.D., D. Lerner and I. de S. Pool (1952) *The Comparative Study of Symbols*. Stanford, CA: Stanford University Press.

Lawrence, G.C. and D.L. Grey (1969) 'Subjective Inaccuracies in Local News Reporting', *Journalism Quarterly* 46: 753–757.

Lazarsfeld, P. (1941) 'Administrative and Critical Communications Research', *Studies in Philosophy and Social Sciences* 9.

Lazarsfeld, P., B. Berelson and H. Gaudet (1944) *The People's Choice*. New York: Columbia University Press.

LeDuc, D.R. (1982) 'Deregulation and the Dream of Diversity', *Journal of Communication* 32(4): 164–178.

Lee, B. (1988) 'Pro-social Content on Prime Time TV', in O. Oskamp (ed.), *Television as a Social Issue*, pp. 238–246. Newbury Park, CA: Sage.

Lee, R.S.H. (1978) 'Credibility of Newspaper and T.V. News', *Journalism Quarterly* 55: 282–287.

Lefever, E.W. (1976) *Television and National Defense: An Analysis of News*. Washington, DC: Brookings Institution.

Leggatt, T. (1991) 'Identifying the Undefinable', *Studies of Broadcasting* 27: 113–132.

Lehman, C. (1984) 'Meeting Readers' Multiple Needs'. Research Report. New York: Newspaper Advertising Bureau Inc.

Leiss, W., S. Kline and S. Jhally (1986) *Social Communication in Advertising*. Toronto: Methuen.

Lemert, J.B. (1974) 'Content Duplication by the Networks in Competing Evening Newscasts', *Journalism Quarterly* 51: 238–244.

Lemert, J.B. (1989) *Criticizing the Media*. Newbury Park, CA: Sage.

Lemert, J.B. and M.G. Ashman (1983) 'Extent of Mobilizing Information in Opinion and News Magazines', *Journalism Quarterly* 60: 657–662.

Lemert, J.B. and R.J. Cook (1982) 'Mobilizing Information in Broadcast Editorials and "Free Speech" Messages', *Journal of Broadcasting* 27(1): 493–496.

Lemert, J.B., B.N. Mitzman, M.A. Siether, R. Hackett and R.H. Cook (1977) 'Journalists and Mobilizing Information', *Journalism Quarterly* 54: 721–726.

Lemon, J. (1977) 'Women and Blacks on Prime-Time Television', *Journal of Communication* 27(4): 70–79.

Lester, M. (1973) 'Generating Newsworthiness', *American Sociological Review* 45: 984–994.

Levin, H.J. (1971) 'Program Duplication, Diversity and Effective Viewer Choice: Some Empirical Findings', *American Economic Review* 61(2): 81–88.

Levin, H.J. (1986) 'U.S. Broadcast Deregulation: A Case of Dubious Evidence', *Journal of Communication* 36(1): 25–40.

Levy, M.R. (1978) 'The Audience Experience with Television News', *Journalism Monographs* 55.

Leymore, V. (1975) *Hidden Myth: Structure and Symbolism in Advertising.* London: Heinemann.

Lichtenberg, J. (ed.) (1990) *Democracy and the Mass Media.* Cambridge: Cambridge University Press.

Lichtenberg, J. (1991) 'In Defense of Objectivity', in J. Curran and M. Gurevitch (eds), *Mass Media and Society*, pp. 216–231. London: Arnold.

Lichter, S.R. and S. Rothman (1986) *The Media Elite: America's New Powerbrokers.* Bethesda, MD: Adler and Adler.

Lichty, L.W. and G.A. Bailey (1978) 'Reading the Wind: Reflections on Content Analysis of Broadcast News', in W.C. Adams and F. Schreibman (eds), *Television Network News*, pp. 111–138. Washington, DC: George Washington University.

Lieberman, J.B. (1953) 'Restating the Concept of Freedom of the Press', *Journalism Quarterly* 30: 131–138.

Liebes, T. and E. Katz (1986) 'Patterns of Involvement in TV Fiction', *European Journal of Communication* 1(2): 151–172.

Lippman, W. (1921) *Public Opinion.* New York: Harcourt Brace.

Litman, B.R. (1979) 'The Television Networks, Competition and Program Diversity', *Journal of Broadcasting* 23(4): 393–409.

Litman, B.R. and J. Bridges (1986) 'An Economic Analysis of Daily Newspaper Performance', *Newspaper Research Journal* 7(3): 9–26.

Locke, John (1681/1965) *Two Treatises of Government.* New York: Mentor.

Luttberg, N.R. (1983) 'News Consensus: Do U.S. Newspapers Mirror Society's Happenings?', *Journalism Quarterly* 60: 484–488, 578.

Lynch, M.D. (1968) 'The Measurement of Human Interest', *Journalism Quarterly* 45: 226–236.

Lynch, M.D. and A. Effendi (1964) 'Editorial Treatment of India in the New York Times', *Journalism Quarterly* 41: 430–432.

Lynch, M.D., B.A. Kent and R.P. Carlson (1967) 'The Meaning of Human Interest: Four Dimensions of Judgement', *Journalism Quarterly* 44: 673–678.

McBride, S. (1980) *Many Voices One World.* London: UNESCO/Kogan Page.

McCombs, M.E. (1967) 'Editorial Endorsements: A Study of Influence', *Journalism Quarterly* 44: 545–548.

McCombs, M.E. (1983) 'Newspapers and the Civic Culture', *Newspaper Research Journal* 4(4): 5–10.

McCombs, M.E. (1987a) 'Effect of Monopoly in Cleveland on Diversity of Newspaper Content', *Journalism Quarterly* 64(4): 740–744, 792.

McCombs, M.E. (1987b) 'Comparisons of Newspaper Content Under Competitive and Monopoly Conditions', in R. Picard, M. McCombs, J.P. Winter and S. Lacy (eds), *Press Concentration and Monopoly.* Norwood, NJ: Ablex.

McCombs, M.E. (1988) 'Concentration, Monopoly and Content', in R. Picard, M. McCombs, J.P. Winter and S. Lacy (eds), *Press Concentration and Monopoly*, pp. 129–137. Norwood, NJ: Ablex.

McCombs, M.E. and J.B. Mauro (1988) 'Predicting Newspaper Readership from Content Characteristics', *Newspaper Research Journal* 10(1): 25–30. See also *Journalism Quarterly* 54: 3–7, 49.

McCombs, M.E. and D.L. Shaw (1972) 'The Agenda-Setting Function of the Press', *Public Opinion Quarterly* 36(2): 176–187.

McCombs, M.E. and J.P. Winter (1981) 'Defining Local News', *Newspaper Research Journal* 3(1): 16–21.

McCormack, T. (1980) 'Feminism, Censorship and Sadomasochistic Pornography', in T. McCormack (ed.), *Studies in Communication*, vol. 1, pp. 37–61. Greenwich, CN: JAI Press.

McCoy, R.E. (1979) *Freedom of the Press, a Bibliocyclopedia: Ten Year Supplement (1967–1977)*. Carbondale, IL: University of Southern Illinois Press.

MacDonald, J.F. (1985) *Television and the Red Menace: The Video Road to Vietnam*. New York: Praeger.

McGranahan, D.V. and I. Wayne (1948) 'German and American Traits Reflected in Popular Drama', *Human Relations* 1(4): 429–455.

McGrath, K. (1980) 'Minneapolis Meets New Information Needs', *News Research for Better Newspapers*, ANPA Research Report no. 29.

McGrath, K. and C. Gaziano (1986) 'Dimensions of Media Credibility: Highlights of the 1985 ASNE Survey', *Newspaper Research Journal* 7(2): 55–68.

McGuire, W.J. (1974) 'Psychological Motives and Communication Gratifications', in J.G. Blumler and E. Katz (eds), *The Uses of Mass Communications*, pp. 167–196. Beverly Hills, CA: Sage.

McLeod, J.M., C.R. Bybee and J.A. Durall (1982) 'Evaluating Media Performance by Gratifications Sought and Received', *Journalism Quarterly* 59: 3–12.

McNair, B. (1988) *Images of the Enemy*. London: Routledge.

McPhail, T. (1981) *Electronic Colonialism*. Beverly Hills, CA: Sage.

McQuail, D. (1977) *Analysis of Newspaper Content*. Royal Commission on the Press, Research Studies, 4. London: HMSO.

McQuail, D. (1986a) 'Is Media Theory Adequate to the Challenge of the New Communication Technologies?' in M. Ferguson (ed.) *New Communication Technologies and the Public Interest*, pp. 1–17. London: Sage.

McQuail, D. (1986b) 'From Bias to Objectivity and Back: Concepts of News Performance and a Pluralistic Alternative', in T. McCormack (ed.), *Studies in Communication*, pp. 1–36. Greenwich, CT: JAI Press.

McQuail, D. (1987) *Mass Communication Theory*, 2nd edn. London: Sage.

McQuail, D. (1990) 'Caging the Beast: Constructing a Framework for the Analysis of Media Change in Western Europe', *European Journal of Communication* 5(2/3): 313–332.

McQuail, D. (1992) 'Vulnerable Values in Multi-Channel Systems: the Case of The Netherlands', in J. Blumler (ed.), *Television and the Public Interest*, pp. 96–111. London: Sage.

McQuail, D., J.G. Blumler and R. Brown (1972) 'The TV Audience: a Revised Perspective' in D. McQuail (ed.), *Sociology of Mass Communications*, pp. 135–165. Harmondsworth: Penguin.

McQuail, D. and J.J. van Cuilenburg (1983) 'Diversity as a Media Policy Goal', *Gazette* 31(3): 145–162.

Mandell, L.M. and D.L. Shaw (1973) 'Judging People in the News – Unconsciously – Effect of Camera Angle and Bodily Activity', *Journal of Broadcasting* 17: 352–362.

Mander, M.S. (1984) 'The Public Debate about Broadcasting in the Twenties: an Interpretive History', *Journal of Broadcasting* 28(2): 167–185.

Manoff, R.K. and M. Schudson (eds) (1987) *Reading the News*. New York: Pantheon.

Marquez, F.T. (1977) 'Advertising Content: Persuasion, Information or Intimidation?', *Journalism Quarterly* 54: 482–491.

Marquez, F.T. (1980) 'How Accurate are the Headlines?', *Journal of Communication* 30(3): 30–36.

Martell, M.U. and G.J. McCall (1964) 'Reality Orientation and the Pleasure Principle', in L. Dexter and D.M. White (eds), *People, Society and Mass Communication*, pp. 283–333. New York: Free Press.

Martin, L.J. (1981) 'Government and News Media', in D.D. Nimmo and K.R. Sanders (eds), *The Handbook of Political Communication*, pp. 445–465. Beverly Hills, CA: Sage.

Martin, W.P. and M.W. Singletary (1981) 'Newspaper Treatment of State Government Releases', *Journalism Quarterly* 58: 93–96.

Mattelart, A. (1984) *International Image Markets*. London: Comedia.

Mazzoleni, G. (1987) 'Media Logic and Party Logic in Campaign Coverage: The Italian General Election of 1983', *European Journal of Communication* 2(1): 81–103.

Meadow, R.G. (1973) 'Cross-media Comparison of Coverage of the 1972 Presidential Campaign', *Journalism Quarterly* 50: 482–488.

Meadow, R.G. (1981) 'The Political Dimension of Non-product Advertising', *Journal of Communication* 31(3): 69–82.

Melody, W.H. (1990) 'Communication Policy in the Global Information Economy', in M. Ferguson (ed.), *Public Communication: The New Imperatives*, pp. 16–39. London: Sage.

Merrill, J.C. (1965) 'How Time Stereotyped Three U.S. Presidents', *Journalism Quarterly* 42: 563–570.

Merrill, J. (1974) *The Imperatives of Freedom*. New York: Hastings House.

Meyer, P. (1983) *Editors, Publishers and Newspaper Ethics: A Report to the American Society of Newspaper Editors*. Washington, DC: ASNE.

Meyer, P. (1987) *Ethical Journalism*. New York: Longman

Meyer, P. (1988) 'A Workable Measure for Auditing Accuracy in Newspapers', *Newspaper Research Journal* 10(1): 39–52.

Meyrowitz, J. (1985) *No Sense of Place*. New York: Oxford University Press.

Miller, S.H. (1975) 'The Content of News Photos: Women's and Men's Roles', *Journalism Quarterly* 52: 70–75.

Miller, S.H. (1977) 'News Coverage of Congress: The Search for the Ultimate Spokesman', *Journalism Quarterly* 54: 454–465.

Miller, S.H. (1978) 'Reporters and Congressmen: Living in Symbiosis', *Journalism Monographs* 53.

Mills, C.W. (1956) *The Power Elite*. New York: Oxford University Press.

Mills, R.D. (1983) 'Newspaper Ethics: A Qualitative Study', *Journalism Quarterly* 60: 589–594.

Mitnick, B.M. (1980) *The Political Economy of Regulation: Creating, Designing, and Removing Regulatory Forms*. New York: Columbia University Press.

Molotch, M. and M.J. Lester (1974) 'News as Purposive Behavior', *American Sociological Review* 39: 101–112.

Montgomery, K.C. (1989) *Target: Prime Time: Advocacy Groups and the Struggle over Entertainment TV*. New York: Oxford University Press.

Morgan, M. (1986) 'TV and the Erosion of Regional Diversity', *Journal of Broadcasting* 30(2): 123–139.

Morin, V. (1976) 'Televised Current Events Sequences or a Rhetoric of Ambiguity', in *News and Current Events on TV*, pp. 172–184. Rome: Edizioni RAI.

Morris, R. (1980) 'Reporting for Duty: The Pentagon and the Press', *Columbia Journalism Review* July/Aug: 27–33.

Morrison, D. and H. Tumber (1988) *Journalists at War*. London: Sage.

Mowlana, H. (1985) *International Flow of Information: a Global Report and Analysis*. Reports and Papers on Mass Communications 99. Paris: UNESCO.

Murdock, G. (1984) 'Reporting the Riots', in J. Benyon (ed.), *Scarman and After*, pp. 73–95. Oxford: Pergamon.

Murdock, G. (1990) 'Redrawing the Map of the Communication Industries', in M. Ferguson (ed.), *Public Communication: The New Imperatives*, pp. 1–15. London: Sage.

Murphy, D. (1976) *Silent Watchdog*. London: Constable.

Nacos, B.L. (1990) *The Press, Presidents and Crisis*. New York: Columbia University Press.

Neuman, W.R. (1976) 'Patterns of Recall among Television News Viewers', *Public Opinion Quarterly* 40(1): 115–123.

Neuman, W.R. (1982) 'Television and American Culture: The Mass Medium and the Pluralist Audience', *Public Opinion Quarterly* 46(4): 471–487.

Neuman, W.R. (1986) *The Paradox of Mass Politics: Knowledge and Opinion in the American Electorate.* Cambridge, MA: Harvard University Press.

Nieuwenhuis, A.J. (1991) *Persvrijheid en Persbeleid.* Amsterdam: Otto Cramwinckel.

Nimmo, D.D. and J.E. Combs (1985) *Nightly Horrors: Crisis Coverage by Television Network News.* Knoxville, TN: University of Tennessee Press.

Nisbet, R. (1967) *The Sociological Tradition.* London: Heinemann.

Nixon, R.B. (1945) 'Concentration and Absenteeism in Daily Newspaper Ownership', *Journalism Quarterly* 22: 97–114.

Nixon, R.B. (1960) 'Factors Relating to Freedom in National Press Systems', *Journalism Quarterly* 37: 13–28.

Nixon, R.B. (1966) 'Trends in US Newspaper Ownership Concentration', *Gazette* 14(3): 181–193.

Nixon, R.B. and T. Hahn (1971) 'Concentration of Press Ownership: a Comparison of 32 Countries', *Journalism Quarterly* 48: 5–16.

Nixon, R.B. and R.L. Jones (1956) 'The Content of Non-competitive vs. Competitive Newspapers', *Journalism Quarterly* 33: 299–314.

Nordenstreng, K. (1974) *Informational Mass Communication.* Helsinki: Tammi.

Nordenstreng, K. (1984) *The Mass Media Declaration of UNESCO.* Norwood, NJ: Ablex.

Nordenstreng, K. and H. Topuz (eds) (1989) *Journalist: Status, Rights and Responsibilities.* Prague: IOJ.

Ogan, C.L. and S.A. Lafky (1983) '1981's Most Important Events as Seen by Reporters, Editors, Wire Services and Media Consumers', *Newspaper Research Journal* 5(1): 3–12.

O'Keefe, G. and K. Reid-Nash (1987) *Communication* 14: 147–163.

Olien, C.N., G.A. Donohue and P.J. Tichenor (1983) 'Structure, Communication and Social Power', in E. Wartella and C. Whitney (eds), *Mass Communication Review Yearbook,* vol. 3, pp. 455–461. Beverly Hills, CA: Sage.

Osgood, C.E., P. Tannenbaum and G. Suci (1957) *The Measurement of Meaning.* Urbana, IL: University of Illinois Press.

Ostgaard, E. (1965) 'Factors Affecting the Flow of News', *Journal of Peace Research* 1: 39–55.

Owen, B.M. (1975) *Economics of Freedom of Expression: Media Structure and the First Amendment.* Cambridge, MA: Ballinger.

Owen, B.M. (1977) 'Regulating Diversity: The Case of Radio Formats', *Journal of Broadcasting* 21(3): 305–319.

Owen, B.M. (1978) 'Diversity in Broadcasting: The Economic View of Programming', *Journal of Communication* 28(2): 43–47.

Owen, B.M. (1982) 'Radio and Television' in D.L. Brenner and W.L. Rivers (eds), *Free But Regulated: Conflicting Traditions in Media Law,* pp. 35–51. Ames, IA: Iowa State University Press.

Paletz, D.L., J.Z. Ayanian and P.A. Fozzard (1982) 'The I.R.A., the Red Brigades, and the F.A.L.N. in the New York Times', *Journal of Communication* 32(2): 162–171.

Paletz, D.L. and R. Dunn (1969) 'Press Coverage of Civil Disorders: A Case Study of Winston-Salem, 1967', *Public Opinion Quarterly* 33(3): 328–345.

Paletz, D. and M. Elson (1976) 'Television Coverage of Presidential Conventions', *Political Science Quarterly* 9: 109–131.

Paletz, D. and R. Entman (1981) *Media, Power, Politics.* New York: Free Press.

Palmgreen, P. (1979) 'Mass Media Use and Political Knowledge', *Journalism Monographs* 61.

Park, R. (1940) 'News as a Form of Knowledge', reprinted in R.H. Turner (ed.), *On Social Control and Collective Behavior,* pp. 32–52. Chicago: University of Chicago Press, 1967.

Pasadeos, Y. (1984) 'Application of Measures of Sensationalism to a Murdoch-Owned Daily in the San Antonio Market', *Newspaper Research Journal* 5(4): 9–18.

Pasadeos, Y., G. Key, S. Hall and C. Morville (1987) 'Information Content of Newspaper Advertisements', *Newspaper Research Journal* 8(3): 1–10.

Pasadeos, Y. and P. Renfro (1988) 'Rupert Murdoch's Style: The New York Post', *Newspaper Research Journal* 9(4): 25–34.

Patkus, J.P. (1984) 'The Newspaper Preservation Act: Why it Fails to Preserve Newspapers', *Akron Law Review* 17: 435–452.

Patterson, T.E. and R.D. McClure (1976) *The Unseeing Eye: The Myth of Television Power in National Politics.* New York: Paragon.

Peacock, A. (1986) *Committee on Financing the BBC.* Report. Cmnd 9824. London: HMSO.

Pearlin, L.I. and M. Rosenberg (1952) 'Propaganda Techniques in Institutional Advertising', *Public Opinion Quarterly* 16(1): 5–26.

Peers, F.W. (1975) 'Canadian Media Regulation', in G.J. Robinson and D.F. Theall (eds), *Studies in Canadian Broadcasting*, pp. 70–84. Montreal: McGill University.

Perry, D.K. (1987) 'The Image Gap: How International News Affects Perceptions of Nations', *Journalism Quarterly* 64: 416–421, 433.

Peterson, R. and D. Berger (1975) 'Cycles in Symbol Production: the Case of Popular Music', *American Sociological Review* 40: 158–173.

Peterson, S. (1979) 'Foreign News Gatekeepers and Criteria of Newsworthiness', *Journalism Quarterly* 56: 116–125.

Peterson, S. (1981) 'International News Selection by the Elite Press: A Case Study', *Public Opinion Quarterly* 45(2): 143–163.

Phillips, D. (1980) 'Airplane Accidents, Murder and Mass Media', *Social Forces* 58(4): 1001–1124.

Phillips, E.B. (1977) 'Approaches to Objectivity', in P.M. Hirsch (ed.), *Strategies for Communication Research*, pp. 63–78. Beverly Hills, CA: Sage.

Picard, R.G. (1985a) 'Patterns of State Intervention in Western Press Economics', *Journalism Quarterly* 62: 3–9.

Picard, R.G. (1985b) *The Press and the Decline of Democracy: The Democratic Socialist Response in Public Policy.* Westport, CN: Greenwood Press.

Picard, R.G. (1987) 'Evidence of a "Failing Newspaper" Under the Newspaper Preservation Act', *Newspaper Research Journal* 9(1): 73–82.

Picard, R.G. (1989) *Media Economics.* Newbury Park, CA: Sage.

Picard, R.G. (1991) 'News Coverage and the Contagion of Terrorism', in A.O. Alali and K.K. Eke (eds), *Media Coverage of Terrorism*, pp. 49–62. Newbury Park, CA: Sage.

Picard, R.G., M. McCombs, J.P. Winter and S. Lacy (1988) *Press Concentration and Monopoly.* Norwood, NJ: Ablex.

Picard, R.G. and R.S. Sheets (1986) *Terrorism and the Media: Research Bibliography.* Columbia, SC: AEJ.

Pilegge, J.C. Jr (1981) 'Two-Party Endorsements in a One-Party State', *Journalism Quarterly* 58: 449–453.

Pilkington, H. (1962) *Committee on Broadcasting (1960).* Report. Cmnd 1753. London: HMSO.

Poindexter, P.M. and C.A. Stroman (1981) 'Blacks and Television: A Review of the Research Literature', *Journal of Broadcasting* 25(2): 103–122.

Pool, I. de Sola (1984) *Technologies of Freedom.* Harvard, MA: Belknap Press.

Porter, M.J. (1983) 'Applying Semiotics to the Study of Selected Prime-Time Television Programs', *Journal of Broadcasting* 27(1): 69–75.

Poulos, R.W., E.A. Rubinstein and R.M. Liebert (1975) 'Positive Social Learning', *Journal of Communication* 25(4): 90–97.

Powe, L.A. (1987) *American Broadcasting and the First Amendment.* Berkeley, CA: University of California Press.

Powell, J.T. and W. Gair (eds) (1988) *Public Interest and the Business of Broadcasting: the Broadcast Industry Looks at Itself.* New York: Quorum Books.

Pragnell, A. (1985) *Television in Europe: Quality and Values at a Time of Change.* Manchester: European Media Institute.

Preston, E.H. (1990) 'Pornography and the Construction of Gender', in N. Signorielli and M. Morgan (eds), *Cultivation Analysis*, pp. 107–122. Newbury Park, CA: Sage.

Preston, W., E.S. Herman and H.I. Schiller (1989) *Hope and Folly: the US and Unesco 1945–1985.* Minneapolis: University of Minnesota Press.

Pride, R.A. and D.H. Clarke (1973) 'Race Relations in Television News', *Journalism Quarterly* 50: 319–328.

Pride, R.A. and B. Richards (1974) 'Denigration of Authority? TV News Coverage of the Student Movement', *Journal of Politics* 36: 637–660.

Pride, R.A. and G.L. Wamsley (1972) 'Symbol Analysis of Network Coverage of Laos Incursion', *Journalism Quarterly* 49: 635–640.

Prisuta, R.H (1977) 'The Impact of Media Concentration and Economic Factors of Broadcast Public Interest Programming', *Journal of Broadcasting* 21(3): 321–332.

Rachlin, A. (1988) *News as Hegemonic Reality*. New York: Praeger.

Rarick, G. and B. Hartman (1966) 'The Effects of Competition on One Daily Newspaper's Content', *Journalism Quarterly* 43: 459–463.

Real, M. (1989) *Super Media*. Newbury Park, CA: Sage.

Reese, S.D. (1984) 'Visual-Verbal Redundancy Effects on Television News Learning', *Journal of Broadcasting* 28(1): 79–87.

Reese, S.D. (1991) 'Setting the Media's Agenda', in J. Anderson (ed.), *Communication Yearbook 14*, pp. 309–340. Newbury Park, CA: Sage.

Renfro, P.C. (1979) 'Bias in Selection of Letters to the Editor', *Journalism Quarterly* 56: 822–826.

Repass, D.E. and S.H. Chaffee (1968) 'Administrative vs. Campaign Coverage of Two Presidents in Eight Partisan Dailies', *Journalism Quarterly* 45: 528–531.

Riffe, D. and E.F. Shaw (1982) 'Conflict and Consonance: Coverage of Third World in Two U.S. Papers', *Journalism Quarterly* 59: 617–626.

Rikardsson, G. (1978) *The Middle East Conflict in the Swedish Press*. Stockholm: Esselte Studium.

Rivers, W.L. and M.J. Nyhan (1973) *Aspen Notebook on Government and the Media*. New York: Praeger.

Roach, C. (1982) 'Mexican and U.S. News Coverage of the IPDC at Acapulco', *Journal of Communication* 32(3): 71–85.

Roberts, C.L. and S.H. Dickson (1984) 'Assessing Quality in Local T.V. News', *Journalism Quarterly* 61: 392–398.

Robinson, G.J. (1983) 'Changing Canadian and US Magazine Portrayals of Women and Work', in E. Wartella, C. Whitney and S. Windahl (eds), *Mass Communication Review Yearbook*, vol. 4, pp. 229–249. Beverly Hills, CA: Sage.

Robinson, J. (1972) 'Mass Communication and Information Diffusion', in F. Kline and P. Tichenor (eds), *Current Perspectives in Mass Communication Research*, pp. 71–93. Beverly Hills, CA: Sage.

Robinson, J. (1974) 'The Press as King-maker', *Journalism Quarterly* 51: 587–594.

Robinson, J.P. and M. Levy (1986) *The Main Source*. Newbury Park, CA: Sage.

Robinson, M.J. (1983) 'Just How Liberal is the News? 1980 Revisited', *Public Opinion* 6(1): 55–60.

Robinson, M.J. and A. Kohut (1988) 'Believability and the Press', *Public Opinion Quarterly* 52(2): 174–189.

Robinson, M.J. and M.M. Sheehan (1986) *Over the Wires and on TV*. New York: Russell Sage.

Rogers, E.M. and J.W. Dearing (1987) 'Agenda Setting Research', in C. Berger and S.H. Chaffee (eds), *Handbook of Communication Science*, pp. 555–594. Newbury Park, CA: Sage.

Romanow, W.I. and W.C. Soderlund (1979) 'The South American Press Acquisition of the Windsor Star: A Canadian Case Study of Change', *Gazette* 24: 255–270.

Rosenberg, B. and D.M. White (eds) (1957) *Mass Culture*. New York: Free Press.

Rosengren, K.E. (1977) 'International News: Four Types of Tables', *Journal of Communication* 27: 67–75.

Rosengren, K.E. (1980) 'Bias in News: Methods and Concepts' in C.G. Wilhoit and H. de Bock (eds), *Mass Communication Review Yearbook*, vol. 1, pp. 249–263. Beverly Hill, CA: Sage.

Rosengren, K.E. (1983) 'Communication Research: One Paradigm or Four?', *Journal of Communication* 33(3): 185–207.

Rosengren, K.E., M. Carlsson and Y. Tagerna (1991) 'Quality programming: Views from the North', *Studies in Broadcasting* 27: 21–80.
Rosengren, K.E., P. Palmgreen and L. Wenner (eds) (1985) *Media Gratification Research*. Newbury Park, CA: Sage.
Roshco, B. (1975) *Newsmaking*. Chicago: University of Chicago Press.
Roshier, R.J. (1973) 'The Selection of Crime News by the Press', in S. Cohen and J. Young (eds), *The Manufacture of News*, pp. 28–39. London: Constable.
Rosse, J.N. (1980) 'The Decline of Direct Newspaper Competition', *Journal of Communication* 30(2): 65–71.
Rosse, J.N. and J.N. Dertouzos (1979) 'The Evolution of One-Newspaper Cities', *Federal Trade Commission, Proceedings of the Symposium on Media Concentration*, vol. 3. Washington, DC.
Rosten, L.C. (1937) *The Washington Correspondents*. New York: Harcourt Brace.
Roszak, T. (1968) *The Making of a Counter Culture*. London: Faber and Faber.
Rowan, F. (1984) *Broadcast Fairness: Doctrine, Practice, Prospects*. New York: Longman.
Rowland, D. and M. Tracey (1990) 'Worldwide Challenges to Public Service Broadcasting', *Journal of Communication* 40(2): 8–27.
Royal Commission on the Press (RCP) (1949) Report. Cmd 7700. London: HMSO.
Royal Commission on the Press (RCP) (1977) Report. Cmnd 6810. London: HMSO.
Rubin, B. (1978) *Questioning Media Ethics*. New York: Praeger.
Rubin, B. (1980) *Small Voices and Great Trumpets: Minorities and the Media*. New York: Praeger.
Rubin, D.M. and M. Cunningham (eds) (1983) *War, Peace and the News Media*. New York: Gannett Foundation.
Rundell, H.A. and T.H. Heuterman (1978) *The First Amendment and Broadcasting: Press Freedom and Broadcast Journalism*. Pullman, WA: Washington State University.
Russo, F.D. (1971) 'A Study of Bias in TV Coverage of the Vietnam War 1969 and 1970', *Public Opinion Quarterly* 35: 539–543.
Rutkus, D.S. (1982) *The Public Trustee Concept in Broadcast Regulation*. Washington, DC: Congressional Research Series.
Ryan, J. and R.A. Peterson (1982) 'The Product Image', in J. Ettema and D.C. Whitney (eds), *Individuals in Mass Media Organizations*, pp. 11–32. Newbury Park, CA: Sage.
Ryan, M. (1979) 'Attitudes of Scientists and Journalists toward Media Coverage of Science News', *Journalism Quarterly* 56: 18–26, 53–54.
Ryan, M. and D. Owen (1977) 'An Accuracy Survey of Metropolitan Newspaper Coverage of Social Issues', *Journalism Quarterly* 54: 27–32.
Sachsman, D.B. (1976) 'Public Relations Influence on Coverage of Environment in San Francisco Area', *Journalism Quarterly* 53: 54–60.
Said, E.W. (1981) *Covering Islam: How the Media and the Experts Determine How We See the Rest of the World*. New York: Pantheon Books.
Salman, C.T. and J.S. Lee (1983) 'Perceptions of Newspaper Fairness: A Structural Approach', *Journalism Quarterly* 60: 663–670.
Scanlon, J. (1989) 'The Hostage Taker, the Terrorist and the Media: Partners in Crime', in L.M. Walters et al. (eds), *Bad Tidings: Communications and Catastrophe*. Hillsdale, NJ: LEA.
Scanlon, T.J. (1961) 'Media Coverage of Crisis: Better than Expected, Worse than Necessary', *Journalism Quarterly* 38: 441–452.
Scanlon, T.J. (1969) 'A New Approach to the Study of Newspaper Accuracy', *Journalism Quarterly* 49: 587–590.
Scherer, F.M. (1980) *Industrial Market Structure and Economic Performance*, 2nd edn. Chicago: Rand McNally.
Schiller, D. (1979) 'An Historical Approach to Objectivity and Professionalism in American News Reporting', *Journal of Communication* 29(4): 46–57.
Schiller, D. (1981) *Objectivity and the News*. Philadelphia, PA: University of Pennsylvania Press.
Schiller, H. (1969) *Mass Media and American Empire*. New York: Augustus M. Kelly.

Schlesinger, P. (1978) *Putting 'Reality' Together: BBC News*. London: Constable.

Schlesinger, P. (1986) 'Trading in Fictions: What do we Know about British TV Imports and Exports?', *European Journal of Communication* 1(3): 263–288.

Schlesinger, P. (1987) 'On National Identity', *Social Science Information* 25(2): 219–264.

Schlesinger, P. (1990) 'Rethinking the Sociology of Journalism' in M. Ferguson (ed.), *Public Communication: The New Imperatives*, pp. 61–83. London: Sage.

Schlesinger, P., G. Murdock and P. Elliott (1983) *Televising 'Terrorism': Political Violence in Popular Culture*. London: Comedia/Marion Boyars.

Schmid, A.P. and J. de Graaf (1982) *Violence as Communication*. Beverly Hills, CA: Sage.

Schmidt, B.C. (1976) *Freedom of the Press vs. Public Access*. New York: Praeger.

Schramm, W. (1955) 'Information Theory and Mass Communication', *Journalism Quarterly* 32: 131–146.

Schudson, M. (1978) *Discovering the News*. New York: Basic Books.

Schudson, M. (1982) 'The Politics of Narrative Form: The Emergence of News Conventions in Print and Television', *Daedalus* 3: 97–112.

Schulz, W. (1988) 'Mass Media and Reality'. Paper at Sommatie Conference, Veldhoven, Netherlands.

Schweitzer, J.C. and E. Goldman (1975) 'Does Newspaper Competition Make a Difference?', *Journalism Quarterly* 52: 706–710.

Seggar, J.F. and J.K. Hafen (1981) 'Television's Portrayals of Minorities and Women in Drama and Comedy Drama', *Journal of Broadcasting* 25(3): 277–288.

Seldes, G. (1938) *Lords of the Press*. New York: J. Messner.

Sentman, M.A. (1983) 'Black and White: Disparity in Coverage by *Life* Magazine from 1937 to 1972', *Journalism Quarterly* 60: 501–508.

Sepstrup, P. (1989a) 'Research into International Television Flows', *European Journal of Communication* 4(4): 393–408.

Sepstrup, P. (1989b) 'Transnationalization of Television in Western Europe', in C.W. Thomsen (ed.), *Cultural Transfer or Electronic Imperialism?*, pp. 99–136. Heidelberg: Carl Winter Universitätsverlag.

Seymour-Ure, C. (1974) *The Political Impact of Mass Media*. London: Constable.

Seymour-Ure, C. (1991) *The British Press and Broadcasting since 1945*. Oxford: Blackwell.

Shapiro, M. and W. Williams (1984) 'Civil Disturbance in Miami: Proximity and Conflict in Newspaper Coverage', *Newspaper Research Journal* 5(3): 61–69.

Shapiro, S.P. (1989) 'Caution! This Paper Has Not Been Fact Checked'. Working Paper. New York: Gannett Center, Columbia University.

Shaughnessy, H. and C.F. Cobo (1990) *The Cultural Obligations of Broadcasting*. Manchester: European Media Institute.

Shaw, D.L. (1961) 'News Bias and the Telegraph', *Journalism Quarterly* 38: 3–12.

Shaw, D.L. and M.E. McCombs (1977) *The Emergence of American Political Issues: The Agenda-Setting Function of the Press*. St Paul, MN: West Publishing Co.

Shaw, E.F. (1973) 'Media Credibility: Taking the Measure of a Measure', *Journalism Quarterly* 50: 306–311.

Shaw, M. and R. Carr-Hill (1991) 'Public Opinion, Media and Violence', *Gulf War Project No. 1*. Hull: University of Hull Centre for Security Studies.

Sheley, J.F. and C.D. Ashkins (1980) 'Crime News and Crime Views', *Public Opinion Quarterly* 45: 492–506.

Shoemaker, P.J. (1983) 'Bias and Source Attribution', *Newspaper Research Journal* 5(1): 25–32.

Shoemaker, P.J. (1984) 'Media Treatment of Deviant Political Groups', *Journalism Quarterly* 61: 66–75.

Shoemaker, P.J. (1991) *Communication Concepts 3: Gatekeeping*. Newbury Park, CA: Sage.

Shoemaker, P.J., T.K. Chang and N. Brendlinger (1987) 'Deviance as a Predictor of Newsworthiness – Coverage of International Events in the US Media', in M.I. McLaughlin (ed.), *Communication Yearbook*, vol. 10, pp. 348–365. Newbury Park, CA: Sage.

Shoemaker, P.J. and E.K. Mayfield (1987) 'Building a Theory of News Content: A Synthesis of Current Approaches', *Journalism Monographs* 103.

Siebert, F.S., T. Peterson and W. Schramm (1956) *Four Theories of the Press*. Urbana: University of Illinois Press.

Sigal, L.V. (1973) *Reporters and Officials*. Lexington, MA: D.C. Heath & Co.

Sigal, L.V. (1986) 'Who? Sources Make the News', in R.K. Manoff and M. Schudson (eds), *Reading the News*, pp. 9–37. New York: Pantheon Books.

Sigelman, L. (1973) 'Reporting the News: an Organizational Analysis', *American Journal of Sociology* 79: 132–151.

Signorielli, N. (1985) *Role Portrayal and Stereotyping on Television*. Westport, CT: Greenwood Press.

Signorielli, N. and M. Morgan (eds) (1990) *Cultivation Analysis*. Newbury Park, CA: Sage.

Sills, P.L. (1968) 'Public Interest', in *International Encyclopedia of the Social Sciences*, pp. 170–174. New York: Macmillan.

Simmons, B.K. (1991) 'U.S. News Magazines Labelling of Terrorists', in A.O. Alali and K.K. Eke (eds), *Media Coverage of Terrorism*, pp. 23–39. Newbury Park, CA: Sage.

Simmons, S.J. (1978) *The Fairness Doctrine and the Media*. Berkeley: University of California Press.

Singer, B.D. (1970) 'Violence, Protest and War in TV News', *Public Opinion Quarterly* 34: 611–616.

Singer, E. and P. Endreny (1987) 'Reporting Hazards: Their Benefits and Costs' *Journal of Communication*, 37(3): 10–41.

Siune, K. and W. Truetzschler (eds) (1992) *Dynamics of Media Politics*. London: Sage.

Slater, J.W. and M.E. McCombs (1969) 'Some Aspects of Broadcast News Coverage and Riot Participation', *Journal of Broadcasting* 3(4): 367–370.

Smith, A. (1974a) *The Shadow in the Cave*. London: Allen and Unwin.

Smith, A. (1974b) *The British Press Since the War*. Newton Abbot: David and Charles.

Smith, A. (1974c) *British Broadcasting*. Newton Abbot: David and Charles.

Smith, A. (1977) 'Subsidies and the Press in Europe', *Political and Economic Planning* 43. London: PEP.

Smith, A. (1989) 'The Public Interest', *Intermedia* 17(2): 10–24.

Smith, R.F. (1984) 'How Consistently do Readability Tests Measure the Difficulty of Newswriting?' *Newspaper Research Journal* 5(4): 1–8.

Smith, R.R. (1979) 'Mythic Elements in Television News', *Journal of Communication* 20(1): 75–82.

Sparkes, V.M. (1983) 'Public Perception of, and Reaction to, Multi-Channel Cable Television Service', *Journal of Broadcasting* 27(2): 163–175.

Sparkes, V.M. and J.P. Winter (1980) 'Public Interest in Foreign News', *Gazette* 26: 149–170.

Sparks, C. and M. Campbell (1987) 'The "Inscribed Reader" of the British Quality Press', *European Journal of Communication* 2(4): 455–472.

Sproule, J.M. (1991) 'Propaganda and American Ideological Critique', in J. Anderson (ed.), *Communication Yearbook 14*, pp. 211–238. Newbury Park, CA: Sage.

Sreberny-Mohammadi, A. (1984) 'The "World of News" Study', *Journal of Communication* 34(1): 121–134.

Stamm, K.R. (1985) *Newspaper Use and Community Ties: Toward a Dynamic Theory*. Norwood, NJ: Ablex.

Steiner, P.O. (1952) 'Program Patterns and Preferences, and the Workability of Competition in Radio Programming', *Quarterly Journal of Economics* 66: 194–223.

Stempel, G.H. III (1973) 'Effects on Performance of a Cross-Media Monopoly', *Journalism Monographs* 29.

Stempel, G.H. III (1981) 'Readability of Six Kinds of Content in Newspapers', *Newspaper Research Journal* 3(1): 32–37.

Stephens, M. (1986) *Broadcast News*. New York: Holt, Rinehart and Winston.

Stevenson, R.L. and M.T. Greene (1980) 'A Reconsideration of Bias in the News', *Journalism Quarterly* 57: 115–121.

Stevenson, R.L. and D.L. Shaw (1973) 'Untwisting *The News Twisters*: A Replication of Efron's Study', *Journalism Quarterly* 50: 211–219.

Stevenson, R.L. and D.L. Shaw (eds) (1984) *Foreign News and the New World Information Order*. Ames, IA: Iowa State University Press.

Stoler, P. (1986) *The War against the Press*. New York: Dodd Mead.

Stone, G. (1987) *Examining Newspapers*. Newbury Park, CA: Sage.

Stone, G.C. and E. Grusin (1984) 'Network T.V. as the Bad News Bearer', *Journalism Quarterly* 61: 517–523, 592.

Stone, G.C., B. Hartley and D. Jensen (1987) 'Local Television News and the Good/Bad Dyad', *Journalism Quarterly* 64: 37–44.

Sullivan, D.F. (1985) 'Comprehensiveness of Press Coverage of a Food Irradiation Proposal', *Journalism Quarterly* 62: 832–837.

Swanson, D.L. (1987) 'Gratification Seeking, Media Exposure, and Audience Interpretations: Some Directions for Research', *Journal of Broadcasting* 31(3): 237–254.

Syvertsen, T. (1991) 'Public Television in Crisis: Critiques Compared in Norway and Britain', *European Journal of Communication* 6(1): 95–114.

Tankard, J.W. and K. Peirce (1982) 'Alcohol Advertising and Magazine Editorial Content', *Journalism Quarterly* 59: 312–315.

Tankard, J.W. and M. Ryan (1974) 'News Source Perceptions of Accuracy of Science Coverage', *Journalism Quarterly* 51: 219–225.

Tannenbaum, P.H. and M.D. Lynch (1960) 'Sensationalism: The Concept and its Measurement', *Journalism Quarterly* 37: 381–392.

Tannenbaum, P.H. and M.D. Lynch (1962) 'Sensationalism: Some Objective Correlates', *Journalism Quarterly* 39: 317–323.

Taylor, W.L. (1953) 'Cloze Procedure: A New Tool for Measuring Readability', *Journalism Quarterly* 30: 415–433.

Thayer, L., R. Johannesen and H. Hardt (eds) (1979) *Ethics, Morality and the Media: Reflection on American Culture*. New York: Hastings House.

Thomsen, C.W. (1989) *Cultural Transfer or Electronic Imperialism?* Heidelberg: Carl Winter Universitätsverlag.

Thoveron, G. (1986) 'European Televised Women', *European Journal of Communication* 1(3): 289–300.

Thrift, R.R. Jr (1977) 'How Chain Ownership Affects Editorial Vigor of Newspapers', *Journalism Quarterly* 54: 327–331.

Thurston, C.M. (1981) 'A Comparison of Attitudes about Social Responsibility among Dutch and American Journalists and Lawmakers', *Gazette* 27: 123–138.

Tiemens, R.K. (1970) 'Some Relations of Camera Angle to Communicator Credibility', *Journal of Broadcasting* 14: 483–490.

Tiemens, R.K., M.O. Sillars, D.C. Alexander and D. Werling (1988) 'TV Coverage of Jesse Jackson's Speech to the 1984 Democratic Convention', *Journal of Broadcasting* 32(1): 1–22.

Tillinghast, W.A. (1983) 'Source Control and Evaluation of Newspaper Inaccuracies', *Newspaper Research Journal* 5(1): 13–24.

Tomlinson, J. (1991) *Cultural Imperialism*. London: Pinter.

Tracey, M. (1986) *The Public Service Idea in Broadcasting*. London: Broadcasting Research Unit.

Trenaman, J.S. (1967) *Communication and Comprehension*. London: Hutchinson.

Trenaman, J.S. and D. McQuail (1961) *Television and the Political Image*. London: Methuen.

Trim, K., G. Pizante and J. Yaraskavitch (1983) 'The Effect of Monopoly on the News: A Before and After Study of Two Canadian One-Newspaper Towns', *Canadian Journal of Communication* 9(3): 33–56.

Tuchman, G. (1978) *Making the News: A Study in the Construction of Reality*. New York: Free Press.

Tuchman, G., A.K. Daniels and J. Benet (1978) *Hearth and Home: Images of Women in Mass Media*. New York: Oxford University Press.

Tumber, H. (1982) *Television and the Riots*. London: British Film Institute.

Tumin, M.M. and W. Plotch (eds) (1977) *Pluralism in a Democratic Society*. New York: Praeger.

Tunstall, J. (1970) *The Westminster Lobby Correspondents*. London: Routledge.

Tunstall, J. (1971) *Journalists at Work*. London: Constable.

Tunstall, J. (1977a) *The Media are American*. London: Constable.

Tunstall, J. (1977b) 'Letters to the Editor', in Royal Commission on the Press, *Studies in the Press*, Working Paper 3, pp. 203–258. Cmnd 6810–4. London: HMSO.

Tunstall, J. (1991) 'A Media Industry Perspective', in J. Anderson (ed.), *Communication Yearbook 14*, pp. 163–186. Newbury Park, CA: Sage.

Turk, J.V.S. (1986a) 'Information Subsidies and Media Content: A Study of Public Relations Influence on the News', *Journalism Monographs* 100.

Turk, J.V.S. (1986b) 'Public Relations' Influence on the News', *Newspaper Research Journal* 7(4): 15–28.

Turow, J. (1974) 'Advising and Ordering: Daytime, Prime Time', *Journal of Communication* 24(2): 138–141.

Turow, J. (1981) *Entertainment, Education and the Hard Sell: Three Decades of Network Children's Television*. New York: Praeger.

Turow, J. (1984) *Media Industries: The Production of News and Entertainment*. New York: Longman.

UNESCO (1975) *Getting the Message Across: An Inquiry into Successes and Failures of Cross-cultural Communication in the Contemporary World*. Paris: UNESCO.

UNESCO (1977) *Ethnicity and the Media: An Analysis of Media Reporting in the United Kingdom, Canada, and Ireland*. Paris: UNESCO.

Varis, T. (1984) 'The International Flow of Television Programs', *Journal of Communication* 34(1): 143–152.

Varis, T. (ed.) (1986) *Peace and Communication*. San Jose, Costa Rica: Editorial Universidad para La Paz.

Veljanovski, C. (1989) *Freedom in Broadcasting*. London: Institute of Economic Affairs.

Vestergaard, T. and K. Schrøder (1985) *The Language of Advertising*. Oxford: Blackwell.

Vilanilam, J. (1989) *Reporting a Revolution*. New Delhi: Sage.

Wackman, D.B., D.M. Gillmor, C. Gaziano and E.E. Dennis (1975) 'Chain Newspaper Autonomy as Reflected in Presidential Campaign Endorsements', *Journalism Quarterly* 52: 411–420.

Wagenberg, R.H. and W.C. Soderlund (1975) 'The Influence of Chain-Ownership on Editorial Comment in Canada', *Journalism Quarterly* 52: 93–98.

Wakshlag, J. and W.J. Adams (1985) 'Trends in Program Variety in the Prime Time Access Rule', *Journal of Broadcasting* 29(1): 23–34.

Walters, L.M., L. Wilkins and T. Walters (eds) (1989) *Bad Tidings: Communications and Catastrophe*. Hillsdale, NJ: LEA.

Wartella, E. (1988) 'The Public Context of Debates about TV and Children', in S. Oskamp (ed.), *Television as a Social Issue, Applied Social Psychology Annual*, pp. 59–68. Newbury Park, CA: Sage.

Watt, J.H. and R. Krull (1974) 'An Information Theory Measure for Television Programming', *Communication Research* 1(1): 44–68.

Weaver, D.H. (1979) 'Estimating the Value of Newspaper Content for Readers: A Comparison of Two Methods', *Newspaper Research Journal* Prototype: 7–13.

Weaver, D.H., J.M. Buddenbaum and J.E. Fair (1985) 'Press Freedom, Media and Development, 1950–1979: A Study of 34 nations', *Journal of Communication* 35(2): 104–117.

Weaver, D.H. and M.E. McCombs (1980) 'Journalism and Social Sciences: A New Relationship?', *Public Opinion Quarterly* 44(4): 477–494.

Weaver, D.H., M. McCombs, D. Graber and C. Eyal (1981) *Media Agenda Setting in a Presidential Election: Issues, Images, and Interest*. New York: Praeger.

Weaver, D.H. and L.E. Mullins (1975) 'Content and Format Characteristics of Competing Daily Newspapers', *Journalism Quarterly* 52: 257–264.

Weaver, D.H. and G.C. Wilhoit (1979) 'Personal Needs and Media Use', *News Research for Better Newspapers*, ANPA Report no. 21.

Weaver, D.H. and G.C. Wilhoit (1980) 'News Media Coverage of U.S. Senators in Four Congresses, 1953–1974', *Journalism Monographs* 67.

Weaver, D.H. and G.C. Wilhoit (1986) *The American Journalist*. Bloomington, IN: University of Indiana Press.

Weaver, P. (1972) 'Is Television News Biased?', *Public Interest* 26: 57–74.

Weimann, G. (1983) 'The Theatre of Terror: Effects of Press Coverage', *Journal of Communication* 33(1): 38–45.

Weimann, G. (1987) 'Media Events: The Case of International Terrorism', *Journal of Broadcasting* 31(1): 21–39.

Weis, R.J. and K.R. Stamm (1982) 'How Specific News Interests are Related to States of Settling in a Community', *Newspaper Research Journal* 3(3): 60–68.

Wenner, L.A. (1985) 'The Nature of News Gratifications', in K.E. Rosengren and P. Palmgreen (eds), *Media Gratification Research*, pp. 171–193. Newbury Park, CA: Sage.

Westen, T. (1978) 'Barriers to Creativity', *Journal of Communication* 28: 36–42.

Westerståhl, J. (1983) 'Objective News Reporting', *Communication Research* 10: 403–424.

Westerståhl, J. and F. Andersson (1991) 'Chernobyl and the Nuclear Power Issue in Sweden', *International Journal of Public Opinion Research* 3: 115–131.

Westley, B.H. and C.E. Higsbie (1963) 'The News Magazines and the 1960 Conventions', *Journalism Quarterly* 40: 523–531, 647.

Westley, B.H. and M. MacLean (1957) 'A Conceptual Model of Mass Communication Research', *Journalism Quarterly* 34: 31–38.

White, D.M. (1950) ' "The Gatekeeper": A Case Study in the Selection of News', *Journalism Quarterly* 27(4): 383–390.

White, L.L. and R.D. Leigh (1946) *Commission on Freedom of the Press: Peoples Speaking to Peoples*. Chicago: University of Chicago Press.

Whitney, D.C., M. Fritzler, S. Jones, S. Mazzarella and L. Rakow (1989) 'Geographic and Source Biases in Network TV News 1982–1984', *Journal of Broadcasting* 33(2): 159–174.

Wieten, J. (1979) 'Media pluralism', *Media, Culture and Society* 1: 166–180.

Wieten, J. (1988) 'The Press the Papers Wanted? The Case of Post-War News Print Rationing in The Netherlands and Britain', *European Journal of Communication* 3(4): 431–455.

Wilensky, H.L. (1964) 'Mass Society and Mass Culture: Interdependence or Independence?', *American Sociological Review* 29(2): 173–197.

Wilhoit, G.C. and D.H. Weaver (1983) 'Foreign News Coverage in Two U.S. Wire Services: An Update', *Journal of Communication* 33(2): 132–148.

Williams, A. (1975) 'Unbiased Study of TV News Bias', *Journal of Communication* 25(4): 393–408.

Williams, R. (1958) *Culture and Society 1780–1950*. London: Chatto and Windus.

Williamson, J. (1978) *Decoding Advertisements*. London: Marion Boyars.

Willoughby, W.F. (1955) 'Are Two Competing Dailies Better than One?', *Journalism Quarterly* 42: 197–204.

Wilson, C.C. and F. Gutierrez (1985) *Minorities and the Media*. Beverly Hills, CA: Sage.

Wilson, C.E. and D.M. Howard (1978) 'Public Perception of Media Accuracy', *Journalism Quarterly* 55: 73–76.

Winick, C. (ed.) (1978) *Deviance and Mass Media*. Newbury Park, CA: Sage.

Wirth, M.O. and L. Cobb-Reiley (1987) 'A First Amendment Critique of the 1984 Cable Act', *Journal of Broadcasting* 31(4): 391–407.

Womack, B. (1981) 'Attention Maps of 10 Major Newspapers', *Journalism Quarterly* 58: 260–265.

Woodall, W.G. (1986) 'Information Processing Theory and Television News', in J.P. Robinson and M. Levy (eds), *The Main Source*, pp. 133–158. Newbury Park, CA: Sage.

Wright, C.R. (1960) 'Functional Analysis of Mass Communication', *Public Opinion Quarterly* 24: 606–620.

Wulfmeyer, K.T. (1982) 'A Content Analysis of Local Television Newscasts: Answering the Critics', *Journal of Broadcasting* 26(1): 481–486.

Wulfmeyer, K.T. (1983a) 'The Interests and Preferences of Audience for Local Television News', *Journalism Quarterly* 60: 323–328.

Wulfmeyer, K.T. (1983b) 'Use of Anonymous Sources in Journalism', *Newspaper Research Journal* 4(2): 43–50.

Zettl, H. (1973) *Sight, Sound, Motion: Applied Media Aesthetics*. Belmont, CA: Wadsworth.

Zillman, D. and J. Bryant (1982) 'Pornography, Sexual Callousness, and the Trivialization of Rape', *Journal of Communication* 32(4): 10–21.

INDEX